Christianity in England
from Roman Times to the Reformation

Kenneth Hylson-Smith

Christianity in England from Roman Times to the Reformation

Volume I: From Roman Times to 1066

SCM PRESS

0 334 02769 1

First published 1999
by SCM Press
9–17 St Albans Place, London N1 0NX

SCM Press is a division of
SCM-Canterbury Press Ltd

Typeset by Regent Typesetting, London
and printed in Great Britain by
Biddles Ltd, Guildford and King's Lynn

Contents

Preface

This is the first volume of three on the history of Christianity in England from Roman times to the Reformation. It can be read as a separate work, complete in itself, or taken as part of the wider story of Christianity covered by the whole series, and indeed by this set of volumes and my three previously published books on the period 1558 to 1998.[1]

There has been a massive outpouring of research, theses, articles and books on the history of Roman and sub-Roman Britain and Anglo-Saxon England in the last half century, especially in the sphere of archaeology and related subjects, so that our understanding of all aspects of life in the millennium from the Claudian invasion to the Norman Conquest has been transformed. A glance at the bibliography and notes to the present work will attest to this, and to my almost total dependence on the labour of others. A great amount of light has been cast in particular on the religious, and more especially the Christian, scene in this foundational period for the evolution of the country. Nonetheless, there has been no attempt to bring all this fruitful work together: to bridge the Roman, sub-Roman and Anglo-Saxon periods and present a comprehensive synopsis of the history of Christianity throughout those formative centuries which takes account of all the major relevant post-Second World War scholarship.[2] The greater understanding which we now have of all aspects of Roman, sub-Roman and Anglo-Saxon life also allows Christianity to be more adequately related to the political, economic and social facets of life at the time; and this is one of the aims of the present work.

I have a broad readership in mind. Undergraduates and postgraduates of history and theology should be helped by the subjects covered, and the extensive notes and bibliography; clergy, informed lay people and, hopefully, a wide range of the general public should find the style and approach to the matters described and assessed both congenial and informative.

My debt to various institutions and individuals is immense. First and foremost I wish most sincerely to thank the Managing Director of SCM Press, the Revd Dr John Bowden, for his courageous commitment to such an ambitious publishing enterprise, and for his invaluable encouragement and support over many years. I want to express my deep appreciation, too, to Margaret Lydamore, Associate Editor and Susan Molyneux, Promotion Manager, for their highly effective and valued combination of efficiency, tact and kindness. Cox Computer Services Ltd of Tetbury have provided most useful technical assistance. Finally, I am grateful to the Librarians and staff of the Ashmolean Library, Oxford, the Bodleian Library, Oxford, the library of the Modern History Faculty, Oxford, the libraries of Bristol University, Trinity College, Bristol, Wesley College, Bristol, and the public library at Tetbury, Gloucestershire.

Introduction

Much of the history of Christianity in England in the period from Roman times to 1066 is still shrouded in mystery. There are many questions left unanswered, and many topics on which there has been more speculation than confident assertion. New, especially archaeological, knowledge has shed some light and helped to pierce the mist, allowing fresh glimpses of that tantalizingly interesting period, but the historian has to be cautious in what is portrayed as reasonably assured knowledge of personalities and events. This is not a counsel of despair. There is no need for almost unrelieved pessimism, or for academic gloom. Great strides have been made in a short time. Archaeology has been radically improved as an academic discipline by 'the application of new techniques, new theories and exciting new discoveries. The result is that an image of the past has begun to emerge that has called into question many basic assumptions about the lives and times of our ancestors. We are now better equipped than ever before to grasp how society, culture and landscape developed into their present form.'[1] An additional aid to increased knowledge of the period has been the growth in inter-disciplinary studies. The practitioners of the various related disciplines have been communicating with each other as at no time before; 'historians, archaeologists, and placename scholars do talk to each other, increasingly coordinate their studies and combine the results'.[2] New perspectives have also resulted in new understanding: the frame of reference for considering insular British or English affairs has been widened as such scholars as Michael Wallace-Hadrill, James Campbell and Patrick Wormald have looked at problems from a continental viewpoint and in a continental context.

Enough is now known for a general picture to be portrayed, and for details to be added for certain times and particular episodes in the story. What has to be acknowledged is the tentativeness of a great deal of the existing understanding. Much of the attractiveness of studying Christianity in England in its first few centuries is the participation in this process of unfolding knowledge and awareness. The religious historian of the period is embarking with others on a voyage of discovery. It has been well said that 'Christianity in Roman and sub-Roman Britain is a subject with peculiar attractions for the scholar, for it contains quite enough darkness for him to imagine that there is much for him to discover, but enough evidence for him to decide that the task of discovery is not a hopeless one.'[3]

Because of the paucity of evidence, and the contention among scholars over the interpretation of much of the material which is available, there is an ever-present danger of conveniently ignoring problems, cutting corners, and indulging in an excess of speculation. On the other hand, the archaeologist and the historian must not be paralysed by the lack of data; they must use their imaginations and allow themselves the liberty of filling in some gaps with warranted reconstructions. While it is true that 'few would be as bold as the late John Morris in constructing a coherent narrative',[4] there is also the danger of unattractive and, I think, unjustified inertia in the face of incomplete knowledge. This book will attempt to steer a course which carefully avoids these two potential pitfalls, and to provide a comprehensive account of the history of Christianity in Roman, sub-Roman and Anglo-Saxon times which is securely based on sound scholarship and a vast amount of research, undertaken especially by historians and archaeologists during the latter half of the twentieth century. It will try to provide an overview, in order to discern the most important elements and trends in that history, and to give a more detailed description and analysis where this is justified by the current state of knowledge. There is value in such works as they give a framework for more particular and specialist studies and also make the relevant findings and theories of scholars known to a wider audience than would otherwise be the case.

A quite cursory reading of this book will reveal a distinct contrast in tone and content between parts 1 and 2, covering Roman and sub-Roman Britain, and part 3, which deals with Anglo-Saxon England to 1066. This is because far more is known about the history and character of Christianity in England from the late sixth century onwards than for the preceding centuries. For Roman and sub-Roman Britain I will be seeking clues from whatever sources I can, but mainly from among archaeological and literary material, in order to discern the vague skeleton of the origin, growth and nature of early British Christianity. The picture which emerges will inevitably be frustratingly patchy and incomplete. But something of those pioneer days for the planting and development of British Christianity is discoverable, and will be described and discussed. In part 3 I will be able to construct a more connected and detailed narrative. I will still be seeking whatever evidence I can which will illuminate the period, but I will be on much firmer ground. At last I will be able to identify trends, specific events, and the relationship of these events one with another. Prominent individuals, with distinctive characters, attitudes and policies, will be encountered, and their lives and activities will be depicted within a fairly full and relevant political, social and religious setting. History will start to assume the form which we have come to accept as the norm, when we can describe patterns and movements, and have a sense of interconnectedness and coherence.

Themes

To encompass such a wide span of time and topics as attempted in the present work demands a few connecting threads.

First, although the book will be divided into Roman, sub-Roman, Saxon and Viking periods, I am aware that time and events are not in reality so neatly apportioned and compartmentalized. There were persistent features as well as newness and contrasts between one age and that which superseded it. This was so even when the move from one major division to another was marked by radical upheavals. There was continuity as well as discontinuity after the departure of the Romans, with the incursion and occupation in great numbers of the Anglo-Saxons, and later with the raids and settlement of the Vikings. The history of the whole period was not a series of completely fresh starts, with little dependence on or relationship with what went before, even in the case of the Roman and the sub-Roman centuries, or between these and the following Anglo-Saxon era. The total span of the thousand years covered by this book was a single connected saga; and this is discoverable, even if at times it is difficult to unearth connections and relationships as we move from one age to the next.

The attempt to distinguish and describe such a historical thread, or series of threads, is made more complicated and hazardous because the period has conventionally been divided into four both academically, and in the general awareness of those with little historical sense or knowledge. Specialists on the Roman, sub-Roman, Anglo-Saxon and Viking periods frequently restrict themselves to their chosen field with little regard for what went before or what came after. This is evident in the spheres of archaeology, history, iconography, art, and more particularly from my viewpoint the history of Christianity. There are, of course, very distinguished exceptions, but a long tradition takes some changing. I acknowledge that archaeological and historical scholarship must be based on concentrated studies of fairly limited periods. I am simply saying that there is value in a broader perspective and in surmounting the normally observed time spans. So every effort will be made to demonstrate the wholeness of the thousand years covered. I will try to appreciate the continuities and discontinuities, especially in the evolving history of Christianity.

Secondly, I will bring a number of academic disciplines to my aid on all the topics covered throughout this book. At the heart of what I aspire to achieve is a historical narrative. But this will be illuminated by archaeological discoveries and the work which has helpfully been undertaken in other cognate disciplines. This is an opportune time to bring together much valuable scholarship in various pertinent academic fields. Frequently such fruitful work remains confined to theses, articles and monographs with a very restricted readership, and books which are of a specialist nature. Periodically it is useful to incorporate often disparate scholastic contributions into a hopefully helpful synthesis.

Thirdly, I will endeavour to integrate the story of Christianity into the general history of the country, relating it to political, economic and social events and trends. This is vital in covering a period where the separation of 'church and state' or 'church and society' is unthinkable, and even the concept is anachronistic. It is only with the modern, post-Reformation, process of 'secularization' that such a dissection could even be contemplated; and it would have been nonsense to anyone living before 1066. Such a weaving together of the different ingredients in the history of this period also makes us aware of the importance of Christianity in what was a nation-forming millennium. The romanizing process, which left permanent marks on society after the departure of the legions; the establishment of Germanic peoples in an island whose core population was Celtic, or by then to a large extent Romano-Celtic; the development of English as a spoken and written language; the emergence of an embryonic distinctive social structure and culture; the creation of the kingdom of England as a political unit; and the replacement of multi-faceted religion by a dominant, vigorous and well-entrenched Christianity: all of these were part of one overarching process, and should be seen as such.

The notion of 'England' as a national community barely existed before the tenth century. There were a number of rulers of kingdoms such as Kent, Northumbria and Mercia who, in the seventh, eighth and ninth centuries may be considered as bretwaldas, in that their rule or sway extended well beyond their own kingdoms, to embrace a very large part of what became England; and Alfred the Great ruled over an especially large proportion of 'England'. But there was no period when the major part of the ultimate political entity known by that name acknowledged its permanent unity under a recognized king or overlord. It was not until after the Norman Conquest that the boundaries of the country were finally fixed. In the meantime, however, there was a growing sense of the identity of interest and the unity of the area bounded on the west by Wales and on the north by the land of the Picts. Because only 'Britain' was recognized as part of the Roman Empire I will use that term until the settlement of the Anglo-Saxons, and then I will use the term 'England'.

Nonetheless, as long as the reality of the political situation is appreciated it is not anachronistic to restrict my concern to 'England', and to make reference to 'England', even in the Roman and sub-Roman periods, although clearly I will frequently allude to those parts of Britain which eventually became Wales, Scotland and Ireland. The emerging national consciousness in the pre-1066 centuries can be seen in retrospect as laying a foundation for the nationhood which was to blossom in the succeeding Norman period. The time from the arrival of the Romans to the conquest of the Normans was the foetal stage for the attaining of this fully-fledged national status.

Fourthly, and as a rider to the previous theme, the pincer movement represented by the Celtic mission from the north and the Roman mission from the south will be described and evaluated in a hopefully dispassionate manner so that due weight is given to each as components in what can be viewed as a single process. They will both be seen as contributors to the evolving English nation, whereby it was made Christian in its professed religion, with its laws, values, ethical and moral standards and social norms securely founded on Christian principles.

Fifthly, the development of Christianity in England will be considered within the continental context. At no time during the period covered by this book was England an island from the point of view of its developing Christian commitment and life. In the Roman period the country was part of a wider Roman Empire. Later it was drawn into mainland continental political, economic, social and religious life through the

Anglo-Saxons and Danes. The Christians were involved ecclesiastically in continental church affairs during Roman times, and the papal influence was magnified from 597 onwards, after the initiative of Pope Gregory in sending St Augustine. The English continental mission of the eighth century, which was epoch-making in the history of the church in northern Europe, made the relationship with continental Christianity more of a two-way process. The links with continental monasticism from the time of St Martin of Tours onwards, and especially during the period of the tenth-century English monastic reform movement, were crucial at important stages in promoting the Christian faith in England, and in determining its characteristic features. And in the time of the Viking supremacy the involvement of Cnut as a Christian king in the church affairs of his other, north European, territories, ensured that England did not stand aloof from the continent in Christian matters. It would be parochial in the extreme, and indicate a somewhat myopic view of English Christianity, if such a wider frame of reference was ignored.

Lastly, and hopefully without falling into the trap of reading back into history what was not there at the time, an attempt will be made to discover certain overall features in the development of Christianity throughout the period taken as a whole. There were unavoidably a countless number of 'unintended consequences of intended human action', which in total produced patterns of development only to be perceived in retrospect and with hindsight. The identification of any such possible configurations must be undertaken with caution, and the exposition and elucidation of them must be hedged about with qualifications. What is suggested must be acknowledged as merely provisional, based on a reading of the history of the period. But the analysis is worth attempting.

Sources – prehistoric, Celtic and Romano-Celtic

The sources for presenting a comprehensive account and analysis of prehistoric British religion are somewhat thin and inadequate. The people concerned left insufficient evidence of their religion to allow much confident interpretation of their religious beliefs and practices. But the clues are sufficient to justify an imaginative but informed reconstruction.

Nevertheless, it is well that I acknowledge the provisional nature of what is portrayed. New material is constantly coming to light; the scene is for ever changing; interpretations are subject to frequent modifications, or even have to be jettisoned in the face of further evidence. Although an immense amount of work has been done in recent decades on the religion of pre-Roman Britain, as far as the pre-Iron Age period is concerned it 'has served to show that most of what we had formerly believed that we knew is either wrong or unprovable'. The discovery of a tremendous variety of religious architecture and artefacts over both space and time 'may reflect an equal diversity of belief' and this 'almost defies generalization. The peoples of our remote past have emerged as more creative, more dynamic, more fascinating and more baffling'[5] than was formerly appreciated.

When we come to the Iron Age and to the Roman period the foundations of knowledge are somewhat more impressive. The last seven decades have seen a remarkable growth in archaeology as a discipline, and in its competence and confidence to understand Iron Age and Roman Britain. This expertise and cumulative knowledge spread from an initial focus on material culture to such non-material spheres of life as religion. As a consequence of an impressive series of excavations which took place from the 1930s onwards, bolstered by a number of published books and reports, some leading historians had, by the middle of the century, come to believe that archaeological evidence could be used to reconstruct Iron Age and Roman systems of agricultural production, trade, social structure and political organization with some degree of certainty. 'However, the realms of religious belief, or ideology as anthropologists would choose to say, were thought to be beyond the powers of archaeological interpretation. With the growth in data collection since then, and the development of more powerful frameworks of interpretation, archaeologists have become more daring.'[6] Evidence such as special buildings and enclosures, monuments, the treatment of dead bodies, material offerings found in or near special structures, and references to individual deities displayed in iconography, or inscriptions, has helped to achieve a fuller appreciation of the religion of the Celts, and the non-Christian Romans.

As a supplement to this evidence, there is the testimony of literature. But this has serious shortcomings. The works concerned were not written by the Celts themselves, who had no tradition of a written language, but by Graeco-Romans (among whom the foremost were Caesar, Strabo, Pomponius Mela, Pliny, Athenaeus, Tacitus, Dio Cassius, Diodorus Siculus, Ammianus Marcellinus and Lucan), the Irish and the Welsh. All of this still leaves us with little 'hard' data which can form the basis for uncontrovertible pronouncements. The literature was second-hand, not only because it came from alien people far removed culturally from those about whom the authors commented, but because some of it, most notably the post-Roman literature, was separated geographically and chronologically from the Celts of the later first millennium BC and the Roman period.

It has to be admitted that even with the academic strides forward the 'evidence of archaeology is at best incomplete and ambiguous; at worst, it is misleading and confusing', and that obtained from literature is far more suspect. Any attempt at an explanation of Celtic, religion can therefore be no more than 'extremely speculative – a construction rather than a reconstruction'.[7] Nonetheless, more data is being discovered, there are those in the field who are more optimistic about the possibilities of achieving fuller knowledge, and the prospects for doing so are brighter than at any time in the past.

As with so many matters which I will examine in this book, the former tendency to over-simplification in the portrayal of native cults in Iron Age and Roman Britain is giving way to an awareness and acknowledgment that with every addition to the evidence available modifications need to be made to previous somewhat naive and sweeping statements. 'Only when the complexity of the material is appreciated and attitudes as to the nature of the native element are altered can we hope to attain to a more realistic and convincing picture of the actual state of affairs in Roman and Dark Age Britain, and the real nature of the religious cults of the Celtic peoples.'[8]

Sources – Christianity

When we come to the Christian faith, the dependence of the church historian on Bede's *Historia Ecclesiastica Gentis Anglorum* (*Ecclesiastical History of the English People*) for the period up to its appearance in 731 is quite remarkable. It is in a class of its own as a source of information and comment, and this is enhanced by its fascination and appeal to an incredibly wide range of people.

So deeply are we indebted to Bede for our knowledge of the history of England before the eighth century that it comes as something of a shock to us to realize that if Bede had not written, the names of Chad and Cedd, Hild and Aethelthryth, Edwin and Oswald, Caedmon and Benedict Biscop would be either completely unknown or names known only to scholars, around which to spin cobwebs of conjecture; and our knowledge of the greatest of his themes, St Augustine's mission and the conversion of the English, would be fragmentary.[9]

But even that foundation document cannot be accepted and used uncritically. It was intended as an account of the unfolding tale of the divine plan. History for Bede was *historia sacra*.[10] He consciously stood in the tradition of Eusebius, Orosius and Gregory of Tours, and his principles of historical interpretation were almost exclusively determined by reference to the Bible. Kings were instruments in God's hands, whether they were Christian or pagan; events were but the unfolding of the purposes of a God who is lord of history. For some modern historians such an orientation detracts from the value of Bede's work as an accurate record of 'what actually happened'. It is not 'the nature of the evidence but the quality of its transmission that is in question. The truth of the "facts" had to be accommodated to the higher truth of the programme of Providence, so reaching *historica fides*, which a wide audience could accept and understand.'[11]

Miracles were accepted by Bede as part of God's ways with people, and as one means for authenticating those who were his special messengers, his saints. But this is an obstacle to many. 'How', queries a commentator on the *History*, 'is it that one who is supposed to be our greatest medieval historian can spend so much time telling wonder tales?'[12] The prominence of miracles in the *History* 'has caused them to be either ignored by historians or treated to a cautious defusing so that they become safe to handle; at best they are considered as primitive survivals of white magic or as a different kind of truth.'[13]

Even within the limits of his intentions Bede is not flawless. Most conspicuously, there are a number of chronological errors. The dates he quotes are sometimes mutually inconsistent, and modern scholarship has found him to be wrong in some of his chronology.

But such fallibilities and questionings should not divert attention away from the pre-eminence of Bede's work as a source for the ecclesiastical history of England in Roman, sub-Roman and early Anglo-Saxon times. It should be treated as a basic text of the first importance, but tested in what it says by other works, including those by modern scholars.

The other primary sources of first rate significance are: *The Anglo-Saxon Chronicle*; the *Confessio* (*Declaration*), the *Epistola* (*Letter*), and the *Dicta* (*Sayings*) of St Patrick, together with Muirchu's Life of St

Patrick; the *De Excidio et Conquestu Britanniae* (*The Ruin of Britain*) by Gildas; the *Historia Brittonum* (*British History*) of Nennius; the *Lives* of the saints, Cuthbert, Wilfrid and Guthlac, and the *Vita Sancti Germani* (*The Life of Saint Germanus*) by Constantius of Lyon; and the *Tribal Hidage*.

The Anglo-Saxon Chronicle was compiled over several centuries and is in fact a group of several chronicles written at different times and in different places. But all of them are based on a common stock of entries which means that they stand in close relationship to one another. The end product can be reckoned as the first continuous history of any Western people in their own language. The authority of the *Chronicle* is greatest when the entry is the work of contemporary witnesses, as with the ninth century, and possibly the eighth as well. Some of the compilers had access to sources which are no longer extant, which allowed the record to be carried much further back, but the statements relating to earlier events do not have the same authenticity as those referring to recent or contemporary events. Entries in the *Chronicle* by their nature tend to be dry, factual, precise, in contrast to Bede's *History* which reveals something of the interests, prejudices and character of the author, and also incorporates anecdotes and comments which enliven the historical account.

The writings of Patrick are of great interest as the only British documents to have survived from the century after the fall of Rome. Muirchu's life was composed about two hundred years later, but it drew upon lost contemporary texts.

Gildas wrote *The Ruin of Britain* about AD 540 as the only contemporary comment on sub-Roman Britain. As he was mainly concerned with the religious, and more especially the Christian, scene, the work is of great value to the church historian, although its limitations need to be recognized. The author is an enigmatic figure; and all our trustworthy information about him comes from his own words.[14] It is difficult to comment on the accuracy of his account, and his observations, as our knowledge of that 'Dark Age' remains obscure. 'In brief, we do not yet have the full equipment to read Gildas as historical prose should be read, and consequently we cannot yet say whether or not there is any faltering in the exactitude of his thought.'[15] Recent scholars have been divided over the reliability of Gildas as a witness to events in the fifth century.[16] But despite much questioning one prominent historian concludes that he 'can be treated as a credible and most valuable witness to a broad sequence of events in Britain in the century following the third consulship of Aetius (446–53)',[17] and he is certainly accepted as an important primary source by most historians.

The *British History* by Nennius is a significant collection of documents relating to early British history. It was drawn together in the first decades of the ninth century. Although, as with other sources I am considering, it should be used with reservations, it is in certain respects unique in concept and form, in originality and in quality of scholarship.

Hagiography has its place in the sources for the early history of English Christianity as we will see when we encounter the *Lives* of Cuthbert, Wilfrid and Guthlac. *The Life of Saint Germanus of Auxerre*, was written by Constantius of Lyon in about 480. Largely because it is a near-contemporary source, it has been accorded considerable value by some scholars, but it shows little knowledge of non-religious matters relating to life in Britain, and it is mainly of value for the light it throws on the state of Christianity in the region at the time.

The *Tribal Hidage* was the earliest 'fiscal' document from the mediaeval period in England. It has marginal significance for ecclesiastical history, but it 'has been pressed into service by those seeking to interpret the nature and geography of kingships and of "peoples" in pre-Viking England'.[18]

These are the main primary sources, but they are supplemented by other supporting documents of variable authenticity and authority, such as the poem *Beowulf*, a small but interesting body of Old English poetry, Asser's *Life of King Alfred*, the *De antiquitate Glastoniensis Ecclesiae* and the *Gesta Regum* of William of Malmesbury, and lives of the eighth-century missionaries to the continent of Europe, Willibrord, Boniface, Willibald and Willehad.

Then of course there is the archaeological evidence. Since the Second World War there has been a most impressive array of new, and sometimes spectacular, finds which have changed perceptions of many aspects of the history of the period covered by this present book. This will become evident as our story unfolds. Partly as a result of such increased data, and also as a consequence of a dynamic academic process whose causes are not easy to determine, there has been an extraordinary flow of scholarly works on Roman, sub-Roman and Anglo-Saxon Britain. But the discipline is still young; the archaeological exploration of the pre-Norman Conquest millennium remains in its infancy; and the historical understanding of the first thousand years of the Christian era in England is as yet insubstantial and piecemeal. For example, it was not until 1967 that the first full-scale history of Roman

Britain, Sheppard Frere's *Britannia*, appeared. In spite of all the subsequent major treatments of many aspects of Roman Britain it is salutary
to realize 'that although much is now known about this part of the
Empire of Rome, we are closer to the beginning of work upon it than to
the end, if there ever could be such a thing'.[19]

Examples of such restricted knowledge and comprehension could be
multiplied. For instance Charles Thomas admits 'that no direct contemporary reference to any Late Roman church in Britain is known,
either from history or inscriptions'.[20] Indeed, there are no British church
sites of the period 400 to 700 which have been excavated in recent times
and the evidence for which has been fully published.[21] The same lack
of hard, incontrovertible evidence applies to Anglo-Saxon paganism.
Having made reference to archaeological finds, place-names and written
records bearing on Anglo-Saxon paganism David Wilson concludes that
overall 'it should be admitted that the tenuous and often limited nature
of the evidence is reflected in the interpretations offered: nobody would
pretend to any sort of certainty in such matters'.[22] It is a verdict which
would have to be passed on so many areas of life, and more particularly
of religious life, in the pre-1066 years of the Christian era in Britain.

The deficiency of evidence even applies to small artefacts. In spite of
the enthusiasm of a countless host of amateur hunters armed with metal
detectors, and the consequent impressive increase in the number of
such items available for examination, there is a disappointing lack of
additional material from this source which bears upon Christianity.
C. F. Mawer has provided an exhaustive catalogue of small items from
Roman Britain which have any indication of association with contemporary Christianity, and it does not make very encouraging reading.
She is at pains to separate the facts from the fiction. When she applied
her criteria to the fifty artefacts which in 1953 Toynbee had considered
to be of Christian significance, only twenty were found to be acceptable
as definitely Christian, with a further eighteen possibly so. The
situation had not massively improved since Toynbee did her work.

Forty years later the total of items found to have been considered at
some point as Christian has risen to 260, but only 70 can be regarded
as of definite Christian significance, with a further 60 which future
discoveries may eventually confirm or discredit. An analysis of these
modifications to the overall corpus of small-find evidence suggests
that while the main geographical areas of Christian activity have been
on the whole correctly perceived, Christianity in Roman Britain was

not only far less prevalent but also neither as complex nor as subtle as the claimed evidence indicated. In view, however, of the 'Chinese whispers' which have been found to have affected so many of the claims, perhaps (to misconstrue Hawkes [1973: 154–5]) 'the astonishing thing is not that there are so few Christian art works from (Roman) Britain but that there are any at all'.[23]

We are confronted by a frustrating lack of apposite material at almost every turn. Another illustration is the scarcity of data relating to the origins of Anglo-Saxon kingdoms, and as a consequence of this the minuscule amount of information on the origin of Christianity in these kingdoms. It was in the first century and a half of the English settlements that kingdoms such as Kent, Wessex and Mercia evolved or were forged; and that is an abstruse period for those scholars who study Anglo-Saxon institutions. It is doubtful if we will ever be able to know anything in detail of the beginnings of these kingdoms, and often not even the barest outline. The kingdom of the Hwicce is one such case. Most historians attribute it to the work of Penda of Mercia around 628, but there is very little evidence to support this view. The West Saxon kingdom is a further illustration of the problems involved. Although the foundation period is said to have been in the late fifth and early sixth centuries, the sources for such history only date from the late ninth century. Even when we enter the second millennium of the Christian era there is still much hidden from view. The eleventh century up to the time of the Norman Conquest has a measure of unity; and it 'witnessed the establishment, attenuation, and extinction of the Danish and Anglo-Danish monarchy'. It also saw important developments in the spread and consolidation of Christianity. And yet it was

> an obscure period and exceptionally difficult to interpret. We have little information about the reign of Cnut. Almost nothing is known about the major part of Edward's life, the period before he ascended the throne, and there is an embarrassing conflict or cleavage between contemporary writers on the few events which were considered important at the time or in retrospect, such as the 'revolutions' of 1051–2 and Anglo-Norman and Anglo-Papal relations. Moreover, this poorly and fitfully illuminated scene is then obscured by two great shadows, the one cast by the Norman Conquest and the other by Edward's cult and canonization.[24]

There is no period from the arrival of the Romans to the successful invasion of the Normans when heavy clouds do not obstruct, and quite frequently hide, our view of events. Gone are the days when a historian felt able to write 'as if he had been present at the landing of the Saxons, and had watched every step of their subsequent progress'.[25] But to 'see in a mirror, dimly',[26] does not imply total blindness. Light shines through, and more light is being cast with the passing years, despite the debates over the interpretation of data. We should pursue the quest for more enlightenment with enthusiasm. What is needed is a judicious weighing of the evidence and a bold yet cautious appraisal and presentation of what the course and character of the events, movements and changes might have been.

Part 1

Roman Britain

Non-Christian Religion in Pre-Roman and Roman Britain

Pre-Iron Age culture and religion

The inhabitants of Britain whom the Romans encountered were an ancient people. They were also inheritors of a long religious history. I will not dwell on the prehistoric era, but as it was the cultural and religious background from which the Celts of Roman times emerged, some indication of its main components will help to set the scene for what was to follow.

It has to be acknowledged that the character and content of Neolithic, Bronze and Iron Age religion is obscure, and open to varied and inter-pretations. We are immediately faced with competing explanations and theories when we consider the function and purpose of such stone circles as Stonehenge and Avebury, and the type of people and com-munities associated with them.[1] Once it was thought that although a remarkable feat of engineering lay behind the erection of these awesome monuments, those responsible were simple and unsophisticated in thought and lifestyle. Opinion has, however, changed. It was suggested in the 1950s, especially by Professor Alexander Thom, that the people involved in these constructions during the period from before 3000 to about 1500 BC had considerable mathematical expertise, and employed a measuring system which produced a predetermined ground-plan. The layout was not haphazard or even approximate, but accurate in accord-ance with finely worked calculations. The executors of such intricate schemes also had an advanced knowledge of astronomy by means of which they were able to predict solar and lunar eclipses and to detect minor movements of the moon. 'If Thom is right – and there are continuing doubts in the minds of many archaeologists – then a reassessment of the societies that built stone circles and the related earthen rings known as henges is necessary. An unsuspected, authori-tarian upper class of priests and astronomers might have existed.'[2]

The Thom thesis was supported by Dr Euan MacKie. After excavations of three large earthwork enclosures in Wessex near to Stonehenge and Avebury he wrote that

> the results from these three large henge sites could in my view, have provided the crucially important, direct evidence for the existence of that specialist class of astronomer-priests and wise men in populous lowland Britain which is required by Thom's theories . . . The great henges could have been . . . the exact counterparts of the Maya ceremonial centres of Central America – the residences, temples and training schools of the learned orders which undertook . . . the decades or even centuries of work at the standing stone observatories.[3]

What was proposed by Thom and MacKie demolished the traditional view of simple peasant communities surrounded by unpredictable dangers from which they attempted to protect themselves by performing acts of savagery and sacrifice amongst the bonfires of the autumn. Such concepts needed to be discarded as misleading and old-fashioned.

It is well to recall that by the fourth millennium BC, when Britain entered its most glorious period of prehistory in which the circles and henges appeared, there had already been achievements of considerable magnitude. These included the manufacture of stone tools and weapons which combined utility with beauty; the construction of wooden homes, or sometimes huts of turves and skins; rudimentary clothing; the ability to pursue a seam of flint along a hillside and to excavate horizontal or vertical shafts; the production of pottery without the use of a wheel; elementary trading in stone axes and pottery over hundreds of miles, including continental Europe; and the facility to harness fire for limited domestic and other purposes. Evidence of quite elaborate burial rituals, and surviving religious statuettes, also indicate supernatural beliefs. These prehistoric forebears may have believed in a number of spirits inhabiting the natural world, in a variety of goddesses and gods, in a universal deity, or in differing combinations of these three.

The henges themselves were ceremonial earthworks in which a bank surrounded a spacious central plateau for communal activities. Because of their low-lying location near rivers and their single entrances which may have been astronomically aligned, they seem to have been monuments for open-air cultic practices in which water was important. In some cases round barrows were constructed inside the earthwork, thus linking the dead with the living.

Soon after this there appeared the stone circles, of which the most impressive were Stonehenge and Avebury. Stonehenge is one of the most tragic monuments in the world, despite its fame, for its worldwide reputation has brought about the destruction of the evidence which might have revealed its history. All that can be said with certainty is that a wooden structure of some description existed at about the end of the fourth millennium BC, and that a large number of stones were erected from about 2100 BC onwards, so that their present pattern was achieved by around 1500 BC.[4]

The Avebury circle, which dates from approximately the same time as Stonehenge, is better preserved, and it has also received intensive scholastic attention in recent years. This has allowed fairly precise and authoritative conclusions about its purpose to be annunciated. Although these cannot be definitive, Aubrey Burl can assert with some confidence:

> Death and regeneration are the themes of Avebury. The presence of human bones, the pieces of stone, the red ochre, the pockets of fertile earth, the antlers, the shapes of the sarsens [stones], the architecture of the avenues and circles, all are consistent with the belief that Avebury was intended as a temple in which, at various times of the year, the large population could gather to watch and take part in ceremonies of magic and evocation that would safeguard their lives.[5]

It is reasonable to picture autumn, midwinter and spring communal activities, led by medicine-men or witch-doctors wearing antlers, and a host of people dancing out the themes of death and rebirth, making offerings, using human bones, and engaging in sex rituals to bring back the warmth and richness of the summer soil. The people, dressed in their soft skin clothes, the leather decorated with shell and bone and coloured in bright patterns, would most probably squat on their heels by the stones, intently watching ceremonies they were convinced would make their brief lives safer. Such rites at such set times of the year as the seasons of sowing and harvest, and possibly at midsummer and mid-winter, were harbingers of the future four great nature festivals of the Celts. These later inhabitants of the land had their Oimelg in February at the time when ewes came into milk; their Beltine in May to mark the time when the cattle could be driven out to the spring grass; their Lughnasa at the time of the August harvest; and their Samhuin at the end of October when the ghosts of the dead were reckoned to arise in the night to roam the dark and defenceless countryside.

Celtic life and religion

In fact there seems to have been a definite link between the life and religion of these prehistoric people and that of the succeeding Celts, although the origin of the Celts has long been the subject of speculation and controversy.[6] Miranda Green considers it 'irrefutable that somehow, this group of peoples, whose language and material culture contained sufficient unity to be identifiable to their neighbours, had their roots in the later Bronze Age cultures of Europe'.[7] This is not to say that in Britain or mainland Europe they suddenly appeared from a specific place as a result of a single event. It was more a process of accretion over a long span of time whereby the lineal descendants of generations stretching back as far as the Neolithic farmers of the fifth and fourth millenniums BC were slowly 'celticized'. 'The prehistory of lowland Britain is a long tale of wave after wave of immigrants sometimes surging, sometimes trickling, across the Channel, and the story of the people whom the Romans called Britons has thus no clear beginning.'[8]

Nevertheless, there were key moments in this protracted emergence. By about 700 BC new social and cultural elements may be observed. These included new metal types which were associated with horse harnesses, the distribution of which suggests mobile raiding parties; ironworking on a large scale; and, at least in Central Europe, rich inhumation burial in wooden mortuary houses under earthen barrows or mounds. The grave evidence indicates a warrior-élite. This culture is called 'Hallstatt'. By 500 BC the features just identified became more sophisticated, with an abundance of warrior accoutrements and luxury objects often decorated for the first time with distinctive Celtic art-designs. Such truly Celtic, 'La Tène', culture was also characterized by large sprawling fortified settlements, called oppida, which may be regarded as proto-towns. In Britain a good example is Danebury in Hampshire, excavated by Professor Barry Cunliffe and others.

But although each phase of prehistory can only be dated and its origin understood by such a reference to continental cultural changes, it cannot be satisfactorily described in continental terms only. It is for this reason that in dealing with the prehistoric Iron Age Professor Christopher Hawkes most usefully introduced the letters A, B and C to designate the broad cultural divisions in Britain. The three cultures so depicted were not intended to be strictly chronological, A preceded B, and C came after B, but A also persisted, sometimes with no modification, until the Roman period.

It may be presumed that the various Celtic communities not only inherited a prehistoric Bronze Age and early Iron Age material culture, but also assimilated much of the religious thought and usage of these previous societies. The nature and form of such religion is not easy to determine. 'Archaeology can do no more than uncover the bare bones of Iron Age religion, although Classical writers allow them to be fleshed out a little.'[9] From these somewhat slender clues it appears that the pagan Celts built no grand temples but worshipped their gods at sacred groves, springs and rivers. As with their prehistoric predecessors, their religion seems to have revolved around nature: seasonal and fertility rites and ceremonies associated with those matters which most forcefully and relentlessly impinged upon the daily lives of a people who lived so close to nature in all its often unpredictable variations.

It is fundamental to the understanding of Celtic societies in general, and their religion in particular, to appreciate that their economies were almost exclusively agriculture. Craft specialization, such as metal and pottery manufacture, the exploitation of mineral resources, and the export of slaves, for all of which there is evidence, were apparently no more than marginal activities. This means that the primary focus of the societies was nature. Men and women were occupied and preoccupied with efforts to wrest what they could from the land and animal life. Their religion reflects this. There are signs of the development of oppida, with some centres such as *Camulodunum* (Colchester) being complex, multi-functional settlements, with separate foci for religion, craft activity, and perhaps élite residences. There is also evidence of a more pronounced social hierarchy in the first century BC. But such developments, although highly visible, and leaving material evidence behind them, were not typical for most of the people. The overall structure was countryside-dominated,[10] and the religion was suffused with concerns about man's relationship to the natural world.

By the beginning of the Christian era the various immigrations and internal migrations had produced a fairly stable tribal distribution, and it is possible to recognize most of the tribal names and territories which were ultimately crystallized under the Roman system of local administration. The Catuvellauni were a burgeoning power, inhabiting an area approximately corresponding to the modern Hertfordshire, with their main centre at Wheathampstead. The Trinovantes were possibly the most closely-knit community, and their territory extended through Essex into much of east Hertfordshire. The Dobunni were to be found in Gloucestershire and Somerset. They were derived from the Atrebates who themselves inhabited Hampshire, Berkshire and west Sussex. Also in Hampshire, and extending north-westwards, were the Belgae. The Cantii were made up of a number of smaller groups which had settled in Surrey and eastern Kent. In Dorset there were the Durotriges; in the south-western peninsula of Devon and Cornwall the Dumnoni. The Iceni were to be found in Norfolk and north Suffolk. To the north-west of the Catuvellauni lay the Coritani, and beyond them again the Cornovii and the Brigantes. The uplands and valleys of Wales were held by four major tribes: the Silures, the Ordovices, the Deceangli and the Demetae. This structure of reasonably unified tribal kingdoms did not prevent inter-tribal power-struggles, and the principal aggressor was the Catuvellauni tribe.

There was a sufficient measure of religious uniformity of attitude among all these pre-Roman Celts to allow us to talk about Celtic religion; but this was something less than a system, and should be viewed more in terms of religious attitudes and tendencies. Patterns and a certain fundamental order can be identified despite the complexities and variety of Celtic religious thought and practice. Some generalizations are justified.

Although the pre-Roman Celts did not normally construct permanent, roofed temples, and stone-built sanctuaries are rare in the pre-Roman Celtic world, there is evidence that wooden temples did exist both in Britain and on the continent. One of the most interesting of these insular shrines is Frilford in Oxfordshire. Beneath two contiguous Roman buildings there were found what were interpreted as two Iron Age sanctuaries, used for some sort of cultic activity. The Romano-Celtic shrine at Worth, Kent, was found to contain Iron Age model shields beneath the Roman cella, and this may indicate an Iron Age temple. At Muntham Court, Sussex, Iron Age pits and postholes raise the possibility that the circular Romano-British temple, which was associated with a cult-well and a healing cult, may have had a Celtic precursor. At Hayling Island there was a pre-Roman shrine. Some so-called Iron Age shrines have been identified as such simply because no secular function could be attributed to the structures concerned. This applies to the small buildings in the hillforts at Danebury and South Cadbury. At Maiden Castle, Dorset, a similar identification of a Late Iron Age circular shrine rests on an infant burial just outside the door, but it was located under a late Roman round building and near to a Romano-Celtic shrine, which all means that its context is ambiguous.[11] The area around the Roman temple at Uley in Gloucestershire was sacred in its previous Celtic use, but it is thought that there was no pre-Roman building there, merely a boundary ditch to demarcate the land of the gods from the world of men.[12]

These pre-Roman, Celtic, shrines or temples were largely located within centres of population and none have so far been identified within small farmsteads, although rural shrines are known, with Harlow being a notable example. They typically consisted of a small square central room, the cella, which housed the deity's cult statue, surrounded by an ambulatory, although about a quarter of the known examples were circular. Some of the suggested pre-Roman temples were found associated with villages or sited in their own sacred enclosures. One of the most interesting is attributed to the fourth century BC, and is thought to have been next to a small village which is now the site of Heathrow Airport. It was a rectangular building surrounded by a colonnade, which seems to anticipate the later Celtic temples of Roman Britain. Where a shrine continued to be occupied into the Roman period it was invariably succeeded by a Romano-Celtic temple built in stone.[13]

For the pre-Roman Celts all natural features were endowed with sanctity; the gods were everywhere. Evidence for this is especially to be had for the Roman period, as we will see in a moment; so it has been necessary to allow such evidence to cast light on a former age. There are very few relevant discoveries from the pre-Roman centuries themselves. Many of the finest examples of late Bronze Age and Iron Age metalwork with some apparent religious connotation have been recovered from a watery context or in pits, shafts and wells, and this slightly reinforces the supposed connection of pagan Celtic religion with groves, springs and rivers. During peat extraction at Llyn Cerrig Bach on Anglesey (Gwynedd), at a site which had once been a small lake, various votive offerings were found which possibly date to between the second century BC and the first century AD. They include the bones of pigs, oxen, sheep, goats, horses and dogs, pottery and fine metalwork used for horse harnesses, chariot trappings, swords, spears, ceremonial horns, cauldrons and slave chains. A bronze shield of the second century BC, found at Witham in Lincolnshire bears a bull motif, and various iron objects of the immediate pre-Roman period, like those from Barton, Cambridgeshire, bear unequivocal bull motifs.

Roman Britain – native Celtic religion

As we move on to Roman Britain it is useful for the purpose of description and analysis to distinguish three components of the non-Christian religious scene: the native Celtic religion, the religion of the Romans, and the imported eastern religions. In practice there was a complex interaction between these so that the religious landscape was extremely complicated. There was a process of cultural and religious mixing or collation in which a hybrid religion, called 'Romano-Celtic', was created out of Roman, Celtic and eastern religious elements. The relationship of these three spheres one with another, and the varied way they impinged upon each other, wrought changes, and in many cases fused together, will be considered in the final section of this chapter.

First, the Celts of Roman Britain and their religious life. In the 1990s new discoveries and re-appraisals have abounded; and the Celtic religion of the immediate pre-Roman period, the distinctive Celtic religion which persisted after the arrival of the Romans, and Romano-Celtic religion have been particular subjects of such close and thorough re-examination and re-assessment.

Hill-top sites are a connecting link between prehistoric, Iron Age, Celtic and Romano-Celtic religion. Although these settlements have not been the subject of a comprehensive overall survey[14] they are generally reckoned as having served a military or non-military secular purpose. But there were also hill-top and hill-slope temples and shrines. It has yet to be determined to what extent these and other religious structures and artefacts found at such sites imply a continuity between the beliefs and religious activities of the Celtic, Roman and immediate post-Roman periods, and whether discontinuity was more characteristic.[15]

Certainly native Celtic religion did not remain totally unaffected by the new and powerful religious beliefs and practices of the dominant Romans. The conquerors introduced a range of new attitudes which touched upon all aspects of life, not just religion defined in a narrow way; for the Romans brought with them a total civilization and cluster of presuppositions.

The degree to which Roman values penetrated British society, and indeed swamped almost all native values and religion, has been a topic for long-standing academic debate. As early as 1932 Louis Gougaud wrote:

Opinions are divided as to the importance of the influence exercised by Roman civilization on the Celtic population of Britain. Some writers are convinced that it left only a slight varnish on British institutions, which rapidly disappeared after the withdrawal of the legions. Others, on the contrary, are of the opinion that the Romanizing process was carried very far, especially in the southern and eastern parts of the island, where, they would have us believe, mere handicraftsmen were already speaking Latin before the country was converted to Christianity.[16]

All scholars are agreed that the pre-existing Celtic religion of the British peoples was not totally obliterated by the conquering Romans. In the latter part of the twentieth century archaeologists in Britain, as elsewhere in other former Roman provinces, have given greater attention than at any time in the past to the indigenous native religious element during the Roman period. A former lack of interest in the Celtic population and their religion has started to give way to a more balanced attitude. But this has generated conflicting interpretations of the data available. Ann Ross and Miranda Green have maintained with vigour that the worship of the Celtic gods remained alive and essentially separate from the adoration offered to Roman gods, and they claim that this is demonstrated by the existence of local iconographic traditions.[17] Graham Webster takes the same view as Green, that the coming of the Romans did not entail the absorbtion of the Celtic cults into the Roman religious system.[18] Others, such as Martin Henig, do not dismiss such assertions out of hand, but they deny that there was such a self-contained native culture.[19]

The various Celtic tribal units differed considerably in their degree of cohesion, and in the religion which prevailed among them as they moved into the Roman period. 'It seems possible that each tribe, perhaps each family and even individual locations, had its own particular tutelary deities, whose worship however does not seen to have excluded that of other divinities.'[20] Nevertheless, as in pre-Roman times, 'a study of the whole reveals a basic homogeneity of religious attitude amongst the Celts which overcomes all regional and economic variations and which is surprising in its persistence.'[21]

What is clear is that the Celts of the Roman period, like their predecessors, were gripped by strong and profound beliefs and superstitions. Their religion did not depart from the essential informality and spontaneity which had characterized it for centuries, even when, under the influence of the Romans, spontaneous responses were somewhat more regimented with the adoption of specifically named gods who had defined attributes. The old impulses were not lost. The same felt-needs remained. Romano-Celtic temples were constructed but, in keeping with the pattern of worship of their forebears, the native British peoples most typically continued to worship their gods at sacred springs, wells, rivers and lakes, at mountains or at a particular valley or habitat. Their religion seems to have been essentially informal, largely unstructured, homely and intimate, as it had been from time immemorial.

In the Romano-Celtic period, as in former ages, watery places were sources of peculiar veneration. Water was recognized as essential to life and fertility. There was a fascination with the constant movement of the water of springs, rivers and the sea, and with the welling-up from the hidden deep of the water of springs which were often hot and possessed medicinal properties. It all seemed mysterious and magical. Water which could be beneficent as a life-giver, healer and means of travel, could also be capricious and destructive. In combination with wind it could batter crops to the ground; and, accompanied by thunder and lightning, it could strike and destroy. It could rage and wreck ships, and there was death by drowning. It is little wonder that the Celts cast precious objects into these watery places in an effort to propitiate or appease the powers residing in them.

By the Romano-Celtic period water-cults were assuming a more formalized and identifiable form. At Carrawburgh in the north, the Romano-British goddess Coventina presided over a natural spring and well. As a single or triple water-nymph, reclining on water-lilies and pouring water from a vessel, she was sufficiently regarded to have a temple built in her honour. At the River Wharfe in Teesdale the cult-spirit Verbeia was revered. At Ratham Mill, Funtington, Sussex, a small shrine was adjacent to a brook and the innermost of three concentric squares could have contained a pool or well. During the Roman period the cult-centre at Ivy Chimneys, Essex, had an artificial pool as its focal point. It has been suggested that what has previously been regarded as a Roman villa at Chedworth in Gloucestershire may in fact have been the site for a shrine or *Nymphaeum* to a water-goddess. Romano-Celtic worship linked with wells is suggested by the religious sites at Kelvedon, Essex and Deal in Kent. Then there was the worship of the Celtic healing divinity Sulis at the Bath hot spring, which I will consider towards the end of this chapter. And names also give clues to this adoration of water in its various natural manifestations. In northern Britain the name 'Latis' occurs with the meaning 'goddess of the Pool'; and Abandinus as the name of a Cambridgeshire god may possibly suggest a water-association. The Roman name of 'Aquae Arnemetiae' ('the waters of the goddess who lived at the sacred grove') for Buxton, Derbyshire, implies the veneration of a goddess 'Arnemetia'.[22]

The sea also played a part in the religious life of British Celts in Roman times. The sanctuary of Nodens at Lydney overlooking the Severn river in Gloucestershire was impressive in scale.[23] It was probably built in the third century AD. Its mosaic imagery suggests healing to have been a major function, and associates the cult both with marine and solar symbolism. The cella-mosaic depicts a sea-scene, and a bronze relief displays a sea-god. At Chesterholm in northern Britain an inscription identifies Nodens with Neptune.

Water in its various natural manifestations was the single most revered feature in nature, and the one most frequently connected with the worship of a god or goddess. It was a vehicle whereby religion pervaded the lives of countless people, for it was so often encountered, and it always evoked associations with divinity. 'The Celtic mind regarded the spirits of water (wells, pools, lakes etc) not as major gods but as part of the vast race of minor deities, often nameless and always ill defined, who had to be placated and propitiated.'[24] But the scope for veneration and adoration was as limitless as the various forms taken by nature.

Certain trees and woodland groves of trees were sacred to the Celts and treated with religious awe. The oak was of particular concern to the Druids and used by them in their rites. Place names, the comments of classical writers, and surviving objects show that many Celtic idols were fashioned from wood, and that considerable care was taken in the selection of the wood used. The Celtic timber buildings which preceded the Roman or Romano-British temple at Thetford, Norfolk, may have had a woodland-spirit focus. The Romans uniquely for Britain introduced Faunus, the woodland spirit, to preside over the sanctuary; and this may indicate a similar previous Celtic spirit. If this is so, the elaborate system of timber enclosures round the original sacred area, consisting of close-set palisades, may have represented a kind of artificial grove.

To water and woodland as foci for Celtic veneration was added the animal world in a variety of forms. Birds were especially popular as objects of cultic attention. 'The concept of the bird as an otherworld agent, as a symbol or attribute of the god, as the herald of death or a symbol of good or evil fortune, is a recurrent and persistent theme.'[25] Among the most powerful were the soaring eagle, the goose representing the destructive forces of aggression and magic, and, perhaps most importantly, the crow and the crane which were viewed as mysterious agents of the otherworld, harbingers of death and portents of an evil force. This is likewise with such animals as the dog, the ram, the horned serpent, the bear, the hare and fish. Epona was the Celtic horse-goddess, but does not appear very frequently in Britain. Curious representations of hooded dwarves generally appear in triplicate, and on certain continental inscriptions are named *genii cucullati*.

There was a great deal of variety in the Celtic representations of a sun-divinity. There were depictions of the god himself in different guises, and sometimes there were epigraphic allusions accompanied by such celestial emblems as the wheel. It appears that the Celtic solar-sky god embraced not only the sun and sky, but war, fertility and death as well. There was also a considerable use of such derivative symbols as the swastika, the rosette and concentric circles. All of them represented rotary movement, with the wheel in particular portraying a physical similarity to the sun.

A yet further aspect of the Celtic nature-worship was the stress given to fertility rites. There is considerable archaeological evidence for this in Gaul and Britain. It is clear that a great many of the Celtic divinities had overt and very definite associations with fertility. This is most pronounced in the various 'mother-goddesses'. 'The cult of the matres, personifying the fertility of the earth, of animals, and of women, was one of the most popular and widespread of all the cults of the Celtic part of the Roman Empire.'[26]

No trace has been found of a Celtic goddess of love, 'but all the goddesses share in having marked sexual characteristics, and no matter what their individual departments of influence sexuality and maternity are their fundamental concerns'.[27] A number of written dedications and iconography, generally in stone or clay but occasionally in metal or bone, attest to mother-goddesses, some of which take a triadic form. The cult of the triple mothers (*Deae Matres*) is more familiar than some other cults of Celtic origin because examples of it often bear a descriptive surname which gives a clue to its identity. And of these examples, by far the majority are linked to a locality, which asserts their essentially territorial nature. They all represent both maternal fertility and the earth's fecundity. Especially interesting evidence of single and triple mother goddesses, in the form of epithets and plaques, has been unearthed at Cirencester, Bath and Carrawburgh.

Varied though the features in nature which attracted Celtic religious attention and aroused a religious response may have been in Roman Britain, there were certain personal and corporate religious practices which were common to all the native people. The lives of all the Celts were governed by sets of rules and prohibitions. The latter consisted mainly of what has been given the Polynesian name of *taboos*, but which the Celts called *geis* (*geasa* in the plural). These largely related to food, although other embargoes referred to such matters as not straightening out a spear with the teeth. Of less importance were the objects and actions considered lucky or unlucky (*matis* or *anmatis*), such as certain movements which it was thought should always be in the direction of the sun.

At the community level, public rituals were conducted which were determined by the annual rural seasonal cycle. The Celts of Roman times inherited the four ancient festivals previously mentioned; and continued them with but minor variations. The year opened with the festival of the autumnal equinox on 1 November. It was thought that on the eve of this celebration all the spirits emerged from their dwellings in the hills, springs, lakes, rivers and ancient burial mounds. The following festival on 1 February was based on the old pastoral lambing season, and it therefore had strong fertility associations. The vernal equinox, with the appearance of new vegetation and new life in nature manifesting a sort of natural upsurge, was celebrated as a great Celtic May Day festival. Finally, the mid-summer festival took place on 1 August. It was a prolonged affair, with great assemblies starting in mid-July and lasting a month, and it included an abundance of feasting, mock-fighting and horse racing.

Although almost all the Celtic gods and goddesses of Roman Britain were local, there were some which seem to have commanded wider allegiance and to have been accorded more than local authority perhaps largely as a consequence of the influence of Roman religious beliefs. Taranis, the sky-god, was equated with Jupiter. There is an epigraphic record of him on an altar at Chester, dedicated by a *princeps* of *Legio XX*, and he is also depicted on a pottery mould from Corbridge where he carries a shield and a crooked stick, which represents the *fulmen* (lightning-flash). The horned-god Cernunnos is depicted on a small plaque from Cirencester, and the goddess Rosmerta, together with her male equivalent, Smertios, who are 'providers', are found on various reliefs, including a good example from Gloucester. The deity Sucellos has, as with Taranis, been linked epigraphically with Jupiter, and this has been reinforced by his bearded facial similarity to the Roman god, so that he has been identified by some as a sky god and the father of the Celtic deities.

The horse goddess Epona was very popular in Gaul, but the only epigraphic evidence of her in Britain is from the military zone, as at Carvoran on Hadrian's Wall. Another god Belatucadros (variously spelt), is attested by about twenty-seven dedications, all from Roman forts, with the exception of one at Carlisle, where anyhow there was a military establishment at least in the Flavian period; and this is not surprising as he was attributed with protective or healing qualities. In military areas the god Cocidius is found in the region of the Wall, in the Irthing valley; three altars at Corbridge point to the god Maponus who appears to have been a solar god who was primarily concerned with healing, and who was a protector against disease and plague. Lastly among the gods with military associations, there were the Veteres, the strangest deities on the northern frontier, represented by over fifty small, and normally very crude, altars, almost all of them on Roman Wall forts.[28]

Certain cult symbols were also universal, or nearly so, among the British Celts. Of these perhaps that of greatest longevity and most wide-spread use over the entire Celtic area, insular and continental, was the representation in various forms of the human head. The head was considered by the Celts to be symbolic of divinity and otherworld powers; it was the most important member of the body, and the very seat of the soul. Representations of the head are found in profusion in Britain on metalwork, carved in stone, and on pottery. Some depict local deities, some the more universal gods.

Of only slightly less importance to the cult of the head was that of a horned god. It appears that the cult of a horned god or gods was well-established in Britain by the first century AD. In the Roman period it seems to have been identified with the Gaulish god Cernunnos, to whom I have already referred, or to an indigenous bull or ram horned god. It was part of the fusion of the Roman with the Celtic deities that in its warrior capacity the horned god frequently became equated with Mars.

The Celts commonly made votive offerings to the god or goddess to whom reverence was given, whether the deity concerned was local or more universal, for they perceived their gods and goddesses as powers which required to be wooed or appeased. The oblations included food-stuffs such as fruits or cereals, juices and beverages containing alcohol, the flesh of animals, coins, weapons, jewellery, tools and pots. But as the Roman period progressed this was modified in three respects. First, the carrying of weapons by civilians was made unlawful, and only such items of miniature size were used as offerings. Secondly, items were produced which were designed purely for votive use, the most noteworthy being copper alloy figurines of gods and goddesses. Thirdly, various objects were employed which bear inscriptions revering, or seeking requests from a particular deity. In recent years inscribed tablets known as 'curses' have been found in great quantities at Bath and Uley in particular. These often have engraved on them a message to the god requesting retribution against someone for an offence, most commonly theft of items varying in face or sentimental value from a piece of clothing to a draught animal, or even a much-loved wife.

Finally, in this brief review of Celtic religion in Roman times, mention must be made of the Druids. On the evidence so far accumulated, it appears that Druidism was the only manifestation of Celtic corporate religion at the time of the arrival of the Romans. From their centre in Anglesey the Druids held some sway over all the tribes in the midlands and south-east. The extent to which Druidical ritual was adopted by the population as a whole is a matter of surmise; and whether the predominantly aristocratic religion of the Druids was imitated by more lowly people is open to conjecture. It is quite possible that even if there were official Druidical tribal ceremonies, once they were concluded ordinary people may have given honour to more low-key, less politically charged deities of their own. The implacable hostility of the Druids to the Romans, which expressed itself in political interference, had already resulted in them being outlawed in Gaul by the edicts of several emperors. The opposition of the Romans was maintained in the British context, and they attempted to abolish the Druidic caste. The Druids seem to have fulfilled the role of a Celtic intellectual élite, and as such were the repository of Gaulish and British cultural as well as political and military opposition to the Roman conquerors. Augustus excluded them from Roman citizenship, and he forbade Roman citizens to practise Druidical rites; Tiberius banned them by a decree of the Roman Senate; and Claudius attempted to 'wholly abolish' them in AD 54.

Roman writers implanted a picture of Druidical fanaticism which has persisted to this day. Most of the literary works concerned belong to the first or second centuries AD, and they often merely repeated the somewhat lurid ethnography of the late second-century BC Greek historian Posidonius. They were almost entirely composed for political or other Romano-centric reasons. They are, however, still worthy of summary

because they produced a mind-set in at least many of the Roman leaders
which was an important element in the total religious scene in Roman
Britain, and they need to be recognized as evidence bearing on the
religion of this controversial Celtic religious fraternity.

Strabo recorded that human victims suffered death by arrows or
impalement within the Druid temples. He, and also Julius Caesar,
described the gigantic wicker baskets in human shape which were filled
with human and animal victims who were then 'burnt alive in a horrifying sacrificial conflagration'.[29] Tacitus described how the Druids
deemed it a duty to cover their altars with the blood of their captives
and used human entrails as a means of consulting their deities. And it
was Tacitus who vividly dramatized the destruction by Suetonius
Paulinus of the sacred Druidic groves on the island of Anglesey. Perhaps
no depiction of the Druids had greater influence than his description of
them ranged in order against the Romans with hands uplifted, invoking
their gods, and pouring forth ghastly imprecations.

The Celtic religion in its various forms and manifestations was deep-
rooted. It persisted as an element in the religion of England, albeit in
many cases in a much adapted or altered form, and it permanently
coloured the Christianity which confronted it and finally emerged
triumphant over it.[30]

Roman Britain – the classical Roman gods

The Romans in Britain adopted a policy of religious toleration towards
all faiths. Their sole concern was that no religion should threaten the
Roman political and social values, and Roman overlordship. The only
known exception was the policy regarding the Druids, who were feared
and despised for what were perceived as their barbaric beliefs and
behaviour, including, so the Romans thought, human sacrifice; and who
were thought to exercise an unduly great and hostile influence on the
population at large. Such toleration demanded little of the Romans who
were themselves polytheists, or perhaps polydaimonists, worshippers,
that is, of an infinite number of minor deities, each of whom was defined
as regards their functions but in other respects were mere names. Even
the official religion of the Roman state was not exclusive; although
observance of it was required of individuals and groups before freedom
for indulgence in any other form of worship was granted, and this presented problems for Christians on occasions, as can be seen from the
martyrdom of Saints Alban, Aaron and Julius.

The Romans were not so much theorists as practical men of action. They were concerned that non-Roman religions should not interfere in the Roman control over conquered people, and in the loyalty of such subject people to the Roman authority. Civil obedience was of prime concern to them. What any subjugated people believed was of little interest to them, as long as it did not undermine Roman government and control, or lessen in any way the allegiance of the people to the Roman rule and all that it entailed. This may be more relevant in the British religious scene from the first to the early fifth century than their toleration. It may be, as one scholar has stated, 'that the Roman attitude towards the religions of the Celts was not so much that of toleration, but more a pragmatic acceptance of the existence of a multitude of local spirits, which they felt obliged to treat as realities'.[31]

The Roman state religion itself was more a relationship of citizens with their emperor and all that he represented than a personal system of belief and faith. It was contractual, designed to reinforce the loyalty of subjects to the empire. The gods, so it was believed, would protect the state if the necessary rituals were performed; and any individual or corporate nonconformity would, it was thought, detract from and even put in peril the fulfilment of the divine side of the transaction. The worship of the Capitoline Triad of Jupiter Optimus Maximus, Juno and Minerva was therefore given a high priority both in the army and in officially founded Roman towns. Although no trace has been found of any *capitolium*, or joint temple to all three of these deities, it would certainly have existed in each of the four colonies and in the municipia of the province, with statues and altars to the deities concerned.

The focus of imperial sentiment was strengthened early in the Roman period in Britain, as elsewhere, when the cult of the Capitoline Triad lost ground to a new state religion, the Imperial Cult. It was the blatant development of such a cult at Colchester that so provoked many of the native Celtic tribes, and resulted in the fearful uprising under the leadership of Boudicca in 60. But even this important centre of Roman state religion was linked with the obscure Celtic cult of Mercury Andescociuoucus; an example of the syncretism which was so typical of Romano-Celtic religion.

It was common in the Roman *coloniae* or chartered towns, to have a temple in honour of both living and deceased members of the Imperial House. The worship was the function of a statutory group of six priests who were selected from among wealthy freed-men traders and possibly old-established citizen families, it being considered by the community that such duties were a reasonable burden for new or rich citizens. The Imperial Cult was intended to promote the security and welfare of the Roman state; and it was therefore considered imperative that it was regularly observed by means of annual public vows for the emperor's safety. Between the emperor and the gods stood various personified virtues; such *numina* as Virtue, Victory, Discipline and Fortune. And it is pertinent that many of the Roman coins portrayed the emperor on one side and one of these qualities on the other.

When we come to the Roman gods other than the deified emperors, we start to move from the dry formulae of government regulations to something far more personal to the individual Roman subject concerned. We begin to be transported into the realm of the great powers of nature; and we find that countless people owed fealty to the three state gods, Jupiter, Juno and Minerva, to Mars, Mercury, Apollo, Venus and Diana, and offered deep and passionate prayer to them.

Of the three gods of the state, Jupiter was the most important to the Romans. He was essentially a sky divinity, but he also fulfilled the roles as both the head of the Roman pantheon and, in the form of Jupiter Best and Greatest, as representative of the spirit of Rome itself. There is, however, but meagre evidence for the cult of Jupiter Optimus Maximus in the towns of Roman Britain. One of the temples added to the Forum of Verulamium could have been for his worship. A very small temple beside the earlier forum of London could have been for the same purpose, and other evidence points to this state cult in the chief town of Britain. A bronze eagle found at Silchester may have been associated with a statue of Jupiter.[32] The paucity of surviving signs of the worship of the pre-eminent god of the Roman state is remarkable. Perhaps it is an indication that on the fringes of the empire state religion was less influential than nearer the centre of governmental power on the continent.

Juno was Jupiter's consort, and as such shared his dominance over other deities. She was, in addition, the leading goddess of women and femininity. Iconagraphically she is of least significance in Britain. She occurs relatively infrequently, but she is represented on small figurines in London, Chester and possibly York.

Minerva appears not only in an unadulterated Roman form, as in bronzes at Canterbury, Plaxtol in Kent and elsewhere, but also in Celtic guise or in association with a Celtic deity. This is most prominently demonstrated at Bath where she is fully equated with the Celtic goddess Sulis.

Both Mars and Mercury were especially popular in Britain, as they were in Gaul. Understandably, as the god of war, Mars was to be found in areas where there was a large military presence, most notably in the north and west.[33] But he was also influential and popular as the patron of farming. Even if some of the quite prolific dedications to him which have been discovered on stone betray Celtic influence in style, they almost universally seem to represent a classical rather than a Celtic Mars.

Mercury, like Mars, lent himself to a wide variety of celticisms but occurs, as the best represented divinity in Roman Britain, in his classical role as the messenger and, more importantly, as a trader-god. Over fifty small figurines of the god are recorded for the lowland regions, mostly in bronze, with a dozen or more from northern and western areas. Of special significance is the cult of Mercury at the Uley (Gloucestershire) temple site.

> These excavations have led to the first clear identification and extensive investigation of a later prehistoric ritual enclosure in Britain. The associated votive finds, form one of the most extensive assemblages ever recovered from a temple site in Britain, which are mainly dedicated to Mercury. The five fragments of the head indicate an amazingly high standard of workmanship for a figure carved in coarse stone. Possibly the sculptor came from a workshop in Cirencester or Bath and artists were peripatetic in antiquity.[34]

Although Apollo, the classical Roman god of healing, prophecy and, later, of the sun, was not particularly common in Britain, a shrine to him has been found at Nettleton Shrub in Wiltshire. Venus usually occurs, as at *Verulamium*, as a small bronze figure, or as a white pipeclay statuette. Diana, the huntress, is found in figures of bronze and on stone reliefs. Evidence of her cult comes from Maiden Castle (Dorset), a temple at Nettleton Shrub, on the same site connected with the worship of Apollo, and at Bath.

Other classical Roman gods who have been discovered include Aesculapius (a healer), Cupid, Neptune, Faunus, Silvanus, Vulcan, the demigod Hercules, and the goddesses Fortuna, Victory, Ceres (a corn-goddess), Luna, Flora and Vesta (keeper of the hearth and fire). In fact there is evidence for the practice of almost all the main classical cults in Britain, either in the form of inscriptions or of statuary.

Within the confines of the Roman home it was often the *penates* or *lares* who were of greatest importance in daily life. The former were 'dwellers in the store-room', which embraced little household deities who watched over the food-supplies of the household. The latter were also domestic gods, but they were of more importance, for their worship extended beyond the houses and land of individuals, although their identity and character have remained vague. It seems that in traditional Roman religion every head of a household carried out priestly functions within his own home and family. The family worship would be focussed upon the *lararium* or shrine within the house. The gods of the home might be joined by images of other more personified deities, and especially those associated with family life and fortune such as Vesta, Venus, Juno Lupicina, goddess of childbirth, and any gods particularly venerated by the family in question.

At the heart of Roman religion were the rustic and family festivals. These related, as with the Romano-Celts, to the annual cycle of rural events such as the lambing season and the end of autumn harvest. By attributing a religious significance to the pivotal periods in the working and domestic life and experience of ordinary people the Romans drew upon primitive and deep-seated impulses; and this was 'overlaid by Greek or Graeco-Italian religion replete with gods and goddesses and young human heroes.'[35]

For the Romans the infinite number of divine beings touched upon every facet of life, so that they could be invoked for all and in all circumstances. Every grove, spring, wood, cluster of rocks or other natural feature, as well as all activities of life, had an attendant spirit. The locals were at liberty to give such entities personal names, but a stranger in ignorance of these would refer to each simply as the *genius loci*, 'the spirit of the place'. Furthermore, each individual was born with a divine entity attached to him or her throughout life. It was a luxuriant polytheism which knew no bounds. For the Romans as well as for the indigenous British this multiplicity of spirits represented very real forces for good or evil; spirits which needed to be propitiated with gifts and libations. They lived in 'a world peopled by witches and little hooded figures, by hunchbacks and animal-headed men'.[36] It is understandable that this Roman religious orientation was underpinned by the conviction that men parleyed with the gods by means of sacrifice for protection from a host of actual or potential enemies, known or unknown, and for a range of favours in the hard grind of daily life.

Buildings associated with classical religion are quite rare in the British *civitas* capitals. Classical temples were absent from most *forum-basilica* complexes, and there are few signs of them in most cities.[37] In contrast,

Romano-Celtic temples were frequently found in towns. They are evident at Silchester,[38] *Verulamium*,[39] at the Gosbecks site, Colchester,[40] and at Canterbury.[41] They varied in ground plan. Some consisted of a simple enclosed space, others were made more elaborate by the inclusion of subsidiary chambers or ambulatories.[42] The most basic were normally small, often rectangular, such as at Springhead or Scargill Moor, near Bowes. Some introduced a semi-circular apse at one end of the building forming the *nymphaea*, as at Chedworth and Housesteads. Others were circular, for instance at Maiden Castle and Frilford. The more complex buildings seem to have included an inner unit, in a variety of shapes, which rose as a tower above a surrounding portico and acted as repository for the cult figures. It was lit by clerestory windows. In some cases additional wings or porticoes seem to have been added, for example in one of the principal temples near the centre of *Verulamium*. The frequent eccentric placing of temples within their enclosures indicates that they may have been of secondary importance to some totem or tree which has subsequently disappeared. In some towns or other settlements, temples were grouped together, as at Caistor-by-Norwich.

The primary purpose of pagan temples was not congregational worship. They were first and foremost homes of their divinities, and the services in them, including the sacrifices, were designed for the sustenance of the deity. Individual worshippers made votive offerings in the hope that the god or goddess would grant a request, in order to fulfil a vow or as an act of thanksgiving, but these were secondary purposes for the temple. Coins were the most popular of the gifts offered, but personal ornaments and small idols were also given.

Roman Britain – pagan eastern deities

The official divinities of the Roman state were worshipped by the administrators, the army and by the public at large in a somewhat formalized way as a patriotic duty. They made little impact on the hearts and minds of most of Rome's subjects. The more exotic eastern mystery cults promised more for their convinced and dedicated adherents than the cold, impersonal Roman state religion. The Roman state religion largely took the form of corporate vows rather than individual allegiances. Even the other gods worshipped by the Romans increasingly appeared to some as somewhat undynamic, to a certain extent locked into the archaic era of Roman, or even a past age of

Greek, mythology. They had perhaps become too 'established' and static to please the more spiritually adventurous members of the population. They remained fine for perhaps the majority of the people who sought conservatism in their religion, but they did not meet the needs of others, albeit a minority, who looked for something with greater mystery and momentum.

The eastern cults in contrast had a more developed and elaborate basis of appeal and called for greater individual response. They held out the promise of unknown and promising experiences of present fulfilment and future joys. They had about them the aura of the exotic and the extravagant. As the Roman period progressed people increasingly turned to these religions, which were probably introduced by soldiers, foreign traders or craftsmen into the cosmopolitan towns. Their popularity was already increasing under the late Republic, but it gained further impetus under the early Empire.

Mithras was a Persian god, an emissary of light and truth from the Iranian cosmic deity Ahura Mazda. Mithras captured and slew a divine wild bull by means of whose death all manner of blessings were released upon the earth. From the blood of the bull sprang all animal and vegetable life, so that an apparent act of destruction was transformed into one of creation. Mithraism was a dualistic religion in which the light, represented by Mithras, confronted the dark element of evil and disorder.

Mithraism first became prominent in the Roman Empire during the age of the Flavians. Its early chief propagators were members of the army and travelling merchants from the east. In Britain traces of the cult are to be found near military forts at Caernarfon, Housesteads, Rudchester and Carrawburgh, at York and London. Although it has attracted attention, especially because of the well-publicized discovery of an important Mithraeum and its sculptures at a site in the valley of the Walbrook in London, for the majority of the inhabitants of Roman Britain the cult must have been almost as unfamiliar, secret and bizarre as it appears to us today.

The worship was dramatic and intense; and it was usually conducted in small buildings designed to hold perhaps a score of devotees at one time. The places where they gathered were long in proportion to their width. A single door in one of the narrow ends gave access to an anteroom which was separated from the nave by a screen. In the nave the worshippers were seated on long, shallow benches attached to the side walls of the building. At the far end from the entrance was the sanctuary of the god. This characteristically incorporated a great sculptured relief commemorating the exploit of Mithras in slaying the bull (the tauroctony). Two torch-bearers accompanied Mithras and, together with the altar fires, must have created a dramatic effect in the semi-darkness, which would have been intensified by the pungent aroma of smouldering pine cones. In such a setting the followers of Mithras ate their ritual meals and endured the ordeal of the graduated initiation rites through which they were admitted to the several degrees of their cult.

Membership of a Mithraic temple was commonly restricted to some twenty or thirty initiates. These were divided into seven grades, of which the six that are known were the Raven, the Lion, the Soldier, the Bride, the Persian and the Father. Initiation into each successive grade was through tests of courage and endurance, all of which took place within the temple.

In common with all ancient religions, with the exception of Judaism and Christianity, the Mithras cult was tolerant of other deities. This is indicated by the naming of Olympian and Romano-Celtic deities in close proximity to mithraea, as at Carrawburgh, and the wide range of sacred objects around the area of the London mithraeum. Nonetheless, the cult had a distinctive character which set it apart from most of the other eastern religions of the time. The believer was required to commit himself or herself totally and for life to Mithras, who was addressed as 'The God'. Contemporary friends and foes alike made an analogy to service in the army; and the third grade of initiation was that of Miles, the soldier. 'Mithraism was a religion of "Enthusiasm" and of "Religious Theatre". It concerned itself with a spiritual journey from obscure darkness to the most brilliant light; from death to eternal life; from chaos to order. Its practice required effort and discipline.'[43]

In the course of the third century the prestige of Mithras was greatly enhanced by his identification with Sol, the Invincible Sun God, who was likewise of Persian origin. The worship of Sol grew in popularity with the Romans. The Emperor Aurelian built an impressive temple to him in Rome in 274, he was frequently depicted on Roman coins, and Sunday was named after him. At Carrawburgh the Mithraic temple was rebuilt and enlarged in the late third century for the unified worship of Mithras and Sol, and was reconstructed after it had been destroyed a few years later by raiders.

Other religions from the east, such as the worship of Cybele and the cult of Isis appealed to the emotions and offered salvation, but they were not secretive and confined to initiated devotees as with Mithraism.

The worship of the Phrygian mother-goddess Cybele and her young shepherd lover and consort Atys appears to have centred around a cyclical myth personified by the castration, death and rebirth of Atys. Driven by remorse and madness for infidelity towards Cybele, Atys castrated himself in her service. The cult was introduced to Rome in 205 BC, but an embargo was placed on Roman citizens participating in its orgiastic rituals; and these bans were only lifted in the reign of Claudius. In Britain the cult seems to have been practised mainly in towns. Objects relating to it have been found at London, in the *colonia* at Gloucester and in the region of Hadrian's Wall. There is no record of shrines for Cybele worship (*metroons*), but they probably existed in London, Gloucester and Corbridge. Other shrines in southern Britain are suggested by a fragmentary torso of Atys found at a villa in Froxfield (Wiltshire) and by a mosaic depicting Cybele at the Whatley Roman villa (Somerset). A bronze jug portraying the head of Atys on the handle, discovered at Hockwold (Norfolk) suggests a rural East Anglian temple, and shows that the cult may have penetrated to relatively unromanized parts of Britain.

The theogeny of the cult included the belief that Cybele, like Isis, enjoyed universal sovereignty, being 'the Mother of the Gods, Peace, Virtue, Ceres, the Syrian Goddess, weighing life and laws in her balance'.[44] In the ceremonies of the cult a festival of mourning was followed by the *hilaria*, a joyous celebration of the rebirth of Atys and the new year. Less explicable as an attraction to Romano-British taste were the rites involved in the *taurobolium* or bull-sacrifice, if these were introduced into Britain, when the eunuch priests, the *Galli*, led ecstatic dances accompanied, in some cases, by the self-flagellation of initiates to the priesthood, and their castration by means of fearsome clamps otherwise used by farmers for gelding their horses. In the ceremony the faithful bathed in the blood of a bull which was sacrificed on a slatted floor over a pit in which the worshippers stood, eager to receive the blood all over their bodies as the principle of life. The only possible evidence yet for *tauroblia* in Britain is the ox-scull which was buried behind the altar in the court of the temple at *Verulamium* which may have been the remains of such a sacrifice.[45]

The cult of Isis, who was originally a moon and fertility goddess, Sarapis, the god of sky and death, and Harpocrates, their son, originated in Egypt. Sarapis and Harpocrates were Graeco-Roman versions of the ancient Egyptian gods Osiris and Horus, and the cult retained much of its ancient Pharaonic character and mythology. Osiris had been killed and dismembered by the evil god Seth and restored to life by Isis. The triad represented the power of creation, as rulers of all restoring life to the earth; and Osiris, because he had died and been restored to life, was seen as an underworld god. At the end of the Republic this religion was discouraged in Roman territories, but the emperor Gaius and his successors actively encouraged worship of the Egyptian pantheon and these divinities were introduced to Britain at the time of the occupation.

As with other eastern deities in Britain, these gods were most commonly found in towns. There are indications that a shrine to Sarapis existed, and in London an *isaeum* (shrine to Isis) is implied by a jug, possibly dated before c.AD 75, scratched with the graffito, *Londini ad fanum Isidis*, by a third-century AD stone inscription, a bronze figurine of the seated goddess, a bronze steelyard weight, a bust of Isis on the head of a bone hairpin and an altar re-used in the foundations of the late riverside wall at Blackfriars. Evidence of the worship of Sarapis includes iron models of *sistra* (tinkling rattles carried in procession by priests) from London, and a bronze full-size rattle from Exeter; a fine marble head of Sarapis from the excavated London *mithraeum*; a marble head in porphyry from a grave at Highworth (Wiltshire); a stone head, probably of Antonine origin, from Silchester; a bronze ring decorated with a head of Sarapis from Stone (Buckinghamshire); a statuette depicting the goddess, recorded from Dorchester (Dorset); and a figurine from the vicinity of the Romano-Celtic temple precinct at Thornborough (Buckinghamshire). Portrayals of Harpocrates include statuettes mainly in London. Nevertheless, despite this body of evidence, the quantitative significance of these cults can be over-stressed. They did, however, show qualitative merits. The cult of Isis was characterized by prayer and praise, with a rich litany in which ceremonies employed incense, flowers and light, and there was joyful celebration; for its followers thought that Isis controlled fate and promised salvation.[46]

Bacchus was probably much better known to Romans and to most romanized Britons. He was the theme of many works of art. For instance, a standing Bacchus was carved in relief upon the altar of Sulis Minerva at Bath, together with Apollo, Hercules, Jupiter and other deities, and Bacchus figures adorn a very large Corinthian capital from Cirencester.

Bacchus is said to have rescued Ariadne after her abandonment by Theseus on the Isle of Naxos. He was a saviour god, and his *cantharus* (wine chalice) designated both physical and spiritual refreshment. It is possible that the Walbrook mithraeum was taken over by his followers in the fourth century. It is difficult to determine if the silver openwork plaque showing Bacchus standing beside his panther and the Leadenhall Street mosaic depicting the god riding upon a panther indicate a prominent body of worshippers, but it does appear that he was known and taken seriously as a source of spiritual life by a significant number of Roman subjects.

The eastern gods so far considered originated in Persia, Anatolia or Egypt. The Syrian deities were not ordered into any form of pantheon; instead there were local, omnipotent city-deities, Baals and goddesses, who sometimes attained a wider status and were exported to Rome, and from thence to the western provinces. The most important Baal introduced to Britain was Jupiter Dolichenus, together with his consort Juno Regina. Dolichenus, like Mithras, was a soldier god, but his cult was not so complex. Almost all Dolichene material comes from areas of Britain which had an important military presence, notably Corbridge in the region of Hadrian's Wall. The cult was frequently connected with the health and safety of the emperor and his family, and it fostered loyalty to the emperor and to the state.

The interaction and fusion of religions in Roman Britain

It is common to find classical Roman gods closely associated by name, and therefore in worship, with Celtic and, less frequently, eastern deities. The best known and most investigated of such examples of syncretism is that of the goddess Sulis with the Roman Minerva at Bath.[47]

The site had many attractions as a focus for religious sentiment. It nestled in a bend of the river Avon and was protected on all sides by the steep limestone scarp of the southern Cotswolds. The Cotswold ridge provided a natural corridor of communication, as did the river. Bath was also located at a crossing point guarded by the Iron Age hill-forts of Bathampton and Little Solsbury. But, most importantly from a religious point of view, it was made awesome by hot mineral waters from three natural springs which broke through the surface of Lias clay within a hundred metres of each other, disgorging vast quantities of supposedly healing waters, in the case of the King's Bath spring at a rate of nearly a third of a million gallons a day. With all these advantages it is perhaps not surprising that the Roman army was firmly established on the site by the winter of AD 43, and that during the following few generations they and their successors responded to the presence of the remarkable springs and of the native goddess who presided over them by helping to make it a prime example of Romano-Celtic religious co-operation. This merging of religions from the two cultures is epitomized in the pediment to the temple, discovered in 1790, in which the Gorgon, who in classical mythology was always female, was depicted as male, and moreover as a Celtic male. It was a diplomatic scheme politically as well as religiously.

> The monumentalizing of an ancient sanctuary and the conflation of its deity with the Roman Minerva would have been a shrewd act, legitimizing the Roman presence and demonstrating the unity of the province. The scheme would have been in nice contrast to the politically inept creation of the temple of Divus Claudius at Colchester – one of the sparks which ignited the rebellion. It may even be that the complex iconography of the pediment with its blatant Celtic centre-piece set within the framework, and amid the symbols, of classical mythology, was deliberately contrived to represent the coming together of Roman and native culture.[48]

The original Romano-Celtic temple was constructed at the end of the first century AD, and an extension was built probably in the second half of the second century or a little later.

In addition to the main Sulis Minerva complex there were other deities worshipped at Bath. An inscription mentions Loucetius Mars and Nemetona, and these two deities, together with three *Genii cuculati*, appear on a small relief discovered in excavations of the bath. An altar to Diana and reliefs of Mercury and of Aesculapius were also found. 'Leaving aside the Aesculapius (if the identification is correct) and allowing Diana to be a conflation with a local huntress deity, then the entire collection has a distinctly rural, Celtic fringe, flavour.'[49] There were a variety of ways that Celtic, Roman and eastern religions interacted in the Roman period. Some may appropriately be designated as assimilation while others are best described as syncretism, conflation or association. Of the Roman pantheon it was Mars who was most easily assimilated with Celtic deities, because his association with war made him widely popular. Thus, we find Mars Camulos, Camulos being the war god after whom the Catuvellauni called their chief city Camulodunum; Mars Toutates, who was possibly introduced to the

Catuvellauni from north-eastern Gaul; Mars Cocidius, who attracted a strong following in Cumberland; Mars Loucetius, who was a Rhineland deity found at Bath; Mars Rigonemetos, from near Lincoln; and Mars Medocius, from a temple outside Colchester, as well as several more.[50]

A few other examples will help to establish the widespread nature of the linkage I am describing. The Celtic goddess Briganta, who is attested in the neighbourhood of Hadrian's Wall, was associated with Jupiter Dolichenus in the dedication of an altar at Corbridge. An altar at the legionary fortress of Chester to *Jupiter Optimus Maximus Tanarus*, erected in the year 154 by a senior centurion, shows how easily Taranis could be incorporated into the Roman concept of a sky-god. At Carrawburgh votaries of Coventina included the prefect of the First Cohort, whose relief showed the Celtic goddess reclining by a flowing urn and holding a water-plant in the traditional manner of Greek and Roman nymphs.[51] Mercury was to an extent celticized in his association with a non-classical Celtic consort, Rosmerta, and at such places as Chester and Uley where he is horned. Some Roman gods possessed Celtic surnames, as with Silvanus Callirius (Woodland King) and Apollo Cunomaghus (Hound Lord) at Nettleton.

An interesting recent discovery of a temple at Thetford has revealed a fourth-century pagan cult which worshipped Faunus, a minor early Italian god.

> The ancient Latin god Faunus had by this time evidently become totally conflated with similar gods, above all with Pan, but perhaps also with Silvanus and others, and had thus become part of the complex web of mystical religious belief incorporated in the worship of Bacchus. Since he shared many features with certain Celtic gods, for all peasant societies have their agricultural fertility deities, Faunus, like numerous other Roman gods, had been absorbed into Celtic religious belief, and fitting names and descriptions from Celtic mythology had been provided for him.[52]

As a last instance of the interlocking of the religions of two different peoples and cultures I refer once again to the way the Roman god Jupiter was adopted and adapted by the Celtic population. 'The Graeco-Roman sky-god apparently became identified with or linked to celestial powers who were seemingly already venerated in the pre-Roman Celtic world.'[53] The transformation of Jupiter in Gaul and Britain seems to have taken various forms, but three main Romano-Celtic deities may be distinguished. There was the association of the god with a Celtic thunderer; 'he was a representative of light, day and the positive element in a dualistic, possibly seasonal, Celtic mythology, illustrated by the so-called Jupiter-columns';[54] and, perhaps most importantly, he was identified with a Celtic solar divinity.

The Romano-Celtic temples which were the focus for the worship of an association in some form of Celtic and Roman religions functioned in an almost identical way to the temples of the classical type. Much light has been cast on this by studies of West Hill, Uley,[55] Nettleton Shrub,[56] Lamyatt Beacon,[57] Harlow and Springhead.

In this whole process of religious interaction, especially when it entailed a high degree of assimilation, although the Celtic element remained powerful, many archaeologists and historians are of the opinion that there was a tendency for the Roman god to exercise the greater influence. The *interpretatio Romana* was a dynamic concept, and although it did not destroy the ancestral gods it certainly changed them. 'Nevertheless, it is true that a line of continuity in worship and ritual links Romano-Celtic religion with its past. A Briton of the Flavian period must have felt he was venerating the gods of his fathers and grandfathers even though artists from the continent now gave them human (i.e. Graeco-Roman) faces.'[58] It has been argued that many of the Roman influences were shallow and cosmetic. The Romano-Celtic temples of Britain, and indeed of Gaul and the Germanies, were fundamentally non-Roman; and even where major elements of classical architecture were incorporated 'the Romanization was only at the level of a facade'. The 'essentially Celtic nature of the temple was retained'. The traditional Celtic form of architecture implies that 'the religious practices may also have continued in their traditional form. Therefore, whilst the cult may have accepted a Roman epithet for its deity and utilized the full benefits of Roman material culture the method of worship in the Roman period may have been little different from that of the pre-conquest era.'[59] Those scholars who minimize the effect of romanization in the religious sphere assert that three hundred and fifty years of occupation did not subvert Celtic religion, but left it essentially intact. They say that 'it is doubtful whether the influence of Rome on Celtic religion was more than superficial'.[60]

I am of the opinion that both views, namely that the Roman religion was supreme and that Celtic religion remained the most important element, contain elements of correct interpretation. The Romans seem to have been concerned to present the appearance, even if not in all cases the substance, of exercising a dominant influence in any joint enterprise or close interaction, but they were not troubled if the basic content of the Celtic religion, which in many situations differed very little from their own, was maintained. In any case, it was frequently subject to quite important modifications. As another scholar has said in reference to cultural and ritual practices at *Argentomagus*, Indre, France at the time of the Roman presence in Britain: 'imported gods were simply superimposed on established local customs and religious practices.'[61] I can accept the conclusion that for most Romano-Britons, 'although their religion became culturally Roman it seems to have remained ethnically Celtic'.[62]

One reason for the fairly easy accommodation of the Celtic and Roman religions to each other is their shared basic assumptions about the nature and purpose of religion, and the forms it should take. Although the Celts had no organized cosmology in the same way as the Romans, there was much similarity between the religious practices of the two peoples. In the main there was a pervasive acknowledgment of the existence and need for a host of local spirits or spirits who were crucial in specific areas of daily life. Polytheism was long-established in both cultures, and there was a willingness to make adaptations in nomenclature and practice in the interest of harmonious co-existence.

There were differences between the two religious cultures, even on issues of fundamental orientation and practice, but they were not as crucial as might at first appear. The seasons, nature in all its ramifications, and the afterworld, were shared matters of central concern, although they were of more significance to the Celts. The Celtic festivals were, to a greater extent than for the Romans, related to events in the agricultural year, for the Roman calendar was much more complex and it was centred more on the veneration of individual gods and goddesses. Even so, the Roman Lupercalia of mid-February carried some of the features of the great Celtic farming festival of Imbolc; and the Parilia of 21 April, together with the Floralia from 28 April to 3 May, included elements formerly contained in the fertility and purification rituals of the May Day Beltine. The Romans celebrated harvest in common with the Celts, although it was rather later in the year.

The same applies to burial practices. The impact of Roman religion on the native population was considerable, and not least of all in the matter of burial rites. But this was as a consequence of example rather than coercion. 'On the evidence available burial custom, like religious thought, was a matter of personal choice, partly because the Romans did not attempt to prescribe funerary practice, except in the law relating to the positioning of cemeteries, and partly because of the strong influence of Celtic religious belief surviving in Roman Britain.'[63]

Initially, after the arrival of the Romans, cemeteries, in line with imperial law, were located outside the town limits along the roadside, and cremation was the dominant practice. The ashes were customarily placed in a glass or pottery urn, together with a few coins and a lamp or small pot as grave goods. For the more wealthy inscribed gravestones were often provided.

The pre-Roman Celts and the Celts of the early years of Roman Britain largely if not universally adopted cremation, with local variations in the details of burial practice. Under the Romans, the rite became more standardized, without the former Celtic variations. Gradually inhumation replaced cremation until it became the almost universal method of burying the dead. Wood, lead or stone coffins were used, and the corpse was laid out fully clothed and shrouded. But there was no single required and used burial method or procedure. Supine inhumation or cremation were most popular, but by the late Roman period the large inhumation cemeteries were not entirely uniform in their detailed characteristics. Some show a virtual absence of grave goods, while others include many furnished graves. Some were apparently arranged in an elaborate way with focal graves, while others were arranged very neatly in parallel or slightly converging rows. These variations may reflect the growing diversification of religious beliefs as classical pagan and Celtic religions were joined by eastern mystery cults, and as Christianity achieved a more dominant position. Certainly, 'while the methods of Roman burial were followed in Britain, the native practices were not totally abandoned. Indeed, in the fourth century, even with the advent of Christianity, burials in Britain reflected a strong Celtic influence.'[64]

So, despite differences of belief and practice between the Celts and the Romans they understood each other. They seem to have recognized that what they had in common in basic matters of religious outlook, in the spiritual needs they felt and in the ways they sought to meet those needs, outweighed the religious differences between the two cultures, especially when it came to the ordinary subject living a not easy life, mostly in a rural or small town setting.

In the light of this, name tags to distinguish one god or spirit from another were of secondary importance. The preoccupation of the ordinary Celt or Roman was with the cycle of birth, youth, decline and death, with the relentless and essentially unchanging round of the seasons, and with the considerable demands of daily living. The Romans may have developed, from their strong legal background, the practice of coming to terms with the gods by means of oath-taking, and by the fulfilment of contracts, as their altars from all over the Roman world confirm; and this may have contrasted with the more spontaneous and non-legalistic approach of the Celts. It is arguable that indigenous Celtic religion was at a more primitive stage than that of the Romans; and certainly, since there was no overall organized Celtic state, there was no universal Celtic state religion. But the fundamentals underlying the spiritual outlook of the two peoples were almost identical. 'It is in the nature of Romano-Celtic culture in general and of religion in particular that hybridization, conflation and interaction between Roman and Celtic ideas took place.'[65] The way this worked in practice has been well described by one historian.

> . . . the Roman army, containing men from many parts of the empire, all with their own beliefs, and certainly no less superstitious than resident Britons, not only introduced new cults to Britain, but also did not hesitate to make appropriate gestures to the local cults they found here. Consequently, there grew in time a broad spectrum of religious beliefs which incorporated both classical and native deities, in which gods and goddesses of one canon were often identified or equated with those of the other. So it can be seen that an almost infinite number of conjoint deities became possible, and, in the process, Celtic beliefs received a classical veneer, while at the same time classical cults became acceptable to the Britons. Such a union would not have been possible unless both forms of religion had contained an underlying, common creed, and the people practising them a common basic spiritual need.[66]

This was the religious world of Roman Britain in which Christianity was planted, and in which it took root and grew.

2

Christianity in Roman Britain to c.410: Its History[1]

Myths, legends and history

And did those feet in ancient times
Walk upon England's mountains green?
And was the holy Lamb of God
On England's pleasant pastures seen?

And did the Countenance Divine
Shine forth upon our clouded hills?
And was Jerusalem builded here
Among these dark Satanic mills?[2]

However earnestly and lustily William Blake's stirring hymn may be sung by assembled school children, and regardless of strong and persistent supporting legends or considerable, mostly ill-informed, speculation, the answer to William Blake's series of questions is a resounding, unhesitant and assured 'No'. There is no authentic evidence which in any way encourages belief in the visit of Christ to Britain. Here is one question on the early history of Christianity in Britain about which we can be categorical.

An almost equally dogmatic response can be given to the pious fancy of some that St Paul made his way to this new outpost of the empire between his first and second imprisonments. The sole basis for such an assertion is a single sentence of St Clement of Rome, in which the apostle is said to 'have come to the boundary of the west'; but this has most naturally been interpreted by commentators as an allusion to Spain, or perhaps Gaul.[3]

There is also the legend which tells of the sojourn of Joseph of Arimathea in Britain, with its geographical focus at Glastonbury in Somerset. This is the spot where Joseph's staff is said to have taken root as the Glastonbury Thorn; and it is the area associated with the evocative and fascinating cycle of literary romances to do with the quest for the Holy Grail. William of Malmesbury, the historian who wrote in the twelfth century, plainly placed no reliance on these apocryphal stories. He mentioned them, and then drew a firm line between myth and history, and explicitly stated that the stories were fanciful. But in the Middle Ages the Glastonbury legend became crystallized, with the claim that St Joseph, friend of the Apostle Philip, brought the Christian faith to Britain in 63. Subsequently the story was embellished until in relatively modern times it has been suggested that the first church at Glastonbury was built by Christ the carpenter. This in turn inspired William Blake (1757–1827) to write the rousing hymn 'Jerusalem', quoted at the beginning of this chapter, in which the 'mountains green' are the Mendip and Polden Hills, and 'England's pleasant pastures' are the Somerset Levels. And the intense veneration surrounding the fancied early Christian history of Glastonbury has been resuscitated in the late twentieth century with regular church services and pilgrimages. An extended period of excavation at and around Glastonbury Abbey and the Tor has revealed nothing earlier than a sixth-century monastic foundation. This myth, even in its simplest form, remains unsubstantiated. It is at best highly dubious, and at worse a fabrication which owes more to inflamed imaginations than to historical evidence.

So, when did Christians first set foot on the mountains green and the pleasant pastures of Britain? Was it in the first, the second or the third century? We simply do not know. The possibility of ever knowing precisely is not bright; but there are clues.

The prospect that new purely literary, rather than iconographic, evidence will aid such a search for origins is not very promising. If we exclude minor inscriptions on stone, metal or wood, 'it seems most unlikely that any new written sources of any length or substance will ever come to light'.[4]

In contrast, archaeology has already helped to illuminate the subject in the post-Second World War period. And the potential for adding significantly to the total picture of Roman Britain, and the history of Christianity in those years in particular, by means of that discipline is considerable. To a lesser extent this is true of what is called 'linguistics', which is now widely viewed as a third academic arm in exploring this past age, and is no longer seen as a mere ancillary to historical and archaeological investigations.

Literary evidence

There are some allusions in Roman literature to the presence of Christianity in Britain, although qualifications need to be made about each of them.

The North African Christian scholar and leader Tertullian claimed in his Tract against the Jews (*Adversus Judaeos*) that by about 200 Christianity was already established in the remoter fringes of the empire. He enumerated the lands he had in mind. In doing so, and before he moved in his partly clockwise coverage of the main countries involved from Spain and the diverse peoples of the Gauls to such northern barbarians as Sarmatians, Dacians, Germans and Scyths, he made mention of *Britannorum inaccesa Romanis loca* ('places of the British not approached by the Romans'), which, like other territories, were said to be by then *Christo vero subdita* ('made subject to the true Christ'). This is too vague to have much value, especially as he proceeded to make reference to 'all the peoples I have not bothered to mention and all the many provinces and islands of which we are ignorant'. He appears to have made little effort to ascertain either the extent of the Roman frontiers in Britain, or the precise location of the few Christians who may by then have been resident in Britain. Nonetheless, he made the statement, and it is arguable that he must have had grounds for doing so.

One of Tertullian's contemporaries, Origen, who was an ascetic and a productive Alexandrian writer and philosopher, also portrayed *Britannia*, or *terra Britanniae* as a region on the borders of the civilized world. It, together with several other places, helped to demonstrate the triumph of a church *quae mundi limites tenent* ('which is now established at the very ends of the (Roman) world').

Despite doubts about such indefinite assertions, one is left with a sense that there could have been some basis for Origen's enthusiasm. One historian concludes that the passages from Tertullian and Origen at least 'demonstrate that Christianity was known as a living force in pre-Constantinian Britain'.[5] Could Tertullian and Origen have heard at first or second-hand reports from travellers, especially those engaged in commerce who journeyed to Gaul and Britain from Mediterranean lands? Christianity may have followed the trade routes from Gaul to eastern Britain, or via the ancient passage from the east Mediterranean, round the peninsulas of western Europe to western Britain; and those using these routes may have visited the important commercial centres of

Carthage and Alexandria. There is considerable evidence of such trade. Carvings believed to be of Mycenaean-type daggers and bronze axes have been found on the stones at Stonehenge; Greek coins of the first and second centuries BC from Carthage and Syracuse have been discovered in great numbers in Britain; and swords and sword chapes of the same period have been found on the banks of the Shannon, showing a connexion with Brittany and Gaul. 'There is thus no lack of evidence of sea trade between western Britain, Gaul and the Mediterranean, and the possibility that here also Christianity came with the traders cannot be ruled out.'[6]

Subsequent writers are even less helpful about Christian origins in Britain. Eusebius spoke as if some of the first group of twelve or seventy disciples had 'crossed the Ocean to the isles called British', but in writing his *Ecclesiastical History* he clearly relied heavily on Origen when referring to the mission-fields of the apostles, and omitted Britain altogether. He and a number of Greek patristic writers somewhat later in the third century, even when they alluded to Christianity in Britain, were less concerned with the historical aspects of the church than with the praiseworthiness of its orthodoxy. Another mighty man of letters, St Jerome, like his predecessor Tertullian, was more at home with grand and sweeping generalizations about a church triumphant than with meticulous well-investigated details about the early course of events and, in any case, much of what he said was derivative.

When we come to Bede the hope of some as yet unknown and unauthenticated text is raised, even if it is only a slim possibility. We must assign to the realm of historical fiction the narrative in which he tells of how Lucius, a British king, sent to Eleutherus, Bishop of Rome, a letter, 'praying him that he might be made a Christian by a rescript from him', and how this 'pious request was quickly granted' so that 'the Britons preserved the faith which they had received, inviolate and entire, in peace and quiet, until the time of the Emperor Diocletian'.[7] Lucius is a classical and not a British name, and in the late second century British kings had no role in the ruling of the Roman province of Britannia. But in this case, we are left with a teasing if insubstantial sense of some unrevealed course of events. 'No doubt it is true that Bede derived the Lucius legend from the *Liber Pontificalis* but his gloss on the text – 'et mox effectum . . . in pace servabant' – suggests that he had some other source for his statement that the Britons, and not only Lucius, were converted and practised their Christianity in peace till the reign of

Diocletian. Moreover, British Christianity was in Bede's eyes properly launched by papal mandate to a king.'[8]

If all of this adds up to the possibility that there were some Christians in the country by the beginning of the third century, it does not imply that there was a significant body of believers, or that there was any ecclesiastical organization with particular geographical foci. On the contrary, for it is highly probable that such a state of affairs did not pertain until after the Constantinian conferment of freedom for Christians in the 313 'Edict of Milan', or 'Peace of the Church', as it is sometimes called. Even if to those engaged in trade is added a few Christian soldiers and administrators from among the thousands sent to Britain by Rome it does not probably amount to a very grand total, and they would have been scattered throughout the length and breadth of the land. There was almost certainly only a mere sprinkling of Christians in the years prior to the fourth century, albeit with a likely growth throughout the third century, and this would help to explain the scantiness of archaeological evidence showing any Christian presence in these early centuries of the Christian era. We have to wait until the fourth century for the first indications of corporate Christian life. As one historian has stated: 'Christians had probably been present in Britain since the second century and certainly there were Christian churches in the fourth century.'[9]

Archaeological evidence

In the search for evidence of British Christian origins the fullest and most thorough archaeological work has been on buildings; so I will begin with a summary of the relevant research, findings and archaeological comment.

It is not easy to recognize fourth- and fifth-century British churches. There was no single architectural model which they followed after the Edict of Milan (313). Constantine and his architects favoured the basilican plan, and this was adopted in four of his earliest churches, the Church of the Nativity at Bethlehem, the Church of the Holy Sepulchre, Jerusalem, and St Peter's and St John Lateran at Rome. It was also the pattern imitated in other romanized regions, or it was adapted to the simpler apsed style without aisles. But a rectangular building without any trace of an apse was the norm in northern (Celtic) Italy, and this type of structure was common around Aquileia until about the sixth century. Finally, there was the octagonal form of church building, with internal chambers in a cruciform. This was favoured in the East as early as the fourth century, and it is the style which may have been used in the building at Nettleton, formerly a pagan shrine.[10] It also needs to be born in mind that there were different architectural and liturgical traditions in 'congregational' and 'cemetery' churches, which only started to merge in the fourth century into one standard architectural form. A further difficulty is that even by the fourth century there was not a universally adopted orientation whereby the churches without exception were built on an east-west axis with the altar at the east end.

In order to be reasonably confident that an extant building was a church in Roman Britain, there needs to be 'an absence of domestic, industrial or agricultural evidence and of evidence of any pagan activity; if pagan features are present, they should be seen to have been desecrated or profaned in some way'. Then, to these negative signs, there should be positive indications which make the identification highly likely. There would not be a consensus among archaeologists as to what constitutes a full range of satisfactory data, or even what comprises a long list of features from among which a certain essential minimum number of criteria are necessary in order to establish the authenticity of any building as a Christian church; and clearly some items in any list are of greater importance than others. Nonetheless, most archaeologists would probably agree that, ideally, in order to be accorded the status of a Christian church, any building should include

. . . evidence of religious continuity at the site, either before or after the Romano-British Christian period; and a building of basilican or simple apsidal plan, orientated west-east or east-west. In the town areas, the apsidal plan may be the more common; in the country, particularly in the south-west, a rectangular shape may occur. For extra-mural sites, a fourth-century cemetery with Christian attributes associated with a structure is a likely indicator that the structure was a Christian church; similarly, a later Saxon Christian cemetery may indicate an earlier Romano-British church in the vicinity. On intra-mural sites, a Saxon Christian cemetery may also point to an earlier church. Finally, useful indicators of a church include the apsidal burial or, to a lesser extent, the apsidal feature, the presence of a baptistery or font, and the defiling of a pagan site or artefact, but this last is of little help unless it can be seen that the site or object had been reused in a Christian context.[11]

The evidence from the archaeological investigation of possible fourth-century churches is not extensive and unambiguous, but it does provide interesting possible indications of early Christian history. All the churches I will be considering are of medium or small size. Although large, much finer churches, such as those at Trier, Aquileia, Bordeaux and Cologne, appeared in continental Europe from about 330, no comparable structure has, as yet, been discovered in Britain.

One of the first churches to be excavated in modern times was that at Silchester (Hampshire). Indeed, it has been dubbed by a distinguished archaeologist as 'the first undoubted Romano-British "church" to be explored'.[12] A building with a rectangular nave, side-aisles and an eastern narthex, or entrance, and a small western apse, with tenuous indications of fourth-century construction, seems to be, and has been widely accepted as a prime candidate for categorization as a church originating from Roman times.[13] Ian Richmond, who re-excavated it in 1961, firmly held it to be a church, and S.S. Frere reporting on the site fourteen years later endorsed that view.

> It has been shown that the Silchester building has all the characteristics of a Christian church, and that none of its features present obstacles to this view. Archaeological evidence for the date of its construction is only able to suggest a *terminus post quem* of the middle or later third century. But a free-standing church, and one in so prominent a position, cannot have been built before the reign of Constantine and is more likely to date to the middle or later years of the fourth century.[14]

But the Christian identity of even this widely-considered 'church' has been questioned, and I will give some space to the argument of one archaeologist as an illustration of how much Christian origins are a subject of lively academic debate.

After a full appraisal of the possible use of the building, and an analysis of the ways its layout reflects the organization of the cult which used it, Anthony King concludes that

> . . . only certain eastern cults, or Christianity, or a cult associated with a *schola* are viable possibilities. Of these, the interpretation that fits the evidence best is that the building was for an eastern cult, since the dating is compatible, unlike the chronological problems that a Christian interpretation gives rise to, and the parallels are analogous in form, which is not really the case with *scholae* or contemporary churches.

And King substantiates his argument. He says that there is the possibility that, from an architectural point of view, the Silchester building is one example of a process whereby local temples were adapted to the needs of an introduced cult. He is of the opinion that at Silchester this process was implemented 'to the extent that the new cult-building, although betraying its Romano-Celtic origins, bore little resemblance to a native shrine'. He continues:

> Such an architectural origin would provide the only possible context for the building being Christian, for if a congregation wanted to erect a church soon after Constantine's reform, ie within the suggested dating framework, an adaptation of the local architecture would have been much easier than seeking out distant metropolitan prototypes. However, there is no evidence elsewhere for this type of instant local adaptation, and the building would be much less anomalous if interpreted as pagan, and an adaptation for an eastern cult.

The conclusion to which he arrives is clearly expressed.

> Reconsideration of the Silchester building has thrown into perspective the problems of attempting to interpret a unique building that has yielded no unequivocal evidence of its purpose. The meagre clues afforded by the plan, the dating and the analogous structures allow only tentative conclusions to be made. Nevertheless, enough is known of the building to call into question the existing interpretation of it as a Christian church and to put forward other possibilities for its use.[15]

It must also be said that the data concerning other churches supposedly from the time of the Roman occupation of Britain are inconclusive. They rest heavily on literary allusion or archaeological deductions based on the presence of later buildings. I will take a few as specimens.

A building at Richborough (Kent) has strong claims to be reckoned as a church of the fourth century. P. D. C. Brown thinks that the stone structures revealed by excavations, and foundation blocks suggesting a timber church, show parallels with late Roman churches excavated inside towns and forts along the Rhine-Danube frontier. He is of the opinion that in the continental examples there were congregational churches of a similar type to that at Richborough, with nearby baptisteries inside the forts.[16] An inscribed pottery vessel found in the northwest corner of the walled area at Richborough provides additional evidence of the existence of a fourth-century church.

At Colchester a remarkable monument was unearthed in 1989, which is believed by many to be the remains of a Roman church. A cemetery on one side of the building has been known for a hundred and fifty years, but it seems that there were two successive cemeteries, the first of which was for pagans and the second for Christians. The second was laid out on top of the first, probably during the early part of the fourth century. The graves were oriented east-west, and were laid out in tightly-packed rows. The church, which was a long narrow building constructed in an east-west direction, with an apse at the east end which was added in a secondary phase, was located in one corner of the cemetery. The building was divided internally by a wooden screen, with two rows of posts running down the eastern half, forming aisles. Its date has been suggested as between 320 and 340, contemporary with the second cemetery. The plan of the building and the association with a large fourth-century cemetery are the main indicators of it having been a church. Some grave-like pits at the eastern end of the church may have been the places where important local Christians were buried.[17]

Another important possible Roman church site linked with a cemetery is at Icklingham (Suffolk). The building, which was situated in a Roman rural settlement of unclear status, has been identified from foundation-trenches as having been small, rectangular, on an east-west axis and possibly with an eastern apse. It was surrounded by an inhumation cemetery, and there may have been an associated baptistery.

Other sites which are candidates for being considered as possible Christian churches include Brean Down, where the excavator himself did not ascribe a Christian identity to the building, but this was suggested by the excavator of the nearby Lamyatt Beacon;[18] Nettleton, where an octagonal shrine to Apollo was converted to a cruciform, possibly a church, in the fourth century;[19] Caerwent, Canterbury, Exeter, Lincoln, St Albans, Dorchester and London.

There are also cemeteries which are important in their own right. Much discussion has surrounded the identification of Christian, as opposed to pagan, cemeteries. So it is useful that Dorothy Watts has distinguished certain features which help to determine the Christian nature of cemeteries. They would be generally acceptable to other archaeologists, no doubt with reservations and qualifications both small and great.

In a cemetery of, say, thirty or more inhumations, those criteria deemed essential for a Christian identity are: burials west-east (that is, with the head to the west), undisturbed by other interments, lying supine and extended, in a cemetery in which neo-natal or very young infants are also buried and given equal respect with adults, and with an absence of decapitated burials, and of grave goods of vessels, animals and birds, and hobnailed footwear. It is also desirable that there be an absence of coins in the mouth, or Charon's fee, although this may not be important.[20]

Other criteria may be applied, such as a Christian inscription *in situ*. Also 'the existence of a contemporaneous pagan cemetery, or the presence of a mausoleum, a focal grave, or plaster burials, but not all these features, or any at all, may be present; and all are not of the same value as evidence, particularly plaster burials'.[21] And, of course, it is important to take account of the broader context of the cemetery concerned to see if there are signs of actual or potential Christian influence in the immediate environs.

The cemeteries at Ancaster, Ashton, Bradley Hill, Brean Down, Butt Road, Colchester, Cannington, the Crown Building site in Dorchester, Icklingham, Lamyatt Beacon, Lankhills, Winchester, Nettleton, and Verulam Hills Field St Albans are among the most important of the apparently Christian burial sites.

There has, unfortunately, not been extensive work on Roman cemeteries in general, and even less on early possible Christian cemeteries. In the study of likely Christian sites cemeteries often form only a secondary part in the archaeological report. The nineteenth-century excavations were poorly recorded, there were few detailed descriptions, with a full analysis of plans, for most of the sites concerned, and the evidence has long been destroyed. It appears that the Christians set great store on burial, largely because of their belief that the sleeping dead would be resurrected on the final day of judgment. Christian cemeteries could, potentially, cast considerable light on the presence of Christians in particular areas, and perhaps on the extent of the growth of Christianity; so it is regrettable that traces of them have not so far been more frequent, and the analysis of them more complete and comprehensive.

Cemetery churches, which were erected where martyrs were buried, include St Albans Abbey, which was located on the site of a Roman cemetery. Such *cella memoria* have been found at Wells and Poundbury, with possible examples at Colchester and St Martin's, Canterbury.

Poundbury (Dorset) has been described by P. Rahtz as the only late Roman cemetery to have 'yielded unequivocal Christian evidence'.[22] It was a major city graveyard which started late in the third century or early fourth century. An earlier group of random, probably pagan, burials, with some in a separate area which were deliberately orientated, was superseded in the fourth century by a much larger cemetery which seems to have been dominated by Christian practices. It at least indicates that there were a number of local Christian believers, and that Christian influence may have extended beyond that immediate circle.[23] I will not dwell on either this particular cemetery or Christian cemeteries in general, as I will be addressing the topic in more detail in the next chapter, in the context of the distinguishing marks of the church in Roman times.

So, to return to the churches themselves, in addition to those in urban areas, and buildings which were specifically designated as churches, there were apparently 'estate' churches or rural, private churches within Roman villas. The villa-estate at Lullingstone (Kent) has achieved the greatest fame as an example of one such building. The principal dwelling was expanded, or altered, or both, in the late second, late third and mid-fourth centuries. Behind it were a second-century circular shrine and an early fourth-century temple-cum-mausoleum. For most of the third century there was a family *nymphaeum* in the basement within the house. It seems that at some time in the second half of the fourth century the owners embraced Christianity. A suite of rooms, probably with a new external access, included areas with wall-paintings and chi-rho signs, together with a frieze which may depict the Christian living and dead. Charles Thomas has referred to this part of the dwelling as an 'obviously Christian suite, whose two main rooms could functionally correspond to the narthex and sanctuary of a primitive, free-standing church'.[24] Work on the fragmentary wall-plaster reveals not only friezes of Orantes and chi-rhos but also biblical scenes, although these are unfortunately too incomplete to identify accurately.

The 'house-church' at Hinton St Mary (Dorset) has also become celebrated, largely because it contains a mosaic depicting a male head, which has generally been interpreted as representing Christ himself, with a chi-rho behind it (see cover). There are indications that the mosaic was laid during the fourth century; and if the bust on it does portray Christ it would be the earliest British-made representation of Christ so far known.[25] The mosaic has also led Roy T. Erikson to suggest that it is a 'syncretistic allegory' showing 'something of the syncretistic climate' from which it is likely to have issued.[26] Whether this is so is open to question. But the Christian element is widely accepted.

'The placing of the bust of Christ centrally in the larger area of floor leaves no doubt that the pavement is Christian.'[27]

At Framton (Dorset) there is also an interesting mosaic. In this case the apsidal portion of the mosaic features a cantharus, and in the cord of the apse there is an encircled chi-rho. But the possible nature and function of the room which was so floored is not clear.

Other villas which may have been the residences of Christians, or even centres for Christian worship, include Chedworth in Gloucestershire and Stone-by-Faversham in Kent. 'There can be no doubt that churches, either houses in which rooms were used or set aside for liturgical purposes or halls of assembly for service, existed in Roman Britain.'[28]

The possible Christian buildings of the Roman period are important not only because they are central to our understanding of Christian origins, but because they are the first in a chain of development for both places of worship and communities of believers which continued until the present day. There was no sudden termination of Christianity with the departure of the Romans, and a totally new start when Augustine arrived from Rome in 597, and Columba and Aidan led a mission from Ireland to Northumbria in the sixth and seventh centuries. 'Augustine's brief was to restore the religious life of Britain, very much along the old Roman lines. And that is what he and his followers did, to the best of their ability, with the result that there is an overwhelmingly strong element of continuity between settlements, churches and cemeteries of the Roman era and those of much later date, in both town and country.'[29] I will be examining the evidence for such continuity, and commenting at length on the whole matter of the link between Roman and later Anglo-Saxon Christianity later in the book.

Then, lastly among the evidences of early Christianity in Roman Britain are the hoards of Christian metalwork and various artefacts with apparent Christian connections. The Mildenhall (Suffolk) hoard of silverware adorned with Christian symbolism is immensely impressive, but it must not be counted as evidence of Romano-British Christianity since the treasure was probably imported as the personal property of the Christian general Lupicinus, who was sent to Britain in 360.

But this cannot be said of the Water Newton (Cambridgeshire) hoard of gold and silver items, which is of the first importance as the cache was probably the communal property of an ecclesia or Christian group, and is the earliest such treasure so far discovered. The site may well have lain within the boundaries of the Roman town of *Durobrivae*. Some of the objects bear a gilt Constantinian form of the chi-rho; and one inscribed cup testifies to the presence of a sanctuary or church. It seems clear that the hoard was buried in its entirety, most likely in the early fourth century; and recovery was probably intended. The plate was possibly used by a community of practising Christians perhaps for sacramental purposes. Among the items are leaf- or feather-shaped plaques, which are typical of pagan objects hung up on the walls of Romano-Celtic temples, such as the one at Uley, Gloucestershire. These may have been objects brought to church by new Christian believers as a continuation of a practice which was already familiar to them from before they were converted. This is entirely conjectural, although it is known that the church encouraged such offerings.

Other buried hoards of valuable tableware with Christian significance include those at Appleshaw (Hampshire), where one of the pewter vessels from a villa apparently abandoned in the late fourth century bears a chi-rho; Biddulph (Staffordshire), where a small hoard of silver spoons includes one which bears a chi-rho; and similar spoons which have been recorded at Dorchester (Dorset). In each case the property was owned by a wealthy family living in a settled homestead, and it was hidden away, for an unknown reason, during a period of disturbance in the fourth century.

Christian objects of various kinds have been found scattered all over Britain, but more particularly in the south-east which underwent the greatest romanization, and in adjacent areas westward to Dorset, Gloucestershire and south-east Wales, as well as northwards along the eastern side of Britain. Such items include complete pewter bowls from London, Caerwent and Welney (Cambridgeshire); a pottery lamp from Margate; a late orange-ware bowl from Richborough; potsherds marked with the chi-rho from Canterbury and Exeter; a tile from York; a brick from Leicester; and a small sandstone block from Catterick (North Yorkshire).[30]

There is also the famous word-square which was discovered at Cirencester in 1868. Incised on a piece of red and black-painted wall plaster are five lines of letters which form a true square or palindrome, reading the same horizontally as it does vertically. It was shown in the 1920s that the letters could be re-arranged to read PATERNOSTER, twice, when set out in cross fashion sharing the central N; with A A and O O (alpha and omega, twice) left over. This is impressive, but other such examples have been discovered, widely distributed, and not all are demonstrably in Christian contexts. Its relevance is however increased by its possible date, which may be as early as the second century.[31]

Especially interesting as archaeological evidence are large lead tanks, such as the one from Icklingham. Of the Icklingham site, it has been said: 'The evidence suggests that the cemetery was Christian, in use from *c*.350, and that two of the buildings and the lead tank were associated with the cemetery'.[32] Professor Toynbee was one of the first archaeologists to argue strongly that these tanks with Christian symbols were used as fonts or baptistries,[33] and her suggestion has been widely endorsed. The figured fragment from Walesby, Lincolnshire, has been used as supporting evidence[34] although the scene portrayed is far from clear.

None of this should imply that Christianity was anything more than a minority religion for most of the Roman period in Britain. It may well be that Christians were to be found from the late second century onwards, but that they did not leave much lasting evidence of their existence. The religion was not brought to Britain by means of bands of missionaries, as was to be the case with Augustine and his company of monks, followed by other similar purposely sent groups. No such determined evangelists worked their weary way across the Roman province, converting, baptizing and establishing churches and communities of Christians. The planting of Christianity in Roman Britain was a much more casual and unorganized affair. Christianity was not apparently a publicly organized religious sect until at least the fourth century. In the course of the third century it is quite likely that it was no more prestigious than any other eastern mystery cult. Although 'the sparse and tantalizing records which remain are sufficient to assure us that Christianity was firmly rooted in this island before the Peace of the Church',[35] it was still not much of a force in society. After all almost all the evidence of a Christian presence so far presented relates to the fourth century. By the second decade of that century 'Christianity was established in Britain and the Church was organized on the same lines as elsewhere in the western provinces of the Empire. There is, however, little to show that it had begun to extend its influence to the broad masses of the people.'[36] It appears to be the fourth century which witnessed considerable advance for the church.

Peace and persecution

It is not clear to what extent the policy of persecuting Christians, adopted by a few emperors, affected Christians in Britain. In the third century it was the Emperor Decius (249–51) who ordered a systematic persecution in 250. Everyone was required to possess a certificate (*libellus*) affirming before special commissioners that he had sacrificed to the gods, and in particular shown reverence for the emperor's *numen*. Under Valerian a further persecution occurred (257–9) in which Cyprian was martyred.

These two pagan attempts to induce conformity produced a reaction from Christians. They emphasized their by then wholly evolved and rigid monotheism and widespread unwillingness to compromise this by the acknowledgment of any other deity. In a sense they suffered and died not because they professed a certain belief, but because they refused to worship any other god. This included any emperor who might demand what the Christians regarded as inappropriate and excessive signs of veneration. They were not prepared to budge from their undivided loyalty and faith in the triune God they professed. Such a firm and unyielding stance was the characteristic mark of St Alban which led to his martyrdom.

Christians by the mid-third century had a simple but profound creed which most probably went back to the second century and would have been in use in Britain for the baptism of early converts. It ran as follows:

> I believe in God the Father almighty; and in Christ Jesus his only son our Lord, who was born of the Holy Ghost and the Virgin Mary, who was crucified under Pontius Pilate and buried, rose again the third day from the dead, ascended into heaven, sits on the right hand of the Father, whence he will come to judge living and dead; and in the Holy Ghost, the holy church, the remission of sins, the resurrection of the flesh.

Baptism was the last act of Christian initiation. It was symbolized by immersion in water and emergence out of it; a solemn act performed generally, and so most probably in Britain, by a bishop unless he deputed another for the service. When Augustine conferred with the British bishops at the end of the sixth century he spoke of baptism as 'the service by which we are regenerated unto God', and this was an expression found in the church as early as the *Apologia* of Justyn Martyr. It was almost certainly familiar to British Christians of the third century.

Because of the exclusiveness of Christian belief it is not possible to equate Christianity with other eastern mystery religions. There were characteristics of belief and practice which were common to many of these faiths from the east, and they might have appeared almost identi-

cal in essence to an untutored observer. But there were crucial differences. In particular there was the monotheism and the conviction about
the person and work of Jesus Christ. There was no room for polytheism,
or the acceptance of other gods; there was but one God, and Jesus
Christ was unique as the only Son of God whose birth, life, death,
resurrection and ascension opened the sole way of salvation.

Under the Rescript of Gallienus, from 260 onwards, Christianity
enjoyed a new status as a *religio licita*, an officially approved cult. In
the ensuing peace churches were built, some of considerable size,
cemeteries were openly resorted to, and there was a public and legal
exercise of the full range of Christian worship and life. It was a calm
before a storm.

In the early fourth century, in 303, Diocletian instituted an attack on
Christians which was far more severe, extended and comprehensive
than any since the time of Nero. All churches were to be destroyed, all
Bibles and liturgical books surrendered, sacred vessels confiscated, and
all meetings for worship forbidden. A few months later, and for a brief
period only, the emperor ordered the arrest of clergy, but this seems to
have been confined to the East. The following year all citizens of the
empire were obliged to sacrifice on pain of death, but this also was in
practice limited to the East. The emphasis on the *prisca religio*, the
various forms of state-favoured religion, is a stark reminder that paganism was far from extinct. And, as we will see, it was still very much alive
in Britain.

It was possibly during this final Roman onslaught on the church that
Alban, Aaron and Julius were put to death for their Christian faith, the
first at *Verulamium*, and the other two at Caerleon, although much
scholarly opinion has tended to favour one of the earlier persecutions
under Decius and Valerian. Comments which survive indicate that
Britain was virtually spared the persecution which many other
Christians in the empire endured in the early years of the fourth century.
If it was during the mid-third century persecutions that British
Christians suffered, the extra half-century or so gap between the martyrdoms and the first literary mention of them in the late fifth century
would help to explain the near-total loss of the names of victims when
reference was made to the persecution.[37]

St Alban is known to us from *The Ruin of Britain*, from the *Life of
Germanus* of Constantius, and from one line of the Christian poet
Fortunatus. There is also the intriguing likelihood of a lost, very early
original account or *Passio*, which would have been a description of

Alban's saintly death, rather than a *Vita*, or quasi-biography, possibly composed a short time before 500.[38] But the main source is Bede's *Ecclesiastical History*, where it is given considerable prominence.

The site of *Verulamium* for the death of St Alban is very credible. It has been said that the 'most singular case for possible Christian continuity in the part of Britain which became England is that of St Albans'. Bede confidently asserted that from the time of the martyrdom until his own day, in the early eighth century, acts of healing and other miracles had not ceased at Alban's tomb. 'The case for continuity is strengthened by the situation of the later abbey of St Alban's: outside Roman *Verulamium*, where an extra-mural cemetery, and so Alban's tomb, could well have been; there are many Continental parallels for such a site.'[39]

Bede's account of the martyrdom of Alban is well-known, but it bears repeating in a summary form in such a work as this, bearing in mind that there has, of course, been widespread academic rejection of the miraculous elements in what Bede recounts.

At a time when 'infidel rulers were issuing violent edicts against Christians'[40] Alban, who was not a Christian at the time, sheltered a priest who was fleeing from his persecutors. As a result of seeing the vigils and prayers of the cleric at close quarters he accepted the Christian faith and was instructed in it by his visitor.

After a few days those in authority became aware that a Christian was hiding in Alban's house. When the soldiers came to conduct a search Alban donned the priest's cloak and offered himself to the soldiers in place of the priest. He was brought to the judge who at the time was offering sacrifices at the altars of pagan gods. He was enraged that the man should give himself up in place of the priest at such a great risk to himself, and after having had Alban dragged before the images of the gods he said, 'You have chosen to conceal a profane rebel rather than surrender him to my soldiers, to prevent him from paying a well-deserved penalty for his blasphemy in despising the gods; so you will have to take the punishment he has incurred if you attempt to forsake our worship and religion'.[41] Alban had of his own accord declared himself a Christian before the judge and those with him. He did not fear their threats, and he refused to sacrifice to their gods, but rather told them of the futility of what they did and of the eternal punishment in hell which awaited those who so committed idolatry. Under cruel tortures he remained constant. The judge finally realized that he would not yield and turn from the Christian faith, so he ordered him to be executed.

A great crowd gathered outside when he was led to his martyrdom. On approaching a rapidly flowing river which ran between the town wall and the place where he was to suffer, he raised his eyes towards heaven and immediately the river-bed dried up at that spot. The executioner saw this, and when Alban came to him he threw away his sword and 'cast himself down at the saint's feet, earnestly praying that he might be judged worthy to be put to death either with the martyr whom he himself had been ordered to execute, or else in his place'.[42]

As Alban ascended the flower-bedecked hill, about five hundred paces from the arena, there was hesitation among the other executioners to take up the sword. When he reached the top of the hill he asked God to give him water, and at once a perpetual spring bubbled up, 'confined within its channel at his very feet, so that all could see that even the stream rendered service to the martyr'.[43] The river then returned to its normal course. Alban was beheaded, but 'the one who laid his unholy hands on the holy neck was not permitted to rejoice over his death; for the head of the blessed martyr and the executioner's eyes fell to the ground together'.[44] The soldier who refused to conduct the execution was also beheaded at the same place. 'In his case it is clear', wrote Bede, 'that though he was not washed in the waters of baptism, yet he was cleansed by the washing of his own blood and made worthy to enter the kingdom of heaven.'[45]

Bede adds that 'the judge, who was astonished by these strange heavenly miracles, ordered the persecution to cease and began to respect the way in which the saints met their death, though he had once believed that he could thereby make them forsake their devotion to the Christian faith'.[46] And he concludes his account by stating that Alban suffered death on 22 June near the city of *Verulamium* which the English of his day called St Albans. When peaceful times returned, a church was built there of wonderful workmanship.

Bede also adds that about the same time Aaron and Julius, both citizens of the Legions (Caerleon), suffered as did many others of both sexes in many other places.

When the storm of persecution had come to an end, the Christians who had fled to woods, caverns and other places of refuge emerged. Gildas graphically depicts the coming of better times, in his customary rather flamboyant language:

Glad-eyed, all the champions of Christ welcomed, as though after a long winter's night, the calm and the serene light of the breeze of heaven. They rebuilt churches that had been razed to the ground; they founded, built and completed chapels to the holy martyrs, displaying them everywhere like victorious banners. They celebrated feast days. With pure heart and mouth they carried out the holy ceremonies. And all her sons exulted, as though warmed in the bosom of the mother church.[47]

'The fact that the known martyrdoms occurred at important Roman towns like Verulamium and Caerleon suggests that most bishops and lay Christians went into hiding in the countryside and that only exceptionally energetic officials sought them out.'[48]

In the Edict of Milan of March 313 issued by Constantine the Great and his fellow-Augustus, Licinius, Christianity was raised to a new standing as 'our first and principal concern'. A general tolerance was announced, the restitution of all church property was ordered, and compensation was granted wherever such property had been destroyed. This encouraged local Christians, such as those in Britain, to be more open in the declaration of their faith, and to engage in a programme of re-building and expansion as indicated by Gildas.

Fourth-century councils

One manifestation of the new lease of life enjoyed by British Christians was the attendance of three British bishops at the Council of Arles in 314; the first Christian gathering ever to have been summoned by a Roman emperor. Eusebius preserved one of the letters of summons which were sent to the bishops of Western Europe. It stated that those attending were to travel to Arles at the public expense by means of conveyance provided for imperial officials; and each bishop was to choose two presbyters who would take part in the Synod and three 'servants'.

The main purpose of the Council was to address the question of church discipline which had arisen out of the recent persecution in North Africa. The issue was over what action should be taken regarding 'the fallen' (*lapsi*); that is, those who had shown weakness in the face of possible imprisonment, torture or death, and who had denied the faith by bowing before pagan gods, or in some other way had displayed lack of resoluteness and loyalty to their faith which their detractors thought was unforgivable. Mensurius, Bishop of Carthage, and his archdeacon Caecilian, who succeeded Mensurius, were suspected of having compromised and shown unworthy pliability in the face of persecution. The disaffection was increased because Caecilian had hastily been consecrated bishop by three country bishops, one of whom was generally believed to have surrendered the scriptures to the police, and was therefore a *traditor*. The consecration raised afresh Cyprian's question, which he had addressed in the mid-third century, whether one who by apostasy or schism had lost the Spirit could confer the Spirit's gifts. The opposition to tolerance was led by Bishop Donatus, and those who advocated strict church order and discipline on this and other matters were called Donatists.

Those present from Britain were Eborius, Bishop of the city of York, Restitutus, Bishop of the city of London, Adelfius, Bishop of the city in the *colonia* of Lincoln, who was accompanied by Sacerdos a presbyter, and Arminius, a deacon. Eborius of Eboracum is rather suspicious, and this may represent a misreading of a British name. More problematic is the use of the word *Londinensium* in reference to Bishop Adelfius. It was once proposed that this should have been *Camulodunensium*, what became Colchester. There is also the view that it should read *Legionensium*, to imply that Adelfius came from Caerleon, the camp of the Legion, on the bank of the river Usk. The last suggestion, which I favour, is that there was a scribal error, and it should read *Lindunensium*, Lincoln. The names of the incumbents of these posts are less important than the fact that such orders of episcopus, presbyter and deacon existed in Britain, as elsewhere. It is also significant that the church in Britain was sufficiently well developed and respected for it to be considered as part of western Christendom, and for five of its ordained members to be invited to participate in an important gathering such as the Council of Arles.

The decision went against the Donatists, but they were not satisfied, and the breach continued even down to the time of Augustine of Hippo.

More importantly for the British church was the adoption of twenty-two canons on the life of the church by the members of the Council who came from Britain, Gaul, Italy, Spain, Germany and Africa. The enactments were considered binding on the whole church and, what was becoming of ever greater importance, Rome was acknowledged as unequalled in status and authority. On the controversial matter of the time for observing Easter, as on other topics, the Council were of the opinion that the custom of the Roman Church was that which all churches should henceforth observe. Although he was not present at the Council, it was the Bishop of Rome who was asked, 'according to custom' to 'send letters unto all', stating that Easter should 'be observed by us on one day, and at one time, throughout the world'. Here were British bishops, not only joining in a Council as representing a recognized part of the church universal, but submitting to decisions made by that church in such an official gathering, and, what is more, agreeing that such decisions should be communicated to the universal church, including the churches in Britain, by another church, that of Rome.

No British bishop attended the Council of Nicaea in 325. This may be regarded as the first 'ecumenical' council because of the range of representation, although almost all the 220 or so bishops were Greek. Only four or five came from the Latin West apart from Hosius of Cordova and two presbyters who were sent by Pope Silvester. The Council was confronted by the teaching of Arius that Christ was of like substance with God, but not of the same substance, with all that this implied. It responded by condemning the proposition that the Son is in any way metaphysically or morally inferior to the Father and belongs to the created order. It rather asserted unambiguously that the Son is 'of one substance with the Father'. The creed proposed, which was forthrightly anti-Arian, was signed by all but two of the bishops. This was a highly pertinent decision for Britain as it was about to experience Arianism at first hand.

The Council of Sardica in 347 marks an epoch in that it was the first occasion on which the differences between the eastern and western branches of the church became apparent in a public way. The ninety-five western members, including some British bishops, supported Athanasius and the acquittal of him from any charge of unorthodoxy, and reaffirmed the Nicene creed, whereas the eastern members issued a violent condemnation of the Council, and affirmed their support for an Arian creed.

Twelve years later, in 359, there were British bishops at a further council in Rimini. It was one half of what Constantius planned as a grand universal council: Rimini being for the western, and a council at Seleucia for the eastern part of the empire. It was a vain attempt to forge the church into a united, agreed, faith, at a time when the division caused by Arianism had been accentuated under the impulse of such extreme Arians as Aetius. More than four hundred bishops appear to have assembled, for all of whom the emperor had ordered provisions and lodgings. It seems that almost all of them found this unseemly, so they refused the facilities offered at public cost and preferred to live at their own expense. There were three Britons, however, who, because they lacked private means, made use of the proffered public bounty.

They refused contributions which had been offered by the other bishops because they considered it right to burden the public treasury rather than individuals. Some censured such conduct, while others thought it was a matter for admiration. It indicates that the bishops were very poor, and perhaps by implication that the British church was poor. If this is so, it may have been a result of small numbers of Christians, the fact that the Christians were predominantly from lower socio-economic groups, a lack of liberality among the Christians, or a combination of two or more of these factors.

St Martin of Tours

It was in the course of the fourth century that Martin of Tours (316–397) lived his remarkable life, which had an immediate as well as a medium and long-term impact on much of continental Europe and on the British church.[49] One historian has even stated that: 'The turning-point in favour of Christianity in northern Gaul and perhaps Britain too was brought about by the mission of Martin of Tours.'[50]

After many years as a soldier Martin became a hermit, and then reluctantly but in response to the overwhelming pressure and persistence of the people, Bishop of Tours. He combined the responsibilities of a bishop with a monastic life in a monastery which he established. His sensitive pastoral care, vigorous evangelism and intrepid courage in the face of threats, assaults and imprecations, together with his ministry of counselling, and, perhaps above all else, his simple holiness and the almost universal belief in his powers as a miracle-worker, endeared him to many who became his disciples, and made him a force in church affairs in his own diocese and far beyond. In the decade after Martin had died, one of his disciples, Victricius, who, like Martin, had been a soldier, became Bishop of Rouen. In the spirit and style of Martin he hounded the remains of paganism along the channel coast. So effective was the former work of Martin in that area, and its continuance by Victricius, that Rouen appears to have become a Christian city, with the remotest parts of the diocese Christianized.

Martin's visit to Britain in 396 gave the British Christians first-hand exposure to a type of Christian energy and dedication which they generally lacked. His zeal and example probably inspired the British Christians at the time, and it touched the lives of St Ninian, St Patrick and St Columba in an incalculable way in the following two centuries. He thus made a valuable contribution to the spiritual life of the church in Ireland and Scotland; and it was Christians from those lands who were instrumental in bringing a vibrant Christian faith to northern England. This was illustrative of Martin's main gifts to the church in many lands – vision and inspiration; for he had both in abundance. His life was 'the story of the Romano-Celtic peoples coming face to face with the individual heroism of the primitive Christian church, and ultimately warming to it in a mass conversion'.[51]

Martin's influence was also shown in the development of British monasticism. Christian inscriptions, dating in all probability from the fifth century, together with evidence from the site of the Celtic monastery at Whithorn, suggest 'that the tradition of missionary activity among the Picts of Southern Scotland at this time was not ill-founded'. If such a development were taking place, 'it would indicate the emergence of a strongly monastic type of Christianity even though episcopally organized, in some parts of Britain, parallel to that which was now developing in northern Gaul'.[52] Although there is little evidence of any kind relating to monasticism in mainland Britain in the fourth and fifth centuries, its presence can possibly be inferred from the fact that Constans, son of the usurper Constantine III, 407–11, was apparently a monk.

Arianism

Gildas, and Bede following him, wrote greatly exaggerated accounts of the pollution of British Christianity by Arians. Gildas employed his highly picturesque terminology to portray a very sorry state of affairs. The days of persecution have passed, and the church has enjoyed a period of recovery and harmony. But then heresy arrives:

> This pleasant agreement between the head and the limbs of Christ endured until the Arian treason, like a savage snake, vomited its foreign poison upon us, and caused the fatal separation of brothers who had lived as one. And as though there were a set route across the ocean there came every kind of wild beast, brandishing in their horrid mouths the death-dealing venom of every heresy, and planting lethal bites in a country that always longed to hear some novelty – and never took firm hold of anything.[53]

Bede spoke of 'the Arian madness which corrupted the whole world and even infected this island'.[54] And of all the heresies that he mentions in his theological works this is the one on which he laid the greatest stress.

But both Gildas and Bede seem to have erred on this particular matter. St Athanasius ranks the British bishops among those who took his side in the theological debate over the nature of Christ's relationship with God the Father. Hilary of Poitiers in 358–9 congratulated his British brethren because they had kept themselves 'pure from the contagion of the detestable [Arian] heresy'.[55] In 363 Athanasius could reckon the Britons among those who were loyal to the Catholic faith.[56] Chrysostom attested to the singleness of true faith among the British, as did Jerome. Plummer, in his commentary on Bede's *History* expressed the opinion that both Gildas and Bede over-emphasized the influence of Arianism in the province. He points out that Bede may also have had in mind other examples of departure from orthodoxy, for he 'seems to hint at the existence of various heresies in Britain'.[57]

This is not to say that Arianism was not present in Britain to some extent. Bede's point was 'not the quantity of heresy but its quality'.[58] Gregory of Tours had been as concerned as Bede about the threat to orthodoxy throughout the western world and its seriousness wherever it occurred; and he has also been accused of exaggeration. It may have been one of the issues which caused such dissension among the British bishops at the end of the fourth century that Victricius, Bishop of Rouen, was obliged to cross the sea to restore peace among them. But there is no proof that this was a factor which led to that visit. What seems clear is that the dispute was fairly well contained. There is no evidence that the Christian body as a whole was rent asunder by Arianism or any other divisive issue.

Christianity at the end of the Roman period

The fourth century was a period of advance for British Christianity. But the 'official adoption of Christianity by Rome and the provinces after the Edict of Milan in AD 313 did not mean that British paganism immediately disappeared'.[59] There is evidence that paganism may even have experienced a measure of renewal, although some have questioned this.[60]

Those who champion the view that there was a resurgence of paganism in at least the period 360 to 380 include J. M. C. Toynbee,[61] W. H. C. Frend,[62] M. Henig[63] and Dorothy Watts[64]. Toynbee and Watts link the revival to the measures taken by the Augustus Julian. Indeed, Watts considers that although the little cloud created by Julian would soon pass, his 'legacy was to be a revival of paganism which was to slow down the spread of Christianity in Britain and weaken the Church to the extent that it barely survived in the following two centuries'.[65] She and Frend in particular emphasize the strength and longevity of the pagan British cults, their hold on the native Britons in rural areas, and the chaotic political situation from the mid-380s onward. This, they say, represented a combination of circumstances which so militated against the fragile Christianity of the time that it made its very survival somewhat surprising.

K. R. Dark has convincingly argued that the basis for constructing the relevant histogram for a revival of paganism does not stand up to close scrutiny, as it depends on a very geographically restricted analysis of coin deposits in temples. Archaeological investigation has shown that some of the temples portrayed as late fourth-century constructions were built earlier than that. Also, the indications of greater numbers of people attending the temples could be read as élite involvement, 'providing them with wealthy and datable objects, or having them built afresh – rather than showing overall commitment to paganism among the majority of the population'.[66]

Rather than a revival, Martin Millett perceives a shift from urban to rural paganism. 'Although the number of pagan temples used in the towns declines in the later period', he declares, 'the reverse is seen in the countryside, where the peak is contemporary with that of the villas in the middle of the fourth century. Since the distribution of the rural temples closely mirrors that of the villas, their construction must be as much a function of élite display as of religious practice.' The causes of élite migration to the countryside were probably complex, and related to non-religious factors. Certainly it cannot be assumed that if there was such a migration it was because of harassment by Christians. 'The function of religion and priesthoods in the Roman world was closely tied to the political and social power of the aristocracy, so their transfer should be seen in relation to the other shifts towards the countryside rather than as a result of supposed Christian persecution.'[67]

Perhaps the most that can be said is that paganism in fourth-century Britain and at the time of the Roman departure commanded the allegiance of at least a proportion of the population; and if we include within paganism the whole range of Celtic, Romano-Celtic and Roman beliefs, and a substratum of 'superstitions' and folklore, then it accounted religiously for a substantial part of the population. Christianity was far from being dominant, even after the Edict granting peace to the church. The Emperor Constantine himself, the granter of the Edict, seems to have treated Christianity as a mere extension and refinement of the Sun cult in his own life. 'He thought of himself as the comrade of the sun and his earlier coins bear the legend *Soli Invicto Comiti*. There were natural links between the veneration of a single, glorious sky-god and Christ, the single, divine saviour of mankind.'[68]

As we have already noted, there are indications of a certain degree of religious syncretism in the later years of the Roman period; and this was not just between Celtic, Roman and eastern religions. There was no sudden conversion to Christianity by the bulk of the people, and many of those who were converted from pagan backgrounds retained much of their paganism, or incorporated it into their new faith. As one commentator on the Christian pavements at Hinton St Mary and Frampton has remarked:

> Some of the scenes in these pavements and other analogous motifs are found in mosaics with no apparent Christian significance and analysis of these floors has revealed a recurring pagan concern with salvation or some sort of apotheosis, with many of its representations derived from the repertory of funerary sculpture. One is left wondering whether the age of Constantine and his sons in Roman Britain should be characterized as an age of spirituality or an age of anxiety.[69]

There is interesting evidence for a residue, if not revival, of paganism in the fourth century, and of its continuance until the legions departed in the early fifth century. An inscription at Cirencester attesting to the restoration of a column and statue to Jupiter 'in honour of the Old Religion' could well date from the time of the apostasy of the Emperor Julian in the 360s. Additional pagan temples were constructed in the fourth century, and others were refurbished. A Romano-Celtic type shrine was built at Brean Down in about 340, and another at Maiden Castle was erected after 367. This helps to confirm that paganism was still present in society in an organized and institutionalized form in the decades just before the end of the Roman era.

Not only so, but these signs of persistent paganism appear in all parts of Britain, including those areas in the geographical penumbra of core romanization, such as Cornwall. 'Beyond the civil zone, in Cornwall, Christianity had certainly been introduced by the fifth century, if not already during the fourth, but paganism lingered on into the sixth. The Celtic form of the chi-rho monograph and certain sculptures on the Irish crosses similar to those of southern Gaul suggest this.'[70] The picture is variable for different parts of the country. Some pagan shrines went out of use in the early or mid fourth century, some continued, and others were built in the late fourth century.

This continuance of paganism refers, of course, to its public expression and acceptance. In a more subtle, more covert and perhaps sublimated form it never came to an end and is still prevalent in various manifestations of superstition and folk religion. By the fifth century, when the Saxons first became a major threat, and soon settled as a substantial part of the population, Britain was not, as was customarily believed in the past, a Christian country in which paganism had been totally marginalized.

To what extent paganism declined, suffered from severe atrophy, or was a victim of Christian antagonism is not yet clear; the questions raised have not so far been fully answered, and they call for further academic attention. It is a matter of addressing the whole issue of how Christianity and paganism interacted in the transitional hundred years or so from the mid-fourth century onwards. There has been much debate about whether Christians undertook a campaign of destroying pagan shrines in the late fourth century, or even if this occurred quite frequently but not in a sufficiently co-ordinated manner to be called a campaign. There was the apparent demolition of Mithraea, which could have been by Christians, and in some cases, as with the London Mithraeum, there appears to have been an accompanying concealment of pagan religious objects. Examples of the destruction of pagan sites and artefacts in an area where a Christian presence is known from other evidence include Caernarvon,[71] the Walbrook Mithraeum, London,[72] Carrawburgh[73] Housesteads, Rudchester, Lower Slaughter, Gloucestershire, and the Southwark Cathedral site in London. These last two are typical of others: badly damaged pagan religious sculptures have been found in wells at both places, where they were possibly deposited in the fourth century, but the attributing of this to Christians represents a high degree of speculation.

More valuable as evidence of Christian destruction or profanation of pagan shrines or artefacts are those sites where there seems to have been not only such destruction but the re-use of the site involved by Christians. Again, the interpretation of this sequence of events for any one site has seldom if ever been uncontested, but those with the strongest case for Christian re-use are Brean Down, Chedworth, Icklingham, Lamyatt Beacon, Nettleton, Uley and Witham.

The most spectacular of the deposited pagan hoards has been the Thetford Treasure which, although it contains what seems to be

Christian elements, appears to have been hidden by pagans themselves in the late fourth century, possibly as a consequence of the activities of Christians in the surrounding area.[74] The same explanation may apply to the Hockwold diadems and the Cavenham Heath ritual crowns which were deposited on sites near Thetford.

Ken Dark not only suggests that there was no pagan revival in the fourth century, but, despite the gloom of Gildas and the crisis of Pelagianism which brought St Germanus to Britain, also asserts that 'as soon as the Roman withdrawal from Britain had occurred, Christianity seems to have become dominant' and Britain was rapidly 'transformed from having a pagan majority to a Christian majority'.[75] In support of this he maintains that no 'pagan site seems to have survived as a centre of paganism as late as *circa* AD 450, and to Gildas, living in the sixth century, paganism was a matter of antiquity.'[76]

One thing seems clear. Christianity increasingly came to be seen as distinctive in its beliefs and practices. As we have seen, there were probably few physical manifestations of the Christian faith in its early years and, at least in the period from its origins to the fourth century, it may not, from its external appearance, have seemed to the uncommitted Roman Britons vastly different from other esoteric eastern cults, or from the many Celtic, Roman and Romano-Celtic cults. But in the course of the fourth century its uniqueness became ever more apparent. This was so despite the Christian absorbtion of a great number of pagan influences and the undoubted similarity of Christianity and paganism in a few respects. It may be that even before its fourth-century imperial patronage, its 'monotheism, its rituals, its exclusiveness and the lifestyle it espoused all set Christianity apart from the pagan, even from the Mithraic cult'.[77]

But there has been considerable academic debate about how healthy Christianity was by the time the Romans departed. In 1953 Professor J. M. C. Toynbee published an article which was seminal for modern studies of early British Christianity.[78] She concluded that the range and distribution of the evidence revealed a mixed Christian following embracing town and country, rich and poor; and that Christianity was sufficiently established by the end of the Roman period that it did not evaporate with the departure of the Romans, but remained 'submerged' until the Roman mission under Augustine brought it to flower again. She also asserted that the Celtic church which survived in the remotest northern and western parts of Britain was thoroughly Roman in its origin and creed.

W. H. C. Frend, in another influential article, responded two years later with a rather different picture.[79] He suggested that Christianity in Roman Britain was not as widely accepted or as popular with the mass of the people as it was in other parts of the Empire; that it remained a minority religion until the end of the fourth century, and that it was all but forgotten by 597 when Augustine arrived at Canterbury. By the 1980s he had somewhat modified these opinions. He surmised that there had been a gradual penetration of Christianity among the upper classes, with greater strength in some of the towns and villas compared with the countryside, and that the period 430–50 witnessed the destruction of the episcopally based Christianity which had developed in Britain.

Common to both these scholars is the generally accepted view that Christianity was a minority religion in Britain right up to the time of the withdrawal of the Romans. But when it comes to the degree of distinctiveness of Christianity there are wide divergences of opinion. Scholars have approached the subject with quite widely differing perspectives, and from their studies have come to contrasting conclusions. Henig is quite clear in his assessment as he expounds it in the Prologue to his book *Religion in Roman Britain*.

As late as the 360s, Julian's restoration of Paganism was presented simply as a return to 'normalcy'. At any rate down to this time, it is hardly historical to view Roman religion from the standpoint of Christianity. In this book it will shrink to its contemporary importance – as a minor cult in the earlier Empire ; later it was one of several significant sects and from the reign of Constantine it was favoured politically. It requires a real effort of imagination and reconstruction to understand cults which vanished, or left only obscure shadows in folklore, in the way that we can with the Christian religion but an attempt must be made to do so, if the past is not to be falsified.[80]

This differs from the stance taken by Charles Thomas in his *Christianity in Roman Britain to AD 500*. In that important work Thomas treats the history of the Christian faith in Roman Britain as more than the story of just another sect among many at the time. The emergence and development of the church in Britain was, he says, part of a wider process 'whereby Christianity rose to become the principal religion of the Later Roman Empire, and thus the main highway (together with a remnant administration) along which Roman civilization could propel some of its accomplishments towards early medieval Europe'. Christianity was able to offer so much more than Roman paganism, Thomas asserts. It was open to all; it asked for belief in one God who had become manifest as Man; Christ had overcome Death; his followers spoke of a Second Coming in which the dead would be resurrected; and salvation was a gift available for everyone.

> If this spiritually ideal picture of the Faith in its first centuries refers to Roman Britain at all, it refers to the earlier third century, between the most likely date of a Christian foothold in Britain (give or take a generation, AD 200), and the trauma of the first full persecution in the middle of that century. One might even propose that the later story of British Christianity is one of decline, a steady fall from grace in the face of worldliness, down to that disgraceful position described – without specific detail, but in adequate degree – by Gildas, writing in the later fifth century.[81]

Despite the decline, Thomas stresses that there was a line of continuity from Romano-British to Anglo-Saxon Christianity.

Dorothy Watts tends 'to confirm the generally accepted view of Christianity as a minority religion in Britain at the time of the withdrawal of the Romans', but she expresses the wish that her investigations might result in 'a more accurate assessment of the extent of Christianity, and of its place in the religious tradition of Roman Britain'.[82]

I conclude that when Roman Britain came to a sad end in the early fifth century, with the withdrawal of the legions to cope with what proved to be intolerable military pressures on various fronts, British Christianity was well established but patchy, and at no place does it appear to have won the allegiance of the mass of the people. We are not in a position to hazard a guess at the percentage of the population which was Christian. Nonetheless, 'the archaeological evidence of churches and, to a lesser extent as yet, cemeteries, does suggest that Christianity in Britain attracted a smaller proportion of the population than in the western empire or Africa. Undoubtedly, it remained a minority religion, even at its peak during the Roman period.'[83] It was a small, even if expanding, religion, but it 'is abundantly clear that even in the fourth century, Christianity did not oust more traditional forms of religion. The startling formula *seu gentilis seu Christianus* scratched on a lead tablet from Bath illustrates a world in which beliefs and expectations were mixed.'[84]

At the time the Romans departed Christianity was not only unevenly and thinly spread over what was to become England, but it had hardly reached some areas. It had barely touched the south-west region. In *Dumnonia* there are but faint signs from *Isca* (Exeter), the only sizeable Roman town in the *civitas*, and little else. In Cornwall and the Isles of Scilly there are mere traces of Christian activity immediately around St Ives bay. The Christians do not appear on the scene in the south-west until about 450, and even then they may have been brought into the Christian fold as a result of seaborne contact with some part of Christian Gaul rather than as a consequence of the evangelistic efforts of Christians from other parts of Britain.[85] England north of the Tees seems to have been in the same parlous state with the same seemingly minuscule Christian presence. Both regions had substantial Roman military installations, but they were virtually devoid of towns, villas and temples. So it is not surprising that there is little evidence of Christian activity.

3

Christianity in Roman Britain to *c.*410: Its Main Features

The Romano-British Christians – who and where were they?

There is little in the history of the church in Britain in Roman times which is spectacular or dramatic. Other than the martyrdoms of Saints Alban, Aaron and Julius, there is no event or sequence of events which immediately and vividly captures the imagination. This is in stark contrast to what occurred from the late sixth century onwards. The mission of St Augustine in 597 was a very public affair which has been well served by written history. 'The 'great arrival' has been much overplayed, largely as a result of ignorance of what came before.'[1] It is the same for the attractive and highly evocative story of the northern Celtic mission, and much of what was to follow both these stirring events. Indeed, many people, including archaeologists and historians, have treated the arrival of St Augustine and the work of Columba as the beginning of Christianity in England. But this is to ignore or lessen the importance of preceding events and Christian activities. What we are largely concerned with in Roman times is the pioneer, unostentatious, and largely unsung story of ordinary Christians living their lives in an unheralded way, but in the process doing a significant work as a basis for future developments.

The focus of attention must therefore be upon the unsensational life of Christians as they went about their daily business, as they tried to live out their faith, and as they met together for worship and elementary teaching. But this should not imply monotony and insipidness. The picture to be painted is full of colour and interest, largely because these were the people, and this the community of believers, which laid the foundations of an enduring Christianity in what was formerly a pagan country. We are looking back to the life and witness of those who, however quietly and unglamorously, blazed a trail, but who were hardly conscious of the vital part they were playing in the history of the Christian faith in England.

Prior to the fourth century Christianity in Britain appears to have consisted of scattered small groups, and even in places isolated believers, who were encompassed and greatly outnumbered by those of other faiths. The archaeological evidence suggests that there was greater strength of numbers and commitment in the towns than in the country-side. But this conclusion is largely based on the discovery of buildings in what were Roman towns; and it is possibly a somewhat biased yard-stick. After all, the greater number and concentration of Roman subjects in a small area in the towns of itself increases the chance of Christians being present. Also, the general greater prosperity of town dwellers compared with country folk heightens the possibility that they would have built churches, with those churches being of a more expensive, and more durable, stone construction than would have been the case in the countryside. In addition, because the location of Roman towns is generally known, and modern building and other works entail digging to some depth in the modern towns which in many cases have super-seded them, there is a far greater likelihood of finding Roman remains than in what were widely dispersed and small rural communities, with churches which may anyhow have rotted away because they were built of wood. As a final consideration, it needs to be remembered that Christianity came to Britain as a Roman religion, and it would therefore probably have been stronger in the urban areas which were the most romanized parts of the country. Charles Thomas rightly concludes that 'it is quite unsafe to claim that Christianity in fourth-century Britain was either predominantly urban, or predominantly rural, in its emphasis'.[2]

What is much clearer, and less open to dispute, is the seemingly greater number of Christians in the more intensely romanized south-east of the country. This was the region which contained the administrative capital and the largest number of towns, and which because of its proximity to Gaul and the continent was the first to receive most forms of import, including ideas. From this hub, Christianity seems to have spread particularly in a westerly direction as far as Dorset, Gloucester-shire and south-east Wales; and in a northerly direction, following the line of the major road systems on a route which passed Lincoln to York, Catterick and Corbridge, as well as west of the Vale of York. It is mysterious that little evidence of a Christian presence has so far been found in some areas such as that stretching from the Chilterns to the

Cotswolds, Hereford and Worcester, and the most northerly parts of Gloucestershire; and it seems logical that this will be forthcoming in the future.

There is also evidence that Christianity was first introduced, possibly at an early stage of the Roman occupation, and was clearly present throughout the Roman period, in and around Roman frontier and other military establishments, and especially in the neighbourhood of Hadrian's Wall. W. H. C. Frend strongly promotes such a view. He points out that Mithraism and local cults held sway soon after the arrival of the legions and throughout most of the second century. But there are signs that after the great Pictish invasion of 297, and the subsequent assaults, there was a marked decline in the life and vitality of the fifty-eight known temples in the vicinity of the Wall, with Coventina's Well standing out as the sole place which continued to attract offerings down to the fourth century. Frend sees all this as pointing in one direction.

> It would seem a reasonable supposition that the advance of Christianity was a cause of this decline of interest. Ever since he ordered his troops to inscribe the Chi-Rho on their shields before the battle of the Milvian Bridge, Constantine had favoured Christianity in the Roman Army. Even pagan troops were obliged to recite a prayer to the *summus deus*. His policy was continued by his successors, except Julian, and its effectiveness may be illustrated perhaps by the fact that Jovian and Valentinian, both Westerners and in Julian's army, were nonetheless devotedly Christian. Later, Magnus Maximus, the commander of the Wall to 383, was a fanatical upholder of the Nicene orthodoxy and the last usurper whom Britain provided, Constantine III, was also a Christian. If therefore the impact of Christianity was to be felt anywhere in Britain in the fourth century one would expect it on the Wall and at other military sites, such as Richborough or Caernarvon (Segontium), and at Richborough two Romano-Celtic temples near the fort seem deliberately to have been destroyed in about the middle of the fourth century.[3]

Other scholars are less convinced of the role of the Roman army in spreading the Christian faith, and therefore of the military sites as among the clearest centres of early British Christianity. R. P. C. Hanson considers it almost certain that the Roman army played a minor part in bringing Christianity to Britain. He asserts that 'though it did have its proportion of Christians as time went on', it 'must have offered during the first few centuries of Christianity stony ground for the seed of the Gospel'.[4]

What can we say about the quite small number of dispersed intrepid believers? Dorothy Watts[5] and others have helped to revise the once widely accepted view that Romano-British Christianity was essentially not only an urban but also an aristocratic, or at least upper-class, religion. It was the religion of the poor as well as of the rich, and the owners of villas and silver plate. Britain was not out of line with other parts of the empire where the church membership was socially heterogeneous.

One historian is of the opinion that although 'there were high-status fourth century Christians in Britain, as the evidence from Lullingstone and Hinton St Mary villas shows, the social composition of the Christian community was predominantly low-middle-status'.[6] I agree with this, providing that allowance is made for the arguably anachronistic terminology of class. In the rural areas in particular, and perhaps to a somewhat lesser extent in the towns, many of the believers would have had a lowly social status. This means that especially in the countryside the Christians could afford only modest churches and artefacts which are unlikely to feature prominently in historical sources, simply because most of them would not have survived. Nonetheless, some objects have been discovered. There are a considerable number of humble items which almost certainly had low-status owners. 'It was surely poorer men and women who scratched *Chi-Rho* and *Alpha-Omega* symbols on the pots, tiles, pewter plates and cups and other everyday articles that have come to life.'[7] Such artefacts have been unearthed throughout Britain, and the impression given is of a faith which was socially comprehensive.

Charles Thomas and Dorothy Watts have suggested that Christianity was also far more widespread in the British countryside than elsewhere in the western part of the empire, as, for example, in Gaul.[8] Supporting evidence for this includes the fact that a number of low-status rural, or small-town, Christian cemeteries have been excavated, as at Bradley Hill,[9] Shepton Mallet, Icklingham,[10] and Ancaster, which it would be hard to parallel in fourth-century Gaul. Such sites are good indicators of the fact that Christianity was attracting converts in the Romano-British countryside when it was still predominantly an urban religion in the Gallic provinces.

It is possible that the number of churches in fourth-century Britain has been greatly under-estimated, and that many more, including perhaps some rural stone churches, remain to be discovered. Some of those rural Christians without a purpose-built church may have worshipped in nearby towns which had a place of worship. It is also likely that the early Christian habit throughout the empire of gathering in house-churches would have persisted in Britain at least until the fourth century, and especially in rural areas. All these factors detract from a true estimate of the number of Christians living in the countryside.

The difficulty in recognizing buildings as churches is increased by the possible reluctance of the Christians to use religious symbols: none of the free-standing buildings identified with confidence as a church with a possible low status membership includes a Christian symbol. The symbols which do occur are all in high-status churches.

So, too much should not be made of the absence of rural archaeological evidence. In itself it does not prove that there were few rural Christians, or that they were less significant either in numbers or influence compared with their urban brothers and sisters. Neither does the relative paucity of archaeological evidence relating to rural churches show conclusively that the rural poor had been unreached by the gospel, or had not responded to it. The evidence collected by Thomas and Watts and others indicates the very reverse.

I think this stress on low-status Christians is a healthy corrective to the previous emphasis upon higher-status believers, but I think the pendulum can be made to swing too much. The social profile of late Roman Britain constructed by some archaeologists and historians 'with Christianity strongest among the poor, but rarely found among the rich, and paganism still widespread, perhaps, among the poor, but dominant among the élite'[11] is perhaps in danger of going somewhat beyond the evidence. After all, the signs of a significant allegiance of low-status believers are slender, and the evidence for the adhesion to the faith of higher status citizens is comparatively quite convincing, even taking into account the qualifications about the evidence which I have made. An alternative profile, therefore, would be an increased acceptance of both paganism and Christianity among the higher social status groups in the late fourth century, especially in the countryside, with new Christian inroads into the middle to lower ranks of society, producing a socially mixed Christian community with perhaps a majority in the middle and lower social orders. But the Christian leadership may well have come predominantly from among those of higher social status. This is seen most clearly in the rural areas.

In the countryside it seems that villas were increasingly a focus for

Christian worship. It is surely significant that the evidence of fourth-century 'estate' churches points to an important Christian presence in the classes represented by the villas. This was just at the time when the class concerned showed some movement from the towns to the countryside.

> Even when compared with the larger houses which are characteristic of the Public Towns during the fourth century, it is clear that the villas represent the prime places for status display and were thus the principal residences of the élite, the heirs of earlier decurions, now exercising their power from their rural seats. Taken with the evidence of the relative decline in public buildings in the towns, we may conclude that a fundamental change had taken place.[12]

This is not to say that many of the Christians, including those in higher-status groups, did not continue to reside in the towns. As we will see, the Pelagian controversy indicates that there were still a number of influential, high social status, Christians in Britain in the early fifth century, with some, and even possibly the majority, to be found in the towns. What is being claimed is that the fourth century and the early fifth century witnessed a re-distribution of Christianity socially and probably geographically. There was an increase in the number of lower-status believers, especially in the rural areas, but also a continued and possible growth in the number of higher-status Christians, together with a movement among this latter group from towns to country villas.

But regardless of this percolation of the faith downwards socially, there was no general turning of people to the faith throughout the land. For whatever combination of reasons Christianity did not gain the popular support and the allegiance of the people which was typical in other parts of the empire. 'Despite official recognition there was no mass conversion.'[13] Even so, the Christian faith made enough progress to ensure that by the end of the fourth century there was a distinct prospect that it would emerge triumphant. 'The wide distribution of Christianity and its appeal to both rich and poor suggest that, had Rome not withdrawn from Britain and the Western Empire not fallen, Christianity would have become as strong as it had in Gaul in the fourth and fifth centuries, and would have emerged as the predominant religion of Britain centuries before it finally did.'[14]

The Romano-British Christians – what did they believe?

The early British Christians lived in a society which was dominated by the range of Celtic, Roman, Romano-Celtic and eastern mystery religions and cults which I have reviewed in chapter 1. They were not only members of a minority religion, but they lived in one of the outposts of the Roman Empire, remote from the major centres of the Christian faith and the teaching which emanated from such churches. Gradually the influence of these important and powerful foci of Christianity, and especially the authority of Rome, began to assert itself, but in the first formative decades, and among the first few generations of Christians, it needs little imagination to picture individual believers, or small groups of Christians, struggling to grasp the essentials of the faith, and to grow in spiritual understanding in the midst of an overwhelmingly pagan environment. Indeed, many if not most of the converts themselves must have experienced one form or another of the various pagan beliefs before they became Christians; and the beliefs and practices of generations of ancestors were not readily discarded. It must have been an uphill struggle for those early Christians to maintain their distinctive faith and to put it into practice in their daily lives.

A high proportion of them in the second and third centuries, and to a lesser extent in the fourth and early fifth centuries, would probably not have totally abandoned their belief in the pagan gods and their powers. The Christians had come to accept and to put their trust in the one they were convinced was the true God, and had found salvation in and through Jesus Christ. The pagan gods they had once worshipped were no longer regarded as true gods, but they had not ceased to exist. 'Instead, they were relegated to the ranks of the ancient Enemy of a jealous God who would brook no rivals, but whose worshippers, like their rivals the Mithraists, recognized the age-old struggle between the forces of good and evil. Their own God would inevitably be victorious but the hostile powers were not to be treated lightly.'[15]

From the beginning the British Christians were therefore fervent in their opposition to what they now regarded as false, but real and not imaginary, other gods. 'The church in Britain must have been a harder taskmaster than were the Romans in the sphere of native beliefs, actively destroying material traces of the old cults, while nevertheless continuing to enjoy the old cult legends in modified form. Idols would be ruthlessly defaced and broken up, old venerated stones cleansed with the sign of the Cross, and old sacred places purified by the erection of new Christian shrines.'[16]

Some archaeologists consider that the most striking example of deliberate Christian defacement and destruction of pagan cult objects comes from Uley, Gloucestershire, probably in the period soon after 380. The site shows evidence that a rectangular Roman temple, perhaps built about fifty years before, was cleared of its votive and cult objects and demolished, together with its associated buildings. The resulting refuse, including the bones of goats, sheep, cattle and fowls, was then scattered over the demolished structures, and a small rectangular stone building with apse to the south-west was erected over the eastern corner of the former temple. The principal cult statue, a limestone figure of Mercury with purse and caduceus, which was accompanied by a ram and cockerel, was at that time deliberately mutilated. The head, broken at the neck, was carefully placed in a small pit near the new building. Some archaeologists read into all of this Christian hostility to the pagan Roman god and the replacement of the pagan temple by a Christian church. In spite of the problem of somewhat odd apsidal alignments, the replacement buildings have been viewed as shrines or chapels of a cult antagonistic to the worship of Mercury, and it is maintained by those who favour this interpretation of the sequence of events that at the end of the fourth century this could only have been Christianity.

It is possible that this Christian hostility to paganism, and determination to abandon it, increased as Christians grew in numbers, as Christianity became more established and the Christian community gained greater confidence, and as news was circulated of martyrs who had died for refusing to sacrifice to pagan deities. It was common on the continent, and could very reasonably be reckoned as usual in Britain, for pagan cult objects to be slighted and defaced, and then incorporated into Christian structures, where their power might be neutralized. Representations of pagan deities were not treated in a cavalier manner. They were not left lying around. They were disposed of with some care. Many were dropped down disused wells, which was practical in that they were out of sight and almost irretrievable, and symbolic, in that such action could be viewed as consigning them to the underworld of demons where Christians thought they belonged.

Such deposits have been found in a late Roman well excavated under Southwark cathedral, where the deities represented were a hunter-god conflated with Apollo, a genius spirit of a locality or community, and a fragment of some maritime god. The largest and most complete of these was the hunter-god, and this had been broken across the thickest part of the body by a heavy blow. It also shows signs on the broken surface of having been burnt. This is all consistent with the shrine in which it stood having been set alight after the figure had been broken. Building debris had been dumped with the sculptures, much of it caked with soot. This may have been from a late Roman temple on the site. It is perhaps not coincidental that there was later a Christian church on the same site, although we do not have either archaeological or historical evidence which bridges the gap of several centuries between the destruction of pagan objects and the later Christian use of the site for worship.

A similar series of events can be surmised for Lower Slaughter in Gloucestershire in its rural environment. In that case three altars, two headless figures and three stone votive tablets with reliefs which depict multiple gods, were thrown down a well which seems to have been part of a fourth-century farmhouse. These objects were, as at Uley, accompanied by a quantity of stone rubble, which presumably came from the shrine or temple that had contained them. At Embleton, Buckinghamshire, a crude relief of Mercury was found in a well, and this may point to the same fate at the hands of Christians as suggested by the other examples cited.

Akin to this was the throwing of statuettes of deities into rivers, often after mutilation. The Thames near London Bridge has yielded a number of bronze figurines, of the type commonly kept in Roman domestic shrines or used as votive offerings in temples; and from most of these limbs have been amputated, while the heads have been removed in two of the finds. Other desecrated pagan religious objects have included stone reliefs and altars, either unmolested or subject to mutilation, as from the Thames at Bablock Hythe near Oxford. Almost identical discoveries have been made on the continent, for instance from the Rhine near Xanten, the Mosel at Metz, and the Saone near Macon.

Of course it is impossible to be certain about the circumstances leading to such deposits in wells or rivers, let alone the motives of those who may have been responsible for such actions. The problem is confounded by the fact that the burial of pagan images in the earth beneath a building or in a deep well, or the casting of them into a river, was used by the devotees of those cults concerned as a means of making offerings to the deities of earth and water that they represented. These were the accepted methods of communication with the nether-world of spirits which the Christians identified as hell. It is, for example, very difficult if not impossible to know for certain whether the reliefs of water-nymphs thrown into Coventina's Well at Carrawburgh were offerings to the goddess who dwelt in it, like the many other votive offerings which have been found in the well, or pagan sacred images that had once been displayed on the surface site above the well until they were cast down by Christians. Where there was the infliction of deliberate damage before deposition, it seems not unreasonable to see in the act the hand of a Christian iconoclast.

When the iconoclasm appears to have been directed against representations of human beings, there may have been some conscious, but in some cases arguably wrongly-aimed, religious animosity. Where this involved deceased emperors and empresses who claimed divinity, or to whom divinity was attributed, it is understandable, for this was not only abhorrent to Christians, but such claims had entailed the death of many Christian martyrs who refused to offer sacrifices to deified rulers. This even applied to emperors who otherwise had a good reputation, such as Hadrian, whose head was hacked from the body of his bronze statue in Londinium and cast into the Thames near London Bridge. The motive is less clear when the same fate befell representations of people who were not apparently deified or hostile to Christianity, as with a smaller head of Agrippina which ended up in the Avon near the line of the Fosse Way at Bath.

In all these examples, with the possible exception of Uley, it is difficult to be precise about the date when the deposit was made. It is a reasonable assumption that the disposal of pagan images on a large scale by Christians, especially where mutilation was involved, would not have taken place until the fourth century. On the other hand, it is highly doubtful if such objects would have been available in the quantities indicated later than the fifth century, at least in towns or accessible locations. So, the fourth century is the favoured period for such acts if they were perpetrated by Christians.

It is apparent that the church generally became more antagonistic to rival cults with the passage of time, and one must presume that this applied to Britain as well as other areas. This may have been due to an increase in the number of Christians, their official recognition, and their greater status and standing in society, which may well have given them a sense of security and more confidence to be bold and assertive.

At worst the gods had been morally neutral, but they now had to be regarded as evil powers or demons; if they were just non-existent, the deaths of the martyrs for refusing to perform a meaningless ceremony could be regarded as suicide rather than glorious, and this was an unacceptable proposition.

Increasingly pagan beliefs and practices were perpetuated as part of an ever more elaborate and explicit portrayal of the powers of evil.

> Even minor attributes of the gods were taken over for the new demonology, and are recognizable in mediaeval iconography. The horns of some Celtic and eastern gods and the cloven-hoofed feet of Pan became characteristic features of devils, and the pitch-forks they used to propel damned souls into hell may well have originated from a misrepresentation of the caduceus carried by Mercury, guide of the pagan dead.[17]

There was thus a certain hardening of attitude. But in other respects there were signs of accommodation. This mainly took the form of sanctifying pagan convictions and conduct, and incorporating them into a Christian body of belief and practice in one way or another. As we saw in chapter 1, much Celtic religion focussed on water in the form of sacred streams, pools, lakes, wells, springs and the sea. The Christian church in Britain seems at first to have tried to combat such veneration of natural objects, but later it found it better to come to terms with those spirits rather than to defy them. Certain Christian saints were associated with holy wells, springs or other former Celtic holy places. It is not possible to calculate the number of examples where, as it were, the water spirit donned the mantle of the Christian saint, but it was probably considerable.

The christianization of springs and other watery places which were previously venerated by pagans, and the frequent appointment of a saint to preside over them, was a recognition of the value of continuity of association, and probably made a positive contribution to the promotion of the Christian faith without too much negative effect. The superstitious veneration of water never ceased, and there was the ever-present possibility of this being inherited with the Christian use of such sites, but the balance of advantage seems to have been in favour of such a policy. A significant number and proportion of the saints were also associated with healing, which harmonized with the Celtic belief in the healing power of water.

A further Christian adaptation which was arguably not detrimental to the faith, but rather strengthened it as a force in society, was the location of churches on sites which were formerly pagan centres of worship. This probably helped to emphasize in the minds of the people a continuity with ancient religions; a gesture which they respected. Thus, at Goodwood in West Sussex, a chapel of St Roche was located inside the Neolithic enclosure, which in turn had been enveloped by an Iron Age hillfort. At Knowlton in Dorset a church was sited in the centre of a Bronze Age henge monument.

But accommodation could easily become dilution. Excessive compromise may have been a major contributory element in an undermining of the distinctiveness, effectiveness and cutting-edge of the church as a worshipping and witnessing body. 'Such syncretism was, no doubt, a factor which assisted in the absorbtion of Christianity into the mainstream of the Romano-British religion, but it was also a weakness which probably contributed to the failure of the religion to maintain its momentum into the fifth century, particularly in the rural areas.'[18]

It was perhaps in the rural areas that the Celtic influences were most harmful. It has been observed that features which the Christians of the time shared with Celtic cults were more evident in the countryside than in the romanized towns. It was in rural areas that cemeteries were more likely to reveal Celtic rather than Roman elements. In rural settings more than in towns, the Christians appear to have too often made undue concessions to pagan beliefs, values and practices which blunted their otherwise clear cut testimony. 'While there is a danger in over-emphasizing this factor, it would seem, particularly in the rural areas, that the hold of Christianity was at times slight and the depth of commitment not great.'[19]

Nevertheless, on balance the church in Roman times seems to have been strengthened rather than weakened, and to have gained rather than lost by its response to the various forms of non-Christian religion which surrounded it; although at times this precarious balance of advantage seems to have faltered. By its mostly adroit adaptations, and despite the pressures from paganism, the syncretism, and the fact that it was located on the very fringe of the Empire, far from the main centres of the western church, it seems that the British church remained true to the main tenets of orthodox Christian teaching. As we have already noted in the previous chapter, it appears that it was largely free from heretical beliefs. Perhaps the main failing of the church, to which syncretism and undue accommodation may well have contributed, was the poverty of its evangelism. It may have been commendably quite orthodox, but lacking in concern to reach out to surrounding pagans with a clear, uncompromising, unambiguous and challenging call to discipleship.

The Romano-British Christians – their church life

By the fourth century at the latest there were groups of congregations, not necessarily gathering in specially-constructed buildings, but usually to be found in large or small towns, who were directed in all ecclesiastical affairs by a clerical hierarchy headed by a bishop.[20] In other parts of the Empire the structure of the church was uniform, so that it may be assumed to have been the same in Britain. The existence of a local bishop does not necessarily mean the contemporary presence of any building which can be archaeologically recognized as a church, although it became increasingly likely that any British town with its own bishop would have at least one intra-mural church. If the episcopal location was a place acting as a centre, focus, or capital of a civitas, and this includes London and the coloniae, and certain other towns which were of similar standing to civitas capitals, and if such Christian focal churches as the kind found at Icklingham were also used as episcopal seats, then a minimum total of twenty such centres and bishops is conceivable by the end of the fourth century. Each bishop would have covered the urban area and the immediately-dependent areas.

This territorial episcopacy may well have been fairly well developed by the time of the Council of Arles in 314 with its representation by three British bishops. An alternative possibility is that the organized church in Britain was only just being formed, perhaps by imperial command.[21] Those who attended the Council were most probably chosen by a synod of bishops and senior clergy which may well have met regularly in some important centre. The synod was possibly quite large by the time the British church contacted the church in Gaul to invite Victricius to visit Britain in 396, and later, shortly after the departure of the Romans but before 429, issued a plea for help over the Pelagian heresy. In recording his journey to Britain, Victricius states that he was called upon by the British church to make peace. 'Precisely what dissensions required Victricius' presence as an arbitrator or mediator we are not told; but the clear implication of a British episcopate, sufficiently numerous both to form opposing parties and to require a Gaulish metropolitan's prolonged visit, carries us to an equally clear implication of an established Christian presence – and a corresponding range of actual churches.'[22]

In the last chapter I considered such churches, but I want to focus on them again from the point of view of the worshippers. In towns the Christians would have gathered together either in houses or, most usually, and by the mid- or late-fourth century probably universally, in specially constructed basilica buildings. The central feature of these buildings would have been an oblong nave, probably about a thousand square feet in area, sometimes with an apse at the east end and more unusually with side aisles, and approximately aligned in a west-east manner. Such places for formal worship, liturgical use, baptismal instruction and, ideally, with episcopal or clerical domestic quarters attached, have been designated congregational churches. Few, it appears, were as large or complex as the one discovered at Flaxengate, Lincoln, which may have been a five-bay basilica, with an eastern apse and a narthex across the western end. In the earliest of these intra-mural churches the font would have been at the east end, but in the late Roman period it was just as correct for it to be placed at the west end.

The rural churches, such as those at Icklingham and Witham, were much smaller than those in the towns. They were more likely to be simple in design and of timber construction. Estate-churches, or house-churches, we have already described. The extra-mural, suburban or cemetery churches are a feature of the fourth century. They began as martyrial or episcopal tombs, located in conventional Roman cemeteries outside the bounds of any town or city, presumably, in most instances at least from the fourth century onwards, in parts of the cemetery set apart for Christian use. They may have been successively enlarged until they possessed facilities for full congregational use.

Not all churches were purpose-built. The complicated mix of religions, of pagan syncretism and of Christian accommodation, expressed itself in the use of buildings. An example is the suggested sequence for the use of the shrine of Apollo at Nettleton, Wiltshire. I will describe this as it illustrates the high level of religious fluidity typical of the Roman period. It also shows the kind of setting in which Christians commonly found themselves, and in which they sought places in which to assemble.

From the archaeological findings it has been conjectured that soon after AD 69 a small circular shrine was built in the valley alongside the local river.[23] It was probably dedicated to the god Apollo, and it possibly superseded the shrine of a Celtic religious cult already established in the locality. The construction of a large hostel by the side of the nearby Fosse Way and a spacious rectangular hall in close proximity to the central building points to a growing interest in the shrine. The site was further improved in 230 by the erection of a large octagonal podium to encompass the shrine, and a precinct wall with a gateway to enclose the whole complex. A fire in about 250 destroyed the shrine; and it was subsequently replaced by a large octagonal temple, comprising an inner *cella* surrounded by eight chambers and an ambulatory. Later still a larger hostel was erected and the settlement was developed in various ways at an astonishing rate.

Just after 330 the shrine ceased to be used for pagan worship and the building fell into disrepair. 'The decline of interest in the pagan temple was probably due to the increasing adoption of the Christian religion, and evidence suggests that the building was used as a Christian church.'[24] But this did not last long. By about 370 the site had been abandoned, and the now derelict building was adapted for use as a homestead. Around that time a small part of the former central shrine was set up and used for a brief resurgence of pagan worship.

In the late fourth century it seems that the settlement was raided on two occasions, possibly by Irish pirates who came by way of the Bristol Channel. Some of the invaders may have settled with the inhabitants of Nettleton. 'These later inhabitants buried their dead in stone-lined graves orientated east-west in wooden coffins, with no grave goods, suggesting Christian burial.'[25] Around the turn of the fifth century the settlement came to an abrupt and violent end as a result of what seems to have been a vicious attack in which the inhabitants met with violent deaths.

The Nettleton story shows something of the multi-faith society, and the sometimes harsh and perilous circumstances, in which the Christians of Roman Britain lived. Nevertheless, for much of the time they were able to have fellowship together, and to worship in their chosen way.

In common with other Christians throughout the Empire, those in Britain would have met each Sunday, either in a church building, in the home of a Christian or in the open air, to commemorate the resurrection of Christ. They would have gathered to celebrate Pentecost and Easter.[26] By the fourth century they would also probably have included Ascension Day and the nativity of Christ in their annual calendar of services. They may have joined together on days of fasting, which were customarily Wednesdays and Fridays. The fast before Easter lasted forty days in the West; and this was the time during the church year associated with baptism. The period of Lent was especially used for instruction, when the bishop would give lectures for catechumens. From the fourth century onwards the church generally had evolved a ceremonial structure for Holy Week which included the special observance of Maundy Thursday.

The earliest second-century texts, such as the *Didache*, and the works of Ignatius of Antioch and Justyn Martyr, are at one in portraying the regular Sunday worship as first and foremost *eucharistia*, thanksgiving; and this term gradually replaced the more primitive 'breaking of bread'. The British Christians probably conformed to this. They were also probably disciplined in only admitting the baptized to the sacred meal. There was no set pattern for the eucharist, but that described by Justyn Martyr was widely followed. After readings from some apostolic writings and from the Old Testament prophets, the president, who was usually the bishop, preached a sermon, at the end of which everyone stood for a solemn prayer and the kiss of peace. The bread and wine were then handed to the president who gave thanks to the Father through the Son and Holy Spirit, to which the people responded with the word 'Amen'. The communion followed, with the elements distributed by deacons to all the people. In conclusion, pieces of the sacred bread were taken to those who were absent because of sickness, and to those in prison. Attendance at this service every Sunday was considered obligatory for all believers, despite the dangers that this might entail in times of persecution.

The liturgy tended to be extended during the fourth century as the congregations swelled. Towards the end of the century many churches started using greatly enriched ornaments and vessels in worship; although liturgical elaboration proceeded at a slower pace in the West than in the East.

By the beginning of the fifth century it was customary, at least in some of the important cities, for the eucharist to be celebrated daily. In this, as in so much of the liturgy which I am describing, it is not known to what extent the British church conformed to the universal practice of the church, but as it was generally conformist there is a high probability that it adopted similar liturgical forms.

Of central importance in the life of the church was the sacrament of baptism. In these early centuries this implied in most cases adult baptism. It was crucial as an initiatory rite of passage for those who had made a definite decision to seek membership of the local ecclesia. Those who wanted to become Christians and to partake in the life of the local fellowship of believers, started as catechumens. They were instructed by means of scriptural readings, homilies, and teaching about certain practical matters to do with the rites of the church and duties of church membership. By the time of the Edict of Milan, in settled urban churches, this training-period or catechesis may well have been prolonged; and it would most commonly have been conducted in the church building outside the times of the regular services.

The baptism itself would have taken place during one of the major church feasts such as Easter or Pentecost. Shortly before the appointed date those seeking to be baptized became known as competentes, persons who were 'sufficiently prepared' to dispense with the old life and be born again. In Roman Britain, as in other areas, the actual baptism would most probably have been supervised by a bishop. It may have been preceded by exorcism, during which one of the lower grades of clergy, exorcista, used prayer and a set formulae to expel any lingering evil spirits. At the actual baptism the competentes would assemble with the bishop, clergy, and their own sponsors in or by the baptistery. The candidates would remove their worldly clothing, and be conducted to the receptacle of water, where the central part of the sacrament would take place either by a total plunging of the whole body under the water (submersion), by submerging of the head (immersion), by pouring of water over the head so that it streamed down the body (affusion), or by sprinkling water on the head (aspersion). Those newly baptized were known as neophytes. Affusion was probably the form adopted in Roman Britain.

Detached baptisteries of the fourth and fifth centuries have been recognized in southern Britain, for instance at Silchester, Icklingham, Witham, Richborough and Uley. They consisted of separate baptismal tanks or fonts, often made of lead, and quite frequently with inscribed Christian symbols on the outer surface. The Silchester evidence consists of what appears to have been a rectangular platform or setting of flint blocks to the east of the 'church', with a base of large tiles at its centre, and immediately to the west of this a small pit, carefully built with flints and tiles, and clearly intended as some kind of soakaway; the whole forming an integral part of the larger structure.

At Icklingham a D-shaped cistern made of coursed tiles was discovered, which was sunk in the ground. Internally, a third of the space was occupied by a shallow step, and the entire inner face showed traces of white plaster lining. Although the cistern was 1.7m east-west and 1.6m north-south, it was only 30cm deep.

At the Witham site the supposed church was found to have the hint of a detached baptistery adjacent to it, which involved a masonry cistern in a flimsy building, somewhat reminiscent of the Icklingham arrangement.

To the north-east of a purported church at Richborough the excavators encountered a tile-built structure just below the surface of the ground. It had a thick stone and cobble foundation, on which tile-and-mortar walling had been erected to form a hexagon with six incurved faces. Internally and externally it had been coated with a hard pinkish plaster. A large cut or gash made through the walling suggests an inlet or outlet pipe, possibly made of lead. The whole construction was obviously intended to hold water. Bushe-Fox, who excavated the site in 1923, thought it might have been a garden tank or a fountain. But P. D. C. Brown, after careful consideration of various European parallels, shows that it was most likely to have been a font or baptismal cistern.

If the building at Uley has been correctly identified as a church of the Roman period, then the apsidal stone-paved extension which was attached to the northern corner of the timber basilican structure may have functioned as a baptistery. Later, following the demise of the basilica, this area alone was remodelled, and it may then have acted as a free-standing, detached baptistery to serve new stone churches constructed on the site.

When it comes to burials and cemeteries we are confronted by a double problem: fragmentary and dispersed evidence and great difficulty in interpreting what evidence is available. I mentioned cemeteries in the previous chapter, but now, as with churches, I want to consider what light our knowledge of them casts upon the church as a religious community.

Archaeologists, with varying degrees of pessimism, think that there were few, if any, distinguishing features which enable us to identify Christian, as opposed to pagan, burials and cemeteries. Some are dismissive of any sure and reliable data.

For the mainstream of late Romano-British burial practice, it is difficult to conclude other than that there is nothing distinctive about Christian burials. In this respect, in the vast majority of late Roman burials, religious faith and afterlife beliefs receive no distinctive material expression. It seems certain that Christianity adopted late Roman burial practice as it had evolved by the 4th century . . . Whilst on occasion it may be possible to identify Christian family groups or individuals on the basis of amulets or iconography, in general the search for a distinctive Christian burial rite or cemetery is likely to prove fruitless, since in many cases in late Roman Britain pagan and Christian were buried in an identical fashion in the same cemeteries.[27]

This view is to an extent endorsed by Charles Thomas. 'It still remains true', he writes, 'that the task of identifying any *Christian* cemetery – that is, a cemetery of persons whose Christian allegiance necessarily resided in their minds not their cadavers – is a formidable one.'[28]

And, of course, 'formidable' does not mean hopeless as some maintain. Indeed, if it is hopeless then a number of able archaeologists have been pursuing the impossible. From Sir Ian Richmond[29] and Jocelyn Toynbee,[30] via such archaeologists as C. A. R. Radford,[31] those who contributed to a symposium on the subject published in 1977,[32] and a number of scholars who have studied large and small settlements,[33] to such recent experts in the field as P. Rahtz[34] and R. Philpott[35], there has been a great amount of research and academic comment on the subject. Some archaeologists, such as C. A. R. Radford, place great emphasis on the continuity of Christian tradition, as represented in names, dedications, records of proprietorship, and the avoidance of disturbance by later secular buildings, rather than archaeological evidence *per se*.[36] For Roman Britain St Albans Abbey is possibly the only site to pass this test, with a question mark over the problematical sites of St Martin's and St Pancras' at Canterbury. This contrasts with continental European studies which have been able to demonstrate Christian continuity in regions such as the Rhineland.

Confidence has waned over the identification of Christian burial sites simply from their ability to conform to a set of simple criteria. It was once thought to be a sure sign of a Christian cemetery if it was 'composed entirely of extended inhumations – bodies, wrapped or unwrapped, laid full-length in the ground in trenches or in coffins of lead, wood or stone – with these graves being *oriented* (or, to use a later and now commoner form, *orientated*), that is laid with the axis of the body and the longer axis of the grave on a line approximately or precisely east-west'.[37] Such features are no longer regarded as sufficient to attribute unquestioned authenticity to a cemetery as a solely Christian burial site. This does not mean that the former criteria should be abandoned. Indeed, these distinguishing marks, plus an avoidance of overlapping or disturbance between successive graves, and attempts at preserving the body by plaster encasement, are seen by Ann Woodward as of considerable cumulative importance. She is of the opinion that although no single characteristic can be taken as proof of Christian burial, the features I have enumerated, 'if they occur together on one site, may be indicative' of Christian burial.[38] I concur with this, but with the caveat that the test should be applied with caution, and should be supplemented where possible with other evidence, such as continuity, as previously mentioned, and a relevant historical and geographical context for the cemetery concerned.

Clearly, it is unlikely that a public and exclusively Christian inhumation-cemetery will ever be found, even if it could be recognized, in a Romano-British town before 313; and the present evidence is thin for any potential Romano-British Christian cemetery. The hope is to find further, more satisfactory, evidence. So far, the cemeteries at Poundbury in Dorset, Ancaster in Lincolnshire, and Butt Road, Colchester, have yielded the highest level of probability, so I will take a closer look at them.

The Poundbury cemetery lay just east of the ramparts of the Iron Age fort. It has been excavated over many years and a total of approximately 1450 burials have been recorded.[39] Rows of large graves ran along the field boundaries behind a Roman farmstead. They were probably initiated in the second century AD, and they contained a fair number of grave goods and hobnails, making them, in this respect, similar to other burials such as those beyond the western suburb of Ilchester, and not Christian. But contemporary with at least some of these graves were many rows of uniform west-east graves, and they continued probably into the fifth century. They were neatly arranged with minimal overlapping; some of the bodies were in substantial coffins of lead or stone, and there were only a few with grave goods. A small number of the burials had apparently been treated with special care, and these were singled out for separate enclosures. There is one grave within which there is a disputed inscription on a lead coffin which may have Christian significance. It is also highly relevant that this extra-mural cemetery was closely attached to a civitas capital in a region which contained the Framton and Hinton St Mary villas. Charles Thomas assigns Poundbury nine out of ten on a scale of probability as a Christian cemetery,[40] and Ann Woodward is able to add her conviction of its probable authenticity. Taking into account the far-reaching criteria to which I have alluded, she is able to affirm that 'the cemetery that is most likely to have been Christian is Poundbury'.[41]

The late Roman inhumation cemetery at Ancaster lay to the west of the town and began probably not later than the early fourth century.

The vast majority of the burials examined were extended and orientated with their heads to the west. Although Malcolm Todd has expressed scepticism and would prefer to leave the matter open,[42] and P. A. Rahtz views Ancaster as a case where the religious connotations remain unproven,[43] Charles Thomas is again able to be affirmative. Even though it was not 'susceptible to rigid proof', he asserts, 'one would suspect that Ancaster may well be as near as we can get to a fourth-century, Romano-British 'small-town' cemetery of mainly Christian character'.[44]

Lastly, with Butt Road, Colchester there was a cemetery which was similar to that at Pondbury. Related to it was a building of aisled construction with a small eastern apse, and a ritual pit near the eastern end which is known to have been associated with a primary grave. This could have been the burial place of a martyr or Christian leader. Outside the western end of what may have been a church there was a timber structure containing a setting of tiles which could be the remains of a baptismal tank.

The cult of saints and martyrs

Martyrdom was prominent in the life of the church of the Roman Empire. It was the means by which the church achieved some of her most conspicuous triumphs. The blood of the martyrs was, to this extent, the seed of the church. The martyrdoms were highly public demonstrations of Christian fortitude. The martyrs attested before an often astonished and confounded public that the Christians in many respects differed from the followers of other faiths. They were prepared to undergo torture and death in order to remain loyal to their beliefs. They were not prepared to bow to any other so-called god. What, asked the bemused authorities and onlookers, was so precious and sacrosanct to them that they could not accommodate other faiths. Why could they not tolerate and accept other deities? What was so final, all-embracing and wonderful about Christianity that it alone was, according to its martyrs, worthy of the full and undivided dedication of Christian believers. Why were the martyrs prepared to undergo such horrific ordeals, when, in so many cases, a simple gesture of reverence to another 'god' would suffice to give them release. And not only so, but the more ardent spirits among the Christian brethren actually longed to obtain the martyr's crown. If death was not the result of a true witness, then to have confessed Christ before men at a time of persecution was, they believed, to have won a glory which was second only to that of their brethren who died for the faith. It was all very baffling to the pagans who witnessed such Christian attitudes, actions and testimony.

For the church itself, the martyrs were an inspiration and example. They were a spur to greater dedication. And more than that, they achieved a place of supreme honour. In some instances they were accorded powers of intercession on behalf of the living, and the place of their martyrdom or burial was linked with miracles of healing. By the third century this veneration of martyrs was well advanced in the western church. 'The prison doors were besieged by crowds of believers, anxious to pay their respects to those who were suffering for conscience sake.'[45] The graves of the martyrs were frequented by pious Christians, and the anniversary of a martyr's death, called his 'birthday', was commemorated at his grave by a celebration. Initially, this veneration was, in the majority of cases, a matter of private devotion. As it became increasingly popular so the church assumed responsibility for the celebrations; special prayers began to be composed and were collected. At an early time, which cannot be identified accurately, relics of the martyrs started to become an integral part of the life of the church.

'The development of the cult of saints and relics must also have affected Britain.'[46] There may well have been other Romano-British martyrs and saints than Alban, Aaron and Julius. 'It is possible that the English cult of saints may have rested on Romano-British foundations elsewhere than at St Albans.'[47]

Gildas resolved to 'bring to light the ills suffered in the time of the Roman emperors'. But he said that he was hindered from doing so by the paucity of literary remains from Britain itself 'which, such as they were, are not now available, having been burnt by enemies or removed by our countrymen when they went into exile'. He said that he was largely dependent on foreign tradition 'and that has frequent gaps to blur it'.[48] Nevertheless, despite these difficulties, Gildas, who wrote *The Ruin of Britain* in about 540, after the inroads of the Saxons, was able to declare that in the time of persecution God 'lit for us the brilliant lamps of holy martyrs'. And he continued:

> Their graves and the places where they suffered would now have the greatest effect in instilling the blaze of divine charity in the minds of beholders, were it not that our citizens, thanks to our sins, have been deprived of many of them by the unhappy partition of the barbarians. I refer to St Alban of Verulam, Aaron and Julius, citizens of Caerleon,

and the others of both sexes who, in different places, displayed the highest spirit in the battle-line of Christ.[49]

There is a further pointer to the way the cult of the saints grew in the western church in the Roman era, indicating that Britain had its own martyrs other than Alban, Aaron and Julius. In the replies of Pope Gregory the Great to St Augustine in the early seventh century, Gregory wrote saying that he was 'sending relics of the holy martyr Pope Sixtus II, to replace the cult of a local martyr also named Sixtus, whose sanctity was uncertain because miracles were not performed at his shrine and because the elders (*antiquiores*) did not know anything of his *ordo passionis* from their forebears'.[50] There is no information on where the local Sixtus was venerated. Nonetheless, it is unlikely that the pagan English settlers would have perpetuated the veneration of a Romano-British Christian martyr. The implication therefore is that a sub-Roman population survived in the area of St Augustine's missionary authority who continued to revere their martyr after a hundred and fifty years of pagan rule. If that is so, it would show that there was a strong tradition, maintained by people who at least were well disposed towards Christianity if not committed and active believers.

In addition to written sources there is the testimony from archaeology to support the existence of British martyrs, albeit probably in small numbers. It seems that at such places as Stone-by-Faversham in Kent early martyr-tombs may have influenced the siting and even the architecture of English churches. In that case the building has been interpreted as a pagan temple converted into a Christian church, but it might, alternatively, and in view of the evidence, have been a chapel built around a martyr's tomb in the same way as in certain sites on the continent.[51] At Wells a similar explanation could apply for 'the minster is now known to have been associated with a sunken canopied structure of Roman date, almost certainly a martyr's tomb in an extramural cemetery'.[52] Slightly less convincing, but still relevant, is the fact that churches such as St Cecilia and St Lawrence at Cirencester, and St Mary de Lode and St Oswald at Gloucester, are now widely recognized as standing on Roman extramural cemeteries.

It is far from certain that the cult of saints as one aspect of Romano-British Christianity had a powerful and significant impact on English Christianity, and provided a tradition which was perpetuated and developed in the Anglo-Saxon church. At present it is no more than a hypothesis. With the exception of St Alban and his co-martyrs Aaron and Julius, Bede gives no support to such an influence. But his virulent opposition to the British who 'would not proclaim to the English the knowledge of the Christian faith'[53] may mean that he omitted such a reference as a result of a biased view.[54]

Evangelism

Whether there was much justification in Bede's censure of the Romano-British Christians for lacking evangelistic zeal is difficult to assess. It does seem that Christianity in Britain at the time of the Roman departure was less well represented in the population as a whole, less an established part of society, and less vigorous in its outreach to its neighbours within Roman society and to adjacent alien territories than in many of the continental European countries where pastoral care, evangelism and growth were more conspicuous. The fundamental problem seems to have been that despite its gains, for instance in the comparative decline of paganism, it had not taken a firm grip on society as a whole. This might mean that there were a high proportion of 'nominal' or 'lukewarm' Christians who were content to be identified as Christians after the Edict of Milan, but who were not especially committed to the Christian faith, and were not prepared to exert themselves unduly either in efforts to transform the culture and social norms of their society, or in any form of aggressive evangelism. The evidence for the state of Christianity in sub-Roman Britain, and the later reprimands of Gildas would support such an interpretation.

Nonetheless, the fact that the faith had spread throughout a wide social and geographical spectrum in a society in which paganism was actively represented by a host of deities speaks well of the outreach of many Christians to their non-Christian neighbours. The martyrs to whom I have just referred were possibly but the most extreme representatives of a witnessing body of believers. It is also of some significance that when Germanus came to the country in 429 and 435/6 he encountered groups of Christians in considerable numbers, and that when Augustine arrived in 597 he found a British church with its own bishops.

Certainly, the faith which had been planted in the Roman era was not extinguished in the course of the following two hundred years. If a sufficient degree of christianization endured to provide a seedbed for the evangelization of the sixth and seventh centuries, then it shows that something of lasting quality and value was achieved in the Roman era. I will suggest later that much of the Christianity of the early fifth century was insubstantial and somewhat superficial, but this cannot be the whole story. Here and there, in pockets and patches, there must have been individuals and groups of believers whose faith was strong and secure enough to last; and it was a faith and way of life which was passed on to subsequent generations. Some of the seed sown did not perish. It was able to survive the sub-Roman period when some degree of Christian solidity was followed by attrition, and this in its turn by at the best a retaining of the status quo.

As far as the Celtic lands beyond the Roman province are concerned, there is only circumstantial evidence of any evangelistic outreach into Ireland, Scotland or Wales by the Christians living in what became England. Gougaud was confident that the 'Christian faith was first propagated in the insular Celtic countries from Roman Britain as a base'.[55] He quite reasonably considered that the intercourse between Roman Britain and the nearby Celtic lands would inevitably have resulted in the spreading of Christianity. The extent and quality of this evangelization is open to question, but something may well have been accomplished. By 400 Christianity had penetrated to the Solway Firth and the banks of the Clyde, and it would, Gougaud said, be strange if Ireland, which was so close to Britain, had remained untouched by any Christian influence. 'The commercial relations of the Irish Scots with the Britons and with the peoples of the Continent, their hostile raids outside their own country, the foundation of Gaelic colonies in Great Britain, the slave trade, actively carried on at the time, and war, which brought captives of whom many were Christians to the shores of Ireland – all these opportunities of contact were likely to disseminate the Christian religion from individual to individual and from nation to nation.'[56] But, like so much of the history of Christianity in Britain in the Roman period, much of this must, in the present state of knowledge, be speculative.

Part 2

Sub-Roman Britain

4

Sub-Roman Britain

Historiography and sources

The whole period of some two hundred years after the departure of the Romans in about 410 has been a fruitful field for theories and conjecture, frequently out of all reasonable proportion to the slender evidence available.

Some historians are pessimistic about the validity of any historical account of sub-Roman Britain. One of the most distinguished, Sir Frank Stenton, has expressed this uncompromisingly:

> Between the end of Roman government in Britain and the emergence of the earliest English kingdoms there stretches a long period of which the history cannot be written. The men who played their parts in this obscurity are forgotten, or are little more than names with which the imagination of later centuries has dealt at will. The course of events may be indicated, but is certainly not revealed, by the isolated or incidental references to Britain made by writers of this or the following age.[1]

Although this presents a gloomy prospect for any aspiring historian of the period, it is partially endorsed, albeit in less absolute terms, by a sub-Roman specialist of note, J. N. L. Myres. 'The period of some two centuries which lies between the collapse of Roman government in Britain and the arrival of St Augustine in AD 597 has', he writes, 'long been recognized as the most difficult and obscure in the history of this country. Between Roman Britain and Christian England there is a great gulf fixed, a void of confusion which remains a standing challenge to historical enquiry.' And yet, it was a formative time of fundamental importance to the whole evolution of the country; two hundred years in the course of which, according to the historian just quoted, 'changes more profound and far-reaching than in any other corresponding period took place'.[2]

James Campbell, in a classic work on the Anglo-Saxons, refers to the years 400 to 600 as 'the lost centuries', and he also sounds a cautionary note when approaching them historically:

> The natural vice of historians is to claim to know about the past. Nowhere is this claim more dangerous than when it is staked in Britain between AD 400 and 600. We can identify some events and movements; make a fair guess at others; try to imagine the whole as a picture in the fire. That is all. Knowledge will creep forward by the accumulation of facts, especially archaeological facts, and by the dialectic of hypotheses. But what really happened will never be known.[3]

Some historians have, nevertheless, cast caution to the winds, and have undertaken ambitious schemes of reconstruction for this, until recent times, much under-explored era. Of these, perhaps the most contentious and, one must say stimulating, has been John Morris. He does not hesitate to advocate boldness in detailing the course of events:

> These centuries are a historical period in their own right, more than a transition or interlude between Rome and the Middle Ages. To be understood, a well-defined period needs a name, as clear in meaning as Roman, Norman or Tudor. The fifth and sixth centuries in Britain are properly termed the Age of Arthur, for modern historical convention normally labels periods according to their principal rulers . . . The Arthurian age is the starting point of future British history. Thereafter, Britain has comprised England, Wales and Scotland; previously these three countries did not exist.[4]

They are certainly enigmatic years. Some historians have regarded the destruction of the Romano-British world as virtually total, and have depicted a full-scale transformation, in which most of the features which typified the Roman era were swept away in a comprehensive process of saxonization. Others have understood the Anglo-Saxon incursion as superficial; as providing little more than the veneer of a new language and a conquering élite on a British population which was not fundamentally changed, but remained in place despite military defeat, economic depression and cultural deprivation. And, as we will see, the religious, and more especially Christian, history of the period is riddled with queries. A painstaking search for clues has to be undertaken in order to fathom even the rudimentary historical outline of what took place in every sphere of life.

Primary written sources, and extant material evidence are meagre for Roman Britain and later Anglo-Saxon England. They are, however, sufficient to provide a reasonably firm basis for constructing a general history of both these periods. But for the intervening centuries there are no contemporary records of comparable quality and thoroughness. The Anglo-Saxons were illiterate, and so it had to await their conversion to Christianity before they began to record in writing some of the oral traditions handed down from their pagan ancestors; and the archaeological data is scanty in the extreme.

For the native Britons Gildas is the only contemporary writer who attempted a general survey of British history from the latter days of Roman rule until the middle of the sixth century. His work suffers from inadequacies, largely because the author did not intend it to be history. 'It is a fierce denunciation of the rulers and churchmen of his day, prefaced by a brief explanation of how these evils came to be.'[5] Just enough is known from other sources to make his narrative intelligible. Chief among these are the *Historia Brittonum* (British History) and the *Annales Cambriae* (Welsh Annals) of Nennius. Unlike almost all ancient, mediaeval, and early modern historians who gave their own interpretations of their sources, or compiled annalistic chronicles of events, Nennius selected extracts from each of his sources and simply arranged them, usually in what he thought was their proper chronological order.

Bede's *Ecclesiastical History* does not dwell at length on this sub-Roman period, but it offers some useful information and comment for the church historian.

In recent decades these literary sources have been helpfully augmented by the archaeologists. But archaeological work on the period is in its infancy. James Campbell is especially concerned about the onus on archaeology to illuminate these dark centuries. Despite this, he is realistic about the daunting task and the degree of potential for success. 'Those', he writes, 'who wish for certainty in history and who like to feel the ground firmly under their feet are best advised to study some other period. For those who care to venture into a quagmire, the archaeological evidence, and the truly remarkable intellectual effort of archaeologists to make sense of it, are of basic importance.'[6] The need is to integrate and give appropriate weight to literary, archaeological and historical evidence. This will be attempted in the present study of religion, and more particularly Christianity, in the period, as it has, for example, been achieved most successfully by K. R. Dark in a refreshingly insightful general study.[7] He not only adopts a fully interdisciplinary approach, but places Britain within the broader European perspective and, perhaps most significantly, tries to concentrate on the British, rather than the Anglo-Saxon, part of the story. He summarizes this succinctly.

> Rather than stressing the importance of the Anglo-Saxon East against a 'Celtic fringe' to the West, it seems, therefore, that until the Anglo-Saxon expansion in the seventh century it was Anglo-Saxon England which constituted the periphery (whether to the British or Continental Franks), rather than the Britons of the West. If we are to place fifth- to seventh-century Britain in clearer focus it is, therefore, important to emphasize its British, rather than Anglo-Saxon, aspects.[8]

It is stimulating and encouraging to know that the study of that problematic age is being undertaken with renewed vigour and heightened prospects of fruitfulness.

History of the period – c.410 to the late sixth century

At the very beginning of this historical review we are confronted with the fundamental question of the general state of the country after 410, and what course of events moulded its destiny in the succeeding century and a half. Myres provides what many others would regard as a reasonable summary of what occurred:

> All that was apparent by the end of the sixth century was the destruction of the whole fabric of Roman imperialism in Britain, the disappearance of its civil and military administration and of many of the arts of life. Instead there was being built up a group of precariously founded barbarian kingdoms whose rulers were still living largely on the spoil of their neighbours, even if many of their dependents, along with the surviving remnants of the British population, were already slowly settling down to the ceaseless routine of subsistence agriculture.[9]

By the late 1980s there was a growing academic confidence which allowed this picture to be given somewhat greater precision. There was a sense of unravelling some of the secrets of the age, albeit in a very tentative and small-scale way. At least it was thought by many scholars that there was some greater understanding of the condition of the Britons in the fifth century, and of the Anglo-Saxon settlement among them which would eventually lead to a hybrid society, Anglo-Saxon in name and in language but a fusion of the blood and culture of the two peoples.[10]

At the heart of the work on sub-Roman Britain has been the question of whether there was essentially continuity or discontinuity as one moves from the fourth century to the seventh century.

Until about the Second World War archaeologists, and some historians, wrote in terms of catastrophic events: of the sudden and fearful end of civilized life after the departure of the Romans, and of a country overrun by hordes of barbaric Saxons with the Britons fleeing to the western highlands for refuge. It was thought that the Anglo-Saxons must have shunned the decaying works of the Romans and virtually razed Roman Britain to the ground in their frenzied onslaught. Such a picture may contain some elements of truth, and it is not to be totally discarded; but it does require radical readjustment.

Archaeologists and historians in the second half of the twentieth century have come to realize that if there was a complete break between Roman Britain and Anglo-Saxon England, then that contrasts starkly and unrealistically with the utterly different situation on the continent. And this seems highly unlikely despite some crucial differences in the circumstances of the two territories. There has also been a growing appreciation that other comparable historical events such as the Norman Conquest did not entail a total, or near total, break with the preceding political, economic, social and religious order.

It is now almost universally agreed that the historical sources portray a long drawn-out process around and after the withdrawal of the Romans in the early fifth century, in which there was a survival of *Romanitas* during a time when Germanic groups arrived, settled and took over most of the country. Vestiges of romanized society continued. Sub-Roman Britain was far more romanized than was once thought.[11] Much of the archaeological excavations and fieldwork during the last ten years or so has emphasized that 'the transition from post-Roman Britain to Saxon England involved a considerable degree of continuity rather than a complete break with the past'.[12]

Perhaps the most cogent case for continuity, or more precisely a whole new way of viewing the issue, has been presented by Ken Dark. He asserts 'that Roman Britain ended not in the fifth century, but the seventh, and, in a sense, not even then'. He points out that until the seventh century 'by far the majority of Britain was outside the area of Anglo-Saxon control, and even in that part of Britain which may be considered Anglo-Saxon, there may have been substantial British enclaves'.[13]

The argument for continuity has been extended backwards in time by some scholars who suggest that there were many continental barbarians, and especially north Germans, in the Roman army in the fourth and early fifth centuries, if not earlier. These, as in other parts of the Roman Empire, were recruited from beyond the frontiers of the Empire in order to help cope with a desperate situation. In Britain, so the case goes, they were stationed in eastern and southern Britain. The Saxon Shore (*Litus Saxonicum*) was a defensive chain of late Roman coastal forts located between the Wash and Portsmouth Harbour, so named because Saxon troops were employed in the fortifications. There was thus a process of Anglo-Saxon infiltration before the impact of Anglo-Saxon assaults and settlement. The apparent concentration of Anglo-Saxon cemeteries around Roman towns has been used in support of this thesis.

But continuity at least went hand in hand with discontinuity. The economic superstructure and the social organization established so efficiently by the Romans were quite rapidly destroyed after they left, so that, for instance, the material symbols of *Romanitas* had gone by about 420; and this is corroborated by the archaeological evidence. The prosperity which had characterized much of the late Roman period did not survive the disruptions after the withdrawal of the legions, or the political collapse of the western empire. The dislocation of the former Romano-British military and civilian administration, if not its total disappearance, demolished the previous money economy and the spending power which had maintained the internal markets for food and manufactured goods. The barbarian pirate fleets also wrought havoc with the profitable export trade as they increasingly infested the coasts and harbours on both sides of the Channel. It is not clear if this traumatic collapse was accompanied by a great loss of life or a massive migration of Germanic peoples to Britain in the fifth century.[14]

What is most questionable in this particular view of events is the extent to which there was decline and collapse from a peak of economic and material abundance to widespread deprivation and disintegration on a major scale. Certainly, the economy and the material well-being of the country as a whole were buoyant for much of the fourth century, but was there a marked recession in the last quarter of the century. If so the transition to the new depressed economy and poor general state of

affairs in the first half of the fifth century may not have been as severe
and dramatic as it might appear to some observers. There may simply
have been an accelerated economic decline, without the previous
administrative underpinning of the economy to help apply the necessary
breaks.

A considerable body of evidence shows that the towns, the villas
and the pottery industry in particular did experience such a slide. This
was manifested in the abandonment and non-replacement of buildings,
and a decline in the quality and level of maintenance of both public
amenities and private residences. Work on *Verulamium*, Chichester,
Winchester and Canterbury, as well as other larger towns, and on such
smaller towns as Brampton, Ilchester, Kenchester, Water Newton,
Alchester and Catterick has revealed such trends, which may be taken
as symptomatic of economic stagnation or worse. The same may have
been true of villas; for there is no sign of any villa being built *de novo*
in the last quarter of the fourth century, and no evidence that there were
any major extensions or refurbishments of existing ones. As far as the
best-known of the British industries, pottery, is concerned, two of the
most important late Roman fine ware industries, those of the New
Forest and Oxfordshire, show no additions to their volume of production, or to the range of their forms or decorative styles in the late
decades of the fourth century. Overall, there is evidence that in the last
quarter of the fourth century there was a decline in the most romanized
sectors of the economy and culture; and this was not checked in the first
few decades of the following century.

A reasonable conclusion is that romanization was deep-seated, especially in the eastern parts of Britain, and that it did not rapidly evaporate
and disappear in the first half of the fifth century. But there was economic and cultural sluggishness or even deterioration in the decades
before the Romans departed and this, added to the internal divisions
within the post-Roman political and social community, made the
country even more vulnerable to external attack than it might otherwise
have been.

The denouement came in 406–10. According to the Greek historian
Zosimus, who drew upon earlier authorities, at some time in 406 the
army in Britain set up a usurping emperor, Marcus, who was slain by
troops the following year and immediately replaced by another usurper,
Gratian, a Briton. He was killed within a few months, and a third
usurper, a common soldier who entitled himself Constantine III, led
most of the army out of Britain to Gaul to help meet the threat from the

Vandals, Alans and Sueves who had crossed the frozen Rhine and were pillaging Gaul.

It appears that Britain was attacked by Saxons in 408–9 and that the military did not cope effectively with the crisis, in part because by then there were such enormous pressures on the Empire from other invading forces on the continent. This may have forced the British élite to take control of their own destiny, which entailed removing the barbarians and then ousting the Roman government in 409. But, left to their own devices the Britons were soon in trouble, and in 410 they appealed for Roman military assistance. The emperor Honorius wrote to the cities of Britain telling them to take responsibility for their own defence. In effect, Britain was no longer a part of the Roman Empire.

There is evidence that early in the fifth century two of the signal stations on the Yorkshire coast were destroyed by fire and slaughter; and the sack of the two frontier forts of Birdoswald and Chesterholm shows that Hadrian's Wall was no longer an effective barrier to Pictish invasion. There may have been a brief period during which the Britons gained some success against these marauding Picts and Scots. But this short-lived respite was followed by civil war, pestilence, and another series of barbarian raids. In response, a certain 'tyrant' negotiated assistance from a body of Saxons for the defence of the land against attacks from the north. Gildas refrains from naming the person, but Bede, Nennius, and traditions which go back at least to the seventh century assign him the name Vortigern. Both Bede and Nennius also supply the names of the leaders of the mercenaries (Hengest and Horsa), and the place where they first arrived and settled (Kent). They served their British employers for 'a long time',[15] but a dispute over their rations led to a revolt (which Bede says occurred between 449 and 456).

It appears that substantial numbers of Germanic settlers began to arrive from about the mid-fifth century; and, according to Gildas, they ravaged the whole land as far as the western sea. If his account is accurate, the effect was devastating, with the wholesale destruction of towns, especially in the south where the situation became intolerable. Isolated villas, such as North Wraxall (Wiltshire) and Lullingstone went up in flames, and archaeological evidence indicates that at the former two bodies were thrown down a well.

Whatever the extent of devastation may have been, it seems that there were large numbers of immigrants in total from northern Germany and southern Scandinavia who came to Britain in this wave, and in other Saxon incursions in the course of the fifth century. Some archaeologists have depicted a small number of well-armed warrior bands who successfully mounted a series of *coups d'état*, and thereby took over British regional 'kingdoms'. This hypothesis flies in the face of contemporary and slightly later commentators who to a person tell of large numbers. The emergence of a variety of Germanic dialects which are ancestral to modern English argues strongly for a large Anglo-Saxon presence, as does the widespread use of Germanic place-names.

A breathing space was granted to the British when many of the mercenaries returned to their own country, and the British defences were reorganized under Ambrosius Aurelianus. He seems to have used to good effect the local and national administrative structures which remained, probably in depleted form, from the Roman era. At the end of the Roman period there had been about thirty *civitas* administered by bodies of about a hundred local men of consequence who constituted the *ordo*. It was to these that Honorius had probably written. In the fourth century there had been a central council, with largely ceremonial functions, for all the *civitates* of Britain, but it is not known if this continued after 410. It may have remained, and there may have been a series of British emperors who had authority over all or most of Britain, working through this administrative network, of whom Ambrosius Aurelianus was possibly one.

Gildas speaks of the terrible time of slaughter, plunder and suffering with the onslaught of the Saxons, and then proceeds to make reference to Ambrosius Aurelianus, whom he describes as a gentleman, and perhaps the only surviving Roman. Gildas also wrote of his parents who had worn the purple, and this could mean that they had been emperors of Britain. He was certainly a person of stature and ability. According to Gildas, he is said to have inspired the people to regain their strength and to successfully challenge the oppressors to battle, once more probably using the local administrative structure in order to gain widespread support.[16] This depiction of events is substantiated by Nennius who alludes to Ambrosius as 'the great king among all the kings of the British nation'.[17] It may have been Ambrosius and his supporters, or those immediately before them, possibly between 446 and 453, who directed the final appeal for help to Rome, the so-called Groans of the Britons: 'To Aetius, thrice consul: the groans of the Britons . . . The barbarians push us back to the sea, the sea pushes us back to the barbarians; between these two kinds of death, we are either drowned or slaughtered'. Gildas, who quotes this pathetic plea for help, adds, 'But they got no help in return.'[18]

Bereft of external assistance they took action to mobilize their slender resources, and when the Saxons returned they were confronted by a much more united and ordered society and military force. For a time there was a struggle which was on equal terms, but it ended with a British victory at a place called *Mons Badonicus* (Badon Hill), probably at some time during the last decade of the fifth century. The triumph was elevated by later writers to a pivotal position in the history of the period. This is understandable in view of the fact that it is the only conflict which Gildas chose to name. It is portrayed by him as the climax of the struggle between Britons and Saxons, and a turning-point in British history which ensured forty years and more of freedom from war.[19] Crucial and critical it may have been, but it must be said that our knowledge of the battle and the events which surrounded it are woefully defective.

Seen in retrospect Badon Hill ended one phase of the war, but it was the last victory vouchsafed to the Britons. The balance of power henceforth shifted not in favour of the Britons but of their opponents.[20] The seven hundred years between the withdrawal of the Roman garrisons and the consolidation of the Norman feudal mastery saw the making of England. The battle of Badon Hill was one of the nodal points in that process, but mainly as a last defiant act of an ancient people who were gradually to yield centre stage to the triumphant Anglo-Saxons.

In recording this historic defeat of the Saxons, Nennius, under the mistaken date 516, gives prominence to 'Arthur', who 'carried the Cross of our Lord Jesus Christ for three days and three nights on his shoulders [i.e. shield] and the Britons were the victors'.[21]

So it is at this stage in the narrative that we are faced with one of the great mysteries of British history; the person and work of King Arthur. Did he or did he not exist, and if he was a historical person, what do we know about him? Historians are divided in their opinions. It weighs heavily with all of them that Gildas makes no mention of any such character. But such silence is not conclusive proof. Nennius refers to Arthur fighting against the Saxons, 'together with the kings of the British; but he was their leader in battle',[22] and he notes 537 as the date of his death: 'the battle of Camlann, in which Arthur and Medraut fell'.[23] The only other reference to Arthur outside Nennius is the observation of an earlier Welsh poet that a certain warrior, though brave, was not an Arthur.

The views of three historians will give a flavour of differing historical opinion. Sir Frank Stenton is cautious and judicious. 'The silence of

Gildas', he writes, 'may suggest that the Arthur of history was a less imposing figure than the Arthur of legend. But it should not be allowed to remove him from the sphere of history, for Gildas was curiously reluctant to introduce personal names into his writing . . . He was a prophet, not a historian; he wrote with passion, and the world he addressed was small.'[24] James Campbell is almost entirely dismissive. 'Arthur's late and continuing fame owes almost everything to a fictional history of the kings of Britain written by Geoffrey of Monmouth in the 1130s.' In an attempt not to be totally cynical, he tries to glean some benefit from the search for the historic Arthur. 'There is', he writes, 'at least this to be said for the inexhaustible, if rather ridiculous, interest in trying to work out who the 'real' Arthur was. By provoking speculation it forces realization of how many great men and great events there must have been in the fifth and sixth centuries of which we know nothing at all.'[25] Finally, and in startling contrast there is that champion of Arthur and all things Arthurian, John Morris. He leaves us in no doubt about his enthusiasm:

> The personality of Arthur is unknown and unknowable. But he was as real as Alfred the Great or William the Conqueror; and his impact upon future ages mattered as much, or more so. Enough evidence survives from the hundred years after his death to show that reality was remembered for three generations, before legend engulfed his memory. More is known of his achievements, of the causes of his sovereignty and of its consequences than of the man himself. His triumph was the last victory of western Rome; his short lived empire created the future nations of the English and the Welsh; and it was during his reign and under his authority that the Scots first came to Scotland. His victory and his defeat turned Roman Britain into Great Britain. His name overshadows his age.[26]

I have great respect for Morris and all he has done for historical scholarship, but I think that he is incorrect in the stress he lays on the person of Arthur, which he allowed to dominate his academic work. I think the true assessment lies in the former two views stated.

By the early sixth century a concord seems to have been established between the British and the Saxons. The British had demonstrated their ability to defend themselves if unduly provoked. The Saxons did not, as it was once thought, indulge in a wholesale and nationwide takeover. They did not clear the forests and establish the nuclei of modern villages.[27] Recent research has shown that Roman Britain was so intensively farmed and densely populated that there was little virgin land left uncultivated. Also, a few tens of thousands of immigrants would not have been able systematically to massacre or enslave millions of native people. In the east of the country, in the land which was to become England, where most of the Germanic cemeteries and settlement sites have been discovered, there may have been a genuine folk movement as part of a process of transition. Elsewhere the most aggressive acts seem to have taken the form of a forceful assumption of control by a small ruling group; so that one set of masters was substituted for another. But even in these situations everyday life seems to have gone on much as before, but under new management. 'For the Saxons came not to destroy, but to share in the good life.'[28]

So, in spite of much aggression there was an underlying, and what was to prove lasting, process whereby two cultures were gradually merged.

> As areas came under Saxon control one assumes that most of the previous Romanized élite fled or were slaughtered, although the remainder of the population may well have remained to work the land under their new masters. These people henceforth came to emulate Germanic customs and habits, so their Romanization was replaced by what we may call Germanization. We can thus see the new culture as the result of positive choices, resulting in a fusion of Romano-British and Saxon elements to produce something new and Anglo-Saxon.[29]

The extent and pace of Germanization can generally and very crudely be measured by the degree to which Saxon place-names were introduced. The greater number of such names diminishes as one moves from east to west, in the same way that the intensity of settlement also lessened.

By the middle of the sixth century, the Saxon advance had resumed, and the communities of Anglo-Saxons, which by then were often well-entrenched, were expanded. By the end of the century the Saxons had established themselves in all areas of the country except the Celtic regions of the south-west, Wales and northern Scotland. England was increasingly becoming Anglo-Saxon in character. Roman Britain was increasingly becoming a thing of the past.

The politics, economy and social structure of early Saxon Britain

Bede made various guesses about the date when the Saxons first arrived, on the basis of the inadequate data provided by Gildas, and concluded that it was between 445 and 455. The Nennius collection opts for 428, and archaeological evidence confirms that this is rather more accurate. Germanic objects which have been found in a number of areas seem to belong somewhere near the beginning of the fifth century; and some of the pottery discovered in England is sometimes judged to be even earlier. There may well have been Germanic settlers in scattered parts of England from the Channel coast to north of the Humber in the earliest decades of the fifth century.[30]

Little is at present known about the origins of Anglo-Saxon kingdoms. Information gleaned from the *Anglo-Saxon Chronicle* and a handful of annals preserved in twelfth- and thirteenth-century chronicles points to the mid-fifth century origin of Anglo-Saxon Kent; and to 477 as the beginning of the history of Anglo-Saxon Sussex with the landing of Aelle. These were the natural points of entry to the country in view of the geographical location of the homelands of the settlers.

The origin of Wessex is traced to the landing of Cerdic and Cynric in 495, Port in 501, and other 'West Saxons' in 514. But it is also to be traced to the settlement of the upper Thames valley from Goring to Oxford, in the region covered by the modern Berkshire and Oxfordshire, in which Dorchester-on-Thames was the focal point.

After the establishment of these bases there was a line of entry into the deeper mainland through the Fens. The origins of East Anglia and ultimately Mercia are associated with a Germanic invasion in 527, and with the beginning of the kingdoms (or dynasties) of Essex, East Anglia, and Mercia in 527, 571, and 585 respectively. Archaeologists have often stressed the importance in the early Anglo-Saxon settlement of the territories occupied by the Middle Angles in what became the modern shires of Northampton, Huntingdon and Cambridge, as equal to that of the better-chronicled, and in some respects apparently more spectacular, exploits of the Germanic peoples in the Thames valley.

A further inland area of early settlement was around the Warwickshire Avon. This region was occupied in the first instance by the Saxons of the Thames valley, though at an early stage it received a strong Anglian admixture. Although its recorded history is even more obscure than some of the other regions, it appears that the initial group of Saxons directed the advance to the west along the Severn valley. They thus created the kingdom of Hwicce, which was soon overshadowed by the rise of Mercia, but which at the height of its power probably stretched from Worcester to Wychwood in Oxfordshire.

Beyond the Humber Bernice and Deira were established at some stage in the fifth and sixth centuries, so that they appear as distinct kingdoms by the end of the sixth century. Although such dates are very much open to question, it is significant that the annals and the *Chronicle* all attribute the Anglo-Saxon rule in England of all dynasties north of the Thames to the sixth rather than the fifth century.[31]

The Anglo-Saxon sphere of settlement and influence, like that of the Romans, did not extend to the extreme west and north of Britain to the same degree as in other areas. For the whole of the period at present being reviewed, covering the fifth and sixth centuries, the south-west peninsula probably remained under British control.[32] At a later date the south-west, the nearer parts of Wales, and most of Cumbria did pass into Anglo-Saxon hands, mainly when there was the consolidation of powerful new kingdoms in Northumbria, Mercia and Wessex. But in the meantime the British population in all these western regions managed to retain cultural individuality. The people concerned possessed a culture which had been far less effectively transmuted by the influence of Rome, and they developed a remarkable resilience both to Roman and Anglo-Saxon pressures. They remained unbowed and unyielding when confronted with the dramatic changes taking place in the east and south. They held on to their own languages, much of their pre-Roman social structure, their settlement patterns, and their legal system. They held on to their Christianity, but also modified its organization to fit their own cultural needs, and found it to be both a powerful unifying force and a continuing reminder of their spiritual links with Gaul, Rome, and the Mediterranean world.

The whole movement I have outlined was closely associated politically with the slow consolidation of Frankish power in the north-east of Gaul, and possibly with the failure to establish a Saxon Normandy. Archaeological evidence confirms that the invaders and settlers were Angles, Saxons and Jutes. The Angles came from the southern part of the Danish peninsula and some of the Danish islands; the Saxons were from the North Sea coastal plain further west to just beyond the mouth of the Weser; and the Jutes, despite the prolonged scepticism of many philologists, are now widely reckoned as having emanated from Jutland.

The Anglo-Saxons introduced important modifications to the settlement patterns which had evolved over many centuries. They retained the largely rural pattern of the Romans, but old settlements were abandoned and new ones appeared on new sites. It sometimes happens that a later Saxon or mediaeval village is found to overlie a Roman site, but there is seldom any reason to believe that the one directly succeeded the other.

The differences between the Roman and Saxon farming sites and farming procedures were considerable. The farms and settlements of Roman times typically clung to higher contour lines; light soils were chosen; the field patterns tended to follow the small rectangular fields of the Celts; and the ploughs were light. With the arrival of the Saxons farms and settlements frequently moved to the valleys; light gravelly soils were favoured, especially in the early days of settlement; and the ploughs used were heavy. Although great skill was demonstrated in clearing woodland and waste, and field systems were introduced which show large open fields divided in such a way as to suggest communal enterprise, the new sites of the early Saxons were often little more than random clusters of huts; they showed little of the regular planning which characterized later mediaeval villages.

In addition to farmsteads and hamlets, important administrative centres were frequently sited in rural areas. Even the kings of the time did not generally reside in one urban capital or palace. They were peripatetic, and constantly on the move from one royal estate to another. Typically, a complex of large, well-built halls, with associated outbuildings seem to have served as royal centres, for this seems to have been the function of such structures found at Yeavering (Northumberland) and Cheddar (Somerset). Some of these, as at Goltho (Lincolnshire) appear to have been adapted for use by a lord.

Although the sacked Roman towns were not completely shunned by the Saxons, as once thought, the settlements which continued on the sites appear to have been on a much-reduced scale. The little archaeological evidence which exists shows that where there was continued habitation, it generally consisted of attempts to maintain or refurbish the defences. Military weakness was a problem in early fifth-century Britain, but there was a greater underlying problem.'Far more disruptive was the collapse of the towns, and consequent upon that collapse the disappearance of the romanized economy and the society and culture that depended on that economic underpinning. That the towns of Roman Britain ceased to fulfil the functions that they had in the fourth century somewhere in the first half of the fifth century is now generally agreed.'[33] No convincing signs have been found of urban civilian life continuing on any level but that of bare subsistence, and this is so even as late as the end of the fifth century. Administrative, and later ecclesiastical, centres may have been located within the walls of towns, but little else. Thus, at Winchester (Hampshire) the Roman walls were maintained during the early Saxon period, but the area so enclosed consisted mostly of open space, with a few scattered compounds which belonged to the king, the church and some nobles.

This discontinuance of the Roman centrality of towns in the life of the country in the fifth and sixth centuries was matched by the tendency for villas to be abandoned. There is archaeological evidence that some may have survived as local centres of romanized life far into the fifth century; but these were the exception, as the majority of them and of the large working farms seem to have gone completely out of use. Almost none of the many hundreds, if not thousands, of late Roman rural estates that dotted the countryside of lowland Britain can be shown with certainty to have left any trace of a name in recognizable form. This, with other changes mentioned, is in marked contrast to Gaul, where family names of countless Gallo-Roman proprietors have survived all over the country. Early Anglo-Saxon pottery or metal objects are but rarely found on the sites of former villas, and hardly ever in stratified contexts which make it certain that there was continuity of occupation. It all points to the fact that whereas in Gaul the Frankish settlement was carried out largely within the framework of existing estates, whose identity was preserved, probably in part at least in order to facilitate their partition in accordance with prevailing legal principles, in Britain no such arrangement applied.

A yet further discontinuity was seen in the means of travel and transportation. Except in Kent and possibly Lincolnshire, it seems that Roman roads were not as crucial as in former times in determining the pattern of settlement. River valleys assumed a greater relative importance.

Lastly, in this brief survey of sub-Roman Britain, mention needs to be made of changes in the relationship of Britain with the continent. For most of the fourth century British administrators looked to Trier in Gaul, rather than to Rome, as the imperial capital; soldiers and administrators who ran Britain and Gaul may well have felt a primary loyalty to Britain and Gaul as a single administrative unit with the focus on Trier, for this was how the governance of Britain and Gaul was regarded by the Romans themselves. And this wider allegiance continued into the fifth century.

Throughout the Saxon period, however, there was a gradual development of kingdoms or dynasties within Britain, and these almost
inevitably became the main focus of political and community life. But
the continental link remained, even if it shifted somewhat into the
background; and it was crucial, not least from the point of view of the
long-term history of kingship, which gradually assumed a central role in
the development of Christian kingdoms.

> The clearest connection between England and the Continent in this
> problem of the origins of kingdoms is not to do with the realities of
> political power but with the way in which English kings and their
> subjects came to regard kingship, as closer contact and eventually
> Christianity brought them the triple image of Roman emperor,
> Merovingian king and Hebrew monarch. As soon as we have written
> sources in England, that triple image dominates the literary version of
> kingship which is often all we have to guide us, or mislead us. The
> continental evidence reminds us of the wide range of possibilities
> available to those who speculate on the realities, on the origins of
> Anglo-Saxon kingdoms; it teaches us also perhaps how flexible our
> concepts of 'kingship' and 'kingdom' actually have to be.[34]

The emergence of a distinctively Christian concept of kingship was one
key to the future establishment and consolidation of the Christian faith
throughout the length and breadth of the land.

5

Christianity in Sub-Roman Britain

Pagan religion in early Anglo-Saxon Britain

Not much is known about the religion which the pagan Anglo-Saxons brought with them to Britain.[1] The prehistoric Ingaevonic tribes included ancestors of the Angles and Saxons. They worshipped Nerthus the Mother Earth. Peace and festivity were supposed to reign wherever she went. In historic times the cult passed from the Danish islands to the Swedes, and the place of Nerthus was taken by the god Frey, the son of Njorth. The Scandinavian traditions tell of a war between the Njorth-Frey family (the Vanir) and the family of Odin (the Anses). It was a struggle between the cult of the Mother Earth, with her gods who gave peace and who blessed agriculture with a plentiful increase, and the heroic gods, the gods of war who gave victory.

The chief god of the warriors was Woden. It seems that he was driving out Thunor, the Thunderer, who was the weather-god beloved by ordinary people, much as Thunor had come in an earlier age from the west and had ousted Tig, the oldest of the great gods, who had faded into the background of men's minds by the fifth century AD. The kingly families looked to Woden, from whom they traced their descent. His character was variable. He had originally, it was said, been a wind-god, a god of the homeless dead, who was followed through the air by the Wild Hunt of disembodied spirits. He was the lord of life and death; the lord of fighting and the inspirer of battle fury. It was a medley of qualities and characteristics which appealed to the kingly dynasties and the aristocrats, but also more widely. Six out of the eight Anglo-Saxon royal houses traced their descent from him, and as that of the South Saxons is missing, only the one for the East Saxons definitely did not. By the time of the migrations to Britain he was probably becoming the master of potent spells which could arm men with the mysteries of the Futhorc, the new runic alphabet. Arrayed with such authority it was easy for Woden to dethrone his rivals among the gods, Tiw and Thunor, and the peaceful prolific Vanir gods. His personality makes him identical to the German Wotan and the Norse Odin. He, and a number of the Celtic gods of Gaul, were identified with the Roman god Mercury, and this may have helped in Britain where a residue of the Roman belief in that god may have persisted.

Place-names in Kent, Essex, Hampshire, Wiltshire, Somerset, Staffordshire, Bedfordshire and Derbyshire attest to Woden's powerful influence in those areas. And in certain spots, such as the Wiltshire Vale of Pusey, these occur in clusters, indicating local centres of particular enthusiasm for his worship. The British Wednesday was named after him.

Thunor was also very popular. There are fewer places named after him. They are found in Essex, Sussex, Wiltshire, Somerset, Hampshire, Kent, Surrey and Hertfordshire, and they are more common in the first five of these counties than those associated with any other deity. He tends to be identified with the Roman Jupiter, and has therefore been given his character as god of the sky and the thunderer. In Anglo-Saxon and Roman calendars he presided over what became the English Thursday. He fulfilled a similar function as the Scandinavian Thor, the German Donner, and the Rhenish Celtic god Taranis. Thunor's symbols seem to have been the hammer and the swastika; and miniatures of the former have been unearthed in graves at Gilston and Kingston in Kent, with the latter motif being very common in cremation urns.

Other Anglo-Saxon gods included Tiw, who was almost certainly a god of war, and who gave his name to the English Tuesday. Archaeological evidence of his presence includes his rune on weapons found in Kent, and more especially swords from Faversham and Gilston and spears from Holborough. In addition to those places, his name appears in Surrey, Hampshire, Worcestershire and Warwickshire. The goddess Frigg or Friga probably had love or festivity as her special area of concern. Her name was given to the English Friday; and it possibly provides the derivation for place names in Hampshire, Sussex and Yorkshire. The remaining deities were less prominent. They included Frey, who in Norse literature was a handsome young god; Seaxnet, from whom the East Saxon kings traced their descent; Ing, whom the Icelanders identified with Frey; Hreda and Eostra, possibly the gods from whom the months of March and April were named before the English adopted the Roman names, but with the latter providing the enduring English name for the Christian feast of Easter; and Geat, mentioned by Asser, the biographer of Alfred the Great.

Little is known of the holy places, the temples, religious officials and the festivals of the Anglo-Saxons. Again, we are largely dependent on place-names. A large number of sites have been identified which were undoubtedly centres of heathen worship, but to which the name of a particular deity was never attached. The best of the evidence comes from the widely dispersed use of such place-names as *ealth*, meaning 'temple', *hearh*, with the connotation 'hilltop sanctuary', and *weoh*, 'idol', 'shrine', or 'sacred precinct'. There is an almost complete absence of archaeological evidence of early Anglo-Saxon temples, so the wooden rectangular building discovered at Yeavering in Northumbria assumes considerable importance. It had a roof, and the complex included a fenced enclosure around the temple entrance containing posts, perhaps for images or trophies. A large pit within the temple was filled with animal bones, and especially ox sculls. The ground on one side was also strewn with such bones, a massive post had been placed at one corner, and an inhumation cemetery was sited nearby. The whole structure had been consumed by fire, but it cannot be said whether this was the work of Christians, the result of war, or the consequence of some other circumstance.

Bede often mentions pagan Anglo-Saxon priests, and the Yeavering site shows evidence of them. Bede also makes reference to pagan worship. It seems that the greatest sacred occasion was the winter solstice. This was known as the *Modranicht*, the 'Mother Night', and it heralded the beginning of the year. In February the people appear to have offered cakes to the deities; in April there was the great spring feast of the goddess Eostre; September was *Halegmonath*, 'Holy Month', and was no doubt celebrated; and November was *Blod-Monath*, 'Blood Month', when cattle were slaughtered prior to the onset of winter, with some used as sacrifices.

The Anglo-Saxons adopted both cremation and inhumation for their funerals. The concern was to bury their people in the earth, and often with goods to accompany them to the after-life. In cremation there was a standardized use of urns; in inhumation a customary posture for the body was considered essential, as was the inclusion of dress and a range of artefacts and equipment sufficient to ensure that the person buried fared well in the next world. Many thousands of inhumations have been recorded by archaeologists, and there is much evidence of cremations. It remains true that we know more about the Romans living and the Saxons dead.

From what has been said it can readily be seen that there was much in common between Celtic and Germanic deities. The greater localization of the former, and the concentration on a few venerated deities of the latter may be more apparent than real. Perhaps the main difference was the sense of an all-powerful destiny (*Wyrd*) which runs through early Anglo-Saxon literature. But, overall, the Anglo-Saxon gods may well have been accommodated by the native British with no great difficulty, except for the Christians. And it is to these that I now turn.

Christianity in fifth and sixth century Britain – an overview

We must immediately address a dilemma, and an apparent contradiction. It is between what many scholars have reckoned as the seemingly reasonable health and even at times vitality of Christianity in the fifth century, and up to at least the fifth decade of the sixth century, and its apparently parlous condition when St Augustine arrived on his mission from Rome in 597.

R. H. Hodgkin spoke in glowing terms of the persistence and even flowering of Christianity in the ninety years from 360 to 450:

> If the growth of the spiritual life of man counts for more than changes in political systems or the distribution of material wealth, then it may be held that this period, which witnessed a transition in Britain from the Roman culture of the later Empire through sub-Romanism to a Celtic and a Christian renaissance, was a period of creation rather than of destruction ... The world had changed. The Romano-Britons who were about to be submerged by a new flood of barbarians had, by the middle of the fifth century, obtained a source of spiritual consolation for the loss of the lands and goods of this transitory world.[2]

Ronald Hutton points out that the religions imported by the invading and settling Anglo-Saxons were insubstantial and short-lived when confronted by vigorous Christian evangelism, as in adjacent fifth- and sixth-century countries, and he proceeds:

> By the middle of the sixth century, only about a hundred years after the immigration had become significant and while it was still in progress, the new kingdoms were almost surrounded by Christians. To the north and west were the native British and Irish, while to the south and east the Franks, who had overrun Gaul, had accepted the new faith. It seems probable that only the haughty refusal of the

British Church to preach to the newcomers allowed English paganism to survive as long as it did.[3]

Hutton also maintains that the text of *The Ruin of Britain* 'gives an inescapable impression of being composed at a time when Christianity was wholly triumphant among the inhabitants of the former Roman province'.[4] Of course Gildas was highly critical of the state of Christian morality and leadership at the time he wrote and in the preceding period, but in what he wrote there is an assumption that Christianity was the prevailing faith and the one which was generally acknowledged as supreme.

If it is indeed true that Christianity was alive and well from about 410 to about 540 and yet was apparently weak and ineffectual at the end of the sixth century, then the only explanation can be a rapid decline in the last half of the sixth century. I propose an alternative possible understanding of this period of nearly two centuries.

I suggest that Christianity was battered by the events of the early fifth century and, although it survived far better than the various former Romano-British pagan cults, it was not as strong or as well organized and led as has sometimes been depicted. There were still many pagans, especially among the peasant community, in the third decade of the fifth century when Germanus of Auxerre visited Britain; and they were still present, possibly in considerable numbers, a century later. 'There is abundant evidence to show that paganism and pagan practices and beliefs were exceedingly widespread among the peasantry of Gaul and Spain in the sixth century and beyond; and there is certainly no reason to think that the country people of Britain were different in this respect.'[5] There was much nominal Christianity right through to the sixth century. Members of the population who had identified themselves with Christianity after it became the officially sanctioned religion of the Roman Empire, passed on to their children and grandchildren a faith which was in many cases somewhat shallow. Their descendants carried on the faith of their fathers out of respect and as a convention, with fewer and fewer optional belief systems as paganism dwindled in the early fifth century. Many of these Christian adherents, and others who were more committed to the faith but badly taught because of a lack of theologically trained local or national leaders, were vulnerable to heresies such as Pelagianism. This was particularly so with the high proportion of nominal or even serious believers who lived in rural areas. The church displayed purple patches of pastoral care and evangelism, but this was interspersed with much lethargy and torpor. In the early years of the fifth century Christianity was widely, but in a great many cases superficially, adopted. It was not deeply-rooted, with a well-established leadership and a large body of well-taught and mature members.

It may be objected that such insubstantial Christianity has character-ized great numbers in society in all ages, and this is so. Even in times of Christian revival, when the faith has made massive progress and there has been abundant evidence of Christian commitment of a high order, it has been the few who have borne the torch, with the majority of the population at best indifferent, and at worse actively hostile. But in the period with which I am dealing there was not that core element of dedicated believers who could blaze a trail. There was an overall some-what uninspiring flatness and lack of vision or evangelistic concern among the conformist but unenthusiastic company of those who called themselves Christians, but were so more in name than in practice. This sounds harsh, but it is a state of affairs born out by what is known of that age.

It seems that in the first half of the fifth century, and then at a reduced pace during the next century or so, the movement whereby individuals were prepared to identify with the Christian faith proceeded down-wards and outwards from the aristocracy and the higher social groups in the towns and the villas, as it had begun to do in Roman times. The more vibrant spiritual life possibly centred as much upon houses as upon churches. But this whole process may well have been slow and piecemeal. There is no evidence of an overall and co-ordinated advance in evangelism, teaching or pastoral care. And in the act of filtering downwards the faith may have become enfeebled and suffered from enervation; with dispersion it appears to have become debilitated.

Then came the Anglo-Saxon invasions and settlements; and with them a new infusion of paganism. With the dominance of Anglo-Saxons in local leadership, and with them determining the norms of social life in many areas, new pressures were brought to bear on the native Christian population. The majority of the Christians did not have a deep enough conviction of the uniqueness of their faith and of its value to engage in evangelism to these newcomers. On their part, the Anglo-Saxons were not concerned to proselytize or to deprive the Britons of the faith they had. So the status quo was largely maintained.

As the numbers of immigrants multiplied, and as the tone of society became increasingly Germanic with the advance of the sixth century, so the Christianity of the country was watered-down, until by the end of the century it was in the kind of condition that concerned St Augustine and his fellow missionaries. The Christian faith had been present in the land for over four hundred years, and its message and code of conduct were well known and appreciated, but it was weak. It had left a substratum of belief, but it was rather vague and ill-defined. There were no doubt fervent Christians in small numbers throughout the length and breadth of the country, but they were probably for the most part in somewhat isolated tiny local fellowships, and the testimony they bore to their faith was perhaps not very effective, and was almost certainly confined to a very circumscribed area.

Set against this somewhat pathetic Christian presence was a Celtic paganism which had lost most of its former hold on the British people, but which continued to exercise a subtle yet powerful influence. It had also by the fifth and sixth centuries been a component of the ideological baggage of society for a thousand years and more, and it had been supplemented by Anglo-Saxon paganism. Paganism of one kind or another was a well embedded feature in society in general, for the native British and for the Anglo-Saxons, and in certain pockets of the population it had a strong grip on people of all social ranks, especially in the countryside. 'It would be the crudest mistake, then, to imagine that the pagan religion was no more than a picturesque adornment of life, to be cast off at the first moment that the Anglo-Saxons were presented with a *real* religion in Christianity . . . All in all, the struggle between Christianity and paganism was not like an evening's game of *Kriegspiel*; it was a genuine engagement of two life principles.'[6]

With the coming of the Irish missionaries in the north and St Augustine and his companions in the south there was not a quick and spontaneous conversion of the masses of the people. As we will see the work of spreading the Christian faith was protracted, and there was occasional fierce resistance encountered. What is simply being stated here is that Christianity had made its impact, and it had established a foothold throughout society by the end of the sixth century. But at that stage it was in a sorry state. The Christian flame was in desperate need of being rekindled; and paganism was open to the possibility of responding to the Christian faith if it was presented in a forceful yet strategic and sensitive way.

Taking this as my framework, I will now examine the history of Christianity in the sub-Roman era in some detail.

Christianity in the fifth century

In the twilight years of the first few decades of the fifth century, when the Britons were coming to terms with a new situation without the presence of the Romans and before any very clear alternative political, economic and social pattern had been inaugurated, when they were at loggerheads among themselves, and when they were beset by the barbarians, it appears that Christianity was one of the elements of the former Roman state which had managed to survive, and even to make progress. One commentator has remarked that by the second quarter of the fifth century, when St Patrick was writing, 'it seems pretty clear that most Britons were Christians, so much so that he [Patrick] can identify Christians with Roman citizens, and Christianity has reached far enough to convert many of the people of the remote Kingdom of Strathclyde . . . There can be no doubt that the Church in Britain was gaining in numbers and influence during at least the first half of the fifth century.'[7]

Of great importance to the early fifth-century British church was the impact of St Martin of Tours. As we have seen, he was the central figure in a vigorous Gallic assault on paganism, and in the promotion of monasticism, although both of these developments, and especially the latter, encompassed Egypt and Italy as well as Gaul. Instead of gradual conversion, which had hitherto been the most typical policy adopted, militants now wanted to eradicate paganism swiftly, and if necessary they were prepared to use force to achieve their end. Temples and cult images were destroyed. The curse tablets of late Roman Gaul attest to this public Christian confrontation with pagan cults, and such action was most impressive when the destruction of statues was not greeted by vengeance of any sort from the pagan god or goddess concerned.[8] There is some evidence that the somewhat élitist indigenous church in Britain was inspired to greater pastoral and evangelistic concern by disciples of St Martin.[9]

The essentials of St Martin's monasticism were perpetuated in the monastery at Marseilles, and by the monasteries lying in the lower part of the Rhone valley. This included Lerins, which was founded by Honoratus in 410 on an island lying a short distance from the coast in the Bay of Cannes.

Of special and specific importance was the influence of St Martin on the lives of three British monks: St Ninian, who probably lived in the fifth century, St Patrick, and St Columba, the latter of whom I will consider when reviewing the sixth-century renewal of Christianity in Britain.

The life and works of St Ninian are largely concealed and unknown, but Bede states in his *Ecclesiastical History* that he was a person of distinction and importance.

> The southern Picts who lived on this side of the mountains had, so it is said, long ago given up the errors of idolatry and received the true faith through the preaching of the Word by that reverend and holy man Bishop Ninian, a Briton who had received orthodox instruction at Rome in the faith and the mysteries of the truth. His episcopal see is celebrated for its church, dedicated to St Martin where his body rests, together with those of many saints. The see is now under English rule. This place which is in the kingdom of Bernicia is commonly called Whithorn, the White House, because Ninian built a church of stone there, using a method unusual among the Britons.[10]

The only other faintly reliable source bearing upon the person and life of Ninian is a tortuous Latin poem of the eighth century. The archaeological and literary evidence indicate that he established his community near Galloway around the middle of the fifth century. There were a number of sub-Roman kingdoms in the region between the Tyne and the Tay with a British church apparently organized on a diocesan basis, with centres which included Carlisle, Glasgow, and perhaps Edinburgh and Old Melrose, in addition to Whithorn.

Then there is St Patrick, who was born about 415 and died about 493. He was certainly a beacon in his day and generation, and no church which gave birth to a Christian of that calibre, and nurtured him in his spiritual life, could have been moribund. But views differ on whether the British church can lay claim to such an honourable role. It has been asserted that he 'was a product of the British Church, and that he is more completely representative of it than any other historical figure'. The same commentator continues:

> The British Church of Patrick's day converts savage barbarians; the British Church of Gildas's day merely abuses them. Gildas shows quite a wide acquaintance with theology, rhetoric, and learning, but in his day they appear to be in danger of degenerating into verbosity and pedantry. Patrick certainly has very little learning and no rhetoric whatever, but he is aware of his deficiency and honest about it, and succeeds in a surprising way in compensating for his lack of these

things. Gildas writes much about God's wrath and punishment, Patrick constantly harps upon God's loving care.[11]

A counter view has been expressed, in which it is said that the British church opposed Patrick's career at all stages. The church authorities, so it is maintained, refused him as a candidate for the priesthood when he longed to prepare himself for missionary work in Ireland, and thus compelled him to train abroad. British bishops opposed his appointment as head of an Irish mission in about 429, and they resented his consecration as a successor to bishop Palladius in the early 430s. Their antagonism to him became acidic after he excommunicated their protector Coroticus. In this reading of events it is reckoned that no unequivocal evidence exists to show that Patrick's mission had been sponsored by the church of Britain; a view greatly enhanced by the silence of Bede, who records the mission of Palladius but makes no mention of Patrick.[12] It is but one more of the enigmas of this age.

But to return more especially to the religious condition of Britain, there are signs that Christianity did thrive at the expense of paganism in the early years of the fifth century. For example the replacement of temples by what appear to be Christian religious sites is well attested at such places as Brean Down, Nettleton, Uley and Lamyatt Beacon. Pagan religious buildings and artefacts also seem to have been destroyed at Witham, Colchester, Great Chesterford, Springhead, Segontium, Housesteads and Rudchester. And, as further supporting evidence for the parallel decline of paganism and surge of Christianity, 'not a single major cult statue from a late fourth-century Romano-British pagan temple has survived undamaged to be excavated by modern archaeologists'.[13]

Nevertheless, these indications of aggressive Christianity, and perhaps therefore a vibrant church, need to be placed in context and interpreted cautiously. Although Christianity continued, and even to an extent made advances, in the first half of the fifth century, it was possibly not very thoroughly grounded either in society as a whole or in the lives of the people; and it may have oscillated considerably in its quality as a witness to the faith. Bede is scathing about this. He says that Christian behaviour too frequently conformed to the prevailing social mood. There were economic fluctuations. Hard times were followed by considerable prosperity because of an abundance of corn, and he continues:

With this affluence came an increase of luxury, followed by every kind of foul crime; in particular, cruelty and hatred of the truth and love of lying increased so that if anyone appeared to be milder than the rest and somewhat more inclined to the truth, the rest, without consideration, rained execrations and missiles upon him as if he had been an enemy of Britain. Not only were laymen guilty of these offenses but even the Lord's own flock and their pastors. They cast off Christ's easy yoke and thrust their necks under the burden of drunkenness, hatred, quarrelling, strife, and envy and other similar crimes.[14]

In times of plenty and ease the Christians thus yielded readily to temptations; but they did not amend their ways when hardship struck. Bede adds that a virulent plague killed many people around the middle of the fifth century. 'Yet those who survived could not be awakened from the spiritual death which their sins had brought upon them.'[15]

The leadership of the church does not appear to have been especially effective in raising standards of Christian discipleship. It was not that there was no effort made. There were bishops, although the number is not known; and some at least did not neglect their teaching ministry. One of them, Fastidius, addressed a book 'on the Christian life' to Fatalis, a devout widow, some time during the third decade of the fifth century. The teaching is simple and direct. He exhorts Fatalis not to despise the rustic bread he has set before her, reminding her that rustic bread can give strength and help to the weary. As Christ means 'anointed', so, he explains to her, Christians are anointed with the oil of gladness. The true Christian is he who keeps Christ's commands and who despises earthly things. Shall he be called Christian who has never fed the hungry with bread, who has never given drink to the thirsty, who has never invited guests to his table, and who has never sheltered a stranger or pilgrim under his roof? The man is a Christian who follows the way of Christ and imitates him in all things.

Some of the more able men must also have compared favourably with Christian leaders on the continent. At about the time Fastidius' book was issued a certain Faustus, who was probably a Briton, went to Gaul as abbot of the important monastery of Lerins, and in 461 he was consecrated Bishop of Riez. It is worthy of note that here is one more sign that there was a close link between the British church and the church on the continent, and that there were British churchmen available of sufficient calibre to fill such important church posts. It is a useful corrective to any unqualified condemnation of the British church, and more particularly the British episcopate.

The career of Faustus seems to indicate that monasticism existed in Britain, and that there was an especially fruitful association with the monastery of Lerins. From the existing evidence it is reasonable to conclude that in the early decades of the fifth century, in common with the rest of western Christianity, British monasticism was both conceptually and architecturally far removed from the large cloistered communities of the Norman and post-Norman times. 'Fifth-century monasticism in Britain would have been characterized not by communal life but by the eremitical life of the individual, or very small groups ("hermits"). It was probably towards the end of the century – and here we are on very uncertain ground, through lack of material evidence – that enclosed communities began to emerge.'[16]

It is also significant that the teaching given by Fastidius indicates an uncomplicated theology in which works rather than dogma were foremost. If this was typical it may go some way towards explaining the vulnerability of ordinary Christians to Pelagianism, and the inability of the leaders to cope with it without assistance from Gaul.

Pelagianism originated with the heretical teaching of a British teacher and theologian. Pelagius received a good education. He went to Rome about 380, and he lived there until about 409. He subsequently moved to Palestine where he was last heard of in 418. His arrival in Rome almost exactly coincided with that of St Augustine of Hippo against whose theology he was to react with such vehemence. Augustine returned to his native land while Pelagius remained in a city where 'cultivated Christian laymen exercised more influence than at any time previously'.[17]

It was while he was in Rome that he developed his views. According to the teaching of Pelagius, perfection was obligatory; God, above all else, commanded unquestioning obedience. He would condemn to hell-fire anyone who failed to perform a single one of his commands. But Pelagius fervently asserted that man's nature had been created so that such perfection could be achieved. Laymen should seek it through living a life of stern, austere, ascetic Christian rectitude. And in developing such ideas he was led to question the doctrine of original sin. It was this which attracted the condemnation of the church. Opposed to the Pelagian belief was the doctrine propounded by Augustine of the absolute sovereignty of God's grace. Pelagius was especially concerned about a prayer from Augustine's *Confessions*: 'thou commandest continence; grant what thou commandest and command what thou wilt'. The use made of these words appeared to Pelagius to undermine man's

moral responsibility. Pelagius stressed that we sin by a voluntary imitation of Adam's transgression. He strongly resisted the notion that the
nature of man can be so corrupted, or has been by inherited sin, that his
will is powerless to obey God's commands.

> Pelagius was accused of denying man's need for grace. He was much
> misrepresented in the course of the controversy. In fact he affirmed
> that in the forgiveness of sins there is an unmerited gift of grace. But
> otherwise he spoke of grace as divine aid conveyed through moral
> exhortation and the supreme example of Christ. Advance in the moral
> and spiritual life depends on free choices of the will confronted by
> possibilities of either right or wrong.[18]

The teaching of Augustine on grace and works received papal endorsement, and Pelagians were declared excommunicate unless they repudi-
ated their views. When it came to the ears of the orthodox church in
Gaul that Pelagianism was raising its head in Britain, Germanus, Bishop
of Auxerre, was sent to help bring the Christians in line with the
Catholic teaching. The crisis appears to have been precipitated by the
activities of a certain Agricola who acted as a propagandist for
Pelagianism. It is not known what efforts the British Catholics had
made to defeat him and the heretics, but we can say with assurance that
they were dismally unsuccessful. The situation must have been dire
when the Catholics appealed to the Gallic bishops for help. 'It was not
quite an unheard-of action in the West for the Catholics of an entire
political diocese – or what had once been a diocese – to admit their
inadequacy as openly as the British Catholics did in 429, for the Britons
had already done the same thing at the beginning of the century when
they brought over Victricius, Bishop of Rouen, to unravel their
problems at that time.'[19] According to Prosper of Acquitaine, the appeal
was voiced by a deacon named Palladius, and responded to by Pope
Celestine.

The mission of St Germanus in 429, when he was accompanied by
Lupus, Bishop of Troyes, and others, was not evangelistic but pastoral.
His ministry was to the Christians of the land. The same was true of the
follow-up visit sometime between 435 and 444. This assumes that there
was a substantial body of believers, and probably some measure of
organization. Without either it is inconceivable that a heresy would
have taken root to such an extent as to demand an episcopal visit from
abroad, or that such a course of events would have been brought to the
attention of the continental church. But it can also be implied that the

British church was unable out of its own manpower resources to supply the theological expertise and the force of leadership necessary to confront the problem.

There is no hint in *The Life of St Germanus, Bishop of Auxerre*, by Constantius of Lyon, which is our main source of information on the visit of Germanus to Britain, that the bishop attached any importance to quelling the old religions, Celtic or Romano-Celtic. At the same time, it is noteworthy that when he wished to say mass while on one of his tours, he had to construct a makeshift building because there was no place available in the countryside setting at the time. This may show that in such areas there were but few Christians, with no specially constructed buildings in which to meet, and that many if not most of the inhabitants in these places were non-Christians. It is not easy to interpret the evidence.

When they went out and preached, Germanus and his companions did not address the peasants or the *coloni* or the rural slaves. Such members of the population spoke British Celtic, which we may assume Germanus did not, and even if a relatively few had acquired some Latin, they would not have been capable of following a Latin sermon on the nature of grace, or a fiery appeal to accept the doctrine of original sin. And there are no grounds for thinking that Germanus addressed the Celtic-speaking country folk through an interpreter. After an exhaustive examination of the text of *The Life of St Germanus*, E. A Thompson concludes that Latin-speaking congregations addressed by St Germanus, both those who subscribed to the orthodox Catholic view of grace and works and the Pelagians, 'were composed primarily of the towns folk and of the relatively well-to-do, of persons who lived either in towns or in such villas as survived, whereas the poor country folk were heathen'.[20] This does not mean that all the poor rural folk were heathen, but that paganism was the prevailing religion among them. Neither does it mean that all the town- and villa-dwellers were orthodox Christians. Constantius, in his *Life of St Germanus*, describes the Pelagians who met in formal debate with Germanus as rich and well dressed. But this merely tells us that these were the heretics who lived in the centre of population, which we assume was a town, where the debate was conducted.

In any case, heretics or not, they were still professing Christians. And, according to Constantius, they came in droves:

And now it was not long before the apostolic priests had filled all

Britain, the first and largest of the islands, with their fame, their preaching and their miracles; and, since it was a daily occurrence for them to be hemmed in by crowds, the word of God was preached, not only in the churches, but at the cross-roads, in the fields and in the lanes. Everywhere faithful Catholics were strengthened in their faith and the lapsed learnt the way back to the truth. Their achievements, indeed, were after the pattern of the Apostles themselves; they ruled through consciences, taught through letters and worked miracles through their holiness. Preached by such men, the truth had full course, so that whole regions passed quickly over to their side.[21]

The Life of St Germanus also casts light on the bishops, and to a certain extent the priests, of the time. But it does so negatively, in that no such leaders are mentioned. This is strange, and it lends itself to various speculations. Leslie Alcock concludes that the 'absence of any mention of British bishops must represent an omission on the part of Germanus' biographer rather than any authentic historical fact'.[22] I accept this, but it leaves unanswered the question why such an omission occurred. Thompson suggests that the bishops, or the bishop, of the region of Britain concerned had himself joined the Pelagians, and that Constantius was being discreet in suppressing the fact as it would reflect badly on the church. This is, of course, possible, but I wonder if in such a situation Germanus would have held such a conference in the diocese of a fellow bishop who was at variance with him theologically. Perhaps a simpler explanation is that there was either no bishop for the area, and Germanus deliberately chose neutral ground, or that none of the British bishops was sufficiently equipped theologically to participate in any such confrontation of theologies, and they were aware of their shortcomings. Whatever the solution, the silence of Constantius does not indicate a powerful, well-trained, British episcopate or body of clergy.

During his visit, Germanus also encouraged the British in their resistance to the barbarian attacks from the Picts and the Anglo-Saxons. He was not chiefly concerned with the political and military situation *per se*, but the menace from these enemies was a threat to the church. He might also have thought that the circumstances required a very dramatic demonstration that the sovereignty of God about which he was preaching and teaching was not just a theoretical and abstract theological matter, but stood the test of working in a real and dangerous situation. The incident in which Germanus assumed the role of a military leader and led the British to a notable Alleluia victory was seen by Bede as having spiritual significance as it was a witness to the power of God. It certainly was public and impressive.

Germanus was with the Britons in the midst of a war situation, when they were confronted by a large, fearsome and formidable army of Picts and Scots. He immediately took control and assumed the role of commander. He also displayed all the skills of a military leader in the field. He quickly assessed the situation and devised a strategy. He explored the country surrounding the British and saw a valley with hills on either side, which lay in the direction from which the enemy was expected to approach. There he stationed the untried British army. As the enemy forces advanced Germanus ordered the men to repeat his call in one great shout. The bishops shouted 'Alleluia' three times, and all the army in ambush shouted 'Alleluia'. The call echoed from the encircling hills, and this multiplied and increased the sound.

> The enemy forces were smitten with dread, fearing that not only the surrounding rocks but even the very frame of heaven itself would fall upon them. They were so filled with terror that they could not run fast enough. They fled hither and thither casting away their weapons and glad even to escape naked from the danger. Many of them rushed headlong back in panic and were drowned in the river which they had just crossed. The army, without striking a blow, saw themselves avenged and became inactive spectators of the victory freely offered to them. They gathered up the spoils lying ready to hand and the devout soldiery rejoiced in this heaven-sent triumph. The bishops thus overcame the enemy without the shedding of blood; they won a victory by faith and not by might.[23]

It was reminiscent of other bishops of the same genre, who were men of action and who boldly put their faith to the test, including St Martin of Tours, and St Wilfrid, whom we will be encountering in part 3 of the present work.

Lastly, regarding the visit of Germanus, it is significant, as mentioned elsewhere, that he and his companions made an effort to visit *Verulamium*, the scene of St Alban's martyrdom, in order to pay homage to the saint and his memory. It was indicative of a tradition of honouring the martyrs and saints, which may have remained important in the life of the British church until that time, and which was to be resurrected from the seventh century onwards, until it became a highly prominent feature of the mediaeval church.

As the century advanced, and as the number of Anglo-Saxon settlers increased, with an accompanying greater germanization, Christianity did not universally sink into oblivion. It generally failed to evangelize the newcomers, but that was not total. There were considerable variations from one region of the country to another. The faith appears to have been more completely integrated into society in many of the western areas of the country. When the Anglo-Saxons first penetrated the West Midlands, and this includes both the area of the future kingdom of Mercia and those territories further west and to the south-west which eventually became the satellites of Mercia, they probably encountered an active British church. It was a church which by the end of the sixth century had been quite successful in converting the immigrants.

This all amounts to a reasonably coherent picture of Christianity in early sub-Roman Britain. The Christian faith seems to have been well established in the country as a whole. It apparently commanded the loyalty of a substantial number of the population, but this does not infer that Britain was mainly Christian. The church appears to have lacked theologically sophisticated leadership. It was confident of being able to stand up to paganism while doing very little to convert the unbelieving neighbours. British Christianity in the fifth century was by no means a lost cause, but it was frail. There was a large proportion of the population which did not even give lip service to it; it was patchily distributed throughout the land; and it contained far too many Christians who were either mere hangers on, or who had but a slight grasp of the faith they professed. Such Christianity was vulnerable to heresy, or worse to pressures which might lead to defections. It was in dire need of a new injection of life; but it had to wait until the latter part of the sixth century before this was forthcoming.

British Christianity in the sixth century

Three lights pierce the overall darkness which envelops the story of the British church in the sixth century. There is the dazzling life and work of St Columba, and the mission instituted by Pope Gregory the Great and implemented by St Augustine, from which so many date the beginning of a connected history of Christianity in England; both of which I will leave to the next chapter. But thirdly, there is the emergence and flowering of the so-called 'Celtic church', which came quite suddenly, and very remarkably, and of which St Columba was but one shining and splendid example.

One of the achievements of British Christianity was the part it played in the conversion of Ireland. It was an important contribution not only to the Christianization of Ireland but, in the long run, to the church in England, for the very country which was evangelized by the British was, within two centuries, to be a powerful missionary agent in the coming again of Christianity to England. I will therefore give some prominence to this seminal work.

The taking of the gospel to Ireland in the first four centuries of the Christian era was a piecemeal process, and the scanty, indirect evidence available suggests that the Irish Christians before the arrival of St Patrick were few in number and unorganized.[24]

According to the Chronicle of Prosper of Aquitaine, in 431 a deacon of the church at Auxerre named Palladius was ordained and sent as the first official bishop of the fledgling Christian community in Ireland. The church in Britain sent St Patrick as a bishop possibly during the following year. The task of instituting an effective church, geared to evangelism and pastoral care, fell almost entirely to Patrick.

The most important part of St Patrick's ministry was his evangelism, the baptisms, the confirmations, and the ordination of clergy. But next to these there was the foundation of churches. These were small and simple. Even the 'great church' on the lands of Conall Gulban in Meath only measured sixty feet in length. As a rule the buildings were constructed of wood, and where this was not the case, the walls were made of clay or mud.

It was of great relevance for the future that the Christian mission in Ireland was promoted jointly from Gaul and from Britain. From the start both streams of influence were committed to the diocesan structure of organization for this was the type of church with which they were familiar. And such episcopacy entailed territorial dioceses ruled by bishops with their administrative officers, with the bishop responsible for church government, evangelism and pastoral oversight. But the circumstances soon highlighted anomalies. The territorial arrangement which had been based on the former Roman military regions, with headquarters in the larger towns or cities, was not readily applicable to the non-romanized, rural Irish society. When it was introduced each diocese was made coterminous with the *plebs* or *tuath* (the petty kingdoms). Each bishop was assisted by a hierarchy of secular clerks, and all priests who wished to officiate in the diocese required the prior permission of the bishop. No bishop was to meddle in the internal affairs of another bishop, and travelling clerics needed letters of introduction. Each bishop was, to the best of his ability, to ensure that the Christian community committed to his charge was kept uncontaminated by the secular world and its values, and he was to discourage involvement with the secular law courts. Any monks in his diocese had no responsibility for church administration other than for their own monastic house.

In a rather uneven and protracted way this system yielded to a church organized on the basis of non-territorial monastic *paruchia* under the control of abbots who were not necessarily bishops. The transition was accomplished mainly in the second half of the sixth century. This was the era when famous and highly influential monasteries were inaugurated. Columcille (St Columba) founded Derry, Durrow and Iona, Comgall established Bangor, and by 615 Columbanus had left the school of Bangor for the continent and had set up monastic houses at Annegray, Luxeuil, and Bobbio. The new system involved less geographical concentration of pastoral responsibility. Both Columbanus and Columcille were heads of *paruchia*. These consisted of monasteries, founded either by themselves or their disciples, which were scattered over a wide area. While Columcille was Abbot of Iona one of his disciples was placed as a ruler, or *praepositus*, over each of his other houses. The heads or abbots also appointed their successors. The *paruchia* or diocese of the priest-abbot under this scheme was by no means the same thing as the former diocese of a territorial bishop. It was such a major change that it is unlikely to have been entirely accomplished by the end of the sixth century, especially as it was a matter of a structure peculiar to Celtic society triumphing over an ecclesiastical institution universally accepted throughout the Christian West.

It was inevitable that, once established, the abbots of the monastic *paruchia* over which they presided, would gain greater power than the previous territorial bishops had exercised within their dioceses, especially as they were not confined to one area and the sphere over which they held sway could continue to expand as new monasteries were added anywhere in the Celtic regions, and even in England or on the continent. The new ecclesiastical structure also had an important political dimension. The rise of the newer-style monastic churches almost certainly went hand in hand with the emergence of the small but dynamic dynastic families who were to dominate Irish politics for the following two hundred years. A very large extant corpus of Irish genealogies preserves dozens of instances in which political and ecclesiastical offices were held in common by the members of such dynasties. A prime example is Leinster, where the fortunes of the rising dynastic family were closely linked to those of the monastery in Kildare. This was the most important church in the province, and the dynasty supplied kings and bishops simultaneously and monopolized high office in the church for several generations. An even more famous example was the island monastery of Iona where this restrictive practice ensured that all but one of the first nine abbots belonged to the same kin-group, and the twelve 'disciples' accompanying the founder were all related to him.

The change to the monastic-centred system seems to have been accomplished in these early years without much conflict between bishops and monasteries, partly because monastic churches may frequently have been founded in places where bishops had acquired little influence. The potential for tension and disagreement increased when the greater monasteries, such as Durrow, Bangor and Clonmacnois, established colonies which were sometimes on unappropriated land and sometimes overseas. On occasions one house would join with another larger and more distinguished foundation.

The story of Christianity in Wales presents an interesting comparison and contrast with what happened in Ireland.

In the second quarter of the sixth century, when Gildas wrote his *Ruin of Britain*, the Welsh church was run by bishops and priests, with some monks who were set aside solely for the religious life and were not involved in the administration of the territorial church. It appears from Gildas that the dioceses radiated out from centres of population. Inscribed stones in various parts of Wales are consistent with the picture of the structural arrangement Gildas paints. The church was sufficiently integrated into society for the bishop to have a recognized and respected social status, with his role accepted and honoured; and the church attracted adequate funding to pay bishops well. Bishops were not necessarily celibate, and not even always the husband of one wife. They and other clergy were frequently guilty of excessive worldly indulgences, such as too much and too lavish feasting, and an over-readiness to attend public entertainments and story-tellings. They showed ignorance about apostolic decrees, but they were exceedingly well-versed in secular affairs.

Some extra details are added by a monk of Dol in Brittany, who wrote the *Life of St Samson*, possibly in the early seventh century. It shows that Welsh bishops attended synods, even on the continent. It also reveals that the bishop's authority was supreme in a monastery within his diocese, and that monks were ordained to major orders by the visiting bishop. The monasteries themselves were often founded on the initiative of lay people out of family property; and they were then frequently regarded as hereditary possessions.

Taking Ireland and Wales together, it is perhaps misleading to talk of 'the Celtic church'. There were operational differences. The territorial episcopate was far more rooted in Wales, and the monastic movement of the late sixth century had a greater organizational impact upon Ireland. In Wales some bishops embraced the monastic life with enthusiasm and new monasteries were also founded by kin groups, but they quite often, if not usually, remained under the jurisdiction of the bishop and, in any case, their estates were often within a confined territory. There may have been monastic bishops, and a system more akin to the Irish monastic *paruchia* in parts of Wales, but the territorial episcopacy seems to have operated in many if not most areas. It can be said with some confidence that 'there is enough evidence to dispute the generally held assumptions that the Welsh system was purely monastic, that there were no dioceses or diocesan bishops, and that bishoprics grew up as a result of Anglo-Norman penetration. Bishoprics were not an English borrowing into Wales: they had never died out. We have not sufficiently recognized the influence of the Romano-British and sub-Roman past on the history of early medieval Wales.'[25]

The Welsh church was more episcopal than the Irish, but it also greatly promoted monasticism. On his second visit to Britain St Germanus may have ordained Illtud as priest. He has been described as 'the first great abbot of the British Church, the first to establish monasticism on a strong and permanent footing, the first to organize a school and studies as a normal complement to ascetical training, and the first to send forth disciples who in their turn would propagate the way of life that he had inaugurated'.[26] His disciples included St Samson, St Paulus Aurelian and perhaps Gildas and St David. David became the national saint of Wales, and he founded the see of Mynyw on a rugged promontory overlooking the Irish Sea. This was but one of the monastic centres which were so crucial in the life of the church. Another great British monk of the sixth century was St Cadoc, who was trained by a Scottic master, and crossed over to Ireland where he recruited a large number of followers, including Finnian of Clonard. On returning to his home country he founded the monastery of Llancarvan. He is also said to have visited Scotland, Cornwall and Brittany.

Throughout the sixth century we obtain fleeting, but attractive, glimpses of Christians who even at this distance of time convey a sense of deep Christian commitment and devotion, and an active life in the service of Christ. St Kentigern was perhaps representative of this resolute band of saints. He was apparently Bishop of Glasgow, but went south to visit St David at Menevia, and afterwards to build a monastery on the river Elwy in North Wales. He left behind him Asaph, or Asa, as abbot and bishop, after whom the monastery, together with its church, was named St Asaph. The monastery appears to have flourished, with the number of monks reputedly reaching 965. 'There must have been here a centre of definite and enthusiastic religious influence and teaching, perhaps, for the British themselves, of even greater significance than it was in the early years of the post-Norman period.'[27] All these activities of Kentigern seem to have taken place in the mid-sixth century, possibly between about 540 and 573. It is a measure of the growth and importance of monasteries at this time, and that the impulse given to monasticism was not ephemeral, that at the end of the century the great monastery at Bangor had increased in size so that it contained two thousand monks ruled by seven abbots.

There were two respects in which monasticism in Wales and Ireland was more intense and well developed than elsewhere. There was a passion for learning and scholarship which was demonstrated in the provision made for the systematic training of the lawyers and poets attached to the court. This was not a secular, but a Christian-centred scholastic tradition, and it was carefully sustained in the scriptoria of Irish and Welsh monasteries. From there it was diffused into England, Gaul and even further afield. The spreading of such knowledge, as well as the Christian faith in total as believed and practised by the monks of Ireland and Wales, was facilitated by the second distinctive mark of the monasticism of those territories – the emphasis placed upon pilgrimage and self-imposed perpetual exile. This was the driving force behind the historic move of St Columba to Iona. It was a tradition which was to bear fruit in the lives of Aidan and Fursa in England and Columbanus in Gaul, as well as many others, with far-reaching consequences for the countries to which they went.

The urge for exile was not infrequently combined with a sense of pressing obligation to convert the pagans, and this added to the impact the pilgrims made. But they did not most commonly go forth as evangelists in any way that this is now understood. Most typically, the specific engagement in evangelism, in the sense of going to the pagans and preaching to them the gospel, was not the central concern. The Irish, and to a lesser extent the Welsh, holy men who went out to other lands, were intent on settling in some remote place where they sought to lead a life of prayer and asceticism which would attract others. To this they sometimes added a concern to revitalize the whole of Christian society through such a way of life. We will see in the next chapter how all these aims were sought and achieved in the life and work of Columba and the monks of Iona.

I mention these developments here as it helps in the realization that monasticism was flourishing in Britain in the sixth century, and that the Christianity of that century was therefore not all corrupt or unworthy of praise, for this is the impression that could be created by Gildas. 'Much may fairly be attributed to the strength of an ascetic movement which gained ground in the sixth century and found its aspirations satisfied by a rigorous monastic discipline.'[28]

The church in Britain as portrayed by Gildas was apparently well established. It had monks and large, to all appearances well endowed, monasteries presided over by abbots; it had buildings, which were presumably churches; it had access to the books of the Bible and some other Christian literature; it had a probably long-established territorial diocesan system covering large areas of the land; it had a hierarchical organization which was headed by bishops and numerous priests; and it had the wealth to support this quite impressive edifice. But, what stands out is the moral laxity, the incompetence, the shamelessness and the greed of a priesthood which failed to provide an adequate example to the laity. The priests were insufficiently diligent in the offices they held and in the priestly duties they were expected to perform. The priesthood as a whole was deeply flawed. They were plunderers, wolves, gluttons and usurpers. They taught bad customs, hating the truth as if hostile to it, and favouring lies. They abhorred the just poor and unblushingly venerated the profane rich. They gave no charity, and they ignored the abominable profanity of the people.[29]

The rebukes of Gildas may hold the key to the apparent state of the church some sixty years later with the arrival in Britain of St Augustine. There is little doubt that those engaged in the Roman mission of 597 were biased in their views of the British church, which they regarded as provincial, on the fringes of western Christendom, and questionable in some of its beliefs and practices. But even making allowance for this, Augustine's cold and rather uncomprehending opinion does seem to reflect the essential deadness and ineffectiveness of the church he found. Perhaps a good proportion of the population at the time Gildas wrote were 'Christian' in the sense that they were not actively pagan, but the

Christianity so espoused was for the most part shallow and without much personal or corporate conviction, so that in the space of sixty years it deteriorated even more, and was in need of a fresh start. This it received, from the Irish in the north and from Rome in the south.

Part 3

Anglo-Saxon England

6

Christianity in England from the Late Sixth Century to 664

It is easy to lose sight of the wood for the trees in recounting the history of Christianity in the hundred years or so after the arrival of St Augustine in 597. The rush of exuberating events is of crucial importance, and these included not only the activities of St Augustine and his companions, St Aidan and his fellow Irish missionaries, and a host of other outstanding Christians whom we will meet in this chapter, but the tangle of political affairs in the various kingdoms of the land. Such exciting epoch-making developments will be central in the narrative which follows, and rightly so, for they constituted both the means and the circumstances whereby the Christian faith was re-planted. They are fundamental to an understanding of how Christianity came afresh to a country where paganism was reasserting itself, and the church had become very nominal and undynamic. This advance of Christianity, and these details of how it was achieved, must occupy our main attention, and they are at the very centre of the story I am attempting to relate in this book, but another process was taking place which was more hidden, less obvious, but equally significant. Into the two centuries after the landing of St Augustine were crowded not only the long-term establishment of the church in England, but 'the first stirrings of a sense of English unity, the beginnings of English literature, of architecture, of education, of Christian civilization in all its branches'.[1] As we turn to these action-packed years it is well that we have in mind these various layers of activity.

The Roman Mission – the first phase

English Christianity owes a great debt of gratitude to Pope Gregory I.[2] During his papacy (590–604), in 596, arguably the single most important decision for the furtherance of English Christianity in the pre-

Norman era was taken by him, when he resolved to send a mission to England. It was not a spontaneous, impulsive, unpremeditated act. He had long had the English and their land on his heart. Here was a supreme manifestation of that combination of spiritual insight, ecclesiastical strategy and, above all else, pastoral concern, which marked him out as such a great Christian leader; although to such qualities must also be added commentator, hagiographer, moral theologian and liturgiologist. He was perhaps 'the most commanding figure in the history of the early mediaeval papacy',[3] but it was his simple Christian compassion for which the English church should be most grateful. He was distinguished by his tenderness and his energetic charity; and England was one of the chief beneficiaries.

Gregory was born in Rome about the year 540, into a patrician family. At the age of thirty-three he became Prefect of the City, with responsibility for its finances, public buildings and food supply. But the following year he concluded that his true vocation was to be found in a full dedication to the church. He espoused the monastic life, expended his patrimony on the poor and on the founding of six monasteries on his family estates in Sicily, and converted the family home on the Coelian Hill into a monastery for himself and some companions. Here he spent what he considered to be the four happiest years of his life in seclusion and contemplation. Pope Benedict I made him a deacon in 578, and the next year Pope Pelagius II sent him as his *apocrisiarius*, or ambassador, to Constantinople. It was on his return to Rome a few years later, possibly in 585 or soon after, that he reputedly encountered the English slave boys, in an incident recounted in the first biography of Gregory, written at Whitby probably between 704 and 714, and re-told by Bede. The authenticity of the anecdote has been questioned, but it is worthy of relating, partly because it may well have a basis in fact, partly because, in any case, it is securely embedded in the mythology of English history, and partly because it is so evocative, and so vividly encapsulates the spirit which motivated Gregory. The Whitby biography tells how the interest of Gregory in the conversion of the English was first aroused, with the event possibly occurring in the Roman Forum:

> There is a story told by the faithful that, before he became Pope, there came to Rome certain people of our nation, fair-skinned and light-haired. When he heard of their arrival he was eager to see them; being prompted by a fortunate intuition, being puzzled by their new and

unusual appearance, and, above all, being inspired by God, he received them and asked what race they belonged to. (Now some say they were beautiful boys, while others say that they were curly-haired, handsome youths.) They answered, 'The people we belong to are called Angles.' 'Angels of God,' he replied. Then he asked further, 'What is the name of the king of that people?' They said, 'Aelli', whereupon he said, 'Alleluia, God's praise must be heard there.' Then he asked the name of their own tribe, to which they answered, 'Deire', and he replied, 'They shall flee from the wrath of God to the faith.'[4]

The details of this account may well be dismissed, as the pun on words has something of the appearance of a story that has improved with the telling, but the core of the Deiran story is by no means incredible. Gregory's interest in the spiritual welfare of pagan English slaves is confirmed by his latter actions.

He apparently went almost immediately to the pope, urged him to send missionaries to the English, and volunteered his service. The offer was accepted, and Gregory started on his way. But the Roman people were adamant that he should not go, for they saw in him their future spiritual head and protector. He was pursued and brought back. During the succeeding few years he no doubt expanded his original idea into a more comprehensive and detailed plan.

In 590 Pope Pelagius died from the bubonic plague which ravaged Rome, and Gregory was chosen by the clergy and people to succeed him. Reluctantly he accepted. The pressures on him were intense and immense. Rome was beset by disease; there was the problem of the encroaching Lombards from the north; and the Donatist heresy was causing havoc in North Africa. But he dealt with each of these issues and, in addition, he unceasingly cared for the Roman people. He also had much literary work on hand. And all the time he had to wrestle with ill-health. But he never forgot the call to evangelize the English.

As a step towards fulfilling his evangelistic scheme, Gregory arranged in 595 for English boys of the age of seventeen or eighteen to be bought and placed in continental monasteries, with the hope that they would prove to be profitable in the service of God in their own country.

And so we come to the St Augustine-led mission of 597. St Augustine was prior of St Andrew's monastery on the Coelian Hill when he was chosen by Gregory to head the precarious undertaking, and he was accompanied by a group of monks.[5] On their journey they became 'paralysed with terror' at the prospect of what lay ahead; and they began to contemplate returning home as they reflected on the 'barbarous, fierce, and unbelieving nation' to which they were travelling 'whose language they did not even understand'. They sent Augustine back to Gregory in order to ask him 'humbly for permission to give up so dangerous, wearisome, and uncertain a journey'. Gregory replied with a letter persuading them 'to persevere with the task of preaching the Word and trust in the help of God'.[6] Augustine was made their abbot, to whom they would owe obedience as to Christ himself. So encouraged and, one may say, commanded, they continued on their way.

Gregory also dispatched other letters. One, inserted in his *History* by Bede, commended Augustine and his companions to archbishop 'Aitherius' (Vergilius) of Arles. A further batch of eight commendatory letters, mentioned in Gregory's register, were for the Bishops of Vienne, Autun, Aix, the Abbot of Lerins, and for the secular rulers of the Franks. In these the pope not only helped to prepare the way for Augustine and his band of monks, but tried to alleviate any suspicion that by sending a party to England he was intruding on the jurisdiction of subject bishops and archbishops.[7] He also enlisted the aid of Frankish priests whom Augustine recruited to assist the Roman monks, and Bede confirms the presence of Frankish interpreters in Augustine's party which arrived in Kent.[8]

On the journey it seems that Augustine was consecrated as a bishop by bishops from northern or north-eastern Gaul. This is attested by Gregory, who by September 597 was referring to Augustine as 'our-fellow bishop', and who wrote about ten months later referring to the fact that Augustine had been consecrated by the 'bishops of the Germanies'.[9]

Immediately after landing in Thanet Augustine sent an envoy to Ethelbert, the powerful king of Kent, whose domains stretched as far as the Humber.

Kent was unique among the southern kingdoms in having already been a kingdom, a state, long before the *adventus Saxonum*. It had been a Celtic Iron Age principality, and subsequently a Romano-British *civitas* with its capital at Canterbury, which was the focus of the Roman road system for the area.[10] By the time Augustine set his feet upon Kentish soil most of southern Britain except Devon, Cornwall and Wales was subject to Anglo-Saxon political control, and the former British dynasties and aristocracies had been destroyed. It had been a gradual process over about two centuries, but it had resulted in a certain degree of unity which, despite the different kingdoms, expressed itself in periods when one ruler, a bretwalda, or over-king, exercised a large measure of control over much of the territory south of the Humber. At first, it was the kingdoms of the south-east, Sussex, Kent and East Anglia, which received most prominence, mainly because of their density of population, and also because of their wealth. Later, the whole of England was to be divided between Northumbria, Mercia and Wessex.

So it was an opportune time for Augustine to arrive. Since the fall of Ceawlin of Wessex in 592, Ethelbert had become the most powerful Anglo-Saxon king of his day. He was reckoned by Bede as the third of the Anglo-Saxon bretwaldas, with authority to summon the other kings to battle and to lead their forces. 'The God or gods venerated by the most powerful overlord of the day would be adopted by those rulers who sought or needed his favour. The support and protection of a powerful overlord was a potential advantage that no early medieval mission could afford to neglect.'[11] The place was right as well. Kent was ideal as a base from which to launch a mission, with the aim of extending the message proclaimed throughout the whole country.

There was the further advantage that the kingdom already had some contact with Christianity. The king had for some time been married to Bertha, who was a Christian Frankish princess. She was a great-granddaughter of Clovis, and she was the daughter of King Charibert of Paris and his wife Ingoberg. She had been resolute in maintaining her Christian faith in the midst of what appears to have been a predominantly pagan society. She had been permitted to bring a bishop named Liudhard with her to Canterbury, where the king and queen resided. Not only so, but the two of them had been able to worship in the church of St Martin outside the city walls.[12] By the time Augustine appeared on the scene Ethelbert had known the close company of Christians for a decade or more; and he was unlikely to be inhospitable, let alone hostile, to a group of monks under a bishop, who had been sent by the pope, and who had been helped at every stage of their journey by the Frankish kinsmen of his wife. By his dexterous diplomacy Gregory had paved the way and given the mission its best prospect of success; for Kent had the closest contact with the Frankish territories of all the English kingdoms. And the Frankish interpreters were a means of reinforcing these advantages.

The reception Augustine and his group received helped to allay most of their worst nightmares. After leaving them on the island of Thanet for a few days while he decided what to do, Ethelbert went there and, sitting in the open air, probably because of the belief of his followers who knew little of Christianity that the might of the magician would thereby be less effective, commanded Augustine and his comrades to come forward and talk to him. They were ordered to preach about their faith to the king and the gathered company. The response of the king was positive but circumspect, the essence of which is well captured by Bede, in the speech he attributed to the king:

> 'The words and the promises you bring are fair enough, but because they are new to us and doubtful, I cannot consent to accept them and forsake those beliefs which I and the whole English race have held so long. But as you have come on a long pilgrimage and are anxious, I perceive, to share with us things which you believe to be true and good, we do not wish to do you harm; on the contrary, we will receive you hospitably and provide what is necessary for your support; nor do we forbid you to win all you can to your faith and religion by preaching.'[13]

Augustine and the monks were provided with a place in which to live in Canterbury. It is recorded 'that as they approached the city in accordance with their custom carrying the holy cross and the image of our great King and Lord, Jesus Christ, they sang this litany in unison: "We beseech Thee, O Lord, in Thy great mercy, that Thy wrath and anger may be turned away from this city and from Thy holy house, for we have sinned. Alleluia".'[14] They had been most successful in the first stage of their enterprise.

The Roman mission – the second phase

The initial success of the Roman mission continued. There were conversions, and most notably the king believed and was baptized. Neither Gregory nor Bede attach any date to these crucial events in Ethelbert's life. It does seem that he was converted in the first few years after the arrival of the Roman mission because Gregory wrote to him in terms which imply that he was a believer. He referred to him as 'most excellent son' and 'my illustrious son'. He encouraged him 'to preserve the grace he had received' and 'to extend the Christian faith among the people subject to him'. And like a new Constantine he urged him to 'suppress the worship of idols'. In addition, he wrote to Bertha, and compared her part in the conversion of the *gens Anglorum* to that of Helena, the mother of Constantine.

At that time the conversion of the king was normally a precondition for the conversion of the folk. So, we read in Bede that every day 'more and more began to flock to hear the Word, to forsake their heathen worship, and, through faith, to join the unity of Christ's holy Church'. He adds that the king, 'although he rejoiced at their conversion and their faith, compelled no one to accept Christianity; though none the less he showed greater affection for believers since they were his fellow citizens in the kingdom of heaven. But he had learned from his teachers and guides in the way of salvation that the service of Christ was voluntary and ought not to be compulsory.'[15] In a letter to the patriarch of Alexandria Gregory states that on Christmas Day 597 Augustine had baptized more than 10,000 converts to the faith. From this it can reasonably be concluded that the king was converted in 597. Perhaps the number of converts stated was an exaggeration, but it at least shows that the people were responding to the gospel in considerable numbers.

With the conversion of Ethelbert the way was opened to extend the mission to other parts of Kent and perhaps to other kingdoms which came under the king's influence. Augustine received another property in Canterbury, which consisted of a more impressive residence and a church which had survived from Roman times. He dedicated the church to Christ, the Holy Saviour, and there he established his see. In answer to an appeal from Augustine for reinforcements to cope with the vastly enlarged, and potentially enormous, evangelistic and pastoral demands, Gregory sent a second party of missionary monks led by the priest Lawrence, an abbot named Mellitus and a priest named Peter. The group also included Justus, Paulinus and Rufinianus; and they brought with them sacred vases, altar cloths, church ornaments and priestly clerical vestments, relics of the apostles and martyrs, and very many books. The men sent seem to have surpassed in experience and stature all those who accompanied Augustine on the first journey, with the exception of the two he had dispatched to Rome. Lawrence was to succeed Augustine at Canterbury; Peter was to become the first Abbot of the monastery of SS Peter and Paul at Canterbury, but he was drowned while crossing the Channel on a mission to Gaul; Mellitus was to be installed as the first Bishop of London, Justus as the first Bishop of Rochester, and Paulinus as the first Bishop of York; while Rufinianus possibly became a later abbot of SS Peter and Paul.

Conversion was no mean step for the king to take: it was fraught with dangers. Nothing shows this more clearly than the fact that his own son Eadbald, and the three sons of King Sabert of the East Saxons, remained pagans. There was thus a court party in each of these kingdoms which was opposed to Christianity. After Ethelbert's death Eadbald led a short-lived pagan reaction in Kent, before he also was converted; and there was a more substantial and prolonged pagan backlash amongst the East Saxons after Sabert's death in 616 or 617. Sabert's sons mocked Mellitus, who was by then Bishop of London, and when he refused communion to them because they were not Christians they drove him out of the kingdom.

Gregory guided the rapidly developing work from a distance. He it was who gave counsel on organizational, ecclesiastical and pastoral matters. He did so in a series of letters.

The way the church was organized was of crucial importance. Gregory and Augustine had fixed ideas and presuppositions. They spoke and planned as if there was no existing ecclesiastical structure to be taken into account. This does not, of course, mean that there were no territorial bishops, for we will see that Augustine summoned some of them to meet with him, with sorry consequences. But it does appear that there was no national scheme. When Gregory sent Augustine the pallium of a metropolitan on 22 June 601, the accompanying letter said that the see concerned was London. Augustine was told specifically to work towards the creation of twelve episcopal sees under his jurisdiction, with a London synod of bishops. A bishop was to be sent to the city of York, and when that city and the regions surrounding it had received the word of God, the pallium and the metropolitan status should be granted to its bishop, who should also have twelve bishops under him. The Archbishop of York should be subject to Augustine during his lifetime, but from thenceforth one of the two metropolitans should have precedence according to which had the seniority of consecration.

Events had pre-empted the use of London as the first metropolitan centre. Ethelbert's sub-king of the East Saxons, Sabert, had not been converted, and London lay in his territory; nor was it practicable to place Augustine's metropolitan see in the capital of an under-kingdom, especially as Ethelbert had already planned for the see to be at Canterbury. Bede tells us that it was in 604 that Mellitus was consecrated Bishop of London, while Augustine remained at Canterbury, and indeed, sometime before 610, knowing that his own death was imminent, he consecrated Lawrence as his successor. So, in this respect, and in few others, the will of Gregory was not fulfilled. From the start of the mission Canterbury was regarded as the metropolitan see.

This account of the foundation of the see of Canterbury has, however, been challenged by the German scholar Archabbot Brechter. He severely questions Bede's veracity. He suggests that Augustine's see was at London, in keeping with Gregory's wishes, and that Mellitus rather than Lawrence was his successor as metropolitan. Canterbury only became the metropolitan see, according to Brechter, after the sees of London and Rochester were abandoned during the pagan reaction.[16] After a thorough, and not unsympathetic examination of the evidence, Nicholas Brooks concludes that there are no adequate reasons to doubt the Canterbury tradition, and I think that is correct.

As far as churches were concerned, Gregory was greatly influenced by the strength of Anglo-Saxon paganism, even if there were signs that it was on the wane. It was still a force in the land. It commanded the allegiance of many of the people, and it was deeply ingrained in the population as a whole from centuries of familiarity. He did not want any unnecessary conflict between Christianity and paganism. When the party headed by Mellitus left Rome in late June 601 they bore with them orders from the pope that pagan temples and idols were to be systematically destroyed. But Gregory countermanded his instruction a month later. He expounded a policy which addressed the whole difficult subject of the relationship of a new and virile Christianity with a far from dead paganism, in a situation in which Christianity was clearly in the ascendant. It is a foundational statement which helped to determine the attitude of the church to paganism for centuries to come, and it is therefore worthy of being quoted at length. Gregory wrote:

> I have decided after long deliberation about the English people, namely that the idol temples of that race should by no means be destroyed, but only the idols in them. Take holy water and sprinkle it in these shrines, build altars and place relics in them. For if the shrines are well, it is essential that they should be changed from the worship of devils to the service of the true God. When this people see that their shrines are not destroyed they will be able to banish error from their hearts and be more ready to come to the places they are familiar with, but now recognizing and worshipping the true God. And because they are in the habit of slaughtering much cattle as sacrifices to devils, some solemnity ought to be given them in exchange for this. So on the day of the dedication or the festivals of the holy martyrs,

whose relics are deposited there, let them make themselves huts from the branches of trees around the churches which have been converted out of shrines, and let them celebrate the solemnity with religious feasts. Do not let them sacrifice animals to the devil, but let them slaughter animals for their own food to the praise of God, and let them give thanks to the Giver of all things for His bountiful provision. Thus while some outward rejoicings are preserved, they will be able more easily to share in inward rejoicings. It is doubtless impossible to cut out everything at once from their stubborn minds: just as the man who is attempting to climb to the highest place, rises by steps and degrees and not by leaps.[17]

Soon after the second group of missionaries arrived from Rome, Augustine acted upon the encouragement received in one of Gregory's letters to form a relationship with the British bishops and their church. There were major obstacles jeopardizing such an attempt. Perhaps those involved in the Roman mission were not aware of some of the hindrances in the way of co-operation; especially their very explicit assumption of Roman superiority and the right of Augustine to receive compliance in all ecclesiastical matters, which was liable to be highly inflammatory to the insular British Christians. The Romans were also probably not alert to the profound hostility which existed between the British church, and the bishops as representatives of that church, and the pagan Anglo-Saxons. Little attempt seems to have been made by the British Christians to convert their pagan Anglo-Saxon neighbours, and they may well have stood aloof from them in spiritual matters.

But there was common ground, in addition to their shared Christian faith. For one thing, the British Christians would have distinguished between the heathen kingdoms and the bretwalda, Ethelbert, who had recently become a convert to the faith. They would also have acknowledged their links with the Roman church, even if these had become more tenuous in the last half of the sixth century. So they agreed to meet Augustine, probably in 602, but possibly in 603, at a place known as Augustine's Oak, on the borders of the Hwicce and the West Saxons.

There were a number of particular points on which the two traditions differed; and they related to customs and not theology. The first and most serious was the mode of reckoning the date for the celebration of Easter. In the words of Bede, the Romans asserted that the British church 'did not keep Easter Sunday at the proper time, but from the fourteenth to the twentieth day of the lunar month; this reckoning is based on an 84-year cycle'.[18] This was not just a difference of mathematical computation; it was a sure indication to which obedience the church thus celebrating belonged. The native British would not accept the Roman method of dating. I will not dwell on this long-standing and contentious issue, but simply note it as the major point of divergence, as I will be returning to the matter more fully when I give an account of the Synod of Whitby.

When they met Bede says that Augustine demonstrated the authenticity of the Roman stance on the question of the Easter dating and other divisive topics by healing a blind man. This was impressive, but the British were adamant that they could not discard their customs without the consent of their seniors. A second synod was agreed which more British Christians would attend.

Seven British bishops went to the second synod, together with a great number of very learned men, notably from Bangor, which can be reckoned as the noblest of their monasteries. Before going they obtained the advice of a much respected holy and wise anchorite as to whether they ought to forsake their own traditions at the bidding of Augustine. He advised them to test whether Augustine was a man of God by seeing if he was meek and lowly of heart. If he rose to greet them when they entered the synod they should listen to him obediently, but if he did not rise they should show no deference to him. 'The advice went to the root of the matter: the Roman magistrate sat on his curule "sella" and did not rise at the entrance of those who sought his judgment: the rhetor taught sitting in his "cathedra", while his pupils stood.'[19] To rise on the British bishops' entrance would be to admit equality: to cede beforehand any claim to teach.

Such a test was perhaps understandable when it is appreciated that long before the arrival of Augustine the British had maintained their Christianity intact. They had a Christian tradition of which they were proud. As we have already observed, in the early sixth century Gildas had reproached the British not with heathenism, which did not enter into his assessment, but with lukewarm Christianity. From the point of view of the Christians in the western parts of the British mainland it might well have appeared that while they remained Christian, carrying on quietly the customs which they had inherited from their ancestors, eastern Britain during the Anglo-Saxon invasions had become heathen, only suddenly to become Christian, in a most orthodox Roman form, with Gregory's mission. In contrast, the sixth century in Wales, 'the age of the saints', had produced such spiritual giants as Illtud, Samson and

David. Neither, in all probability, were the British Christians as tardy in evangelistic outreach as Bede asserts. The British church in the West may have thought that it had also been active in retaining, consolidating and spreading the gospel. For example in the west midlands the Anglo-Saxons found a church which seemingly had not been lethargic and inert. Because of what it had achieved, it had 'left the missionaries from Canterbury and Iona with little to do'.[20] In the light of such a history, it ill-became the Roman missionaries to behave in any way arrogantly in their dealings with the long-established, faithful, British Christians and their leaders.

The British contingent followed the counsel of the hermit. Augustine remained seated. It was one of those many, but no less significant moments in history, when the single, apparently small and unimportant, act of one man, or in this case inaction, had massive, incalculable, repercussions. The situation was lost before the conference even began. Actions had spoken louder than words. The British Christians refused to accept anything Augustine said. They would not comply with his request that they should conform to the Roman dating for the celebration of Easter; they would not adopt the Roman rite of baptism, although it is not known how the Celtic rite was at variance with this; and they would not agree to unite with the Roman missionaries in preaching the word of the Lord to the English. They would not accept Augustine as their archbishop. From his point of view the British church in its isolation and independence had, perhaps inevitably, diverged considerably from the paths followed by Rome, both in matters of form and ritual, and in its whole organization. Rome could not readily brook the continued existence of what was regarded as schismatic ways and a failure to recognize the pope as the church's spiritual head. The British church could not afford to ignore the benefits which Rome, representing by far the greater part of Christendom, had to offer. Some sort of rapport was clearly in the interest of both churches, and, more importantly, of the Christian faith in its pioneer work of evangelism in Britain. But it was prevented by a clash of personalities and by the force of inherited attitudes. It was a tragic case of an opportunity missed, irrespective of how blame should be apportioned.

Augustine was in fact deeply imbued with all things Roman. His theology and ecclesiology were determined by Roman teaching from his youth. By inclination, nurture, schooling and training he had acquired a deeply ingrained Roman perspective. Any other view of Christian belief and practice was beyond his ken. It was to him both incomprehensible and totally unacceptable. There was but one true church. It is therefore perhaps understandable that he reacted to the British Christians and their bishops in the way he did. It is the reason that he looked to Rome and to the pope for guidance in all matters. And he received from Pope Gregory that which he sought.

The pastoral help which Gregory gave is too extensive and profound to summarize adequately, but it is worthy of a close look as it gives some insight into the kind of issues facing the British church at that time. He was presented with a very wide range of questions, and he responded to each with wisdom and biblical insight.

Augustine first asked about how bishops should relate to their clergy, how the offerings of Christians should be apportioned, and how a bishop should conduct himself in the church. The pope referred Augustine to the epistles of Paul to Timothy. It was customary for the apostolic see to give instruction to bishops that all money received should be divided into four portions, for the bishop and his household to allow hospitality and entertainment, for the clergy, for the poor, and for the repair of churches. The pope said that Augustine should adopt the monastic practice with which he was familiar, and follow the biblical example of the early church where the believers had all things in common. But if there were clerics in minor orders who could not be continent, they should marry and receive their stipends outside the community. In fact marriage was forbidden to all clergy above the rank of sub-deacon all through the Middle Ages.

Augustine secondly asked if there were varying customs in the churches, and more especially if there was one form of mass in the Roman church and another in the Gallic church. In answer, Gregory showed a willingness to imitate other churches where this could be seen as profitable. The standard to be followed was that of the Roman church, but if Augustine found any customs in the Gallic church, or any other church, which were more pleasing to God, it was permissable to make a careful selection from them and teach such customs to the church of the English, which was still new in the faith.

A series of very specific queries referred to matters which obviously confronted the church. In response to a question on the appropriate punishment for a person who robs a church, Gregory said that this should not be uniform but according to the circumstances of the thief, and the motives for the theft. Some should be fined, others flogged, and some should receive a more severe punishment. All punishment, but particularly that which was more harsh, should be administered with love and not out of anger. The culprit should also restore whatever had been stolen from the church.

In answer to further questions, Gregory replied that it was entirely permissable for two brothers to marry two sisters provided they belonged to a family not related to them. Marriage was forbidden by the church between people who were of the same kindred. Christians should only marry relations three or four times removed, and it was a grave sin to marry one's stepmother. Those of the English race who had, out of ignorance, and while they were unbelievers, entered into such marriage relationships, should be warned that they must abstain now that they had been converted. But they should not be refused communion because of their marriage, unless they persisted in such a relationship.

Augustine then returned to two ecclesiastical issues. He was concerned to know whether bishops might be consecrated without other bishops being present, if they were living at such a distance from one another that they could not easily meet. And while thinking of the episcopate, he raised the question of his relationship with the bishops of Britain and Gaul. Gregory stated that in the English church Augustine was the only bishop, and therefore it was not possible for him to consecrate another bishop otherwise than alone. This is an interesting reflection on the attitude of Gregory to the existing British bishops. Gregory acknowledged that bishops from Gaul, who might assist as witnesses at the consecration of a bishop, were only very infrequent visitors to Britain. So, Augustine was allowed to consecrate bishops with other pastors present. Once bishops had been consecrated in places near to one another, no consecration of a bishop should take place except in the presence of three or four other bishops. Gregory proceeded to say that Augustine had no authority over the bishops of Gaul, where the Bishop of Arles had received the pallium; but all the bishops of Britain were under his jurisdiction.

Augustine's remaining two questions were targeted at particular and practical matters; addressing the kind of situations which were obviously part of the routine life of the church. The first related to pregnant women. Can they be baptized; how much time should elapse after the birth of the child before the mother can enter the church; when should the child be baptized; after what length of time can the husband resume intercourse with his wife; and was it lawful for her to enter the church or receive communion if she was in her period. May a man who has had intercourse with his wife enter the church or approach communion before he has washed? To all of these Gregory gave precise and definite answers. There was no reason why a pregnant women should not be baptized, nor why any restriction should be imposed on her right to enter the church after she had delivered. Baptism should be administered promptly where there is danger that the person, adult or child, is on the point of death. The husband should not approach his bedfellow until the new-born child is weaned. The woman should not be forbidden to receive communion at these times. A man who has had intercourse with his wife should wash himself before entering the church.

In his final appeal for advice Augustine asked if a person might receive communion after unclean thoughts such as often occurred in a dream; and if the person concerned was a priest, if he might celebrate the communion. Gregory said that a man must wash himself both physically and morally, by banishing any tempting or impure thoughts, and then delay entry to church until the evening.

Such were the type of pastoral queries and questions of church organization and conduct which pressed upon Augustine in his archiepiscopate. And clearly he rested heavily on Gregory as the one to whom he was responsible, and as his spiritual superior and guide. In fact we know far more about Gregory than we do about Augustine.

A true and just assessment of the character and achievements of Augustine eludes us. He remains a somewhat shadowy personality. On the one hand, by any reckoning he must be accorded a prominent place in the history of the Christian faith in England. On the other hand, he is chiefly known by two anecdotes, both of which are not flattering to him: his hesitancy on the way to England, and his seemingly arrogant treatment of the British Christian leaders. There was clearly much more to him than what is revealed by these two incidents. He must have been a man of considerable ability and spiritual standing for Gregory to have chosen him for a task so dear to the pope's heart, the success or failure of which so much depended on the leader of the mission; and he must have possessed considerable energy, and been a man of many-sided talent, in order to accomplish what he did. John Godfrey offers such a balanced and judicious assessment that I will allow him to summarize the man and his achievements:

St Augustine is almost a text-book example of the type of man who has greatness thrust upon him. He has attained his immortality in the annals of the English people not by his personal character and achievements, but as the chosen instrument for the accomplishment of a design quite beyond his capacity and which had matured in the mind of a far greater man. He himself was a legalist rather than an evangelist, a priest rather than a prophet. In his favour must be remembered his loyalty, his perseverance in what may well have been an irksome and unwelcome task – undertaken through a sense of duty rather than in a spirit of missionary zeal.[21]

This should not be taken as patronizing. If he had lived longer, and had been given time to learn from his mistakes, his archiepiscopate may well have been more notable. There are few historical instances of missionaries achieving great things in the space of a few years. Nonetheless, what he did accomplish was of lasting importance. He was the one who executed the policy of the pope in its first, delicate, and crucial stage. Thereby, he played his vital part in restoring the lost connection between the English church and Rome, for good or ill; and he helped to bring the Anglo-Saxons for the first time into the orbit of western ecclesiastical civilization. The mission may also be viewed as initiating among the Anglo-Saxons that 'order and discipline, and those processes of written law and centralization which were to lead them to national unity'.[22] All of this was no mean achievement. But, whatever the true measure of the man may have been, it is fair to conclude that when he died in 609, the first two phases of the rebirth of Christianity in England were over.

The Roman mission – the third phase

Lawrence, Augustine's successor at Canterbury, built on the foundations which Augustine had laid. He 'not only undertook the charge of the new Church which had been gathered from among the English, but he also endeavoured to bestow his pastoral care upon the older inhabitants of Britain as well as upon those Irish who live in Ireland'.[23] Nevertheless, neither he nor the Roman church leaders for the next hundred and twenty years and more were able to bring full harmony of practice between the two traditions, despite the intervening Synod of Whitby. This is evident from Bede, who wrote in 731 that despite the efforts of Lawrence and his fellow bishops to bring the British Christians into catholic unity, the present state of affairs showed that they had little success. Indeed, in this and other ecclesiastical matters, as well as in its attempt to extend its sphere of influence, it is fair to say 'that in the first 15 years of the seventh century the Christian mission was failing to consolidate its position'.[24]

Before his death in 616, Ethelbert had been defeated in war by Redwald of East Anglia who had assumed the bretwaldaship, and had also professed conversion to Christianity. But he did not take a bishop back with him from his visit to Ethelbert's court in order to establish a see in his kingdom. At the instigation of his wife he continued to venerate the old gods and merely placed a Christian altar in his temple alongside those of the pagan deities. His conversion was also shown to be half-hearted as it was not followed by any conversions among his people and, after the death of Ethelbert, there was a relapse to paganism at both the East Anglian and East Saxon courts.

An interesting, and highly publicized, piece of archaeological evidence possibly bearing on this is the Sutton Hoo ship burial. It has been conjectured that the man interred in such splendour was Redwald. But this is controversial; the evidence for it is somewhat thin, and even more open to question is the attempt which has been made to find a Christian element in the burial, or at least some link with Christianity. It largely rests upon inscriptions on the handles of two spoons: one of which clearly reads 'Paulos', and was competently executed, while the other reads 'Saulos', and was the work of a different and far less able hand. The advocates of a Christian interpretation suggest reference to the conversion of St Paul on the road to Damascus. The critics, or sceptics, point out that the Saulos inscription might well be an illiterate attempt to copy the name Paulos, or a mistake in joining up the gouged-out points of each letter, as sometimes occurred with inscriptions on coins, where the same technique was used. They also draw attention to the fact that East Anglia was only on the very brink of conversion in the early seventh century, and it is doubtful if anyone, priest or king, would have been able to interpret the Greek lettering on the spoons. Such questioners suggest that it is more likely that the spoons were imported into East Anglia, together perhaps with the rest of the silver, simply as a gift, and that their inscriptions were of no great consequence to the people who ultimately buried them. Certainly, the case for their significance as a possible symbol of Christianity, let alone Christian commitment by the king or someone else, is far from proven, and should not be overstated.[25]

After Mellitus and Justus were expelled from their sees and had fled to Gaul, Lawrence was about to follow when, according to Bede, he was restrained from doing so by a visitation of St Peter at night, which left him with scourge marks. These he showed to the new king of Kent, Eabald, who was so impressed that 'he banned all idolatrous worship, gave up his unlawful wife, accepted the Christian faith, and was baptized; and thereafter he promoted and furthered the interests of the Church to the best of his ability'.[26] Mellitus and Justus were recalled. Justus was reinstated at Rochester, but the people of London would not receive Mellitus back.

In terms of evangelistic outreach the situation was not very encouraging, not only for East Anglia and among the East Saxons, but more generally. 'There is no evidence that the missioners penetrated beyond the confines of Kent, save momentarily into London and Essex, nor even within Kent itself were they able to secure the banning of idol worship by royal edict.'[27] The church of Canterbury received recognition and honour for the traditions which had already grown around it, and the metropolitan dignity of its head was acknowledged at Rome. But it had lost the initiative in the conversion of the English peoples well before the death of the last archbishop who had known Augustine. Something significant had been achieved. A foothold had been gained, and a basis provided for further inroads into English paganism. The faith was well established in Kent, and the danger of any reversion to heathenism lessened with the passage of time. King Eabald, who reigned until 640, became a respectable Christian ruler, and he was remembered as a benefactor of churches. His son, Eorcenberht, became the first king to order the destruction of idols throughout his kingdom. These were all grounds for comfort. It just needed a vigorous and effective missionary outreach into other English kingdoms. There was not too long to wait. Encouraging developments were soon to take place in the north.

When Lawrence died Mellitus succeeded him at Canterbury. And when he died Justus of Rochester received the pallium from Pope Boniface V as Archbishop of Canterbury. He only held the post for three years, as he died in 627; but in that time he consecrated Paulinus as a bishop to be sent to Edwin of Deira. This was of first importance, not only because the mission under Paulinus led to the founding of the second metropolitan see of Britain, but because it was a move towards uniting the Roman and the Irish missions. The Roman mission to the Northumbrian territories was to come to an abrupt, albeit temporary, end in 633, and the Irish-Scottish St Aidan was to arrive the following year as Bishop of Lindisfarne.

The Roman mission – the fourth phase

The way was opened for an extension of the Roman mission in the north by a fortuitous situation. Power among the northern Angles was divided between the kings of Bernicia and Deira, which correspond roughly with the later Northumberland and Yorkshire. In the late 620s King Edwin ruled Deira, or Northumbria as it is commonly designated by scholars, and he sent suitors to King Eabald, asking for the hand of his sister Ethelburga in marriage. When he was told that it was not lawful for a Christian bride to be given to a pagan, he promised that in no way would he interfere with the practice of her religion. He would additionally allow all who came with her to follow their faith. Lastly, he did not deny the possibility that he might accept that faith if, on examination, it was judged by his wise men to be a holier worship than theirs, and was more worthy of God. On this understanding she was betrothed and sent to Edwin. Paulinus was consecrated bishop and went with her.

But Paulinus was an evangelist as well as a pastor. He was concerned to prevent those who had gone with him lapsing from the faith, but was also passionately committed to the conversion of the pagans in Northumbria. To this end he toiled hard and long in his preaching, but to little apparent avail.

Then there came a break-through. An assassin was sent by Cwichelm, king of the West Saxons, to kill Edwin. The king was saved by the rapid intervention of one of his thegns, who lost his own life in his act of bravery as he interposed himself between the king and the assailant who tried to stab Edwin with a poisoned dagger. The king in gratitude for his deliverance promised to renounce his idols and serve Christ, if God would grant him recovery from the wound he sustained in the assault, and victory over the West Saxon king. These two favours were granted, and in return he abandoned the worship of idols, but he delayed for further consideration any commitment to the Christian faith. Nevertheless, he did learn more of the faith from Paulinus, and he consulted his wisest advisers. He pondered long and earnestly about the religion to which he should adhere. He was encouraged to accept the Christian faith by Pope Boniface in a long and persuasive letter; but still he hesitated.

At that juncture he recalled how, earlier in his life when he was in exile at the court of King Redwald of the East Angles and in great danger, a stranger appeared to him one night and promised deliverance from his present perilous situation if on his part he would follow the stranger's advice on being given a sign on some future occasion. The sign would be the laying of the stranger's hand upon his head. He was delivered and entered his kingdom of Northumbria. As he sat contemplating his religious situation, Paulinus approached and laid his hand on his head, enquiring if he recognized the sign. He then called on him to embrace the faith. It is unproven whether Paulinus was the stranger at Redwald's court, but it is not impossible. 'Whatever lay behind the vision at Redwald's court, Paulinus was using his gifts now in order to play upon something in Edwin's spiritual experience or in the workings of his mind and to point a moral which was perfectly clear. Not Redwald of East Anglia but a higher agency had saved him and set him up in his kingdom, and he, Paulinus, was now the representative of that higher agency.'[28]

Edwin was almost persuaded. But before he took the final step he wished to seek the advice of his council, or witan. If they all agreed that the Christian faith should be accepted, they would all be consecrated together. The ensuing debate was one of the pivotal points in the early years of revived English Christianity in the seventh century.

A meeting was held, and all the men present were asked in turn what they thought about the hitherto unknown doctrine, and the new worship of God which was being proclaimed. Three contributions to the debate are worth quoting in full, as recorded by Bede, as they largely determined the outcome of the meeting, because they give some insight into aspects of the relationship between Christianity and Anglo-Saxon paganism, and because of their momentous consequences for the Christianization of England. The first to reply was Coifi, the chief of the priests. He had obviously given careful consideration to the matter beforehand, and what he counselled was unambiguous, even if apparently tinged with a certain amount of self-interest.

Notice carefully, King, this doctrine which is now being expounded to us. I frankly admit that, for my part, I have found that the religion which we have hitherto held has no virtue nor profit in it. None of your followers has devoted himself more earnestly than I have to the worship of our gods, but nevertheless there are many who receive greater benefits and greater honour from you than I do and are more successful in all their undertakings. If the gods had any power they would have helped me more readily, seeing that I have always served them with greater zeal. So it follows that if, on examination, these new doctrines which have now been explained to us are found to be better and more effectual, let us accept them at once without delay.[29]

Another of the chief men concurred with what Coifi said, and added advice which touched on the non-temporal dimension of the issue confronting the witan:

This is how the present life of man on earth, King, appears to me in comparison with that time which is unknown to us. You are sitting feasting with your ealdormen and thegns in winter time; the fire is burning on the hearth in the middle of the hall and all inside is warm, while outside the wintry storms of rain and snow are raging; and a sparrow flies swiftly through the hall. It enters in at one door and quickly flies out through the other. For the few moments it is inside, the storm and wintry tempest cannot touch it, but after the briefest moment of calm, it flits from your sight, out of the wintry storm and into it again. So this life of man appears but for a moment; what follows or indeed what went before, we know not at all. If this new doctrine brings us more certain information, it seems right that we should accept it.[30]

Other counsellors of the king continued in similar vein. Then Paulinus addressed the witan. After that Coifi made a further, and telling comment:

For a long time now I have realized that our religion is worthless; for the more diligently I sought the truth in our cult, the less I found it. Now I confess openly that the truth shines out clearly in this teaching which can bestow on us the gift of life, salvation, and eternal happiness. Therefore I advise your Majesty that we should promptly abandon and commit to the flames the temples and the altars which we have held sacred without reaping any benefit.[31]

There was little more to say. The king publicly accepted the gospel which Paulinus preached. He renounced idolatry, and he confessed his faith in Christ. Of course there may have been mixed motives which finally persuaded him to embrace the Christian faith. 'The acceptance of Christianity by the barbarian kings of Europe at this time was very much bound up with the establishment of larger units of territory and power and the validation of their right to rule in the eyes of a wider group, through their attachment to late Roman traditions. It was perhaps this appeal of Roman tradition as much as the Christian marriage and the efforts of the queen's chaplain, Bishop Paulinus, which eventually converted Edwin and many of his people also.'[32] But whatever combination of impulses produced such a new religious allegiance, the consequences for Northumbria and for England were momentous.

Coifi declared that he would be the first to profane the altars and the shrines of the idols, together with their precincts. And he acted on this immediately. With the king's permission, he armed himself with a sword and a spear and rode off on a stallion. As he passed through the countryside the people thought he was mad; but he proceeded on his way. He cast his spear into a pagan shrine near York, and set fire to it and the whole enclosure. The effect of his actions must have been electric.

A vast number of the people received the Christian faith. They were baptized and forsook their paganism. The readiness with which paganism was abandoned accords well with evidence indicating that it had less hold upon the people in the north than in certain other kingdoms and areas. It is possible that those who now came to hear Paulinus preach, even as far north as Yeavering, were Celts who were familiar with the Christian faith if not actual believers. The king was baptized in the wooden church of St Peter the Apostle in York, and he established an episcopal see for Paulinus in the same city. Among those who believed and were baptized were Osfrith and Eadfrith, sons of Edwin.

There is not much extant evidence on which to make assured comments on the church buildings where these baptisms took place. There are few recorded church buildings which were constructed in England in the first half of the seventh century. The small number of which there is knowledge were mainly confined to Kent, with a handful of examples in East Anglia and the kingdom of the West Saxons. In Deira there was a flurry of building in the late 620s, but this proved to be premature. The pace began to quicken in Northumbria around the middle years of the century.

Many of the newly constructed churches were probably of wood, as this was the normal Anglo-Saxon building material. Stone buildings were apparently erected when Roman materials were readily available, as at Escomb, Wearmouth, Jarrow, Hexham, Ripon and Brixworth. Edwin started to build a stone church in York which enclosed the original church, but he died before it was completed.

In the seventh century it appears that local services for the rural communities were in the main provided by a relatively small number of minster churches, which took the form of small monastic communities, often including priests with duties to travel around very extensive 'parishes' serving the rural population.[33] It may well be that in the provision of pastoral oversight, the distinction should not be made between town and country, as between important local centres where minsters were built, and other places where there was no such facility. The siting of minsters depended to a large extent on how the church developed under the aegis of the king; for where the *villa regis*, the royal *tun*, was, there most often was the minster, and such dual development frequently determined where a town grew up in later centuries.[34] But there is a difficulty in accepting this theory of the original *raison d'etre* of minsters. 'References to churches at royal *tun* are common enough, and there is no doubt that in the tenth and eleventh centuries such churches exercised considerable pastoral responsibilities. Such evidence as we have, however, points more to the *initial* purpose of these foundations as private chapels for the use of the king, his family and *comites*.'[35] This is an issue which I will be pursuing in some detail later in this book.

The earliest church in the kingdom of Lindsay may be the one said by Bede[36] to have been built by Paulinus on the occasion of his missionary visit to Lincoln in 628/629. According to Bede it was still visible as a ruin at the time he wrote. At least since the twelfth century and the comments of Ralph de Diceto, tradition has linked the site of St Paul-in-the-Bail to Paulinus' foundation. There is general agreement that it 'has become one of the crucial churches in the history of the Christianization of Britain'.[37] But its identification with Paulinus has been a matter of some scholarly debate. There are rival interpretations. Radiocarbon tests, which can be accepted as substantially correct, place the building essentially in the late Roman period. If radiocarbon dating is played-down, or if an existing building is reckoned as having been used by Paulinus, then it can be accepted as his church. In support of this reading of the situation, it has been pointed out that the dedication to St Paul is uncommon later without being associated with St Peter; and this may be an indication of an early date, as in the case of St Paul's Cathedral in London, founded in 604.[38] A further interpretation results from focussing attention on the small, single cell, that forms the core of the probably ninth-century or later Saxon building. Although there are these variations in dating, the one constant is a hanging bowl, found in the cist grave at the end of the nave, which is assigned to the seventh century, and probably the early part of the century. St Paul-in-the-Bail is a persisting riddle.

To return to our narrative, it is evident that Edwin was anxious to translate his faith into action. He undertook various works, and, for example, he made provision for the welfare of his people by such measures as supplying drinking places for travellers. He was held in high regard throughout his territories.

Not only did Edwin encourage the acceptance of the faith in his own domain, but he persuaded Eorpwold, son of Redwald, the king of the East Angles, to abandon his idolatry and to accept the Christian faith. This was followed by the conversion of many of the people in his kingdom.

Eorpwold's brother Sigbert also became a Christian, and when he succeeded his brother as king he made it his business to ensure that the whole kingdom had the opportunity of sharing his faith. In this he was assisted by two helpers from outside his kingdom. A certain Bishop Felix, who had been born and consecrated in Burgundy, had a longing to work among the East Angles, and he was sent there by Archbishop Honorius to support Sigbert in his efforts to spread the faith.

He arrived in 630 full of zeal and compassion to win the heathen English to the Christian faith. He may have been connected with the mission of Columbanus in Burgundy, and so have imbibed something of the fiery concern of Columbanus for the propagation of his faith; an uncompromising concern for truth and moral integrity which brought the Bangor monk into severe conflict with the authorities of both state and church. Even if Felix had not been involved directly in Columbanus' missionary movement in Burgandy, he would certainly have known of the remarkable Irishman, and perhaps learnt from him of the need for the gospel to be proclaimed to the heathen Anglo-Saxons in England. After travelling around and undertaking much evangelistic and pastoral work he established the seat of his bishopric at Dunwich.

It was also at about this time that an Irish man, Fursey, who was a bishop when he came to England some time after 630, served with distinction among the East Angles. Fursey seemingly laboured side by side in harmony with the continental bishop, as they shared a common goal. Descended from the royal house of Munster, Fursey early and assiduously applied his mind to his studies and disciplined himself in following the teaching and practice of the Christian faith. While he was still a young man, he built himself a monastic cell on the shores of Lough Corrib in western Ireland, where he devoted himself to prayer, fasting and the study of the Bible. Such a practice was not uncommon, and these anchorites were sometimes joined by others in a country where there were many monastic institutions. The precipitating circumstance which resulted in him coming to England, and to East Anglia in particular, is unclear.

His wonderful eloquence in preaching and the holiness of his life were rewarded by a number of converts. The existing believers also received encouragement, and a spur to continue and grow in their faith. The king, Sigbert, was delighted at Fursey's success, and gave him land for the establishment of a permanent settlement. On it the missionary built a monastery for himself and his few companions. The site was a disused fortress which the English called Cnobheresburg, and which tradition has connected with the Saxon Shore fort at Burgh Castle near Yarmouth. There he was joined by two of his brothers, Foillan and Ultan. In about 644 Fursey went to Gaul to spread his faith further afield, and Foillan became the abbot. The two brothers fled to Gaul about the middle of the century when the monastery was attacked and plundered by Mercian invaders, and all the monks either escaped or were captured and killed.

The working together of Felix representing the Roman tradition and Fursey the Celtic, with both under royal patronage, shows such tripartite co-operation at its best, and is illustrative of what was to become increasingly common.[39] It was especially impressive when it was in order to undertake pioneer Christian missionary work, as in East Anglia. This, and other similar enterprises, were foundational in terms of the establishment of the faith in formerly pagan areas.

In these early formative years, the Christianity which was introduced into Kent, Northumbria, East Anglia and elsewhere, was largely confined to individual belief and personal morality. But it did not stop there. As more and more of the population accepted the faith, and as the authorities increasingly acknowledged it, so it pervaded every aspect of the life of the community. Over the next decades and centuries it exercised an ever more powerful influence in moulding social norms and mores. There were political, social, cultural, educational and artistic consequences which in total amounted to a radical reforming of society. Christianity acted as a unifying and 'civilizing' force. Such an all-embracing transformation contained elements derived from both the Celtic culture of Ireland and from the continent, especially Italy and Gaul, from where many of the missionaries came. The process did not represent a wholesale replacement of what was there before, but it amounted to a revolution. The indigenous culture of the Anglo-Saxons was transmuted by the imperative personal and community implications of the new faith, and also by its emphasis on education and learning.

Although much of this lay in the future, the religious and social reformation was largely initiated by kings, by outstanding individuals, and by the unheralded efforts of countless ordinary members of society in the forty years after the arrival of St Augustine.

A special place of honour in the Christianizing process should be given to monasticism. It was one of the key elements in the Christian evangelization and transmogrification of society in the seventh and subsequent centuries. Such Christianization was most fruitful when it emanated from co-operation between king, clergy and monks.

> With the coming of the monks and clergy an interaction was established between the Church and society. The secular rulers encouraged the work of the clergy, donating land for churches and monasteries. The Church in turn supported the secular rulers and influenced every aspect of society giving it new insights and perspectives. Nowhere better is this seen than in the contribution of Churchmen towards the reshaping of traditional codes of law which, with the introduction of religion, was infused with a new spirit of humanity and enlightenment.[40]

All seemed to be progressing well in the spreading and establishment of the Christian faith in the north until the death of the king. This was a severe blow. It stopped the growth of the faith in its tracts. Edwin was killed in 633 at the battle of Hatfield Chase, when Caedwalla of Wessex and Penda of Mercia united against him. Penda and all the Mercian race are described by Bede as heathens, and Caedwalla as a Christian by name and profession, but a barbarian in heart and disposition. The victory they gained was followed by a great slaughter both of Christians and of the people in general in Northumbria, in which it seems that neither women nor children were spared.

It was a time of great crisis, when the affairs of Northumbria were thrown into confusion, and there seemed no safety except in flight. Paulinus returned to Kent with the queen, Ethelburgh. Some think this was to his considerable discredit, although he may have been prompted more by his sense of duty towards his Kentish protégée and her infant daughter than by fear and concern to flee from persecution. After a short time he was placed in the vacant see of Rochester, where he remained until his death.

Paulinus left behind him in York 'a certain James, a deacon, a true churchman and a saintly man'. And Bede adds that 'he remained for a long time in the church and, by teaching and baptizing, rescued much prey from the ancient foe'.[41] He continued in his ministry, possibly in a village near Catterick, until peace was restored to the kingdom and the number of believers grew. He then made a rather specialized contribution to the life of the church, instructing many in singing after the manner which prevailed in Rome and Kent, until he died at a great age. And this brings us to a new phase in the unfolding drama of Christianity in northern England: the reign of Oswald, and the bishopric of the Irish monk Aidan.

The Irish mission – phase one: St Columba and Iona

There is a danger of romanticizing, some would even say inventing, Celtic religion. There is an attraction in the Christianity of those early monasteries, in the pilgrimages of the saints, and in the simple communities which were established at places like Iona and Lindisfarne, which is beguiling, and which encourages fantasy and make-belief. Figures like St Columba, St Aidan and St Cuthbert appear out of the mists of early northern Christian history with a sanctity, devotion, and seemingly uncomplicated lifestyle which is entrancing, especially to modern man in the space and computer age. It was even so with those who lived shortly after the evocative events and seemingly romantic age to which I am referring. This is well expressed by Henry Mayr-Harting:

> One of the major puzzles of Bede's *Ecclesiastical History* is that when one puts it down after reading the first three books one realizes that though Bede was a supporter of the Roman Church order it is the Irish missionaries who have made the overwhelming impact on the imagination. The pages about the Romans, who should have been his heroes, rather limp along, while the pages about the Irish or Irish-trained monks, whose church order and calculation of the date of Easter left much to be desired, are full of life and attractive information . . . The pages on the Romans, like their subject, seem dignified and official rather than warm.[42]

This fascination surrounding the early Christianity of the Irish is, to a large extent, based on a valid assessment and interpretation of 'what actually happened', but it needs to be freed from the accretions which have acted as a barrier to a full understanding of its true nature over the centuries, and not least of all in the twentieth century.

Once converted Ireland made rapid progress in the faith. Small and simple churches and monasteries multiplied, and piety blossomed. One feature of this effulgence and dedication was the drive for the believers to go beyond their own country, bearing their faith with them. 'From an early time, strong impulses towards expansion were at work among the religious. Anchorites sought a fuller solitude beyond the seas, monks were inflamed with the desire of carrying their ascetic practices to foreign lands. We need not seek any other motives to account for the movement of emigration which set in from the sixth century among the Irish.'[43] Of course there may have been a dose of *wanderlust* intermingled with these elements of dedication and sacrifice, for the love of adventure was a trait noticed among the Irish throughout the ages. But this should not detract from our recognition and acknowledgment of the driving force which was at the very heart of the lives of these early believers which was manifestly religious.

This urge to serve Christ was seen clearly in that missionary *par excellence* of the late sixth century and early seventh century, St Columbanus (d. 615). He was a monk under Comgall at Bangor, who went to Gaul about 590, where he and his followers were influential in a remarkable monastic movement. Within a few years such famous monasteries as Corbie, Chelles, Jumièges, St Bertin, St Riquier and Fontenelle were founded. The similarities between such developments and the events in England which I am about to consider, and the relationship between the two activities, have perhaps not been given the weight they deserve. Neither have these two developments been sufficiently recognized as part of wider movements which were affecting both Gaul and England at that time.

Nonetheless, while acknowledging such influential currents of thought and action, the story of the impact of Irish Christianity, first on Scotland and then on England, is one of dedicated lives and heroic missions, and it can best be appreciated, at least at the outset, by a consideration of the work of these pioneers. It is especially the tale of St Columba and St Aidan.

St Columba (*c.*521–97) was born into a family of high social status, possibly in Gartan, in a remote and wild district of Donegal.[44] His father was king or chieftain of the region, who belonged to the tribe of the Cinel Conaill, which was descended from the famous fourth-century Irish king Niall of the Nine Hostages. Columba's grandmother was daughter of king Erc, and his mother, Eithne, belonged to the Royal House of Leinster.

Columba's training for the religious life began quite early. He was baptized Colum or in Latin Columba, a dove. As a child he is said to have shown a great fondness for wandering away to the church, reading the psalms and praying. It was a sign that he was destined for the church that while he was very young he was sent as a foster-son to Cruithnechan, the priest who baptized him. There he spent a happy time, later dedicating a church in the area to the memory of his teacher. He went on to the monastic school of Moville where he was under the care of St Finnian. He was ordained deacon and then lived under the tutelage of a Christian bard named Gemman in Leinster. It was from this time that his first 'miracles' are recorded. From Leinster he proceeded to the monastery of Clonard, attracted there by the reputation of another St Finnian, who was one of a succession of Irish scholars who established the fame of Ireland all over Europe.

Around this time, in 561, there was a battle at Cul Drebene which Columba's kinsmen and their allies won against the ruling southern Ui Neill. Some mediaeval and modern commentators have made much of an abstruse reference to Columba which suggests that he was perhaps involved in some inappropriate way in the battle, a suspicion especially aroused by the fact that he departed for Britain two years later. Too little is known for any definitive conclusion to be reached. The mystery is increased because of the allusion of Adomnan to the excommunication of Columba by a synod meeting in the territory of the defeated Ui Neill, at Teltown. Adomnan claims that this was 'for some trivial and quite excusable offenses by a synod that, as eventually became known, had acted wrongly'.[45]

What seems clear is that whether there was a precipitating cause for his departure from Ireland or not, there lay behind his journey the driving force of pilgrimage (or *peregrinatio*, the Latin word which Columba and his contemporaries used) and penitence. This was, as I have mentioned briefly before, an aspect of contemporary Irish monasticism at its best, with its stress on asceticism, holiness, self-discipline and sacrifice. And '*peregrinatio* was the most intelligible form of ascetic renunciation available to Irishmen'.[46] Adomnan puts it simply and succinctly: 'when he was forty-one, Columba sailed away from Ireland to Britain, choosing to be a pilgrim for Christ'.[47]

The sacrifice was to leave what in Ireland at that time, in the kinship group from which Columba came, were attractive, strong family ties and landed wealth, with an emphasis on local patriotism. In Columba's case there was not the radical discipleship which resulted in the solitary life of the hermit, but it was demanding enough as it was.

In or around 563 he set sail northwards in a small boat with a few companions. After a journey of about a hundred miles he arrived at the mainland of Scotland; and he was given the island site of Iona by Conall son of Comgall, the king of Scottish Dal Riata.[48] It met one important criteria, for after climbing the highest hill he found that he could not see his beloved homeland. The island was to be his base for the rest of his life, although he ventured into nearby Dal Riata where he spread his message, supposedly performed miracles, and gave support to the royal house which eventually provided the first rulers of the united kingdom of Scotland. He returned to his beloved Ireland on a number of occasions, on one of which he founded the monastery of Durrow in the territory of the southern Ui Neill.

In fact, by the time of his death Columba seems to have been responsible for the establishment of a number of monastic establishments both in the Ui Neill territories of Ireland and in the mainland Dal Riata region of Scotland. And these were not two separate sets of communities. There was a network of authority and communication which linked the monasteries on both sides of the Irish Sea. This can be deduced from the evidence of the *Vita Columbae*. Columba's authority and jurisdiction extended over all the foundations associated with his name, which evidently included the selection of abbots and other leaders. Among these was Baithene, who was appointed for a time as head of the monastery of *Campus Lunge* in Tiree, and eventually succeeded Columba in Iona. In like manner, Columba's uncle, Ernan, was installed as *praepositus* over the monastery on Hinba. In the *Vita*, Laisren, one of Columba's companions on Iona, is depicted as having charge over the monks of Durrow. This did not prevent Columba from exerting his supreme authority over these fraternal monastic institutions when this was thought necessary; and he intervened on behalf of the Durrow monks when they were overworked by Laisren. In this action he showed that the position he occupied as the *monasteriorum pater et fundator* over his entire monastic community had practical consequences.

This dual legacy of spiritual and temporal prerogatives seems to have continued in the generations following Columba's death. It was but one manifestation of a trend which was to be found in all the Anglo-Saxon kingdoms: the erosion of the barrier between the secular and ecclesiastical realms. Columba had come from royal stock, and he had family ties with people of influence in Ireland. To this was added his involvement in the affairs of Dal Riata. He had the necessary political awareness and spiritual stature to operate effectively in both spheres; and he demonstrated the benefits to be gained from co-operation between church and dynasty. The interests of Ui Neill were furthered by the ecclesiastical association, as when Columba as an ecclesiastic cemented an alliance between his Irish kinsmen and his Dal Riata patrons in Scotland. The organization which he adopted for the governance of his monastic *familia* in Ireland and Iona, also seems to have mirrored Irish secular concepts of overlordship, kinship, and inheritance, and this gave to the system a built-in potential for survival and continuity in Irish society.

On Iona, in the last thirty-four years of his life, he appears to have continued the mix of activities to which he had become accustomed: 'praying, copying manuscripts, offering pastoral care and spiritual leadership, founding and running monastic communities and playing a high-profile role in the dynastic disputes and political rivalries of Irish and British kings and chieftains'.[49]

Throughout his life he maintained a simple lifestyle, as did all the members of the monastic community of which he was part. The monks lived, prayed, slept, ate and worked in a collection of wooden huts and wattle and daub shelters, clustered in an area of possibly twenty acres. It seems that some of them lived alone, while others slept in dormitories. The centre of the site was occupied by the small wooden church, and huddled around it were the guest house, kitchen and refectory, library and scriptorium where the manuscripts were copied and studied, barns for the storage of grain, the smithy, and workshops for working with metal, wood, leather and glass. Beyond the *vallum* were just under five hundred acres of fields on which the community kept cattle and sheep, and grew wheat, oats and other crops.

By the time of Columba's death about one hundred and fifty monks resided on Iona. They were either *seniores*, who were responsible for the church services; working brothers engaged in manual work; or *juniores*, who were novices under instruction.

It is well that I reiterate that Columba was not part of what can be clearly recognized and designated as the 'Celtic church'. He would not have regarded himself in this way. 'The notion of a Celtic Church, conceived of as a distinct ecclesiastical entity clearly distinguishable from, if not actually in opposition to the Roman Church, is profoundly misleading.'[50] There was not the degree of uniformity which this presupposes, nor was there a sense of self-conscious separation and separateness. 'Christianity had its particular aspects in early Ireland and Britain, but its aspects were many and varied from region to region, and from people to people. The ideals that united them, the study of scripture, the imitation of Christ, the ascetic practices of monasteries – these were to be found all over Europe at the time.'[51] It is true that the church of the 'Celtic fringe' had for some considerable time been somewhat remote from the increasing power, authority and centrality in the life of the European church of the church of Rome, but this did not mean a fundamental difference between the two over what was regarded as essential for a healthy individual and corporate spiritual life. This is worthy of mention, as Aidan took the Iona tradition with him in his mission to Northumbria, and the Christianity he planted there appears to have come into direct 'conflict' with the Roman church; but it was over the one major public issue on which there was disagreement – how to calculate the date of Easter; although this was indicative of the more basic question ecclesiastical allegiance.

The Irish mission – phase two: St Aidan and Lindisfarne

The death of Edwin and the consequent ravishing of Northumbria seemed at the time to be a disaster of major proportions for the church. But the situation was quickly and dramatically reversed within about a year with the victory of the Christian king Oswald over Caedwalla at Heavenfield in 633.

Oswald was great-grandson of Ida, the first king of Bernicia. He was the son of Ethelfrith, and during Edwin's reign he had lived in exile among the Irish, where he had been converted to Christianity.[52] When he became king in 635 it was therefore natural for him to apply to the monastery of Iona for a bishop who would further the Christian faith in his kingdom; 'his action contributed, in a perceptible way, to the subsequent history of north-east England'.[53] The first man sent was considered by the English to be rigid and uncouth. In his place the community sent Aidan 'a man of outstanding gentleness, devotion, and moderation',[54] who was zealous and, as seen from his ministry in Northumbria, courageous yet discreet.

The king gave him a place for his episcopal see on the island of Lindisfarne. And there he established a monastery and a base for his activities. He may have regarded himself as a monk subject to an abbot, rather than as Bishop of Lindisfarne, in view of the ecclesiastical struc-ture which prevailed in Ireland, and the discipline he had experienced at Iona; but whatever his self-perception, his influence was immense. In his Christian work he is portrayed by Bede as united with the king in a close fellowship of service.

The king humbly and gladly listened to the bishop's admonitions in all matters, diligently seeking to build up and extend the Church of Christ in his kingdom. It was indeed a beautiful sight when the bishop was preaching the gospel, to see the king acting as interpreter of the heavenly word for his ealdormen and thegns, for the bishop was not completely at home in the English tongue, while the king had gained a perfect knowledge of Irish during the long period of his exile.[55]

There are grounds for rejecting or qualifying the sense in which Oswald can be understood as humble, but 'he clearly was a convinced Christian himself, a man of faith and prayer; and he used his position to promote the conversion of his people, assisting his bishop in a way which associated him intimately with the work of evangelization'.[56]

With such an example at the highest level in society, and with the aid of many who came from Iona, and perhaps Ireland as well, who were mostly monks, the work prospered. People came to faith, churches were built, and great numbers of the population met in gatherings to hear what was being proclaimed. The king also provided land and property for the establishment of monasteries.

Aidan himself set an example of godly living. He was renowned for his abstemiousness and self-control, his freedom from greed or worldly ambition, his poverty, his charity, and his concern to exercise his ministry of evangelism and pastoral care with gentleness and yet firmness wherever he found himself as he walked about his diocese.

It has been suggested that the progress of Christianity in Northumbria at this time, and the high profile it achieved locally and throughout the country, combined with the Northumbrian bretwaldaship, resulted in Lindisfarne superseding Canterbury as the effective ecclesiastical centre of England for thirty years.[57] The northern church under the leadership of Aidan exerted an influence throughout the land which was without precedence. In doing so it was also making a contribution to an evolving sense of nationhood of which contemporaries were unaware. This was one of the unintended by-products of an ever expanding allegiance to the Christian faith and the values it enshrined. Increasingly the people were being drawn towards a common set of beliefs and a widely accepted moral and ethical code.

The partnership between king and bishop was brought to a sudden and violent end when Oswald was killed in a great battle at Oswestry in 642 by the Mercians under the same king, Penda, who had slain King

Edwin. His death was treated by many as martyrdom; and he became a European saint. He has been described as the first English martyr; St Alban being the first British one.[58]

For a short time Oswin was king of Deira. He was a man of fine character, known especially for his modesty. This was demonstrated in one incident which has gained considerable fame. He had given Aidan an excellent horse. Aidan met a beggar, alighted and gave him his newly acquired horse and all its trappings. The king heard of this and asked Aidan why he could not have given the beggar a less valuable horse or something else of lesser worth, rather than the superb animal he had specially chosen for the bishop. The bishop replied that surely the son of a mare was not more precious to the king than the Son of God. The two of them went in to dine. The king came in and, remembering the bishop's words, divested himself of his sword and gave it to a thegn. He threw himself at Aidan's feet and said that he would never again refer to the matter of the horse, and in the future he would not question what the bishop did with any money he gave him, or query any of the bishop's gifts to the sons of God. The bishop raised him from the ground and they sat together at the meal. But Aidan became increasingly sorrowful, and when he was asked why, he replied that the king would not live long, for he had never before seen a humble king, and the nation did not deserve such a ruler.[59] The king was murdered not long after this, and Aidan died twelve days later.

Oswald was succeeded as king of Northumbria by Oswy in 642. The new king took on the overlordship of Oswald, and held sway over English, Britons, Picts and Irish-Scottish. In order to gain and retain supremacy he had to fight hard against other kingdoms, and also against princes of his own Northumbrian dynasty. In doing so, he was guilty of the murder of Oswin in 651, a crime for which he appears to have repented and sought expiation by the foundation of a monastery. It was a blot on what was generally a life of Christian zeal and evangelistic effort. He followed the example of Edwin in his concern for the promotion of the Christian faith in other kingdoms. Thus, when Peada, king of the Middle Angles,[60] came to him and asked for the hand of his daughter Alchfled in marriage, he readily agreed on condition that Peada's nation accepted the Christian faith and baptism. Peada heard the gospel preached and gladly became a Christian himself even if he was refused his request for marriage.

He returned to his kingdom accompanied by three English priests and one Irish priest, who so successfully preached about the Christian faith that many nobles and lower status people gave up their paganism and accepted Christianity.

King Oswy was likewise most effective in his dealings with the East Saxons. The new ruler of that kingdom was Sigbert, and when he came on frequent visits to Northumbria Oswy tried to persuade him that idols made by the hands of men could not be gods. At last he was converted and baptized, together with his followers. At his request Oswy sent him Cedd and another priest who traversed the whole kingdom and went a long way in building up a body of believers. Bishop Finan of Lindisfarne and two other bishops consecrated Cedd as Bishop of the East Saxons in 653. The new bishop carried on the work he had begun as a priest, but with greater authority. He established churches and ordained priests and deacons to assist him in preaching and in the administration of baptism. The surviving chapel of St Peter at Bradwell-on-Sea in Essex may be the monastery he founded there; the other site being Tilbury at the mouth of the Thames. When the king was murdered by two kinsmen, his successor, Swithhelm was baptized, and the work of the church in East Anglia continued to thrive.

Cedd retained his links with Northumbria, and he founded the monastery of Lastingham in Yorkshire on land provided for him by Othelwald, king of Deira, who was the son of Oswald. He died during an outbreak of the plague soon after attending the Synod of Whitby, where he acted as an interpreter between the Roman and Irish parties.

In the meantime Oswy was sorely harassed by Penda of Mercia, who finally refused the offer of a massive payment in order to desist, and attacked the Northumbrian king. Oswy gained the victory, and as part of his thank offering gave six estates in Deira and six estates in Bernicia for monasteries. He not only freed his own subjects from the devastation which threatened them, but used his considerable influence in a successful campaign to bring Mercia and the neighbouring kingdoms into the Christian fold. The first bishop of Mercia, of Lindsey, and the Middle Angles was Diuma, and he was followed by Ceollach, both of whom were Irish. Christianity had by now been re-introduced into most of the kingdoms of the land; although it was at an early stage in any one of them, and it had not percolated downwards to grip the population as a whole.

Towards the end of his life Oswy tried to promote greater unity between the Irish and Roman traditions. The single most contentious issue remained the mode of calculating the date of Easter. The heat had not gone out of the debate on this matter, but had perhaps intensified.

Because it was so crucial to the harmonious life of the church, representing as it did a declaration of adherence to the one tradition or the other, Oswy decided to bring the parties together in order to attempt a resolution of the long-standing bone of contention. He therefore summoned a synod at Whitby in 664 for open and frank debate, followed, he hoped, by a decision which would be universally accepted throughout all sections of the church in Britain.

The Synod of Whitby

'In the long period before the submission of the Celtic Christians to the obedience of Rome and Canterbury, and in the arguments at the Synod of Whitby itself, it is notable that the question of the ultimate obedience of western Christians to the see of Peter was scarcely raised.'[61] Margaret Deanesly is right in making such an assertion. She is also correct in saying that the Celtic and the continental missionaries mainly worked in different areas, and that there was thus minimal opportunity for discussion and argument. The Celtic leaders held the faith as apostolic and the church as one, and reverence was accorded to those who went on pilgrimage to holy places in Gaul, Rome and Palestine. There are examples of confrontation and hostility, as when the British bishops and other leaders refused to accept the authority of Augustine, but this was perhaps a consequence of his attitude rather than because of a fundamental resistance to the Roman tradition – and one wonders what would have happened if he had risen from his chair at that fateful moment! Even in the south, where antagonism was most pronounced, there was co-operation and a close working together of missionaries from both traditions, as we have noted in East Anglia.

But there were different traditions and different senses of loyalty and self-perception, and they were not merely confined to religion. It seems that the issues at stake were bound up with cultural and racial identities. On the one hand there were the Welsh, the Irish and those Britons of the old Celtic order who had long lost sight of any Roman supremacy, if they had ever accepted such authority. All three of these had strong and well-embedded social and cultural norms as well as distinctive Christian usages and practices. And on the other hand there was a comparatively small group of 'foreigners' who had swept in uninvited. From the point of view of the long-resident Celts, these newcomers were encumbered by a whole baggage of cultural and social presuppositions, which initially at least may have been a barrier to full Christian unity and harmony. The recently arrived strangers were inevitably associated with a social and cultural system which was in many respects alien, and perhaps somewhat threatening to the native, Celtic, population. After all it represented not just in name, but in ethos and attitude, much of the former Roman system which had imposed itself on Britain; and this was the regime of a power which had driven many of the Celts to the 'fringes' they now inhabited.

The religious issues at stake may therefore have had an underlying social and cultural component which was as emotive and as important as the purely theological or ecclesiastical differences. The purely ecclesiological questions had all been ventilated for many years before the Synod of Whitby, but not, it seems, as directly bearing on submission to Rome or Canterbury. Perhaps the synod itself made more explicit the whole question of the authority of the Petrine see. It may in the end have done as much to fuel as to solve a problem, at least in the short and medium term.

The synod may never have been held, and the 'crisis' not highlighted, but for the initiative of King Alfrith, Oswy's son, and the under king of Deira. He came into contact with Wilfrid, the future bishop and leading churchmen, in about 660. He heard at length from him some of his impressions from an extended visit to the continent. These included his conviction about how to calculate the date of Easter, which Annemundus, Bishop of Lyon, and Boniface the archdeacon in Rome had helped him to clarify in his own thinking.[62]

As we have noted, at the time of St Augustine, there were two points relating to church practice which were in dispute: divergence in the form of ministering baptism, although it is not known what differences were at stake, and the Easter question. Augustine included both, together with co-operation in converting the heathen, as a basis for unity between the two traditions. We will, said the archbishop, 'gladly tolerate all else that you do, even though it is contrary to our customs'.[63]

But in the ensuing sixty years the shape of the tonsure was added to those issues which caused practical difficulty. After all, it, together with baptism and the dating of Easter, was a very public demonstration of which tradition was being followed. Both parties were agreed that to cut the hair short was a desirable practice for the clergy. The Irish monks, following what they believed was an older custom than the Romans, and one which also obtained in the East, shaved the front part of the head only; while the Romans, tracing their practice back to St Peter, shaved the top part of the head, leaving a tonsure in the shape of a crown. The larger and more well-informed Celtic houses like Iona had conformed to the western usage, but the alternative custom prevailed in many other houses.

By far the most crucial issue was the date for the celebration of Easter. 'The Paschal question is not attractive to the reader of Eusebius; it is profoundly wearisome to the reader of Bede.'[64] Nonetheless, a summary of the highly technical computations involved is necessary if one is to appreciate what was being discussed with such animation. It was agreed on all hands that there should be a yearly festival to commemorate the death and resurrection of Christ; that a fast of some undefined duration should precede this; and that the timing of the Christian Passover and fast should to some extent be regulated by the season of the Jewish Passover. But to what extent? Should the fast be concluded on the fourteenth day of the moon on which the Jews were to kill their Passover, on whatever day of the week it may fall? Or should a Sunday be taken as a fixed point? The majority of the churches adopted the latter practice. The church of Ephesus, and those dependent on it in the province of 'Asia' followed the former dating method, and were consequently called Quartodecimanians.

The question was further complicated in the third century by the query as to whether the festival should always be kept after the vernal equinox, and various canons or 'cycles' were proposed in order to ascertain the true date for the beginning of the 'first lunar' or the 'Paschal' month. The Nicene Council laid down a rule for arriving at the date of Easter. 'Easter is the Sunday which follows the fourteenth day of the moon which attains this age on 21 March or immediately after.' Others who joined in the computing debate used various dating 'cycles' to come to different equinoxes and Easter dates. In 457 Rome favoured the cycle of Victor of Aquitaine, and later, about 525, that of Dionysius Exiguus, a monk who followed the mathematicians of Alexandria. Gaul continued to use the cycle of Victor. The Dionysian calculation was based on a cycle of nineteen years and a spring equinox on 21 March, and according to this reckoning Easter Sunday would fall between the fifteenth and twenty-first day of the month. Augustine had followed this timetable, but the Irish and the Britons were still using the older cycle of eighty-four years, which Rome had abandoned long ago. They departed from the Nicene rule in that they allowed the fourteenth of the moon to be Easter Day, if it fell on a Sunday; whereas, according to the Nicene declaration, in that case they ought to have deferred Easter until the twenty-first.

The synod was for bishops and clergy, and it was to meet under the presidency of Oswy and his court in the double minster[65] at Whitby. It must be said that the king was predisposed to accept the Roman way before the synod gathered. This was not only because he may have been convinced of its inherent truth. In addition to the merits of the argument he saw the advantages of incorporation into the extensive and authoritative Roman church system. He also had the constant domestic irritation of differing from his wife in the timetable for the celebration of Easter as she was the daughter of King Edwin, and had been brought up in the Roman observance in Kent.

The council was held in 664.[66] It was attended by King Oswy, and his son Alfrith; the friend and adviser of Alfrith, Abbot Wilfrid of Ripon; Bishop Agilbert of the West Saxons, with a priest, Agatho; Bishop Colman of Lindisfarne and his Scottish clergy; the venerable Bishop Cedd, who acted as an interpreter; James the Deacon; Romanus, Queen Ethelberga's chaplain from Kent; and the Abbess Hilda and her followers.

Oswy opened the proceedings. It was fitting, he declared, that those who served one God should observe one rule of life and should not differ in the celebration of the sacraments. He called upon Colman to explain what were the customs which he followed and how they originated.

The bishop said that he observed what he had received from his superiors, who themselves were inheritors of what their fathers had practised, and these traditions could be traced back to St John the apostle. Then Wilfrid spoke on behalf of Bishop Agilbert, probably because of the bishop's language difficulties, and because Wilfrid was renowned for his adeptness in conversation and debate. He said that he and those of like mind followed what was universally adopted in Italy and Gaul and generally throughout the world. The only exceptions to such conformity were 'these men and their accomplices in obstinacy, I mean the Picts and the Britons, who in these, the two remotest islands of the Ocean, and only in some parts of them, foolishly attempt to fight against the whole world'.[67] Understandably, Colman was offended by what he interpreted as disparaging remarks against those who followed the example of the apostle John. Wilfrid gave assurances that 'the beloved disciple' was not considered foolish, but he argued that Colman and those who shared his opinion had misunderstood both John and Peter, and they therefore followed neither. The apostle Peter, whose teaching the Church of Rome especially regarded, was the one to whom

Christ said, 'Thou art Peter and upon this rock I will build my Church and the gates of hell shall not prevail against it, and I will give unto thee the keys of the kingdom of heaven.'

King Oswy declared himself in favour of the Roman teaching, and most of those present followed his lead. The incensed Colman was not willing to comply with the Whitby decision, and he returned to Iona in the company of others of like mind. His decision to leave Northumbria, and indeed a key factor in his approach to all the issues raised at Whitby, was his veneration for Columba and the Irish tradition which he epitomized; and this was so for the other Irishmen. They did not depart with a sense of pique, determined to have nothing more to do with the church in Northumbria, and the Christian link between Iona and Northumbria was maintained. But the matters dividing the two traditions were deeply felt on both sides, and the synod did little if anything to change previously held views.

Colman was replaced as Bishop of Lindisfarne by Tuda, one of Aidan's pupils who was willing to conform to Roman belief and practice. Northern Ireland adhered to its traditional opinions and practice, in defiance of the Whitby pronouncement, until 704, when Adamnan, Abbot of Iona and a convert to the Roman interpretations, gained the support of the influential monastery of Bangor. Iona did not change its usage until an Englishman, Egbert, persuaded them in 716. And in the intervening fifty years or so there was much difficulty caused by the confused situation after the synod.

The Roman mission to Wessex

Before moving on to some concluding remarks about the period from the late sixth century to 664, brief mention needs to be made of a further initiative taken by Rome in the Christian affairs of England. The pope concerned was Honorius I, and he decided to institute a mission for the founding of a church in Wessex, but without reference to the Archbishop of Canterbury. The whole enterprise met with limited success.

The missionary selected to lead this venture was Birinus, who was consecrated bishop by Asterius, Archbishop of Milan. He may well have been intended for Mercia, and the pope may have envisaged a future archbishopric in that region. But when he landed in Wessex in 634 he was so alarmed at the heathenism of the Gewisse that he decided to remain there and devote himself to local evangelism.

His initial success was most encouraging. The king, Cynegils, accepted the faith, and he was baptized. As was customary, many of his people followed his lead. Oswald, the godly king of Northumbria, was present at the baptism and stood godfather for the newly-converted king. Birinus was given the Roman *civitas* of Dorchester-on-Thames as his episcopal seat, and during the rest of his life he built and dedicated churches and brought many to faith.

But after the death of the king, his pagan son Cenwalh came to the throne, and there ensued a most unfortunate series of decisions and events. Within a short time the new king fought against Penda of Mercia, and was expelled from his kingdom. In exile he accepted baptism. When he returned to his kingdom he secured a Frankish bishop named Agilbert, who, much to the annoyance of Cenwalh, had not mastered the local dialect several years into his bishopric. The king obtained another bishop, Wini, a Saxon who had received orders in Gaul, divided the kingdom into two dioceses, and appointed Wini to the bishopric of Winchester in about 661. The indignant Agilbert withdrew to Gaul, where in due course he became Bishop of Paris. It was but a short time before the native bishop proved to be unsatisfactory, and he was deprived of his see. It may be an indication of his character that he took refuge with Wulfhere, the king of the Mercians, and purchased from him the see of London, of which he remained bishop until his death. Cenwalh unsuccessfully pleaded with Agilbert to return; but the previous bishop sent his nephew Leuthere in his stead, who was consecrated Bishop of Winchester by archbishop Theodore, and proved to be a satisfactory prelate. The *Anglo-Saxon Chronicle* records that Cenwalh had built the minster church at Winchester, and that it was completed and consecrated in 648, the dedication being to St Peter.

Cenwalh had considerable influence in promoting Christianity in the north through his friendship with Benedict Biscop, whom he supported with generous gifts. Benedict was a scholar from Northumbria who founded the twin monasteries of Monkwearmouth and Jarrow. He was an avid collector of books, and he travelled far and wide over England and Europe in order to obtain precious manuscripts for his libraries. Another friend was the sub-king of Deira, Alchfrid, who was a keen supporter of the Roman church and a close friend and admirer of Wilfrid, Abbot of Ripon and later Bishop of York.

Towards the establishment of a Christian kingdom

One of the greatest dangers in historical interpretation is the discerning of non-existent trends and patterns which are then imposed on un-related and largely chaotic events. But there are developments which are only apparent in retrospect. There are outcomes to disparate historical occurrences, and interconnections between apparently unconnected events, which come into focus only when they are placed within an extended timescale, which were not, and could not have been, evident at the time. There are unifying themes which make sense, and which give coherence and relevance to what might otherwise be a somewhat confusing array of apparently distinct and separate sequences of events. There are unintended consequences of intended human action which can only be recognized much later.

In hindsight there was an emergence over a span of six hundred years or so, if not longer, of the 'Christian' state of England, which only became fully manifested with the coming of the Normans. It may be that 'in the early 8th century, there was not yet a country called England',[68] but it was well on the way to being founded long before that. And, what is more, it was well on the way to being established not just as 'a country', but as a Christian kingdom. Initially there was the formation of individual 'Christian' kingdoms, and then the merging of these.

The period from the late sixth century to 664 was crucial in this process. The main political advance was marked in the south by the triumph of the West Saxons at the battle of Dyrham near Bath in 577, and in the north by the battle of Chester, fought between 613 and 616. Political consolidation for the midlands came with the reign of Penda (632–55). By the time of the Synod of Whitby the England of the so-called Heptarchy had received its major bold outlines. The political hope for the future lay with Wessex, Mercia and Northumbria, as the kingdoms which could provide long-lasting political viability, and which could still expand. 'The achievements of St Augustine and his successors and the energy of the Celtic missionaries, particularly in the north, brought it about that most of the kingdoms of this new England were Christian, or subject to Christian influence, though Penda himself remained a steadfast heathen.'[69]

In its struggle against paganism, and in its appeal to kings and political leaders from the late sixth century to about 664 the tide was in important respects flowing in favour of Christianity. There was no political barrier or disadvantage if a kingdom embraced the resurgent Christian faith. Far from it, for there was much potential gain in being identified with powerful continental Christian dynasties, and with the ever more formidable western Christendom as a whole. At the very least the advocates of Christianity were not hampered by extraneous non-religious considerations. For these reasons it is perhaps not remarkable that kings were often tolerant of the new religion and indifferent to the fate of the old.

Even Penda, the pagan king of Mercia, although he refused to forsake his gods, permitted his son Peada to adopt the new religion and allowed missionaries to work in both Middle Anglia and Mercia. There were not the same political implications to the acceptance of Christianity which hampered its advance in some regions of the continent, and which were to hinder the work of British missionaries in northern regions of Europe during the eighth century.

> There were no martyrs among the early Christian missionaries of England, which contrasts markedly with the history of the missionary activity of the English themselves on the Continent in the eighth century. It was partly a consequence of the incoherence of heathen belief, organization, and practice in England. Perhaps even more it was because the Christian missionaries of the eighth century appeared to the heathen Frisians and Saxons as agents of a Frankish power which wished to subjugate and enslave them, with the result that paganism became identified with the cause of tribal independence. The missions to England were in no way compromised by any connection with a hostile secular power; whether Celtic or Roman their motives were exclusively religious.[70]

Of course it was not just a matter of how great was the success of the Christianization process as measured either in terms of the number of professions of conversion or declarations of belief by rulers. Neither was it a question of just gaining acceptance of the Christian faith alongside a variety of other gods already worshipped. That was not difficult to achieve. Far more impressive was the destruction of heathen temples and idols, and this was a much harder and more telling task. If such action was permitted it showed that the Christian faith had penetrated deeply both for individuals and for society. But there was a further stage with the eradication in large part of the beliefs of the ordinary people in the virtue of magical spells and charms. These were standard means of ensuring good crops and protection against the powers of evil with which men were surrounded; and the worship of natural objects such as trees and stones was not easy to eliminate. Traditional practices had quite a strong grip, or at least they had been incorporated as an accepted feature of life, and even when Christianity finally and fully triumphed there remained a residue of such beliefs which was manifested as superstitions and folklore.

Although by the mid-seventh century paganism was to some extent a matter of conventional practice rather than deeply-rooted belief, it was far from defunct: it was part of the inherited, conventional, time-honoured, way of regarding the world. Few people may have been committed to it as a profound explanation of life, and as a means of entry to a future state of bliss after death, but it still had a treasured place in the lives of countless, mainly illiterate and unsophisticated rural, members of the population. It was accepted and respected for the part it had played in the life of especially country people over many centuries. From time immemorial it had provided a sense of security in harmony with traditional values; and it continued to do so for an innumerable host of people who had been nurtured in a world inhabited by many and varied spirits. It was well ingrained as an integral element in a way of life which was hallowed by values and practices handed down from one generation to another. Paganism may not have offered the kind of life-transforming experience, radical reformation of ethical and moral standards, and assurance of eternal life which characterized the Christian faith, but it persisted as a powerful force.

By the mid-seventh century Christianity had made remarkable strides towards capturing the hearts and minds of many people, but it had not by then to any great extent infiltrated the lower ranks of society; and that is just where paganism was most fully entrenched. The material, archaeological, evidence of this slow but sure advent of Christianity as a popular, widely appreciated, accepted and practised religion is contained in the slow appearance of churches and other Christian buildings, the occasional but increasing use of Christian monuments and other stone objects, and the progressive change of burial practices.

In this whole process of the Christianizing of society, and in the protracted saga of establishing Christian kingdoms which would ultimately merge into one kingdom, the Irish, Scottish and continental contributions were all vital. 'There is little profit in trying to assess the relative importance of the Irish and continental influences in the conversion of the English . . . the spheres of Irish and continental missionary enterprise cannot be closely defined . . . The strands of Irish and continental influence were interwoven in every kingdom, and at every stage of the process by which England became Christian.'[71] The English church after the Synod of Whitby continued to be profoundly influenced by the stress on asceticism and penitential discipline so characteristic of Irish Christianity. The Celtic Christian tradition was perpetuated by St Cuthbert of Lindisfarne, although he married this to an adoption of Roman usages. And, as we will see, such a blending of the two traditions enriched English Christianity in countless ways in the following centuries.

7

Christianity in England from 664 to the Late Eighth Century

The Synod of Whitby did not solve many immediate problems for the church as a whole in England. Its significance was to be felt later. In the aftermath there was crisis rather than confidence, and the Christian concern was with survival rather than revival. It has been suggested that the five years following the council 'form the most critical period in the history of the Anglo-Saxon church', and that 'for the moment the mere continuance of organized Christianity in England was uncertain'.[1] And a case can be made to support such a contention. Although the opportunity for unity had been given, the synod decision was not widely acclaimed at the time, and the men who were to realize that ideal were as yet untried in responsible positions. Even while the synod sat England, together with much of western Europe, was experiencing the deadly effects of pestilence. The plague removed many leaders among the clergy, depopulated whole monasteries, and resulted in a widespread reversion to heathenism.

Politically, the sixty or so years after the synod was a period of instability. The eclipse of the Northumbrian supremacy, combined with the inability of any of the southern kingdoms to take on the bretwalda mantle and assume a comparable hegemony, had dire consequences for the work of the church. This state of affairs resulted in constant warfare: no longer could ecclesiastical leaders depend on the powerful support of kings whose sway extended over all or most of England.

Confusion or worse in church circles was quite common. There was a relapse into general panic among the East Saxons, especially after their bishop, Cedd, died of the plague. Bishops such as Jaruman extended their labours outside their own dioceses in an effort to prevent apostasy. When Wighard, a priest of the late archbishop Deusdedit's *familia* was sent to Rome for consecration by the pope as the new archbishop, he died of the plague after presenting his credentials, together with nearly all his companions. It was a distressing moment for the English church, with the possibility of widespread disintegration.

Bede bemoaned the fact that many remote hamlets and villages in the inaccessible mountains and dense woodlands of Northumbria did not see a bishop for years at a time; and some of the few bishops anyhow failed to preach regularly and neglected their duties. Such Christian communities were also without teachers; and where there were priests, a number were ignorant of Latin, and often ill-instructed in the faith.

Bede additionally, and with justification, lamented the poor spiritual state of some of the monasteries. It was the practice of a considerable number of magnates to secure land under the pretext of founding monasteries. They then lived in them with their wives and children, and by this device they became absolved from secular obligations, but with no intention of conforming to the most elementary standards of monastic piety. Such was the extent of misconceived liberality by kings in support of what were manifestly pseudomonasteries that money was not available for the endowment of new sees. The church of the day could ill afford such a scandal. Even monasteries which had formerly enjoyed good reputations could become lax if they fell under the rule of an over-indulgent abbot or abbess. This happen to Coldingham, which had become degenerate by the beginning of the eighth century.

But despite these various and serious shortcomings, in the seventy years after the Synod of Whitby Christianity prospered and grew in its coverage of the country, in its organizational efficiency and in the way it became more deeply integrated into the life of society. It moved much nearer to becoming the universally recognized religion of the people as a whole; and its teaching and moral code exerted an ever greater influence upon political and social life. This was to a great extent because the age produced some Christian leaders of stature who made a massive contribution to the life of the contemporary church, as well as to the church of future generations.

Three men in particular helped in their very different ways to inaugurate a new period in the history of the church in England: Archbishop Theodore, Bishop Wilfrid and St Cuthbert. They were instrumental in converting what could have been a half century or more of disaster into what can in retrospect be regarded as a golden age for the church. They therefore provide a good starting point in our attempt to understand that age when Christianity was consolidated and extended to such an extent that the process of Christianization became irreversible. They were key players in the drama of those turbulent times for the church and the nation. Their lives helped to determine the course of events, touched upon the most crucial issues and trends in the life of the contemporary church, and decided to a great extent what matters should be given prominence in the lives of Christians throughout the various kingdoms of the land.

After about the fourth decade of the eighth century the story becomes less glowing. The underlying weaknesses of the church which have been noted began to assert themselves. But a sharp contrast should not be drawn between the two halves of the period covered by this chapter. Certainly, and largely because of the outstanding leaders I am about to consider, the first part was more glorious than the second; but the last sixty years of the eighth century were not, as has often been asserted, an almost unrelieved tale of stagnancy and decline. The life of the church had its merits and high points, as we will see.

Archbishop Theodore

When Pope Vitalian in 668 chose the distinguished Greek scholar and monk Theodore of Tarsus to be archbishop of the English he did a service for the English church which was without parallel in the centuries between the pontificate of Gregory the Great and the Norman Conquest.[2] He had chosen a man who was from a very different world and culture than the people to whom he was to minster. 'Whereas in England the energies of churchmen were taken up with spreading the faith in a primitive Germanic countryside and defending the young church from casual extinction at the hands of violent men: Theodore was a Byzantine gentleman, a Graeco-Roman philosopher, as Boniface called him, who belonged to the old, civilized, learned Byzantine world.'[3] There was not only the cultural divide. The new head of the English church was sixty-seven years of age. The situation in England called for a man of vision, energy, evangelistic and pastoral ability and commitment, and sensitivity to local needs, who would build on foundations already laid, and who would take the initiative in many directions in order to promote the work of the church. The appointee seemed to have little to commend him for this particular and demanding task. He proved to be one of the most distinguished and effective primates in the history of the archbishopric of Canterbury. He was the first great organizer on a large scale of the Christian church in England.

Theodore arrived in 669 accompanied by the wise and supportive

Hadrian, an ex-abbot from Italy who had refused the archbishopric for himself and had recommended Theodore. The two of them promptly visited all parts of England and were gladly welcomed and listened to by all. Confidence in the new head of the English church was rapidly and permanently established. He could claim to be the first of the archbishops 'whom the whole English Church consented to obey'.[4]

Both the men were extremely learned, and they promoted learning by their teaching as they travelled around, and by establishing a first rate school at Canterbury, which was a pinnacle of intellectual culture in the early Middle Ages. By what they, and Wilfrid, accomplished, they made possible a most impressive and widespread efflorescence of learning, manuscript illumination and church building.

Theodore rendered no greater service to the church in England than his re-structuring of the diocesan system, and the infusion of new life into it. He, more perhaps than any other person, set the church firmly on the road to comprehensive diocesan pastoral cover. And he started on this work soon after he took up his onerous duties, as he gave it top priority in his agenda. He boldly conducted a shrewd re-organization of dioceses and monasteries, so that there was a more efficient evangelistic and pastoral provision for all the kingdoms. When he took up his work in England Christianity was established in all but one of the English kingdoms, but it had a very precarious formal structure. There were a mere seven dioceses, three of which were unoccupied. In only two of those which were occupied was the bishop canonically unobjectionable. By 690 there were thirteen or fourteen bishoprics, and Theodore's immediate successor added three or four more.

On his arrival in England Theodore also found uncertainty and inconsistency in the principle for determining the extent and nature of episcopal provision. This hinged on whether dioceses should be large or small and whether there should be one or more dioceses for each of the Anglo-Saxon kingdoms. There was confusion about the authority and jurisdiction of even the small number of bishops in post when he embarked on his archiepiscopacy. It was not clear whether Wilfrid or Chad should be Bishop of the Northumbrians. Chad had been appointed Bishop of York in 664 by King Oswy, but Wilfrid had already been nominated to the see of York by Oswy's son. There was one bishop for the East Angles, one at Rochester, none in Mercia, and only the simoniac, Wine, in Wessex. Theodore acted promptly and decisively. He made Chad Bishop of the Mercians with a see at Lichfield; he consecrated Eleutherius from Gaul as Bishop of the West

Saxons, with his see in the *civitas* of Winchester; and he confirmed Wilfrid in the see of York.

He called a synod at Hertford in 672 and proposed the further division of these large dioceses. The gathering brought together such bishops as Bisi of the East Angles, Wilfrid through his two legates, Putta of Rochester and Leutherius of the East Saxons, and Wynfrith, Chad's successor, of the Mercians. But he encountered divided opinion on the thorny question of the bishoprics. This entailed a face to face conflict of attitude between Theodore and Bishop Wilfrid. Theodore proposed that more bishoprics should be created as the number of Christians multiplied, but Wilfrid resisted the division of existing dioceses. Although much time was given to discussion of the matter, no firm conclusion was reached. As we will see, the clash of views rumbled on for many years, although Theodore's policy ultimately and, with the later changes in the number and distribution of Christians, perhaps inevitably, prevailed. But in the interim the archbishop bided his time, and awaited opportunities to move in the direction he was convinced was right for the church. 'When Bishop Bisi of the East Angles became too ill and feeble to object, he divided his diocese into two. When Wilfrid was exiled from Northumbria in 678 he promptly divided his diocese into three, and then, in 681, into five.'[5]

Theodore adopted definite principles in all this diocesan reorganization. In essence two guidelines were crucial: all dioceses should relate to the distribution of the population, and there should be a scrupulous regard for political or tribal divisions. Thus, East Anglia was divided into sees based on Elmham and Dunwich; in Mercia, in addition to Lichfield, dioceses were created at Hereford, to focus on the Magonsaetan, at Worcester, to serve the Hwicce, and at Leicester to minister largely to the Middle Angles; and in Northumbria episcopal oversight was apportioned carefully between Bernicia, with a see at Lindisfarne, Deira, with the bishopric at York, and Lindsey, with a see presumably at Lincoln.

In some if not all of the new diocesan areas the British church may have been quietly at work in the sub-Roman period, so that the newly established Anglo-Saxon dioceses were not, as it were, founded upon virgin territory and in a sea of heathenism. This is well illustrated by the area around Worcester. The Anglo-Saxon diocese of Worcester was established in 679 or 680. When the first Anglo-Saxon Bishop of the Hwicce arrived, he found a place which was already an important Christian centre. The minster established there took over from a well established British church, which was probably a diocese serving a wide rural hinterland.[6]

Theodore exhibited tact and humility as well as firmness, resolve and courage in the whole range of his policies and actions, so that he was able to remain loyal to Rome and the papacy, and yet harness much of the somewhat alienated Irish church tradition into a co-ordinated Christian work throughout the land. As we have seen, the Synod of Whitby had not secured the triumph of Roman authority in England. It was, both in the short, medium and long-term, a pivotal gathering, but it was primarily an affair of the Northumbrian church at a time when Northumbrian political power was beginning to wane. Some of the advocates of allegiance to Rome were notably undiplomatic in their attempts to promote their views, and thereby ruffled many feathers. Wilfrid had asserted in his characteristically strident and abrasive way that papal authority should be recognized as far more comprehensive and complete than was generally acceptable; and he had even suggested that conformity with the Roman dating of Easter was not just a matter of discipline but also one of faith. And he was outdone in the un-equivocal enunciation of papalism by his Irish friend Aldhelm, abbot of Malmesbury, who expressed doubt whether those who did not observe the Roman Easter, and thus spurned the decree and doctrinal mandate of the apostle Peter and his church, could enter the kingdom of God. The moderation and diplomacy of Theodore was therefore a boon in obtaining a measure of consensus.

Despite the lack of agreement over diocesan organization, the synod of 672 was an important step in securing concord and a sense of common aims. Basing himself on a *liber canonum* or 'book of canon law', Theodore gained the assent of the participants to ten canons covering many subjects, including practical issues such as marriage and divorce, as well as major matters on which the Irish belief or practice differed from that of Canterbury. It was the personality of Theodore which was crucial in effecting the measure of agreement which did emerge, and in handling sensitive problems of disagreement. It had been the personality of Gregory the Great, and his apostolic relationship to England, which had been so crucial in those vital years when Christianity was re-planted in England seventy years or so before. Now it was the personal qualities of Theodore in presenting the papal case which won the day. When the personal chemistry was absent, as with Augustine and the English bishops, apostolic authority counted for little.

The new archbishop also exercised a profound Christian influence on secular rulers. This, as with his other work, extended throughout the land. In the north he brought about a reconciliation between kings Ecgfrith and Ethelred after the battle of the Trent in 679, and persuaded them and their people not to engage in a war of vengeance. The ministry of making peace was vital for the life of the church. By such endeavours he was instrumental in providing a stable political framework for the work of the church. The comprehensive approach he adopted, which clearly encompassed both the political and ecclesiastical spheres, was one of the major contributions he made to the growth and wellbeing of the church. 'No action of Theodore was of greater importance at the time than the watch he kept over the bishops, their increase in number, and the peace he provided for them by the respect and affection he inspired in the various kings.'[7]

But he was also concerned with men of low estate; with the spiritual life and the religious practice and morality of ordinary monks, priests and lay people. This is shown in various ways, as with his *Penitential*: a list of penances for the failings of clerics and laymen, 'many of them the sins of rough and barbarous men in a rough and barbarous age'.[8] In issuing these he set his seal of authority on the Celtic system. The older system of penance in the Mediterranean countries was administered solely after a grave sin such as heresy and had no essential connection with pastoral care and the giving of spiritual counsel to ordinary people in their daily lives. In contrast, the Celtic abbot or priest regarded sin as a sickness of the soul which occurred all the time, and for which both penance and salutary counsel were necessary. The *Penitential* was an endorsement of this view, and a further measure of the deep pastoral concern of this remarkable archbishop.

Bede regarded Theodore's time as the climax of magnificent days for the English church:

> Never had there been such happy times since the English first came to Britain; for having such brave Christian kings, they were a terror to all the barbarian nations, and the desires of all men were set on the joys of the heavenly kingdom of which they had only lately heard; while all who wished for instruction in sacred studies had teachers ready to hand.[9]

There is little doubt that Theodore, and indeed his two immediate successors, exercised greater authority than Canterbury was ever to possess again.[10] Certainly there was the papal power in the background, with instructions from the pope, and this was supplemented by the all-important fact that for most of his reign he was working through diocesans of his own appointment.[11] Nevertheless, it needed a man of the right stature and with the appropriate characteristics to accomplish what Theodore did. This was especially so in view of the political chaos of the time, most serious in the south where the archbishop was based. After the death of Cenwahl control of Wessex was shared by a number of minor kings for about ten years until in 685 Caedwalla secured mastery of the kingdom; there were then West Saxon raids on Sussex by Caedwalla carried on by King Ine. To promote the work of the church in the prevailing conditions of late seventh-century England called for ability of a high order. It was well for the English church that at such a critical juncture such a man as Theodore was placed at the helm.

Wilfrid

Theodore had a winsomeness which captured the hearts and evoked the loyalty of many, and he was a healer in the widest sense in addition to all his other attributes. This was not so with Wilfrid. He was one of the most powerful churchmen of the seventh century; but his role in the affairs of the church was dictated by the forcefulness of his character, and the uncompromising way he pursued the aims which he set himself. 'The discreet silences of Bede, and the protestations of his own monk and biographer, Eddius, have both, in their different ways, helped to detract from the saint's reputation.' He is not portrayed as a lovable and attractive character as is the case with almost all the other Christian leaders of the sixth and seventh centuries. Even dispassionate historians 'find the apparently self-centred litigiousness, the pomp and circumstance, and the crusading energy of the man unattractive'.[12] I think such an assessment of his character, with the stress laid upon negative and unappealing traits, although to an extent justified, runs the risk of belittling the achievements of a man of remarkable spiritual stature who was outstanding as an evangelist, church and monastery planter, and promoter of those beliefs concerning the gospel and church matters about which he felt so passionately. He was engaged in controversy, but this was an age when anyone of such dynamic character and convictions was liable to encounter confrontation with those who dissented from his views. It was an age which called for the forthright proclamation of the Christian faith, and he played a most valuable part in forwarding Christianity in various parts of England as well as on the continent. It may be unfortunate that he caused considerable disturbance to a range of people in achieving what he did; but it is arguably a price which, in retrospect, was worth paying in view of the good he did for the church, and for the nation he served.

One of the victims of the plague which caused such havoc after the Synod of Whitby was Tuda, the Bishop of Lindisfarne, who had been appointed when Colman had withdrawn because of the Whitby decision. Wilfrid was chosen to replace him, and was consecrated in Gaul in order to avoid any question of the validity of his orders, for he could not have found three British bishops to perform the ceremony whom he would have regarded as innocent both of simony and schism. He went to Gaul 'in great state', and was consecrated by at least twelve Catholic bishops in a service of pomp where, as the Gaulish tradition demanded, 'he was borne into the oratory aloft on a golden throne by the bishops alone, to the accompaniment of songs and canticles from the choir'.[13] It is unclear whether he was initially appointed to Lindisfarne or York, although it does seem that he was intended to be bishop of all the Northumbrians, like his predecessors, but with his see at York.

It was not long before he was engaged in a serious controversy which was of fundamental importance for the whole organization of the English church in his generation and for the future, and which set the tone for much of his remaining long life. It was all to do with the diocesan policy and actions of archbishop Theodore, which I have briefly described. After allowance has been made for exaggeration and undue adulation by his biographer Eddius Stephanus, episcopal might stands out as a characteristic of Wilfrid. Wherever he went he seems to have loomed large as a personality, as an episcopal authority, and as an enricher of buildings and estates. In the years 669 to 671 he restored his episcopal church at York, supplied it with liturgical vessels, acquired vast tracts of land for the church, and attracted valuable endowments.[14] At Ripon, in the years 671 to 678, he constructed a church 'of dressed stone, supported with columns and complete with side aisles'.[15] At Hexham he built a church of deep foundations, 'crypts of beautifully dressed stone, the vast structure supported by columns of various styles and with numerous side-aisles, the walls of remarkable height and length, the many winding passages and spiral staircases leading up and down'. It was, says Eddius in his enthusiasm, such a place that he and his contemporaries had 'never heard of its like this side of the Alps'.[16] Wilfrid's sphere of ecclesiastical jurisdiction was also enlarged as a result of great victories gained by King Ecgfrith over the Picts and over Mercia which extended the territories under Northumbrian control.

All of this was broadly within the concept of dignity, grandeur and political influence in public activities combined with a certain monastic simplicity in private life, which the Gaulish church held out as the ideal balance for a bishop. But it was somewhat at variance in its emphasis, if not in conflict, with the ideas of the episcopal office which Theodore shared with Pope Gregory the Great. They acknowledged the need for a bishop to maintain a certain external appearance, and not to be so humble and self-deprecating that he lost authority in restraining and disciplining those under him. But he should not be indulgent in outward show in order to gratify his own sense of self-importance. He should always stress his evangelistic and pastoral function and be alert to the danger of growing spiritually cold amidst external works for want of humility or the fire of contemplation. Theodore thought that the bishops trained in the Irish tradition, and in the tradition of St Martin of Tours, who insisted on going round on foot, had neglected their external dignity; and they had to be made to ride on horses. The Gaulish tradition was at the other pole, and it contained the pitfall of excessive stress on externals. It was in keeping with their shared episcopal ideal, that both Gregory and Theodore greatly favoured small dioceses. It all amounted to two pastoral concepts; and the two protagonists in England were Theodore and Wilfrid.

In 678 King Ecgfrith quarrelled with Wilfrid, and enlisted the support of Theodore, who, as we have noted, took advantage of the situation to further his plans for the division of over-large dioceses. The archbishop consecrated three new bishops for Northumbria. The affronted Wilfrid set off to appeal to the pope. On the way to Rome he spent the winter of 678–79 preaching the gospel to the heathen in Frisia. A council presided over by Pope Agatho decided in Wilfrid's favour; so he returned in 680 with papal letters designed to effect his reinstatement in the see of York. King Ecgfrith disregarded these and refused to restore Wilfrid. Instead he flung him into prison for nine months. He was released in 681 on condition that he left Northumbria.

He spent most of his subsequent five years of exile in Sussex preaching to the heathen and founding a monastery at Selsey, but he also spent time in Wessex where he was active and effective in the conversion of the inhabitants of the Isle of Wight.

With the death in battle of King Ecgfrith in 685, Wilfrid and Theodore were reconciled, and the new king of Northumbria, Aldfrith,

allowed Wilfrid to return as bishop of York in late 686 or early 687.
The diocese was much diminished as York was the seat of the bishopric
of Deira alone; Bernicia was divided between the bishoprics of
Lindisfarne, then under Cuthbert, and Hexham. After administering the
see for about five years, the king quarrelled with Wilfrid and he was
again expelled. In his extended exile we hear of him in Mercia, East
Anglia and Kent, but little is known of his activities. In about 703 King
Aldfrith declared his intention of ruining Wilfrid by depriving his
churches and monasteries of all their endowments. In an appeal to
Rome, Pope John VI upheld Wilfrid's case. Shortly afterwards Aldrith
died and his successor Osred allowed Wilfrid back to Northumbria and
to the custody of his monasteries. Although he seems to have spent the
last four years of his life in the northern kingdom, he died at one of his
Mercian monasteries, Oundle, in 709.[17]

In addition to the varied and substantial achievements to which
reference has been made in this brief biographical sketch, the church in
England is indebted to Wilfrid for his part in eradicating the Irish teaching about the reckoning of Easter and the shape of the tonsure. Lastly,
in this catalogue of significant works, in a short passage Eddius pinpointed two unobtrusive acts which help to give Wilfrid a permanent
place in English church history: his introduction of a method of
chanting which was in accordance with the practice of the primitive
church, and the establishment in England of the rule of St Benedict.

Clearly this volatile yet able man played a massive part in an
evolving church; and his talents were immense. 'But his abilities were
thwarted by his identification of his own interests with the cause of
religious order, and for all his insistence on the universal authority of
the Roman church he remained essentially an individualist.'[18] He 'was
an excellent example of how not to succeed in the political and ecclesiastical world of the seventh century when an accommodating and com-
promising disposition together with guile and a flair for skilful intrigue
were prerequisites for professional or personal survival. It was only by
great strength of character that Wilfrid weathered the vicissitudes of ill-
fortune.'[19]

But no account of the church in England in the seventh century
should diminish the part Wilfrid played in almost every aspect of its life.
He was querulous and difficult. 'But he was also monastic founder and
missionary, a builder and an art-patron of considerable importance. Of
his greatness as a pioneer in many fields there cane be no doubt.'[20]

St Cuthbert

When we move from Wilfrid to St Cuthbert we are confronted with contrasts rather than likenesses. Here, despite his commitment to Roman practices, we are aware of the Celtic, and more especially the Irish, monastic tradition rather than the Roman ecclesiastical system; we are conscious of a life confined largely to one geographical area and a fairly circumscribed round of spiritual exercises, pastoral, teaching and healing ministry, and the general avoidance of controversy. The life of Cuthbert is presented to us as that of personal dedication and holiness, in the steps of St Columba and St Aidan, in which personal piety is to the fore, and the world of ecclesiastical politics and activity recedes into the background.

There is little to relate of the events of Cuthbert's life. He was born in Northumbria in about 634. In 651 he became a monk at Melrose. He remained there, except for a brief time at the short-lived colony of Melrose at Ripon, until 664 when he moved to Lindisfarne or Holy Island where he became prior of the community. Approximately eleven years later he went to live as a hermit on Farne Island, roughly seven miles south of Lindisfarne and about a mile and a half from the mainland. In 684, and much against his will, he was chosen Bishop of Lindisfarne, and he was consecrated the following year at York. In 687 he foresaw his death and retired to Farne Island where he died on 20 March.

The character and life of Cuthbert have caught people's imagination for untold ages. It is the fascination of the man who rode armed to the monastery of Melrose after having resolved to become a monk; the paradox of the Anglo-Saxon who was schooled in the traditions of Irish Christianity, but who acquired prominence in the church after the Whitby prohibition of certain Irish practices, at a time when influences from Rome and Gaul were making themselves felt. And there has always been the intriguing story of the out-going pastor who was irresistibly drawn to the solitary life, and who interspersed service as monk, prior and bishop with an extended period as a hermit, and finally went to his much-loved hermitage to die.

Even after making allowance for the excesses of hagiographers, it does seem that Cuthbert impressed his contemporaries with his exceptional sanctity, the quality of his life and his powers which went far beyond the normal, or indeed the natural. He made many predictions of events which seem to have occurred as he had forecast, he appears to have healed a host of individuals from various ailments, and he showed by his style of life and behaviour that he was not only a man of prayer, but had a close affinity with the natural world. One example, as told by Bede, captures something of this.

> He was in the habit of rising at the dead of night, while everyone else was sleeping, to go out and pray, returning just in time for morning prayers. One night one of the monks watched him creep out, then followed him stealthily to see where he was going and what he was about. Down he went towards the beach beneath the monastery and out into the sea until he was up to his arms and neck in deep water. The splash of the waves accompanied his vigil throughout the dark hours of the night. At daybreak he came out, knelt down on the sand, and prayed. Then two otters bounded out of the water, stretched themselves out before him, warmed his feet with their breath, and tried to dry him on their fur. They finished, receiving his blessing, and slipped back to their watery home. He was soon home and was in choir at the proper time with the rest of the monks.[21]

In his dress and means of travelling he did not infringe the standards which Gregory the Great and Theodore recommended. 'He wore quite ordinary clothes, neither remarkably neat nor noticeably slovenly.'[22] In common with the Irish at that time, he had a more Roman image of episcopal dignity than many of his predecessors. Although he often walked he did not have the same concern as Aidan or Chad to avoid horseback.[23] His magnificent pectoral cross, which was placed on his breast when he was buried, is an extant testimony that the monks at his death, and presumably he during his life, did not consider such superb external ornateness to be inappropriate as a sign of his authority.

Cuthbert was also remarkable for the legacy he left, and the posthumous history of miracles which reputedly occurred at Lindisfarne after his burial there.[24] In 698 it is said that the monks exhumed his body and found it to be incorrupt. This was a sign of sanctity which was claimed for a number of saints. The body was reburied in a new coffin and it was claimed that further miracles occurred. After the anonymous *Life* of the saint, and then Bede's *Life*, were issued, a cult was born. Its devotees included members of the Northumbrian royal family, one of whom, Ceolwulf, retired to Cuthbert's monastery when he resigned the kingdom in 737. Cuthbert acquired something of the status of a patron saint of Northumbria.

Bede

I have not included Bede among the prominent churchmen of his day, because he was not to the same extent as those just considered engaged in the life, politics and organization of ecclesiastical affairs. But, of course he was, and has remained, in some ways the pre-eminent Christian of that generation. His name lives because of his abiding contribution to literature, and most particularly because of his monumental *Ecclesiastical History*.

Little is known about his life; nothing beyond what he casually mentions in his *History*. He was born in 672 or 673, somewhere in the region of Wearmouth and Jarrow. When he was seven, he was given into the care of Benedict Biscop, the former soldier turned monk who had founded the monastery at Wearmouth in 674. After the sister-house of Jarrow was established about 681, Bede was transferred there, under the care of Ceolfrith. Soon afterwards a plague struck, and all the twenty-four or so inmates died, except for Ceolfrith and one little boy, who is presumed to have been Bede. He remained as a student at Jarrow for the rest of his youth. A measure of his distinction as a scholar and monk is his ordination to the diaconate at the age of nineteen, six years before the canonical age. He was ordained priest in 703. For the remaining thirty-two years of his life he was a typical scholar-monk; except that he was so outstanding. His spiritual life was marked by constancy in devotion; and his academic life by an outpouring of commentaries, or exegesis, on books of the Bible; works on biblical chronology; hagiography, of which the most famous are his *History of the Abbots* of Wearmouth and Jarrow and his *Life of St Cuthbert*; moral treatises; and, most significantly for future generations, the *Ecclesiastical History of the English Nation*.

Aldhelm

Although not equal in significance for the church in his own time as Theodore, Wilfrid and Cuthbert, or as important in the long-term as Bede, Aldhelm still deserves a place of honour in any review of this period.[25] He was the first Anglo-Saxon to exhibit profound learning, and he just pre-dates the Venerable Bede. He was born in 639, a kinsman of the West Saxon royal family. At the time of his birth the missionary bishop Birinus had been preaching in his home kingdom for several years. Aldhelm was about eleven when Birinus died in 650, so that he may have remembered something of his mission, and may even have been influenced by it.

His education included a period in the 660s at Malmesbury monastery, possibly the finest educational institution in Britain, and a time in the 670s at Canterbury under Hadrian. In 661 he took monastic vows. He received the tonsure from the abbot, Maelduib; and in about 674 or 675 he succeeded him as abbot of Malmesbury. During his thirty years in that capacity he replaced Maelduib's simple church, probably built mainly of timber, with a larger and finer church of stone.

Aldhelm established himself as one of the leading Anglo-Saxon churchmen, and founded other monasteries, possibly at Wareham and Frome, and at Bradford-on-Avon. His complex, extremely flamboyant Latin style of writing is difficult to read, and his two most ambitious treatises, one in verse and the other in prose, were in praise of virginity, which does not encourage their translation for modern readers. He may have been acclaimed as a most important source for the ecclesiastical history of England had he not been overshadowed by Bede.

For the last four years of his life he was also bishop of Sherborne, and he carried out his duties with diligence. But it was the monastery which commanded his first and greatest love, and he remained its abbot until his death in 709.

One thing common to all the lives I have considered was a deep respect for literary, artistic, architectural and educational matters. And, of course they all contributed greatly to one or more of these aspects of English cultural life. What was achieved from about the middle of the seventh century to the mid-eighth century in the development of learning and literature was quite remarkable.

> Within a hundred years England had become the home of a Christian culture which influenced the whole development of letters and learning in western Europe. The greatest historical work of the early middle ages had been written in a northern monastery, and English poets had begun to give a permanent form to heroic traditions. There is nothing in European history closely parallel to this sudden development of a civilization by one of the most primitive peoples established within the ancient Roman empire.[26]

And, of course, this flowering of culture and learning was almost entirely confined to Christian circles, and more especially to the monasteries.

The decades after the death of Bede

Bede died in 735. Many historians have regarded the period after his death 'as an age of increasing degeneration in the English Church'.[27] I think that the picture has frequently been painted in too dark and gloomy colours, and that the situation was not as dire as it has commonly been depicted. I concur with the assessment of D. J. V. Fisher. He conceded that in the period from the death of Bede to the time of the Danish invasions the church in England could not boast of any spectacular achievement and no outstanding figure. Nonetheless, a good deal was done which consolidated the work of the saints of the conversion era.

> The Danish invasion was a catastrophe and a challenge. By its disruption of the organization of the Church over much of England, the supply of clergy was endangered; by its destruction of the greatest of the monasteries, the most impressive monuments of Christianity were annihilated. But because by the third quarter of the ninth century Christianity was firmly rooted in the social order of England the challenge was answered, the conquerors rapidly converted, and a very real danger was not allowed to materialize. Much of the credit for this considerable achievement must surely be given to the men who had been engaged upon the work of the Church in the years before invasion.[28]

The Danes were not only quite speedily won to the Christian faith, but they soon provided dignitaries of the highest rank for the church, such as Oda of Canterbury and Oscytel of York. Monasticism was, for whatever combination of reasons, largely a spent force by the time the Danes arrived and settled in the country, so it was not a powerful source of witness to the new heathen immigrants. In addition, there was apparently no concerted and organized attempt to Christianize the Danelaw, with missionaries assigned to the work, so presumably the task was undertaken by the rank and file of the church. This speaks well of the church, for it could hardly have been either thoroughly corrupt, or in an advanced stage of decay, let alone almost extinct, if it achieved what was a quite remarkable feat of evangelism.

The widely-held view that the church in the period from the death of Bede to the Danish invasions and settlement was in decline and in a moribund state rests upon rather scattered pieces of evidence. These are chiefly Boniface's letter to Ethelbald of Mercia, and Bede's to Ecgbert of

York. In his letter[29] written shortly before his death, Bede complained to Bishop Ecgbert, who later became Archbishop of York, that he was greatly concerned about signs of deterioration in the monasteries. He asserted that some sham monasteries had been founded by men who had no true religious motive, but merely wanted to free their lands from military service and other secular burdens. These monasteries were ruled by laymen, and they were, according to Bede, filled with renegade monks from genuine monasteries, or with the tonsured retainers of the lay abbot. On the other hand there were insufficient bishops to allow for the universal practice of an episcopal visit by each bishop to all his diocese every year.

The period under review was not renowned for any king who promoted Christianity within his kingdom or further afield, which had been a feature of the fruitful early decades of the seventh century, and this was a major handicap for the church. The foremost and most remarkable king, Offa of Mercia, apparently lacked benevolence towards the church, and by his divisive and brash ecclesiastical policy caused confusion and dismay.

A critical and pessimistic view of the post-Bedan century is also conveyed later in the letters of Alcuin with their gloomy picture of England, and more especially of the church. And in a the letter of 808 to Charlemagne, Leo III deplored the hostility in the north between King Eardwulf and his archbishop Eanbald and in the south between King Cenwulf of Mercia and Archbishop Wulfred.

All of this amounts to an apparently degenerate church, with few redeeming features. But caution is called for in making any sweeping statements. What is clear is that in such a long period there were inevitably variations in standards and quality of life for any institution, and the church was no exception. Retrogression and reform, atrophy and advance, could alternate more than once, and also from one region to another. To interpret the whole history of the century or so after 735 from evidence which applies to only a part of the time or country can be most misleading. The golden age of Jarrow during the decades after its foundation may not have been a golden age for the whole church in England. To write of the 'church in England' as a unified entity at this time is unprofitable and deceptive. The churches were still localized, even tribal, and there was often a great difference between the churches north and south of the Humber.

For Northumbria, which can be taken as the barometer for the northern church, the latter half of the eighth century was marked by political upheavals. This made the task of the church more difficult, but there is no clear indication that the church shared fully in Northumbria's decline as a political power. With the restoration of a greater measure of political stability after the return from exile of King Eardwulf in 802, and with some seemingly effective bishops, there was a period when the church appears at least to have been stable if not especially vigorous. This was brought to a sudden and dramatic end in the middle of the century with the renewal of civil discord, and the reappearance of kings who despoiled the church of its possessions.

In the south we are faced with a much more confusing and kaleidoscopic political situation which produced instability and uncertainty, and a not very helpful environment for the church. Mercia and Wessex are the key kingdoms, and Offa the most prominent and important king. Although his liberality to the church is acknowledged, his interference in its affairs has attracted much criticism. But Alcuin had a different view. He rebuked him for his personal vices, but he considered that these were more than balanced by the service he rendered to the church by the establishment and maintenance of a firm peace which was so favourable to its mission. He is most severely condemned for his creation of the archbishopric of Lichfield.

The reign of Offa of Mercia (757–96) represented 'a turning point in English history'.[30] Never before had there been such a decisive and determined attempt to go beyond the traditional powers of an overlord, or bretwalda, by a systematic suppression of subject kingdoms, and an attempt to exercise direct rule over them. 'Offa's policies posed more challenging and dangerous problems for the archbishops and community of Canterbury than they had to face hitherto.'[31]

These difficulties were political and ecclesiastical. The new king of Mercia was determined to rule Kent in person. He took a proprietary attitude to the churches and monasteries of Kent, and his hunger for land hazarded the grants of earlier kings. He 'sought to establish his own line as a hereditary monarchy imbued with religious symbolism through a ceremonial anointing', and he 'planned to create at Canterbury's expense a new midland province of the English church with a metropolitan see at Lichfield'. The threat of this to the existing and established church order was intensified by the fact that Offa exercised unparalleled influence in the courts of Charlemagne and of the pope. 'Offa's ambitions brought the archbishop and the church of Canterbury willy-nilly into the centre of the political stage.'[32] Offa's actions did not spring from hostility to the church, or a cynical indifference to its well-being. He probably regarded what he did as political necessity.

In 786 two papal legates arrived in England, possibly as a result of pressure by Offa on the pope. It is very likely that they were agents in the radical proposal to divide the province of Canterbury, although there is no mention of this in their extant report. Within a year of their visit a new archbishopric had been established at Lichfield, and the pope endorsed this action by dispatching a *pallium* to the appointee, Bishop Hygeberht. Although it is not clear how the bishoprics were apportioned between the two provinces, the arrangement was clearly an insult to the see of Canterbury.

Inadvertently, however, the action may have strengthened the position, and accentuated the honour, status and authority of Canterbury, and cemented its acceptance as the primacy, because the new arrangement only lasted for sixteen years. The archbishopric of Lichfield was abolished by the Council of Clofesho held in 803/4. The reassertion by the Council of the standing of the Canterbury primacy was underscored by the dropping at that time of a scheme for an archbishopric of London. The failure of these schemes and counter-schemes left Canterbury more secure than it might otherwise have been. Later, when the political unification of England was accomplished under West Saxon rather than Mercian kings, there was no question of a challenge to the metropolitan status of Canterbury.

Such acceptance of the ecclesiastical authority of Canterbury had far-reaching consequences. The ramifications were not confined to the sphere of religion. It was a factor of the first importance, if not the single most significant element, in creating a sense of shared 'Englishness'. The remarkable development of English communal identity 'drew its strength from spiritual ideals rather than political realities'.[33] It was not planned or foreseen by most of those concerned, but it happened as if it had been intended. 'Like so much else in the history of the church of Canterbury, the fostering of a concept of an English nation may best be understood as an accidental legacy of Pope Gregory and the hierarchical structure he inspired, rather than as a deliberate creation of the archbishops of Canterbury.'[34]

The close linkage between politics and religion, between the state and the church, in this age is graphically illustrated by this series of events. It is also demonstrated in the way that after the collapse of Offa's political system in the months following his death, some of the kingdoms he suppressed broke away, and in the words of the *Anglo-Saxon*

Chronicle, Bishops Ceolwulf of Lindsey and Eadbald of London who had been intimately associated with the former political regime 'left the country'.[35] The attempt of a powerful king to intrude in the affairs of the church had been a manifest and dismal failure. The message was plain, that for the benefit of both, the state and the church should work together in harmony. Their interests were so frequently identical, or they at least overlapped sufficiently, that mutual co-operation was the wisest course of action in most circumstances. The way the church had developed, for good or ill, meant that it could not disengage itself from politics; and neither could the king treat the church in a cavalier manner.

'As Christianity took root, the church was integrated into political structures where the king already occupied the dominant position. Bishoprics might be seen as part of the resources of royal power.' The interests of the king and of the church were increasingly seen as inextricably interwoven. 'Dioceses and kingdoms were coterminous: the possession of a see appeared to mark a certain royal rank for a kingdom, and conversely the absence of one, political dependence.'[36] As in so many things, Archbishop Theodore had helped to accelerate this linkage. It was, for instance, during his archiepiscopacy that functions formerly exercised by kings, such as the selection and deposition of bishops, were placed in the hands of the primate. Of course the transfer of power was not achieved instantly and without considerable tension. It was a somewhat tortuous redefinition of areas of responsibility. There were many frustrating reverses, as for example Theodore's inability to fully implement his policy of creating more sees, but the trend was becoming ever more apparent.

Theodore's authority had also stretched north and south of the great political, and not infrequently ecclesiastical, boundary of the Humber. So, a re-alignment of authority had been supplemented by its geographical extension and consolidation. There was the complication that the archbishop's suffragans were the bishops of many different kingdoms, and they owed allegiance both to their local king and to their archbishop, but this was a situation which only helped to tease out the implications of a national identity which was slowly but surely being forged. The establishment in 735 of a new archdiocese at York, which was not a rival to the primacy of Canterbury, was a further step in the direction of a unified church and nation.

In the half century or so after Offa's death in 796, there was not the same dominance of the political scene by one king, and Mercia and

Wessex shared power. It was a time of mixed fortunes for the southern church. There were unfortunate situations, as with the quarrel between Cenwulf and Wulfred, but also encouraging developments such as the reuniting of the bishoprics of Dunwich and Elmham, the reform of his cathedral clergy by Wulfred, and the holding of the important Council of Chelsea in 816, which addressed some of the issues and problems facing the church of the day.

Such a concern to redress its own shortcomings had been evident in the church throughout the entire period from 735 to the time of the Danish invasions. It made some genuine attempts to put its house in order. Thus, when it was confronted by what it conceded was the well-founded criticisms of Bede and others, it readily and promptly addressed them. In 747, the Archbishop of Canterbury held a synod at Clofesho, probably near London. From this came a number of requirements for the improvement of pastoral oversight and the tightening of discipline within the church. Bishops were to conduct a visitation of their dioceses once a year. They were also to ensure that there was no monastery without a priest to care for the spiritual wellbeing of the inmates. Other clauses required that both monks and nuns should lead a quiet *regular* life, and observe the seven canonical hours. They were to shun showy clothing in imitation of laymen; and they were particularly to be on their guard against drunkenness. Monasteries were to be retained as places of silence, and they were not to be the homes of poets, musicians and comedians; laymen were not to be tonsured, nor were they to be admitted to monasteries unless their fitness had been proved.

Forty years later, in 786–87, at provincial assemblies called by visiting papal legates in Northumbria and at Celcythe, measures of reform were agreed which provided, *inter alia*, for half-yearly synods and yearly visitations by bishops, for episcopal supervision over the elections of abbots, for tithes, and for the up-rooting of paganism. A novel and more significant feature of these gatherings was the decree that, while monks and nuns should live regularly according to their Rule, the secular clergy of collegiate churches, who were, for the first time, called canons, should live 'canonically', that is, according to the canons of the church.

These councils, and these various resolutions and actions, imply that there were serious problems in the church in these post-Bedan decades; but they also shows that the church was alert enough to recognize and respond to them. Bede, Boniface and Alcuin remonstrated against the slackness, avarice and worldliness of bishops, but no extreme measures were required as in Gaul where, in the sixth century, it was deemed necessary for a bishop to be attended day and night by two of his clergy to watch over his moral conduct. Neither are there recorded scandals such as that of the Bishop of Bordeaux, who it was said kept a harem in his palace. In the Gallic church evil-livers bribed their way into bishoprics, and some called themselves bishops and abbots who in fact remained soldiers, wearing a military cloak, and being girt with a sword. The conclusion of R. H. Hodgkin stands:

> Thus, looking at the evidence against the English Church as a whole, the prima facie case for its condemnation is not very serious. There is a loss of position when comparison is made between England and the Continent, because the Frankish Church at this time made a rapid advance – thanks largely to the work of Boniface and the hundreds of other Englishmen who followed him to the Continent, thanks also to Alcuin, and still more to the fortunate series of great rulers who succeeded one another in the Carolingian family. There is in England an apparent dearth of saints and kings pre-eminent in piety such as the seventh century had produced. There are no spiritual conquests of the few to set against the dead level of the many. But where our knowledge is almost blank, it is idle to lay stress on deficiencies.[37]

Education, literature, manuscripts and charters

Some achievements of the English church were continuous and substantial throughout the hundred and fifty years from the Synod of Whitby to the beginning of the Danish invasions, and were not unduly affected by political disturbance. For one thing the tradition of learning was maintained. In this respect special mention should be made of growth rather than decay at York, and a healthy rival to this at Worcester. Then there were the magnificent upright stone crosses of Northumbria, which unite Irish and Mediterranean features, the most famous of which are those at Ruthwell and Bewcastle; and there is evidence that Mercia and Kent, thanks largely, no doubt, to the strong lead of Ethelbald and Offa, blossomed in learning in a remarkable way. There was also the nascence of English poetry associated with Caedmon, which was perpetuated by Cynewulf, a Northumbrian or Mercian, who appears to have flourished in the latter half of the eighth century or early in the ninth century. Vernacular poetry may have included poems such as *Genesis*, *Exodus* and *Daniel* which were in manuscripts compiled in about the year 1000, but with the poems themselves almost certainly written before the Danish invasions. The *Dream of the Rood* was composed early in the eighth century.[38] Both Caedmon and Cynewulf were churchmen, and the close identity of all branches of learning with the church is ample testimony to its influence in this sphere of life.

There was the prolific and qualitatively astonishing output from the monastic *scriptoria*. Some remarkably produced copies of all or parts of the Bible appeared in the seventh and eighth centuries; masterpieces of illumination. There was the copy of the four Gospels given to the church at Ripon by Wilfrid, which is a splendid manuscript, written in letters of gold on purple-dyed parchment, with a gold case set with precious gems to contain it. The Lichfield Gospels also attest to the superlative quality of such works. And, as a further example, there was the Lindisfarne Gospels, which was a blend of Irish and Mediterranean influences. It was possibly the work of Bishop Eadfrith of Lindisfarne between 698 and 721. The text is of Mediterranean origin, but it is written in an Irish half-uncial hand and the portraits of the evangelists are strongly influenced by Italian models. The decoration is a combining of Celtic spirals, Irish illuminated capitals and decorated 'carpet' page with Germanic ornaments and interlace.[39]

Of course the monasteries were responsible for most of the educational, literary and artistic magnificence of the age. They were the focal points for every aspect of education, writing and art. They were the major patrons of the arts. The very buildings they occupied were examples of fine design and construction, unsurpassed in England; and internally they were outstanding for the richness and aesthetic splendour of their furniture, fittings and decoration. This is encapsulated in the surviving window glass from Jarrow. Liturgical items like the hoard of plate from Trewhiddle, St Austell, Cornwall, the Hexham chalice and the Ardagh chalice from County Limerick give some notion of the excellence of the craftsmanship and dedicated work of the age. Superb items buried with some of the most highly esteemed Christian dead indicate the incomparable quality of what was produced by the monasteries at their best.

Monumental works testify to the skill and fine artistic ability of Saxon stonemasons. Stone coffins, grave covers, standing crosses and pillars abound. Good examples of such work include the Northumbrian and Mercian running-scroll designs, with their copious birds and beasts, which can be seen at Morham, Lothian, Croft, North Yorkshire, and Breedon-on-the-Hill, Leicestershire. There is also the slightly later cross-shaft fragment from Dacre churchyard in Cumbria. In addition to such funerary monuments, there is a less profuse but equally significant collection of church furniture fragments. These include frontal panels of altars, as at Ohillack in Cornwall and Flotta in Orkney; solid stone shrine covers, as with the Hedda Stone at Peterborough Cathedral; side panels of slab-built shrines, a sample of which is the Pictish processional slab from Papil, Burra, Shetland; and thrones, as found in the Frith Stool, Hexham.

Additional and excellent examples of written material emanating from this period are the various, and often superbly produced, charters. These can be dated from about 670, and have been described as 'the most valuable records of the effect of Christianity on Anglo-Saxon society and politics'.[40] They graphically demonstrate the interplay of religion and politics, which we have noted as a feature of the period.

Local church life

Most of the people of England in the seventh and eighth centuries lived in the countryside. There were few towns, and these were mainly very small. In such a situation there were countless communities where there was no provision for Christian witness or worship. It was only by a slow and uneven process that the religious life of all English villages became centred upon a church served by a resident priest. Even by the late eighth century many communities with a large proportion of professing Christians lacked a purpose-built place of worship. It was all symptomatic of a church which was still in a pioneering mode and needed to be built up and established. Everything was on a small scale.

There has recently been a thorough revision of former views on the nature of Anglo-Saxon settlement. One aspect of this which is especially pertinent to church history because of its relationship to the development of pastoral oversight is the characteristic form taken by local rural communities. 'The traditional image of the stable Anglo-Saxon village as the direct ancestor of the mediaeval village is no longer tenable in view of growing evidence for settlement mobility in the early and middle Saxon periods. Indeed, it now appears that most "nucleated" mediaeval villages are not the direct successors of early, or even middle Saxon settlements, and that nucleation itself appears to be a remarkably late phenomenon.'[41] As the Anglo-Saxon period continued there seems to have been a splitting up of the early settlement areas and a concomitant spread of manorialism. 'We can see the emergence of large numbers of separate manors in the later Anglo-Saxon period, and (at a rather slower pace) of a parochial geography which mirrored the manorial one.'[42]

A series of local studies in recent years has raised the possibility that more may have been achieved in the seventh and eighth centuries in providing pastoral care for these evolving settlements than has previously been acknowledged.[43] The existence of superior or 'mother' churches is being recognized, and these exerted control over groups of lesser churches from the eleventh century onwards. It is surmised that such churches once served great 'proto-parishes' which are sometimes called *parochiae* by historians, from which the parishes of the lesser churches were formed. But several scholars have gone further, 'identifying the mother-churches with seventh and eighth-century *monasteria* or "minsters" staffed by pastorally active religious communities, and postulating that a network of "minster parishes" was established in each of the Anglo-Saxon kingdoms within two or three generations of conversion'.[44]

John Blair spells out the implications of such a development of minster churches not only in the sphere of church affairs, but more widely, and especially in relation to the growth and character of local communities:

> Four main hypotheses are offered. First, that in the seventh and eighth centuries most institutions to which the word *monasterium* was applied had their place in a coherent pastoral system, with territorial *parochiae* and responsibility for supporting a ministry within them. Secondly, that early minsters usually lay at some distance from their counterpart royal *villae*, often in Roman enclosures with the *villae* outside on open ground. Thirdly, that minsters are more important than royal *villae* in the origins of small towns, and that such 'minster towns' often show a distinctive topographical development. Fourthly, that centralized control was compatible with decentralized worship: the *parochiae* assimilated a class of heterogeneous and often older cult sites, controlled and served by the minster clergy, where baptism and burial sometimes continued to be practised through the seventh, eighth and ninth centuries.[45]

It seems that already in the seventh century there was a large lay population in England whose lives were profoundly affected by their dependence on minsters. It has been said that 'the conversion of the

English kingdoms was effected largely through the agency of the minsters or *monasteria*', and that this is 'beyond doubt'.[46] The land was almost certainly peppered with minsters. For instance, in Dorset a minster is known at Wimborne, but not known at a host of places whose names suggest such an institution, villages like Iwerne Minster, Charminster, Lychett Minster, Yetminster, Beaminster, Sturminster Marshall, and Sturminster Newton.[47]

The model of minster churches is, however, not without its problems.[48] Its most dubious element is the claim to universality; that it was to be found in all the Anglo-Saxon kingdoms. Insufficient attention has, perhaps, been paid to the different religious histories of individual provinces. Some, such as Sussex, were late in being converted, and were, in any case economically backward. Also, distinctions need to be made between large, wealthy and scholarly establishments such as Wearmouth and Jarrow and small, family houses like Withington in Gloucestershire. They should not all be treated as the same within the minster-network. The timetable for the creation of such a network is also open to question. It was not uniformly rapid with an invariable co-operation of kings and bishops. Such harmony was common, indeed usual, but it was not without exception. And there were also local initiatives such as that by Benedict Biscop, which I will be describing later in this chapter.

The model also implies that the need to provide pastoral care was the driving force behind the founding of monasteries. This may have been so in a few cases, as for example with the house at Breedon in Leicestershire, but in almost all foundations other motives were pre-eminent. Foremost was the concern of founders to win prayers for themselves and their kindred in this life and the next; but other even less worthy reasons seem to have come into the reckoning, such as the desire of some Northumbrian thegns to convert their households into monasteries in order to obtain the benefits of bookland tenure and long-term security of family ownership of the land.

These criticisms suggest not that the minster-model should be abandoned but that it should be applied with greater flexibility than hitherto. 'It seems unlikely that the system was created as uniformly and as quickly as has been suggested. The possibility of a slower development and later modifications should be considered.'[49]

In his topographical study of Surrey, Blair postulates that a number of mother churches were founded after the eighth century. As we will see in chapter 9, the ninth century may have been a crucial period in the

provision and organization of pastoral care, and this included a determined effort by bishops to draw the monasteries of their dioceses firmly
within their control.

In the valiant efforts of the church to provided pastoral care in an age
before the parish system had come into being, much had to be done with
sparse resources. Theodore allowed priests to say mass 'in the field'.
There were scattered standing crosses to mark the spots where services
of prayer were held, and where, perhaps, even a 'field church' had not
yet arisen. Believers must have gathered in the open-air in many areas
where there was not access to some form of church building.

Few parish churches of this period have left remains which can be
identified, but certain tentative suggestions concerning mid-Saxon
churches can be made. That at Escomb by the Middle Wear still stands
to bear witness both to the smallness and yet the simple and austere
dignity of the rare examples of stone-built places of worship. It is set in
a circular churchyard, and it has a tall, long nave and a stubby chancel.
It was largely built out of recycled Roman masonry. A good impression
of the original fenestration of such churches is conveyed by the five
minute windows set high up in the walls. But the apparent plain
simplicity of the building is somewhat deceptive; for excavations have
revealed that there were in its early days porticoes at the west end and
on the north side of the chancel. Escomb has achieved some fame, but
there were a number of other mid-Anglo-Saxon stone churches, albeit in
a minority compared with timber constructions.

It is also worthy of note that many of these appear to have been
superimposed on former Roman villas.[50] This is now reckoned to indicate a complex relationship between the two types of building which
goes beyond the mere proximity of reusable building materials. Use
certainly was made of the pre-existent structure. The later churches are
frequently found to be aligned upon the Roman building, with reuse
of some of the Roman walls, at least as foundations, and use of pre-
existing tessellated floor, as at Widford, near Burford in Oxfordshire.
Examples of the close correlation between villas and churches are widespread from Dorset to the Humber. There are some especially noteworthy sites at Lyminge and Cuxton in Kent, at West Mersea,
Brightlingsea and St Osyth in Essex, at Kedington in Suffolk, in Dorset
(Wimborne, Tarrant Crawford), in Gloucestershire (Kings Stanley,
Woodchester, Frocester), Nottinghamshire (Southwell, Stanford-on-
Soar, Ruddington), in Lincolnshire, at Scampton and Claxby-by-
Normanby, and in Humberside, at Messingham. At Castor in

Cambridgeshire the monastery of St Kyneburga was erected in the middle Saxon period within the existing shell of a very extensive court-yard villa, and the present parish church still stands at the centre of what was the principal court. There is a strong possibility, difficult if not impossible to prove, that many of the churches and claustral buildings of the mid-Saxon period were adaptations of existing Roman structures; and it was only through a prolonged time of rebuilding and modifications that Roman masonry disappeared beneath the ground, to be replaced by the now familiar mediaeval work.

Perhaps the most magnificent of the whole gamut of surviving Anglo-Saxon churches, despite its present decrepit state, is All Saints', Brixworth. In its original form it consisted of north and south aisles with internal subdivisions, which made a range of porticoes. It was a basilican structure on a continental scale; and it probably dates from about the latter half of the eighth century. Other churches of a similar basilican appearance include that at Wing in Buckinghamshire and St Mary's, Deerhurst, Gloucestershire. The latter is known to have been a monastery from 804, but it undoubtedly had an earlier origin. Beneath St Mary's Abbey, Cirencester, the foundations of another basilican church of curious form have been discovered; and this early church seems to have been Anglo-Saxon, or conceivably late Roman.

A further sophistication in the architecture of these stone churches was an apsidal eastern sanctuary incorporating a crypt. At Wing this took the form of an elaborate chambered polygonal structure, and at Brixworth it included a corridor or 'ring' crypt. Perhaps the most complicated structure of this type so far unearthed was at the site of St Wystan's church, Repton, in Derbyshire. The crypt originated as a square, semi-subterranean mausoleum, which was possibly built for king Ethelbald of Mercia, who was buried at Repton in 757. Alternatively, it may have been built for king Wiglaf, who is known to have been interred at Repton in 840. In either case it would have been a Mercian royal burial place.

Crypts were not unusual in the great Anglo-Saxon churches. Others include Winchester Old Minster, Glastonbury and Sidbury church in Devon. A number of the known examples combined with their function of burial chamber that of relic display. And where there was a corridor this permitted pilgrims to process around the area concerned and peer through openings in the wall to see relics contained in a *confessio*. The chambered crypts, as found at Hexham, Ripon, Repton and Wing consisted of two sets of corridors and steps which emerged in the interior of the church; and this allowed for a free flow of pilgrims who were venerating the relics.

By the end of the ninth century there was a quite impressive array of cathedrals and churches. In descending order there were the metropolitan cathedrals of Canterbury and York; the diocesan cathedrals of London, Winchester, Rochester and Dorchester-on-Thames; and the later cathedral churches of Hexham, Lindsey, Lichfield, Elmham, Hereford, Worcester, Leicester, Lindisfarne, Selsey, Sherborne and possibly Felixstowe. Most of the cathedral churches had the status of minsters. Then came what seems to have been a considerable number of local churches, both stone and timber, which I have just described.

Whatever its form, and whether it was quite elaborate and made of stone, or rudimentary and made of timber, the local church and its priest required capital and income. Voluntary financial support from primitive farmers was unstable. From an early date the priest was part of the agricultural community, with a holding, the glebe, which allowed him to obtain his own modest supply of food. In the case of minsters there was patronism by royalty or a rich landowner, and more generous endowments, mostly in excess of an entire hide. This of course reflected the scale of the operation. The 'lesser church' was geared to a single priest, whereas the minster was originally the church of a religious community.

There were other mediaeval sources of revenue for the upkeep of churches and priests which may be traced back to the seventh century, such as the church-scot and the soul-scot. The former was a tax imposed by authority, and consisted of a penny payable within a fortnight after Easter in respect of each plough-team working in a parish. By slow degrees the tithe came to replace church-scot as the basis of parochial financial support for the parish, and there were signs of this change as early as the eighth century. In 786 a legatine council at Clofeshoh enjoined the payment of tithe on all men, but this was apparently not implemented. The soul-scot was a voluntary offering of a proportion of a dead person's goods given for the welfare of his soul. At the open grave at the time of the burial it was handed to the priest of the deceased person's local church. Such a practice may well have represented a heathen custom which had been turned to Christian uses. These ecclesiastical dues amounted to a serious charge on the English peasantry, and became an impossible burden in hard times of famine or war. But it was part of a concerted effort by the church in the seventh and eighth centuries to provide and sustain an effective and comprehensive pastoral oversight.

What was accomplished in this provision of local churches and local ministry in a quiet way in numberless places throughout the land was not outwardly sensational; but it was of fundamental importance in the growth of the English church, and it has not received the attention it deserves. One historian has claimed that 'the development of a parochial system is the central thread of English ecclesiastical history in the generation following the arrival of Theodore'.[51] In a painstaking series of negotiations with kings and nobles, and by initiatives such as field churches and minster churches, as well as in the work and support of simple working people who helped in various ways to sustain local churches, the skeleton of a future impressive parochial network began to be formed.

But what about the priests who ministered in whatever churches were provided? It is notoriously difficult to assess the quality of personal Christian belief and conduct in former ages, and this increases the further we go back in time. Bede gives descriptions of learned and pious clerics, but Theodore's *Penitential* provides a very different picture. In it he shows that secular priests were mostly very ordinary people with failings and shortcomings which constantly needed correcting. And some such inadequacies were perhaps widespread and scandalous. Theodore certainly found it necessary to address specific and serious forms of misconduct as if they were sufficiently prevalent to make action desirable, and even essential. Priests were forbidden to perform pagan divinations;[52] penances were prescribed for sexual offenses,[53] for habitual drunkenness,[54] and for those who had abandoned their religious vows.[55] There are frequent allusions to clergy who had not been ordained or baptized, and there are indications of clergy ignorance and negligence, clergy who could not say prayers and enunciate the readings according to the rites, and others who may not have had a right and orthodox belief in the Trinity.

Without any system for the training of clergy in anything but the basic matters to do with faith and its practice, or in the conduct of worship, and with widespread illiteracy or semi-literacy, the provision of a well-taught and instructed local clergy, who mostly undertook their liturgical and other duties as supplementary to rural work, was at best difficult, and at worse, impossible. Nevertheless, the local ministry system which was developing in such a random way was crucial to the life of the church at the time.

Monasticism

The establishment and growth of the parochial system may have been given far too little attention by historians; but this is not so with monasticism. All are agreed that it was central both to the Roman and Irish missions to England, and in the succeeding life of the English church. It was at the heart of the initial evangelistic thrust, and it continued to be a pivotal institution by virtue of the pastoral care it provided, and the value which society, and the church in particular, placed on communities dedicated to prayer, contemplation, literary and other cultural activities. Monasticism expressed a concept which enthused kings, nobles and lay people, so that the multiplication of monasteries did not stem so much from a deliberate policy of ecclesiastical rulers as from spontaneous national and local initiatives and action.

By 700 a great number of monasteries were in existence in England. They were to be found throughout the length and breadth of the land, from the great foundations of Northumbria to such renowned centres as St Peter and St Paul at Canterbury, and the houses at Folkestone, Dover and Reculver; from the distinguished centre of learning at Malmesbury to the famous foundation of St Botulph at Icanhoe in East Anglia; from the large and internationally distinguished bodies to the small communities of three or four monks who attempted to meet the pastoral needs of a scattered local population. No one rule was adopted for all these institutions. Rather, each had its own character and style of life. This depended to a large extent on the circumstances of its establishment, and the routine of life and the norms favoured by its most dominant patron, abbot or inmate. The physical layout varied, with cells for one or two which formed the nucleus as at Whitby, to the dormitory and absence of cells at Hackness and Jarrow.

Whatever may have been the initial intention of the founder, in the pioneering conditions of the seventh and eighth centuries, the luxury of a totally withdrawn religious house without some responsibilities to the neighbouring villages and monastic estates would have been unthinkable. Preaching and baptizing may not have been listed as required duties in a monastery's foundation charter; but such functions would have been taken for granted. The absence or scarcity of parish priests as such in all localities meant that clerics were needed to undertake the kind of perambulations which Cuthbert, and prior Boisil before him, had made from Melrose, in which they covered vast areas extending even to the remotest farmsteads. Bede conjures up a picture of such ministry. He says that 'it was the custom amongst the English people at that time, when a clerk or a priest came to a village, for all to gather at his command to hear the Word, gladly listening to what was said and still more gladly carrying out in their lives whatever they heard and could understand'.[56] The monasteries would have been one of the main, and in many areas the only, source of such priestly ministration. Even monasteries like Jarrow and Monkwearmouth, despite their dedication to learning as their primary objective, must have had pastoral obligations, especially in view of their extensive estates. Care for the poor and the sick outside the monastic walls is implicit in the anonymous *Life of Ceolfrid*, with its account of Jarrow and Wearmouth, despite the fact that it contains no mention of pastoral work.

Most of the monasteries were independent houses, but some were linked with mother houses. This was the case with the monasteries of Wilfrid, scattered over England between the Tyne and the Channel, each one of which was accountable to him through its abbot. It was true also with the monasteries founded by Aldhelm, which remained under his control even after he became Bishop of Sherborne.

Colonization was not uncommon in the seventh century. Thus, monks were sent out from the monastery of Medeshamstede (afterwards known as Peterborough) to Breedon in Leicestershire, Woking and Bermondsey in Surrey, Hoo in Kent, and probably Brixworth in Northamptonshire, and the daughter monasteries they established were subject to the ultimate authority of the abbot of Medeshamstede, with their muniments being sent to the mother monastery for preservation.

The majority of the monasteries were for men only. There were few if any houses founded at this time which were solely for women. 'Female monasticism was a new development in late seventh-century England. In the mid-seventh century the nobility still sent their daughters to Frankish monasteries.'[57] But from the middle of the century double monasteries, with men and women in separate but close together institutions, invariably under the supervision of an abbess, were to be found in various places, such as Whitby, Lyminge, Minster-in-Sheppy and Minster-in-Thanet in Kent, Barking, Coldingham, Repton, Wimborne and Hartlepool.[58] This concept was an importation from Gaul.[59] It appears that Ely, Much Wenlock and Bardney all had an original double constitution. In such houses the relationship between the two communities was strictly controlled, and they all seem to have had good reputations, with the exception of Coldingham, in an isolated location above the sea in the far north of Bernicia, where there were grounds for scandal. The abbesses were frequently of high social rank with powerful personalities. Hilda of Whitby was a kinswoman of king Oswy; Elffled, her successor, was Oswy's daughter; Wimborne was founded by two sisters of Ine, king of Wessex; Ethelthryth, the founder of Ely, and Seaxburg her successor, were daughters of Anna, king of the East Angles; and Mildburg, abbess of Wenlock, as well as Mildthryth, abbess of Minster in Thanet, were daughters of Merewalh, king of the Magonsaetan. 'Women of this type exercised an influence on the life of their time to which there is nothing parallel in later history.'[60]

The nuns would most probably not have been exempt from the obligation laid upon the monks to baptize and teach in the surrounding area, especially on their estates. But women did not preach, so that a small complement of monks or clerics would be necessary. 'The double monasteries therefore fitted naturally into the general organization which lay behind the evangelistic and pastoral oversight of the English dioceses and kingdoms, at the same time satisfying a demand which arose from the religious enthusiasm of Anglo-Saxon royal women.'[61] It is noteworthy that when the double monasteries disappeared in the general demise of the monastic institution in the ninth century, or in the Viking raids, they were most usually re-established in later Saxon times as local churches. This may infer that the districts which the churches served were exactly or almost the same as those which had come under the pastoral care of the monasteries since their foundation in the seventh century.

In a short time there were many of these double monasteries, and they were accepted by such an ardent disciple of the stricter form of the Benedictine rule as Wilfrid, who was a friend and teacher of Ethelthryth. As we will see, Boniface sent especially for Wimborne nuns to help in his work on the continent.

In the discussion of monasteries a place of special honour should be given to Wearmouth and Jarrow, not only because of their importance at the time, but because of the attention they have attracted generally, and from scholars in particular. Benedict Biscop was a Northumbrian noble, and a gesith of King Oswy. In his twenties he travelled on the continent and was deeply impressed with the monastery of Lerins. He founded Wearmouth in 674 and Jarrow in 681 as one confraternity despite the fact that the former was at the mouth of the Wear and the latter was a few miles away near the mouth of the Tyne. He acquired masons and glaziers from Gaul to help in their construction, and he accumulated an impressive collection of books, relics, vestments, chalices and icons for his new foundations. He also borrowed John, the archchanter of St Peter's, Rome, to teach chant and the manner of reading aloud which was used in the basilican monasteries. The two foundations soon achieved a wide reputation for their spiritual and literary excellence, and they attracted high quality monks, including, of course, the Venerable Bede.

As a sample of a smaller monastery, but one which also rapidly became a centre of learning, I will take Malmesbury. Its foundation helps to underline the variety of origins of these establishments. Maelduib was an Irishman who left his native land to become a pilgrim for Christ and to undertake work in his name. After some wanderings, he arrived at the kingdom of the West Saxons, close to the forest of Selwood, where he built himself a hermit's hut. There he lived as an anchorite, spending his time in prayer, study, and various forms of ascetic exercise which were so cherished by the Celtic monks. Like some other hermits, he soon attracted disciples who were seeking knowledge and spiritual counsel. He offered instruction in the faith, expounded the Bible and the doctrines of the church, and taught reading and writing. A few remained to learn more. They built rough dwellings around his hermitage and began to follow the Rule which he observed and taught. Thus the monastery grew. As the number of disciples increased so individual cells for the monks, a kitchen, refectory, infirmary, and a church for the mass and the reciting of the daily offices were constructed.

It does not appear, as was once asserted, that there was a massive deterioration in the spiritual quality and the overall standard of life of monasteries in the hundred years and more following the death of Bede. All was not well with the English church between 735 and 865 but too much has been made of the so-called 'secularization' of monasteries. During the period significant advances were made, and when there was retrogression it was less serious than is sometimes supposed.[62]

The Christianization of society

Churches, mother churches, priests and monasteries were an integral part of the engagement of the church with the people in their daily lives. Another medium for such influence was the Christianization of the laws of the land. The progress achieved in this is illuminated by a comparison of the code of King Ethelbert of Kent at the beginning of the seventh century with the code of king Ine at the end of the century, composed some time around 694. It also shows how Anglo-Saxon society had advanced in the intervening years, partly under the influence of the church. It had become much more complex and organized, but also much more sophisticated and sensitive in its collective moral consciousness.

> Ethelbert's primitive code, compiled when he and his people were only a step away from their pagan past, reads like a catalogue of penalties and compensations to be paid for injuries, some very trivial, against one's neighbour. Ine's code, on the other hand, covers the whole spectrum of a well organized agricultural society, omitting the trivial and dealing with the basic and important aspects of a multifarious society. Like the Kentish code of Wictred, it reflects, too, the all pervasive influence of Christianity and its impact on culture, while at the same time, Anglo-Saxon society retained its distinctive Germanic character.[63]

And what about the ordinary people themselves? As we have seen, the resources were limited to enable the faith to be proclaimed and sustained among the people as a whole, and there were barriers to overcome. For one thing there was the widespread illiteracy. It was easier to communicate the gospel to a limited number of better educated people, as with the king, his family, friends and contacts, the members of the court and the nobility, who may well have been more open to a message which was contained in written scriptures and which entailed the need for a certain measure of theological appreciation, than to the illiterate or semi-literate and less sophisticated mass of the people in their dispersed, and often isolated, rural areas or small towns.

Then there was the shortness of life, and the demands made upon ordinary people in their world of work and survival. This is well captured by Peter Hunter Blair

> What then did men believe about the world in which they lived? Of the many who have left not so much as a name behind them, we shall scarcely be mistaken in supposing that for those who survived the perils of birth to die a probably painful death perhaps twenty or thirty years later, there would be little opportunity and less inclination for philosophical speculation about the nature of the world in which they struggled to maintain even that brief span of existence.[64]

In such circumstances it is not surprising that the holy life of the saint, the stories of miracles performed, and the wonders associated with relics, and the bones of the saints and the martyrs, should have been popular. There was an understandable response to all that sainthood represented from people who were embroiled in the hard and demanding life of that coarse and in many ways brutal age. Those who had little to relieve the monotony, drudgery and grind of work and home life with its almost totally predicable diet of wearisome labour and few things out of the ordinary, would doubtless have found immense attraction in the colourful and elevated lives of the saints. The world of miracles and remarkable dedication and holiness would have appealed to people who struggled to maintain reasonable moral standards amidst the various pressures upon them to conform to practices and values which fell far below what was their ideal. In a world without penicillin or any of the amenities which give material comfort to modern man, when pain and discomfort were the everyday lot of all the people, but especially of the majority in their primitive homes with their burdensome work, there was a predisposition to accept anything which offered possible relief, and the hope of better things. 'Beyond all question men believed in miracles. The sick were healed by the bones of holy men. Food was provided for travellers in strange deserted lands. Fires were extinguished. The dead were restored to life.'[65]

The whole 'cult of the saints' for which relics were the most visible and tangible expression, was well suited to the Anglo-Saxon world, not only because of the factors just mentioned, but because of the cosmologies of the Anglo-Saxons themselves, which I examined in chapter 5. As one historian has said: 'The concept of saints' relics as a doorway between this world and the next developed in the late antique Roman-Christian synthesis but easily made itself at home in the worldviews of Germanic peoples in the early Middle Ages'.[66]

A good example of a contemporary saint whose life and works would have inspired awe, and aroused the kind of emotions to which I have alluded, was Guthlac.[67] Born about 674, he was of the Mercian royal blood and his father was a Christian. After about nine years as a freebooter, taking advantage of a disturbed period of warfare, which was a lucrative and apparently respectable occupation, he suddenly, as a result of contemplations during the night, decided to become a monk. After two years at Repton, in 699 or 700, he made his way to the remote and desolate island of Crowland in the middle of the fens, and made his dwelling in the side of an old burial-mound, or barrow. His biographer, an East-Anglian monk called Felix, vividly tells of how he experienced fierce temptations and assaults of devils, how he wrestled with demons amidst the bogs and swamps of the fens, but how he persisted in his chosen life of solitude, prayer and fasting, until his death sometime between 715 and 749.

An interesting facet of this cult of the saints was the place in it of the royal saint. A number of kings from the early days of the re-establishment of Christianity in England in the late sixth century onwards were canonized. In addition to all the considerations which would normally apply to sainthood, there was an extra dimension when it came to the canonization of a king. 'There can be little doubt that the creation of a royal saint might further the immediate political objectives of a ruler, might enhance the prestige of a dynasty and might go some way towards conferring legitimacy upon a fictive successor. And there can be little doubt that the church sanctioned this political use of the royal cult. It did so not in order to shore up an otherwise feeble monarchy but in recognition of the centrality of royal power.'[68]

The synthesis of Christian and non-Christian cultural and social, as well as religious elements, which was evident in the cult of the saints in general, if less obviously so with the royal saints, was manifested in a host of ways. One aspect of it in Anglo-Saxon England was the process whereby, for its own benefit, the increasingly dominant Christian culture made concessions to the culture being replaced. It was part of a European-wide evolution, in which pagan practices were accommodated by an ever more pervasive Christian church. 'In terms now familiar to the modern anthropologist and social historian, these practices served, in the early Middle Ages, to hold the forces of too rapid an "acculturation", or cultural dominance, at bay, to prevent the complete "deculturation" of the subject culture, and, through extended exercises in "negotiation", to bring about an enduring fusion of religious sensibilities and behaviour instead.'[69]

The Christian church with all the ramifications of its teaching and practice, which was in the ascendant as a religious and cultural force, had to make concessions if its aims were to be fulfilled. And this meant coming to terms with pagan magic by incorporating some of it.

Magic was important to many in the mediaeval church because it was already believed in by the peoples to whom its missionaries came, and because some of this belief gave hope and supported happiness. The church had need of these peoples. It too supported this hope and happiness; and it could find echoes of this magic, furthermore, when it looked for them, within its own dispensation. Much magic was, then, rescued in the service of human aspiration, and, certainly, in defiance of certain aspects of reason and regulation.[70]

'Popular' religion was complementary to the structured 'institutional' manifestation of the Christian faith. Each had its part to play. 'This dynamic interaction between the formal and the popular at their mutual boundary makes the process of the formation of Christianity visible to us, especially the largely oral popular tradition.'[71]

The higher echelons of society were then, in general, more Christianized than the ordinary people, in these centuries, but this should not imply a clear divide between a Christian social élite and a pagan mass of the population. It was far more complicated than this. It was only gradually, even in the higher socio-economic groups in society, that there was a thorough Christianization. Kings professed belief, and in many cases this was clearly genuine and utterly sincere, as it was with other high ranking and socially important individuals; nevertheless, there was clearly much nominal Christian profession for the sake and benefits of conformity. On the other hand, although many of the general populace most obviously did not even profess belief and commitment, there was a host of ordinary, low social status, people to whom the Christian faith was a precious thing, and who faithfully practised and bore witness to their Christian belief. At no level of society was the Christian faith completely absent, nor fully received and totally endorsed. There was a long drawn-out process of amalgamation, adaptation and replacement, with a residue of old beliefs persisting or assuming new, even perhaps sublimated, forms. This was evident in countless ways.

Clearly, pagan temples were reconsecrated as Christian churches, pagan charms and spells were adapted for Christian prayer, and pagan smiths and jewellers' shops turned their hand to Christian ornament. Anglo-Saxon kingship itself developed into a remarkable amalgam of Christian and pagan elements. By the ninth century kings underwent a Christian ceremony of consecration and anointing, but they continued to trace their genealogies back to Woden. Kings gradually assumed a Christ-like character; yet Christ Himself took on some of the qualities of the old Germanic heroes, so that Christ and his apostles, for instance, could be seen as a lord and his thegns. The kings of the Old Testament also, fighting against the enemies of God, fitted well into the pagan mental framework of man's fight together with the gods against the evil giants.[72]

Perhaps the interplay of Christian and heathen Anglo-Saxon beliefs and culture is nowhere better exhibited than in the poem *Beowulf*.[73] Such is the mixture of the Christian and the pagan elements in that epic that it is difficult to distinguish where the one begins and the other takes over. Taken as a whole, however, it does seem to have a Christian sub-text, and to be pervaded by Christian values and a Christian perspective, but with heathen influences very apparent. Aristocratic traditions are enveloped in a Christian atmosphere. Although there are problems in seeing the poem as a consistently Christian work, such as the lack of a Christian reference after Beowulf has returned to Geatland, it seems that the poet was a Christian, 'and the cosmology and aetiology are largely Christianized. A typical Anglo-Saxon moralist, his traditional gnomic gravity and wryness are modified in places by a Christian note of agonized moral and spiritual concern such as we find in the homilies of the time.'[74] The poem is suffused with morality and a religious tone. The hero's struggles are presented as a cosmic contest between good and evil which is a characterizing element in the Christian understanding of history. The powers of darkness may, and often do, kill the worthiest of champions for light, but God will not allow such contenders for the power of good to bear witness in vain.

The English church and the continent in the eighth century

It is a testimony to the health and non-parochialism of at least some sections of the English church in the eighth century that it could make a massive and telling contribution to mission work on the continent.[75]

In order to place this in context, we need to remind ourselves of the close contact of England with the continent over many centuries. There was continual and important trade between Britain and the continent which can be traced back well into prehistoric times. The whole Roman period and the romanization of Britain, with the intimate political association of Britain and Gaul in those centuries, helped to underline the continental affinity. The links between England and the Roman church were manifested in the Augustine mission and the appointment and oversight by Rome of his successors. It was typified in the application for the pallium and the frequent advice given by popes on church matters, which at times verged on instruction. The various church conferences on the continent attended by English church leaders, and the issues of universal import which were discussed at some of them, helped to emphasis that in Christian affairs Britain was not devoid of strong influences from abroad, or cut off from the mainstream continental Roman church. The frequent assistance given to the promotion and stabilization of Christianity in Britain by such continental church leaders as Germanus of Auxerre, Birinus and Felix, were invaluable to the British church. It was largely as a consequence of continental influences, such as the life, teaching and example of St Martin of Tours and St Benedict, that monasticism was established and became so central to the life of the English church, with some monasteries even under the direct jurisdiction of the Apostolic See.[76] Those who visited Rome, such as Wilfrid, Benedict Biscop, Willibrord and Boniface acquired books, vestments, and relics of the apostles and martyrs which then became an important part of the life of monasteries and churches in England. And the integration of the English church within the Roman tradition was enhanced with the appointment by the pope of Theodore as archbishop of Canterbury.

It was fortunate that the English church, especially in the eighth century, was able to give a great deal as well as being a recipient in Christian ministry. The sphere of this outstanding English missionary endeavour was northern Europe in the region around Friesland, and central Germany.

The Merovingian kingdom had reached its greatest extent by about the middle of the sixth century. It then included nearly all of Gaul and most of the German countries, but the greater part of the modern Netherlands and north-western Germany remained outside it. The decisive battle of Tertry in 687 gave the preponderance of power to the more Germanic parts of the kingdom. During the ensuing four generations, from Pipin II to Charles the Great, there was a great period of reconstruction in which strong central government re-established the Frankish frontiers, and the lands of the last independent German tribes, the Frisians and the Saxons, were incorporated into the kingdom. But in fact they were outside the Frankish borders, and they clung not only to political independence but to the gods and rituals of their ancestors. For these people, as for others at the time, religion and politics were inextricably linked; and the Frankish kingdom was at least nominally Christian. 'Frankish domination and the Christian religion were to them inseparable notions.'[77]

But the conversion of the Franks themselves had been a somewhat superficial affair. Paganism lingered on; and whilst the Franks practised 'an attenuated and sometimes perverted type of Christianity, they persisted in their cult of the old gods'.[78] It is not surprising that they had

little concern to convert the Frisians. There had been no great missionary effort by the Frankish church, and what had been done had been
unsustained and too fitful to overcome the massive problems involved.
The situation called for dedicated pioneer work.

As we have already noted, Wilfrid remained in Frisia during the
winter of 678–79 on his way to Rome. The Frisian King Aldgisl not only
contemptuously declined a proposal by Wilfrid's enemies that he should
either surrender Wilfrid to them or kill him, but allowed him to preach
the gospel to his people. In taking advantage of this opportunity,
Wilfrid did not adopt the confrontational and dramatic method, of
which the classic exponent was Martin of Tours, but the more concili-
atory, but still firm and stern where necessary, approach of Gregory the
Great. 'Wilfrid's whole attitude to missionizing approximated more
closely in spirit to Gregory's mixture of step-by-step mildness, compul-
sion and material inducement than to anything else.'[79] And it seems to
have had some success. Eddius, his biographer, says that 'his preaching
was accepted and that year he baptized all but a few of the chiefs and
many thousands of the common people, thus laying like the Apostle of
the Gentiles the foundation of the faith'.[80] However much this may be
an exaggeration, and however multiplied may have been the attributed
fruits of Wilfrid's preaching, a start seems to have been made in
evangelizing the Frisians. He had 'shown an opening to his fellow
countrymen which was not forgotten'.[81] Seed had been sown. The one
who continued the good work was Willibrord.

Little is known of Willibrord, but what is recorded leaves the
impression of a man who deserves recognition as one of the outstanding band of early English missionaries who were instrumental in taking
the faith to areas of the continent where it had not taken root.[82] He was
born in 658 in Northumbria, and he was educated at the Ripon
monastery. This was supplemented by twelve years of further monastic
education in Ireland. There he was touched by the spirit of pilgrimage;
the calling to a life of monastic devotion in exile. He and some companions were sent to Friesland in 690. They began their work in the
conquered part of the territory under the protection of Pipin. And, most
portentously, Willibrord obtained the sanction, benediction and advice
of the pope; a momentous move as the pope had not up to that time
exercised much influence in the Frankish church. Christianity spread
enough after a few years for Willibrord to be consecrated archbishop in
695, in order to provide a pastoral head, and an authority to coordinate the organization and establishment of the church. The castle of

Triectum, the modern Utrecht, was given to him as a cathedral site and centre of the ecclesiastical province. There monks and other clergy lived side by side; and native clergy were provided with education. It also seems that Willibrord consecrated other bishops. The progress was noteworthy, and the church appeared ready for further growth. But the continuity of the work was to be suddenly and rudely halted.

Willibrord had relied on political support, and he had succeeded in the conversion of the Frisians largely because the Frankish supremacy, and the backing of Pipin, gave him protection. But in 714 Pipin died; and all the enemies of his house joined to overthrow its power. The Frisians took part in the insurrection. The Frankish dominion and the standing of the Christian church collapsed together, and all the work of Willibrord seemed to be undone.

But there emerged from the strife an even stronger man than Pipin, Charles Martel, the 'hammer' as he has been designated because of his conquest of the Arabs. Willibrord was able to resume his work and to make good the loss of the years 715 to 719 in a constructive period which lasted until his death in 739. He even tried, but without success, to convert the Danes.

Despite what had been achieved, Christianity had not spread beyond the Frankish borders. Willibrord had not made any further inroads into Frisian areas other than western Friesland. To the east of the Zuider Zee as far as the lower part of the Weser, in the oldest settlements of the Frisians, the inhabitants adhered tenaciously to their non-Christian ancestral traditions. This was to be the scene for the heroic missionary outreach of Boniface.

Wynfrid, or St Boniface as I will be calling him because he is better known by that name, was born in Wessex about 675 into a family of free landowners.[83] His childhood education was at the monastery of Exeter. There he was nurtured, taught and trained in the spirit of St Benedict, and he imbibed all the nuances of the Roman ecclesiastical tradition.

He became an impressive preacher and an effective teacher, and he displayed practical abilities. He was recommended for responsible posts in England, including the abbotcy of Nursling. But his heart and mind were set on spreading the gospel abroad. This resolve was not deflected by the failure of a first attempt at such service, when he went to Friesland in 716 at the time of the revolt and the persecution of the Christians. He was forced to return to England, but in 718 he sailed a second time. In was the decisive move of his life. He never lost touch with his native country, but neither did he see it again. Until his death in 754 he devoted himself in unstinting service to the work of the church in Germany.

He first of all engaged in missionary activity, like Willibrord with the explicit agreement and help of the pope. Initially it was as a priest, and then, from 722 as a bishop. He received the pallium and was made an archbishop probably in 732. From then onwards, until a short time before his death, he concentrated on the organization of the church. The provincial structure for the church had taken root in England, but it had disappeared in Frankish countries. Boniface now applied it to his archiepiscopal area, and he became head of a new German church. But the organizational plans had to wait, as for several years he was a metropolitan without bishops subject to him and without any dioceses. His main sphere of activity was in central Germany, and this gave him the title of 'Apostle of Germany'. The going was difficult. There was much hardship, privation and danger; but he also experienced success in the war he waged against heathendom, pagan survivals and heretics. The most famous of these exploits was when he destroyed the oak of Donar at Geismar in Hesse, as a highly public and visible manifestation to the pagans that their god was defeated and as a demonstration of the might of Christ. He founded monasteries at Amoneburg east of Marburg and Fritzlar in Hesse as places of prayer, rest and refuge and as Christian strongholds.

One interesting effect of all this was its stimulus in urging others to undertake missionary work. His reputation increased. News of his preaching, and all that he was doing to spread the gospel, reverberated around much of Europe.

> From Britain an exceedingly large number of holy men came to his aid, among them readers, writers and learned men trained in the other arts. Of these a considerable number put themselves under his rule and guidance, and by their help the population in many places was recalled from the errors and profane rites of their heathen gods. Working in widely scattered groups among the people of Hesse and Thuringia, they preached the Word of God in the country districts and villages. The number of Hessians and Thuringians who received the sacraments of the faith was enormous and many thousands of them were baptized.[84]

By 741 Boniface had eight suffragans, and there were a few other bishops of the older dioceses in Alamannia who also accepted his leadership. Of particular significance was the fostering of monasticism. The steady stream of English recruits could not be relied upon to continue after his death. The future stability of the work he had initiated and the spreading of monastic life to all parts of his vast missionary territory depended on mobilizing native Christians to undertake the necessary responsibilities. He sent Sturm and Leoba to Rome and Monte Cassino to learn the Benedictine customs and traditions. The foundation of the abbey of Fulda had a transforming effect on the cultural conditions in Germany. From its school there went forth a long line of notable scholars, and they in their turn established additional centres of learning. These were astounding and far-reaching consequences to issue from the vigour and dedication of a small band of Anglo-Saxon monks.

But even more momentous was the ecclesiastical organization and structure which Boniface bequeathed to Germany. He instilled into the Frankish and German churchmen 'a lively attachment to Rome and a firm belief in the unity of the universal Church'.[85] The idea of a separate, territorial church, which had held sway in Frankish kingdoms for so long and which appeared likely to grow in Germany, was decisively suppressed. At the same time, the freedom of the church to order its own affairs in a fruitful co-operation with the rulers and political leaders was clearly taught and fostered. 'The separation of Church and State and the recognition of the supremacy of each within its own sphere, which has largely conditioned the civilization of western Europe, was brought about at this time, and the freedom of worship, freedom to teach and the right to economic independence, can be traced through the Anglo-Saxon missionaries to the policy of Theodore of Canterbury and ultimately of Gregory the Great.'[86]

In 753 Boniface was over seventy-five years of age, but there still burned within him the missionary zeal which had originally motivated him to bring the gospel to the heathen abroad. The Christian vision of his youth had not died, or even grown dim, in his later years. He was able at his then ripe age to dream dreams. He again took up the plans he once cherished, and with Eoba, the Bishop of Utrecht, and many other helpers, he returned to Friesland, in order to preach to the pagans north-east of the Zuider Zee; for Willibrord had died in 739, and with his death the Frisian church as a separate province had come to an end. Thousands were christened. The onset of winter suspended his work, but he re-started his ministry the following year. He was about to administer communion to a gathering of new Christians near Dokkum when they were attacked by a frenzied mob armed with spears, swords and all manner of other weapons. He forbade resistance and was killed on 5 June 754 with fifty-three companions. A general English synod added the anniversary of his martyrdom and that of his companions to the designated festivals for solemn celebration each year.

A *new age dawns*

The English church in the Saxon period, which I have surveyed in the last two chapters, was to be suddenly and severely rocked and tested from the end of the eighth century onwards. The cause of such trial and tribulation was the Vikings. In a passage from *Historia Regum* (History of the Kings), attributed to Simeon of Durham, the author graphically portrays the horrifying onset of the Viking raids under the date 793:

> In the same year the pagans from the northern regions came with a naval force to Britain like stinging hornets and spread on all sides like fearful wolves, robbed, tore and slaughtered not only beasts of burden, sheep and oxen, but even priests and deacons, and companies of monks and nuns. And they came to the church of Lindisfarne, laid everything waste with grievous plundering, trampled the holy places with polluted steps, dug up the altars and seized all the treasures of the holy church. They killed some of the brothers, took some away with them in fetters, many they drove out, naked and loaded with insults, some they drowned in the sea.[87]

The onslaught was not a temporary affair. After a respite the frequency of the incursions increased and led on to settlement. The age of the Vikings was about to begin; and it would not end until the Normans came to conquer and to settle.

8

The Vikings in England to 1066

In considering the dramatic, and at times bloody and destructive, intrusion of the Vikings which began in the late eighth century it is necessary, as in so many aspects of history, to avoid over simplistic generalizations. One modern historian has expressed this well:

> To be obsessed with the image of peaceful and peace-loving Scandinavian farmers, taken from the history of Scandinavia over the last two centuries, can lead to falsification as great as that provoked by the nursery and early schoolboy image of ruthless Viking axemen, horn-helmeted and heathen, breakers of skulls and despoilers of churches. Reality was much more complex. Not all farmers love peace. A ravager in May can turn a skilful hand to corn-harvest in August.[1]

When we enter the age of the Vikings we are still hampered by poverty of written and archaeological evidence which gives a clear and unambiguous picture of the course and nature of events. 'Evidence of Viking raids, to say nothing of alleged atrocities, is difficult to find . . . From an archaeological viewpoint the Vikings are rather elusive.'[2] Much surmise is founded on slim evidence.

The invasions represented an onslaught on Christian England. This does not necessarily mean that the Vikings were explicitly anti-Christian. In common with the barbarian invasions against Europe in general at that time, the attackers were aggressively non-Christian. But religion was not the motivation which drove them from their homeland to England; or at least it played a minor part in the enterprise. The various groups who troubled to leave their home country to undertake such ventures were driven by the lure of wealth and the understanding that English political weakness made the risk worth taking. Those who embarked on such predatory expeditions were apparently young and energetic, with an eye to the bounty which would result from their foraging. And of course England of all countries was an easy target. The sea-raiders were capable of taking the North Sea in their stride; and they could strike quickly and withdraw, with little danger of being opposed, or, if confronted, of being prevented from escaping.

The Vikings may also have been pushed from behind as well as being drawn to possible rewards overseas. In their home country a rising population was putting pressure on the land and on resources, and 'royal power was curbing the autonomy of fiercely independent local chieftains'.[3]

The raids were at first small-scale opportunistic attacks on exposed and vulnerable coastal sites. It seems that bases were established in the Hebrides, the Isle of Man and Ireland from which hit-and-run attacks were launched all over the coast of the British Isles during the spring and summer sailing season. When little effective resistance was encountered an ever increasing number of Vikings came to join in the lucrative activity, and the intention changed from raids to conquest and settlement.

Again, as the volume of attacks increased, the archaeologists and historians are still faced with lack of evidence, both of the raids and of the alleged atrocities. Jarrow is a case in point. The excavated buildings on the site were covered with a thick destruction layer of charcoal, and it is tempting to identify this with the documented Viking attack of 875, but it may have been a result of other causes. It is assumed that such decorative Irish and English metalwork objects as mounts from reliquaries, and book covers and caskets found in Viking graves in Norway are loot from these raids, but it is difficult to prove the link. Among the most revealing discoveries have been those of a farmstead at Jarlshof in Shetland and a Viking site at Coppergate in York, used by specialist craftsmen and merchants who sold their wares from stalls along the street front. Both excavations are useful in giving a more rounded picture of the Viking settlers, but 'these peaceful traders, craftsmen and farmers should not entirely blind us to their less respectful, free-booting cousins'.[4]

It can, however, be asserted with considerable confidence that settlers such as those at Jarlshof and York followed close on the heels of the raiders; or such settlement may have been part of what happened from the beginning. What is clear is that large numbers of Danes settled in eastern and northern England in the course of the ninth and tenth centuries. The Norwegians showed a preference for the coasts of north-west England, the Isle of Man, Ireland and the Western Isles. And the settlements were far less disruptive for English life than the raids. The immigrants had a similar culture, lifestyle and language to the native English. The process of integration and, indeed, assimilation, was quite rapid. The main barrier was the adherence of the newcomers to belief in their old Germanic gods. Once converted to Christianity, the pace of absorbtion into English society was prompt and thorough.

Viking religion

The Scandinavians were incontestably polytheistic. The religious world of the Vikings was filled with many gods who governed the cycle of the years. The natural world was inhabited by a multitude of gods and goddesses, and nature worship was axiomatic to a people who lived so close to fountains, groves and streams. The oak and the ash were venerated. 'The heavens in their mysteries, sun, moon, thunder and lightning, attracted the worshipper. In more sophisticated form re-generation themes can faintly be traced in the attitudes to the rising sun on the cycle of human growth from conception to death and decay.'[5]

By the early ninth century three cults were coming to the fore within the Northern pantheon: Odin (Woden), Thor and Frey. Of these Thor gradually assumed a predominant place, although Odin continued to appeal especially to poets, nobles and others who cared more for wisdom than strength. Thor was in essence a sky-god, like Jove the Thunderer. The hammer, the axe, and probably the swastika, were his symbols, and physical strength was his major attribute. Odin developed more subtle characteristics, and became the god of cunning, of know-ledge and of craft. Frey continued to be important as the fertility god, the protector of crops, of sex and of the harvest.

Material available for entering into the religious world of the Vikings after their arrival in Britain is somewhat restricted. The main focus of attention of archaeologists has been the contents of graves, but there are serious pitfalls in reliance upon such evidence. 'In our search for the thought world of the Germanic peoples', Wallace-Hadrill warns, 'we are nowadays ready to see symbolism in almost any object among their grave goods.'[6] Viking burials have been unearthed throughout the far north of Scotland and the islands, and in the Isle of Man. Almost all were inhumations and some graves were richly furnished, the men with weapons of war and workshop tools and the women with jewellery. Several were buried in, under or beside boats but, as in the Anglo-Saxon cases, the significance of such burial practices is not clear. Sometimes horses or dogs, whole or burned to fragments, were interred with the humans. Occasionally women accompanied wealthy male corpses.[7] It is possible that Viking burials 'were in some respects sacrifices to honour, and perhaps placate, the dead; there may have been a fear that dishonoured dead would not rest, but return to haunt the living'.[8]

Of the other relevant finds mention should be made of silver amulets dug up near Goldsborough, Yorkshire, and of tenth-century coins minted by the Viking kingdom of York, which bear images of the hammer. Carved stones in northern England and the Isle of Man depict scenes from Viking mythology, and they include representations of pagan deities. But in most cases the episodes appear to have been chosen in order to harmonize with Christian teaching.

The Vikings may have been more ardent pagans than has sometimes been assumed. Life generally for them was tough, crude by modern standards, and short; and their religion may have reflected the need which these conditions engendered. Although, as I have said, the prime motive of those who harassed Britain may not have been religious, there is evidence that they ransacked churches and monasteries and destroyed religious objects and literary items which could have had no monetary value.

> Some of this evidence gives one pause about the modern confidence that Vikings were not fanatically pagan. Some, clearly, were not, since we know of cases of a ready, if somewhat cynical, acceptance of baptism; and Scandinavian settlers seem to have been converted fairly soon after their arrival in England. Yet it may not be coincidence that Scandinavian sagas preserve most of what we know of ancient Germanic religion, whereas *Beowulf* is uncompromisingly monotheist; and that the Christian sculpture of northern England after the Viking settlement draws on pagan myths unlike the Ruthwell Cross. If the memory of paganism survived better among the Scandinavians than other Germanic peoples, it may have been more strongly rooted to start with.[9]

The horrific way that it was reported that king Aelle of the Northumbrians and king Edmund of the East Anglians were sacrificed by Ivarr to Othinn, the Scandinavian Woden, with their lungs being ripped out of their rib-cages and draped across their shoulders like an eagle's folded wings, indicates uncompromising paganism, and helps to explain why Viking attacks struck such terror into Christians.[10]

The course of the Viking invasions to 954

There was a tradition in the south of a raid on Dorsetshire some time in the period 786 to 802:

> When the pious king Byrhtric was reigning over Wessex and the people scattered innocently about the countryside were devoting themselves in all tranquillity to the plough . . . a small fleet of the Danes consisting of three war-ships suddenly arrived; and that was the first arrival. When the king's reeve who was then stationed in the town called Dorchester heard it, he mounted his horse and went forward with a few men to the port, thinking that the new-comers were merchants rather than enemies. He addressed them in a commanding tone and ordered them to be brought to the king's vill. But he was killed there and then, and those that were with him. And the name of the reeve was Beaduheard.[11]

Then there was the raid on Lindisfarne, followed a year later by the sacking of the monastery at Jarrow. The unexpectedness and shock of these attacks, which was felt throughout the Christian world, is conveyed vividly by Alcuin writing to the Northumbrian king:

> Lo, it is nearly 350 years that we and our fathers have inhabited this lovely land, and never before has such terror appeared in Britain as we have now suffered from a pagan race, nor was it thought that such an inroad from the sea could be made. Behold the church of St Cuthbert spattered with the blood of the priests of God, despoiled of all its ornaments; a place more venerable than all in Britain is given as a prey to pagan people.[12]

As I have already noted, there has been considerable scholarly debate about the motives and scale of the Viking assault, about the nature of its leadership and the extent of the destruction it caused and, above all, about the reasons for the whole eruption of activity. I would agree with Peter Sawyer that these initial attacks at least were the work of small and mobile raiding bands, who created an atmosphere of crisis far in excess of what was justified by the actual events, and thereby acquired a reputation of being far more formidable and fearsome than they really were. The reality was gruesome and horrific; but those were harsh and cruel days. The invaders were regarded as devils incarnate because they destroyed churches and monasteries; but they did this because they were pagans who did not regard the sacking of churches, and even the slaughter of priests, as any worse than if the attack was perpetrated against ordinary citizens. In the words of Sawyer, 'once the prejudices and exaggerations of the primary sources are recognized, the raids can be seen not as an unprecedented and inexplicable cataclysm, but as an extension of normal Dark Age activity, made possible and profitable by special circumstances'.[13]

This is not to say that the earliest raids were not serious; they were. They were relatively isolated and sporadic, but they were a foretaste of what was to come, and they spread a sense of alarm which undermined the confidence of the English. And this was despite considerable political and military advances which had left the country in a reasonably strong position.

England seems to have attained to a high degree of unity by the early ninth century. It had progressed further along the path to political unity than the other three nations of Britain. This was reflected in the coinage of the age. 'Before England was partitioned in the 880s, a unified currency had evolved. Coins of a single design were issued by agreement between the kings of Wessex, the kings of Mercia, and the archbishops of Canterbury, and the issues of each mingled freely together throughout most of England.'[14] At the beginning of the ninth century the leading dynasty was Mercia, largely because of the reign of King Offa (757–96), who had established himself as the effective head of all the Germanic people south of the Humber. By his coinage, the style he adopted, *rex Anglorum*, by the nature and constitution of his courts and by his charters he made a positive contribution to the future unity of England. But the policy adopted by Offa and the Mercians had weaknesses which are evident in retrospect. He had used excessive force; he had not been able to exert control north of the Humber, where the traditional enemies of England were ever ready to pounce; and he had alienated such subordinate people as those of East Anglia and Kent by the way he treated them.

The future lay with Wessex. It was restive, and under Egbert and his successors it proved to be better able than Mercia to take the lead in English affairs. Members of the house of Wessex appear to have occupied a strong position even before Alfred emerged on the scene. 'If they did not actually dominate the other kingdoms, they were nearer to doing so than their rivals.'[15] They had established their dominance and reputation in a series of spectacular victories against the Mercians, and at the expense of the Cornish and Welsh. The dynasty was more stable than that of Northumbria, and also, probably, than Mercia.

English society in general, and that of Wessex in particular, was dominated by a powerful and wealthy aristocracy which had profited from government service or favours, and from the labour of a well-subordinated peasantry. The king was the key figure. He it was who most significantly determined the military and political success and tone of the kingdom.

Such, in broad outline, was the situation when the Viking raids resumed in the 830s. This time they were more frequent, and more widespread than forty or so years before. There seem to have been descents upon the south coast from Cornwall to Kent, and on the east coast in Lindsey and East Anglia. The attackers suffered a setback in 838 when King Egbert defeated a coalition of Danes and Cornishmen at Hixton Down, west of the Tamar. The incursions were still on a relatively small scale, with no more than fifty ships involved on most occasions; there seems to have been no settlement other than temporary winter camps, and this appears to have been so for even the Shetlands and Orkneys, where neither archaeology nor place-names nor literary sources prove such pre-850 long-term settlement. The target for the attacks was almost certainly movable wealth in the form of coin, precious objects, or manpower which could be ransomed or sold into slavery. This meant that a high proportion of the raids were upon important trading places, or sites like Sheppy which commanded trade routes. For the same reason, the attacks on monasteries were probably motivated by the expectation of booty and manpower, and because, like ports, they were undefended and easily accessible. 'The evidence does indeed support the view that, in its early phases, the Viking onslaught consisted of sea-borne raids by predatory war-bands of the type familiar in Germanic literature.'[16]

A new phase began in 850–51 when, for the first time, the Danes wintered in England. The momentum of attack grew, and serious colonization began in 865. In that year 'the storm broke upon England with the force of a hurricane'.[17] The Danes were principally under the leadership of the sons of Ragnar Lothbrok, especially Ivar the Boneless, Healfden and Ubba. It is probable that they spent the greater part of 866 concentrating their forces in East Anglia, and organizing themselves into a fighting force which could hope to win battles against the greater English kingdoms. They stormed, captured and sacked York. A powerful Northumbrian force was overwhelmed by the Danes when they tried to relieve the city, and almost all the fighting stock of the north was wiped out.

The ferocity of the subsequent molestation of the English countryside, and the fear which was engendered throughout England, is attested by such evidence as the deposit of coin hoards in England. This reveals that a substantial peak occurred during the decade 865–75. The unrelenting, victorious, march of the Danes included many slaughters and much pillaging. The death at this time of King Edmund of East Anglia is of immense importance as it marked the end of native Christian kingship in that kingdom.

With Northumbria and East Anglia conquered, and with Mercia in submission, from late 870 the Danes turned their attention to the conquest of the southern English kingdoms. They made progress, and won battles against the West Saxons at Englefield, Reading, Basing, fourteen miles due south of Reading, and the unidentified *Meretun*, only losing at Ashdown.

When Alfred became king of Wessex in 871 at the age of twenty-two, the outlook was bleak. The Danes were reinforced by another Viking army. Alfred was defeated and paid Danegeld to obtain a respite. As the result of a second invasion the Danes struck deeper than ever into Wessex, and Alfred was once again forced to buy peace. A third attack in 878 caused Alfred to flee to the west after offering no resistance.

But then the tide started to turn. Alfred took refuge in the marshes of Athelney. He mustered troops, and he advanced eastwards, gathering county levies as he went. He inflicted a heavy defeat on the Danes at Edington, and obtained the surrender of the enemy at Chippenham, their stronghold. Guthram was baptized, and he promised to leave Wessex in peace. The Danes first of all withdrew to Cirencester in English Mercia; then in 879, to East Anglia, where they undertook a systematic settlement. For the remaining years of the ninth century there was an uneasy truce, leaving the Danes in command of most of England to the east and north of Watling Street and the river Lea, the Danelaw, with the house of Wessex in substantial command of unconquered England. But the Danes had won a measure of recognition within the Christian community, and they had regularized their own territorial settlement in the east and the north. It was a step towards a more permanent entente.

After the death of Guthrum, there was a final and massive threat. It largely resulted from defeats on the continent, and pressure forcing the invading forces westwards. A formidable armada of 250 ships was amassed in 892 off the coast of southern Kent, to be joined by a fleet of eighty vessels which sailed into the Thames. Here was an invasion deliberately planned and coordinated, a concerted effort to overthrow Alfred's kingdom, and Alfred's defensive measures were still incomplete. The Danes undertook a three-year campaign, but in the end they were beaten as a result of a combination of factors. There was the fortified ring of *burhs*, which mostly consisted of militarily well-prepared and equipped townships, shielding Wessex itself; there was the loyalty and courage displayed by Alfred; the valour and leadership of his subordinate ealdormen, of his son Edward, and of his son-in-law Ethelred of Mercia; and the stubborn and determined resistance of ordinary Englishmen. By 896 the Danish plans for conquest were abandoned, and Alfred spent his last three years in peace until his death on 26 October 899.

Of course Alfred was far more than just a military leader. He was an epoch-making figure in the spheres of civil law and administration and in a whole range of cultural matters. He and his reign constitute one of those critical times when fundamental changes took place which helped in a substantial way to determine the character and direction of long-term English history. 'When judged in purely military and political terms, Alfred's achievement was impressive, when judged also in cultural terms, it was truly exceptional.'[18] Little justice can be done to his wide-ranging and profound measures for the furtherance of learning and letters in the brief compass of what can be said in the present work. I will leave aside the details of what he and his actions meant to the whole life of the church until the next chapter; but it must be appreciated that religion was at the heart of all Alfred's cultural activities. He was passionately convinced that the nation had relapsed into ignorance and materialism. 'The old ideals were almost extinguished. The culture which had flowed with so strong a stream after the Conversion had now become stagnant.'[19]

His cultural programme was strategic in its conception, and wide in its scope. It arose out of a personal impulse of almost visionary intensity and insight, and yet it was practical and workable. He was passionately concerned that his subjects should be educated, at least in basic reading and writing, and he commenced with those who surrounded him in his court. He gathered together with great care many nobles of his own kingdom and boys of humbler birth and formed them into a school.[20] The officials of the king were compelled to make an effort to educate themselves. Whereupon, says Asser, 'nearly all the ealdormen and reeves and thegns (who were illiterate from childhood) applied themselves in an amazing way to learning how to read, pre-

ferring rather to learn this unfamiliar discipline (no matter how labori-
ously) than to relinquish their offices of power'.[21] In order to extend
such education more widely he devised a scheme for the education of
the children of all free men; but by what means is not clear.

Alfred recruited a number of learned men, rather as Charlemagne had
gathered a circle of scholars about him including the Englishman
Alcuin. His own contribution to the revival of learning was to translate
from the Latin into Old English the *Book of Pastoral Rule* of Pope
Gregory I, the *Soliloquies* of St Augustine of Hippo, and the *Con-
solation of Philosophy* by Boethius. He began, but did not live to
complete, a translation of the psalter into English. His team of scholars
translated other works, of which the most important was Bede's
Ecclesiastical History.

The succeeding half century or so after the death of Alfred witnessed
a complicated series of political and military manoeuvres in which
power swung from one English or Danish king to another. But the overall move was towards the absorbtion of the Danes. The successor to
Alfred was his son, the competent and highly successful Edward the
Elder. His most striking achievement was the conquest of the Danelaw
up as far as the river Humber, by means of a series of campaigns
between 909 and 920. It was fortunate that he was succeeded by his
perhaps equally talented and effective son, Athelstan, who consolidated
what his father and grandfather had accomplished. He was especially
successful in securing the northern frontier against the military might of
Olaf Guthfrithson, a claimant to the kingdom of York, Constantine
king of Scots and Owen king of Strathclyde, whom he defeated at the
battle of *Brunanburh* in 937. He protected his western frontiers with the
Britons as a result of a series of agreements made possible by superior
military might. And by his wide-ranging contacts with European rulers
he gained security, a high reputation, and the satisfaction of attracting
a host of learned men to his court. As with the previous two rulers,
scholars, men of letters, and artists as well as soldiers were the pillars of
his authority.

After the death of Athelstan in 939 there ensued a period of chaos. It
was almost immediately made evident that political stability relied
almost entirely on the strength and ability of the reigning monarch.
Edmund, Athelstan's brother who succeeded him, was a youth of
eighteen. Before he had time to prove his metal, Olaf Guthfrithson, king
of Dublin, led an army of Irish Vikings in a second invasion. Without
any resistance, he entered York in 939, and the following year he

conducted a great raid over the midlands. Before King Edmund could confront him in battle, the Archbishops of Canterbury and York arranged a treaty whereby Olaf received the whole region between Watling Street and the Northumbrian border, the area now represented by the modern shires of Leicester, Derby, Nottingham and Lincoln. At a stroke 'a large Anglo-Danish population which for more than twenty years had been obedient to the king of England and to local officers governing in his name'[22] was abandoned.

The confusion was compounded by the death of Olaf in the following year, and by the transfer of his kingdom into weaker hands. His cousin Olaf Sihtricson was made king. But within two years the new Viking king had lost to King Edmund the lands his uncle had acquired. In 943 the Northumbrians drove him out, and he was replaced by his brother Ragnald. In 944 King Edmund retrieved York, and for the rest of his reign, until 946, the West Saxon house was once more in control of the north.

With the assassination of King Edmund in 946, there was even more confusion. Olaf Sihtricson of Dublin seems to have been received again in Northumbria as king from 949 to 952, when Eric 'Bloodaxe' became king for two years.

The course of the Viking invasions from 954 to 1066

From 954 to 980 England enjoyed freedom from the imminent threat of major foreign invasion.

> Edgar's reign (959–975) contrasts sharply with the confusion which came before and the disasters which followed. Coinciding largely with the thirty years of peace which prevailed between the end of one series of Viking attacks and the beginning of a new wave, Edgar's reign is generally regarded as the period during which the developments in monarchical power and towards the unification of the kingdom inaugurated by Alfred came to a climax and completion.[23]

The *Anglo-Saxon Chronicle* claims, with justification, that Edgar can be credited with support of the church and the maintenance of peace. And, as we will see, the period of peace left a permanent impression on English history in the spheres of religion and culture. This was the time of monastic revival, and these were the years when Dunstan was the central figure in English religious life; but the king played a full part in the renewal of religious life and all that flowed from that rejuvenation by his encouragement of Christianity and cultural expression. The *Chronicle* also, rightly, points to the impressive imposition of his authority on the rulers of neighbouring lands. In 980 a new series of Danish raids began which ended in the Danish conquest of the whole land. They started in the same way as the earlier forays. Small companies descended without warning on coastal sites, pillaged, and departed before they met with any but local resistance. They concentrated on Hampshire, Thanet and Cheshire in 980, added Devon and Cornwall in 981, and Dorset in 982. There was then possibly a lull for six years, after which the south-western shires were again visited, and the thegns of Devon met the attacks with a gallantry which became famous throughout the land. The only national significance of these localized attacks was that the Norman aristocracy, conscious of its Scandinavian origin, made the ports of Normandy open to ships returning from raids on England; and this, understandably, resulted in hostility between the English and the Norman courts. The pope brokered a treaty between the two courts which was agreed in March 991.

In the last fifteen years of the tenth century England was harried by a much larger force than those which had previously ravaged its coast; it was more akin to an organized army. Ominously, the new onslaught compelled the English government to raise a heavy tax in order to buy off the invaders. During the next twenty-five years this precedent was followed on several occasions, and these levies became the prototypes of the recurrent Danegelds imposed by the Anglo-Norman kings.

Despite an heroic local resistance at Maldon in 991, the raids persisted. In 994 Olaf Tryggvasson of Norway, accompanied by king Sweyn Forkbeard of Denmark attacked with a huge fleet, and they exacted an immense geld, despite the fact that London beat them off. At that point Olaf was converted to Christianity, and he agreed to desist from hostility. But others were more aggressive, and from 997 attacks became continuous. The ensuing years were a catalogue of useless English activity and treachery, and repeated incidents when English forces were wrong-footed. The Danes frequently landed, and no part of England was free from ravaging.

By 1014 England was prepared to accept the Danish Sweyn as its own king, and King Ethelred II of England, remembered by his countrymen as Ethelred the Unready, went into exile in Normandy with his family, which included the young Edward, long afterwards to become Edward 'the Confessor'. The untimely death of Sweyn soon after this, opened up the chance of Ethelred's return; and his able son and successor, Edmund

Ironside, achieved a balance of power with Sweyn's son, Cnut. But Edmund died at that time, and the Danish Cnut was universally recognized as king of the English in late 1016.

Cnut and his followers probably encountered considerable resentment from the English. This is understandable after the many years in which the Danes had dealt out death, destruction and devastation to much of the country.[24] Of course, his hold on the country was strengthened by the Danish settlement in many areas of England, and the possession of large estates by his followers and supporters. But the Danish territorial overlordship was far from total.

> Although much is uncertain, and while it is likely that Cnut's men had possessions in nearly every shire in England, it is clear that there was no replacement of native landowners by foreigners on the scale that followed 1066. William the Conqueror ruled the country by giving lands to major Norman supporters who proved more trustworthy than the English. Cnut was in a different position. Not all his Scandinavian warlords were reliable, but this was compensated by the willingness of many Englishmen, exasperated by the traumas of Aethelred's time, either to throw in their lot with Danish rule or at least to tolerate it in return for peace; the rest there were other ways of controlling.[25]

Cnut may have cemented political unity in England had he not died in 1035 at under forty years of age. Nevertheless, his reign transformed the English political scene and made a major contribution to the evolution of England as a national state. He did not promote the interests of the Vikings at the expense of harmonious co-existence between them and the Anglo-Saxons. 'Cnut was one of the great men of the period, and proved to be a powerful agent in bringing the Viking Age to an end. He stressed continuity with the settled English past.' He personally helped to demonstrate the unity between the English and the Danish cultures and peoples by marrying Emma, Ethelred's widow. He also actively promoted the Christian faith. 'He showed all the fervour of the convert in upholding Christianity and Christian kingship. England became his favoured home even after he succeeded to the Danish throne in 1019.'[26]

As king of England, of Denmark, and of the Norwegians, and in part of the Swedes, at the height of his power he was able to exercise considerable influence to promote the well-being of England. In the field of international relations, he established effective links with the pope and the emperor, and negotiated trade agreements to the advantage of

England. 'It is sufficiently clear', writes his modern biographer, 'that Cnut was, by the standards of his day, the most successful of all pre-Conquest rulers in Britain.'²⁷ This is a big and somewhat extravagant claim, but it stands up to examination, if we exclude Alfred.

The continuity after his death was shattered by the fact that none of his sons reached the age of thirty. The last of them died in 1042. In any case, with the succession uncertain, there ensued a series of uneasy compromises between parties which coalesced around Cnut's two sons, Harthacnut and Harold. Out of this came the restoration of the old dynasty, when Edward 'the Confessor' was recalled from his exile in Normandy in 1041 by Harthacnut, his own younger half-brother.

A prevailing deep desire to avoid any recurrence of Viking raids or civil war, helped Edward to benefit from an amalgam of skill and luck to keep his kingdom substantially in peace until his death in the first week of 1066. The international situation also favoured him, as the Danes and Norwegians were engaged in a fierce battle for mastery, which reached a climax with the emergence from the chaotic politics of two master figures, Harold Hadrada, king of Norway (1047–66) and Sweyn Estrithsson, king of Denmark (1047–74).

There was only one major intrusion by these northern powers into the affairs of England, but that was of supreme importance for the whole history of England. In September 1066 Hadrada was able to supplement his own military might by reinforcements from the Earl of Orkney and Harold's disaffected brother, Tostig, in an invasion by a fleet of 300 ships bearing at least 9,000 men. Initial success was followed by comprehensive defeat at Stamford Bridge near York. Hadrada was slain, and a couple of dozen ships sufficed to transport the survivors back to their native lands.

The victor, Harold II, who had succeeded Edward on the throne, hastened south to confront William of Normandy, and was devastatingly defeated at Hastings on Saturday 14 October 1066. A new era in English history was about to begin.

England at the time of the Norman Conquest

By the time of the Norman Conquest England had gone a long way towards achieving unity and identity as a single country. There was one king accepted by all as supreme. He reigned, most people believed, by the grace of God. Beneath him were a small number of highly important, influential earls, who collectively were very powerful. There were other noblemen of lesser, but still considerable, wealth and power, who mattered in English politics. And the nature of the evolving political structure meant that comparatively minor landowners, the thegns, who would later be called gentry, also carried substantial corporate weight.

The mass of the people were the non-landowners. Indeed, a high proportion of them were not even free men. A change had taken place since the Anglo-Saxons first arrived:

> The central course of Old English social development may be described as the process by which a peasantry, at first composed essentially of free men, acknowledging no lord below the king, gradually lost economic and personal independence . . . the general drift of English peasant life in these centuries was undoubtedly from freedom towards servitude, and on the eve of the Norman Conquest, many thousands of Englishmen, each possessing a ceorl's wergild of two hundred shillings, were bound by a strict routine of weekly labour to the estates of private lords.[28]

For many generations before the Norman Conquest there had been a move towards a manorial economy. 'The distinction between the thegn and the peasant was the fundamental line of cleavage in Old English society.'[29]

By 1066 there was a well-developed and well-defined local government structure. The largest of the local units were the shires, with their own life and distinctive features. The shire divisions were to remain almost as they were until the reorganization of 1974. Some of them, such as the old kingdom of Wessex – Hampshire, Wiltshire, Dorset, Devon and Somerset – were in existence by at least the late eighth century or the ninth century, if not well before that. Some, for instance Essex, Kent and Sussex, were former kingdoms. The Midland shires assumed their final form some time between 900 and 1016. It is certain 'that the introduction of the regular system of shires, which was to be the basis of English government for a millennium, was the work of the late Saxon kings'.[30]

The shires were also sub-divided into hundreds, or, in parts of the Danelaw, alternatively, 'wapentakes', before the arrival of William of Normandy. These small geographical units dealt with local affairs through hundred courts, which in the tenth century met monthly and were supposed to be attended by all free tenants. They were increasingly used as a means of implementing, or making real in the daily life of country people, the policies and wishes of royal government. The hundreds also probably always had military functions, and the local tenant militias were important as a new royal weapon. Hundreds were an integral part of an emerging hierarchical system of civil and military administration which focussed on the king. 'The most ancient and traditional institutions, such as the feud, the wergeld, the fyrd, the hundred and the shire, were altered, experimented with and left rather different from what they had been. The change was always in the direction of greater power for the crown.'[31]

Within hundreds, or crossing their boundaries, there were 'not individual villages or farms, but large estates that could produce all the food and raw materials that lords and their dependents needed. They usually included among their appurtenances woodland, arable, pasture, fisheries and, in coastal areas, saltpans.'[32] The fragmentation of estates resulted in a large number of small Danelaw parishes.

The military, political, constitutional, economic and social developments of the immediate pre-Norman Conquest centuries briefly outlined in this chapter provided the context for religious, and more especially Christian, changes of considerable magnitude. Without an awareness of this kaleidoscopic 'secular' history much of what occurred in the life of the church in England becomes unintelligible. As we will now see, it helped to determine the various, quite dramatically fluctuating, fortunes of Christianity in those turbulent times.

9

Christianity in England in the
Age of the Vikings

From the late eighth century to 878

The church in England in the last decade of the eighth century was not suffering from terminal decay, but neither was it particularly healthy and vibrant. It was somewhat stagnant, lacking vision and zeal, and showing little evidence of the kind of vigour and creativity which had characterized it at various periods of renown and distinction since the late sixth century. It was suffering from torpor which was to last for well over one hundred years but for the shining example of King Alfred. The grand time of mission, and of figures like Willibrord and Boniface, who set alight a concern in the English church for spreading the gospel to heathen lands on the continent, was past. It seems to have come to an end as quickly as it began. And while it lasted it may have drawn away from the home church some of its finest sons and daughters. Wilfrid lived until 809, otherwise by the end of the eighth century all the Christians of outstanding stature were dead: St Cuthbert; St Leoba, who went out to help Boniface, and ended her life as abbess of Tauberbischofsheim; St Wilibald, an English monk who travelled widely in the Mediterranean region and finished his life as Bishop of Eichstatt in Germany; St Lullus, or Lul, who was the successor of Boniface as Bishop of Mainz; St Willehad, the first Bishop of Bremen in north Germany; and Albert, an outstanding Archbishop of York.

The only other Christian of comparable standing who survived until the ninth century, Alcuin, died in 804. He was a Northumbrian who was probably born about 740. In 767 he succeeded Albert as director of the school at York, which was the most distinguished centre of learning of its day in Europe. There he found his vocation as a teacher; perhaps the first Englishman to find his full satisfaction, and lifelong career in such work. He was ordained deacon, but he was never admitted to the priesthood, and there is no evidence that he was a professed monk. The curriculum within which he taught was based on the trivium and quadrivium. The study of scripture was the pre-eminent subject, but grammar and rhetoric, law and chant, astronomy, and also probably some biology and arithmetic, were included. Pupils seem to have received teaching in those subjects from this range of options which appealed to them or for which they had a particular aptitude.

In 782 Alcuin was persuaded to join the court of Charles, king of the Franks (Charlemagne), and he remained there for the rest of his life. He relished the urbane atmosphere of the court, and the way all aspects of education and personal cultural development were enthusiastically encouraged. He not only shone as a scholar, teacher and poet, but he used his undoubted administrative talents to make the court school more efficient. In addition, he was influential in persuading higher clergy to establish monastic and diocesan schools. He was an unswerving traditionalist, and thoroughly orthodox in his theology and teaching. Heresies greatly troubled him, and he championed the Catholic doctrines against such unorthodox teaching as Adoptionism, which had spread from Spain into the Frankish realm. He made a monumental contribution to Carolingian culture and to the life of the Frankish church and state. He can be reckoned as the last great name in the line of distinguished Anglo-Saxon scholars in the pre-Danish period. He formed a bridge between the golden age of learning, monasticism and vibrant Christianity in his own country and the Carolingian renaissance. In that role he was also one of those who helped to give continuity between the age of the Vikings in England and what went before.

But with his death there came an extended dearth of inspirational churchmen of outstanding ability. And this reflected the rather flat and uninspiring level of church life as a whole. Nevertheless, local church life, and the life of monasteries did proceed, even if it was at a somewhat mundane and banal level, where the large issues of policy, strategy and exciting innovations gave way to a run of administrative enactments.

The church was, in mostly small ways, trying to put its house in order. At the end of the eighth century there was some preoccupation with the restoration of the status and standing of the archiepiscopacy of Canterbury after the attempt of Offa to establish a third archbishopric at Lichfield, and his successors' effort to gain acceptance of London as an alternative to Lichfield; machinations which I have previously considered. The honour and status of Canterbury were forthrightly upheld at the Synod of Clofesho in 804.

Among other domestic church measures were the reforms of Wulfred,

Archbishop of Canterbury from 805 to 832. Following the example of Bishop Chrodegang of Metz (742–766), Wulfred allowed his cathedral clergy to retain property but insisted that they should regularly attend services of the cathedral church, make use of the common refectory and dormitory, and observe regular discipline. In the same vein, the Council of Chelsea, which Wulfred summoned in 816, condemned the lay lordship of monasteries, and asserted the right of bishops to elect the heads of monastic houses. The council was at pains to safeguard and strengthen episcopal rights and ecclesiastical property.[1]

All these preoccupations and actions are indications that the church was going about its business, and not unaware of its responsibilities, when suddenly the crisis of the Viking raids came like a thief in the night. The effect was traumatic. 'There can be no question that the Danish invasions of the ninth century shattered the organization of the English church, destroyed monastic life in eastern England, and elsewhere caused distress and anxiety which made the pursuit of learning almost impossible.'[2] As we have seen, the first Viking incursions were sporadic and localized, but they were destructive of property and personnel, and they were psychologically very damaging. The fear of raids was undermining and tension-provoking. The wrecking of Lindisfarne was especially devastating.[3] This single act of pitiless aggression sent waves of fear throughout the church, and shudders of apprehension about what might be in store. The Anglo-Saxon Chronicle[4] captures this almost cosmic consternation under the entry for 793: 'Here terrible portents came about over the land of Northumbria, and miserably frightened the people: these were immense flashes of lightning, and fiery dragons were seen flying in the air. A great famine immediately followed these signs; and a little after that in the same year the raiding of heathen men miserably devastated God's church in Lindisfarne island by looting and slaughter.'[5]

To the compiler of the *Chronicle* these marauders and destroyers of monasteries and churches were 'heathen men', 'the heathen army', or occasionally 'the pirates'. And it is understandable that they should appear to the Christian Anglo-Saxons as enemies of true religion.

The Danes were dedicated to their gods. But this was not in the Christian sense of personal piety resulting in a distinctive, sanctified, lifestyle. As we have seen, they acknowledged Thor as almost their national champion, the symbol of personal valour and success, the guarantor of victory in battle. 'How much this made them crueller enemies than, say, Northumbrians to Mercians, cannot be demonstrated: but certainly their exploits are recorded with peculiar bitterness by the Anglo-Saxon chroniclers, and certainly they not merely plundered the minsters (as was indeed natural, for the minsters had much portable plate and other loot) but brutally maltreated such monks and bishops as they captured.'[6] Of all classes of Englishmen it seems that the English clergy, both pastoral and monastic, suffered peculiarly.

As the raids resumed in the 830s, with larger war bands, so the devastation caused became more widespread and serious; and once again it seemed to focus especially on monasteries and churches. Thus, the Anglo-Saxon Chronicle records for 869 how East Anglia was overrun:

> Here the raiding-army went across Mercia into East Anglia. and took winter-quarters at Thetford; and in that year St Edmund the king fought against them, and the Danish (*sic*) took the victory, and killed the king and conquered all that land, and did for all the monasteries to which they came. At the same time they came to Peterborough: burned and demolished, killed abbot and monks and all that they found there, brought it about so that what was earlier very rich was as it were nothing. And that year Archbishop Ceolnoth died.[7]

The occupation and colonization of East Anglia, the eastern half of Mercia and southern Northumbria by armies of heathen Danes must have had a massively detrimental effect on the life of the local church. The administration and pastoral oversight of the church must have been reduced to an extremely low level with the ending of the bishoprics of Dunwich, Elmham and Lindsey, and with the reduction of York to a state of demolition and poverty. In the region beyond the Tees, the sees of Hexham and Whithorn ceased to exist. The cathedral at Lindisfarne was abandoned, and the bishop spent seven years with some of his younger clerks wandering from one insecure refuge to another, preserving the relics of St Cuthbert from destruction until peace was sufficiently restored in the north that a church could be built for them at Chester-le-Street.

There was probably not a complete breakdown of pastoral care in a number of sees in these troublesome times. But although in the worst part of the fighting the list of bishops can be traced with few vacancies, there is no certainty when one succeeded another. Thus, when East Anglia was raided and overrun, the times of accession of the Bishops of Dunwich and Elmham are quite uncertain: either the Easter table and annal perished or no book was kept. The situation is confused. It is not known if Bishop Cunda was consecrated in 836 to the see of Elmham or Dunwich, or whether Bishop Aelfred was consecrated in 934 to Elmham or Lindsey. The names of the Bishops of Elmham are not known for the period 836 to 934, although after that the episcopal succession was continuous until the Norman Conquest. The years of succession for the bishops of Hereford are uncertain in the second half of the ninth century; and the record for the see of Leicester ends with bishop Ceolred, who died sometime between 869 and 888. In the same half century the succession years of the bishopric of Lichfield are unclear: and there is a similar absence of records for the bishops of Lindsey, and even for those of London, Rochester and Selsey. The years of the bishops' consecrations for Winchester are unknown between 871 and 900.

Although the continuity of ecclesiastical organization was not so severely curtailed in the west midlands and the south, as in the other areas just mentioned, innumerable ancient centres of Christianity must have perished, and the disruption to the church must have been immense; as, for example, in the harryings of Wessex between 870 and 878. Likewise, the churches of the Severn valley, which was the safest part of England, must have suffered many evils when the Danes were abroad in the vicinity of the Wrekin or encamped at Gloucester. In all these areas, and throughout England, the Danish raids and foraging of the land must have meant, if not destruction, at least the grievous impoverishment of civilization and the undermining of the church.

It is, however, not known to what extent the local minster provision with the network of dependent churches was affected. By the time of the Danish invasions this was well established. The continued existence of minsters depended on the endowments provided by their patrons, usually a local lord, and clearly many of these were adversely affected by the Danish incursions. What is known is that the system was well developed, with 2000 churches serving 13,000 settlements, by the time of the Domesday Book – a pointer to the fact that the major part of the nationwide church provision remained intact despite the Danish crisis, or was able to recover from dislocation soon after the raids lessened or ceased, and after the Danes had settled down to peaceful community life with their native British neighbours.

There is no indication of religious, or indeed any other form of tension between those who made England their new home and the existing native population. There are good indications that the Vikings quite readily conformed to Christian customs and even to Christian belief once they settled in the midst of the host society. For instance, like the Anglo-Saxons before them, they seem to have 'respected Christian burial grounds and used them for the disposal of their own dead'. They appear to have 'reacted quickly to their Christian surroundings and were soon adapting their burial customs to those of the Anglo-Saxon population'.[8] And this change of burial custom may be reckoned as related to a more general change of religious belief.

The Vikings seem to have taken a reasonably tolerant attitude to Christianity from the early days of the settlement. The church on its part adapted itself to Viking culture. This is illustrated in the north-west, where the famous Gosforth Cross has been convincingly interpreted as showing a reconciliation between the Christian and pagan beliefs.[9] This all supports the conclusion of much recent scholarship, that the shared characteristics of Viking, Anglo-Saxon and Celtic cultures, emanating from the common experience of all three as migratory peoples, helped when it came to negotiating accommodations to one another.

From 878 to the early tenth century

Accommodation does not mean the rapid and total abandonment by the Danes of their traditional religion. Scattered Scandinavian place-names in the region embraced by the Danelaw reveal heathen cults and heathen practices. The hill projecting from the north-western edge of Cleveland, which is now called Roseberry Topping, appears in the twelfth century as Othensberg, which means that it was once sacred to Othin, the Scandinavian counterpart of the Anglo-Saxon Woden. The name Ellough for a village in Suffolk probably represents the Old Scandinavian *elgr*, 'heathen temple'. Then there are place names such as *Leggeshou*, *Katehou*, and *Granehou* which seem to commemorate the burial of Danish settlers in heathen fashion under *haugar*, or mounds, to which their names were permanently applied. 'But in view of the great extent of the region covered by the Danish settlements, the number of place-names which carry a suggestion of Danish heathenism is too small to prove an obdurate adherence to ancient ways of thought.'[10]

How and when the Danish settlers embraced Christianity for themselves, and in what numbers, is hidden from our view. 'Little is known about the process by which the conversion of the Danelaw was actually brought about. But the fact that no traditions of the work have survived suggests that it owed less to the labours of missionaries than to the example of the Christian social order of Wessex and English Mercia.'[11] There was initially no widespread or 'official' reception of Christianity and rejection of traditional Danish pagan gods. It seems that the church as a body was not very evangelistic and did not systematically, or even periodically and haphazardly, set itself the task of converting the newly arrived Danes. We have here shades of a former and similar situation typified by Bede's reprimand of the British for not more readily working for the conversion of the Anglo-Saxon settlers.

How much Christians, and bishops in particular, were to blame for not having been more active in winning the heathen Danish settlers to the Christian faith is almost impossible to determine. A letter survives which purports to be from Formosus, the pope from 891 to 896, in which he chides the English bishops very severely for their past ineffectiveness in taking action against the heathenism of the settlers. Whatever justice there was in attributing blame to them, it is clear that there had been a change in the years immediately prior to the pope's expressed concern. The letter states that the bishops had started to instruct the heathen; and this is one of several pointers to the way King Alfred had begun to transform the whole situation. Until the 870s no king among the English Danish invaders or settlers had abjured paganism and personally accepted the Christian faith. It was therefore an historic moment when Guthram and his chief followers accepted baptism in 878 as the price of a treaty with King Alfred. How deep the personal faith of those concerned went is, of course, open to question, and even cynicism. But the act was, at the very least, hugely symbolic. And it was not limited to that small band of Vikings. Guthfrith, the first known king of Danish Northumbria, who died in 895, was a Christian. The Christian tide was perhaps beginning to turn; and at the centre of all that was happening in England in those critical last three decades of the ninth century was King Alfred.

In the preface to his translation of Pope Gregory's *Pastoral Care* Alfred elaborated on the need for the country to apply Christian values to all aspects of its life. This is therefore a cardinal document in our understanding of his views and policy. It also gives some insight into the literary culture of late Anglo-Saxon England in general, and the religious aspect of that culture in particular. An extensive quotation from it will convey something of the character of the king, and of the encouragement he gave to the renewal of the religious life of England:

I would have it known that very often it has come to my mind what men of learning there were formerly throughout England, both in religious and secular orders; and how there were happy times then throughout England; and how the kings, who had authority over this people, obeyed God and his messengers; and how they not only maintained their peace, morality and authority at home but also extended their territory outside; and how they succeeded both in warfare and in wisdom; and also how eager were the religious orders both in teaching and in learning as well as in all the holy services which it was their duty to perform for God; and how people from abroad sought wisdom and instruction in this country; and how nowadays, if we wished to acquire these things, we would have to seek them outside. Learning had declined so thoroughly in England that there were very few men on this side of the Humber who could understand their divine services in English, or even translate a single letter from Latin into English; and I suppose that there were not many beyond the Humber either. There were so few of them that I cannot recollect even a single one south of the Thames when I succeeded to the kingdom. Thanks be to God Almighty that we now have any supply of teachers at all! Therefore I beseech you to do as I believe you are willing to do: as often as you can free yourself from worldly affairs so that you may apply that wisdom which God gave you wherever you can. Remember what punishments befell us in this world when we ourselves did not cherish learning nor submit it to other men. We were Christians in name alone, and very few of us possessed Christian virtues.[12]

I have already in the last chapter rehearsed the wide-ranging and impressive ways Alfred helped to revive learning and education. My concern now is to focus on those aspects of his staggeringly comprehensive programme which were more directly to do with the church in England. The divide is blurred, because religion was not a separate, compartmentalized, sphere of life or intellectual activity. It was closely identified with matters of culture and education.

The king promoted writing which was very explicitly religious. We have seen how he engaged in translations of religious works; and the availability of Christian literature was a central feature of his whole vision of Christian England. But his example and influence were more subtle and pervasive. He was probably instrumental in helping to Christianize literature generally. It is perhaps not coincidental that in his time, and in the following century, Christian literary works of importance appeared. The king's insistence on the use of English and the learning of English letters by as wide a circle as possible was revolutionary, and it was one of the foundations of the pastoral work of late Anglo-Saxon bishops. In providing this impetus Alfred did not, of course, work in a vacuum; he drew upon a tradition of Old English verse and scriptural poetry which had been handed on to Wessex by Mercia, and which ultimately came from Northumbria.

The great name in the Mercian tradition of religious poetry was Cynewulf. He was the outstanding English Christian poet of these centuries at present under review. The earlier school of Anglo-Saxon religious poetry associated with Caedmon dealt with biblical stories, and it typically had a loose, alliterative, epic verse structure. God, Christ and the saints were praised like kings and heroes. With Cynewulf the subject matter was the legends of saints, homilies, or special expositions; and the structure of the sentences was clearer and less diffuse. The four poems definitely attributed to him are those on the *Ascension*, the martyrdom of *St Juliana*, the *Elene*, and the *Fates of the Apostles*.

Much modern scholarship regards the poem *Beowulf* as belonging to this same genre. Alfred was a great admirer of the traditional poetry of his people. He may have numbered some written version of *Beowulf* among such a corpus of literature, for some have surmised that what was circulated orally assumed its essentially complete present written form in the period 750–800. The epic would no doubt have commended itself to the king. For it was a work which dealt with tales of the pagan past, and indeed perhaps of the contemporary pagan world, and yet was probably written by a Christian poet for a Christian audience. If this is right, then the author may be viewed as a lover of analogy. Beowulf in his fight with the monster Grendel, the sea-burial of Scyld, and so much else, was entertaining, but with a profound meaning. It could be interpreted at different levels. At the highest it can be seen as 'sophisticated poetry, written down for those who accepted the Christian order of things, who could understand allusions to biblical events and needed no explanation of 'noon' as implying a service at the ninth hour, or "the great doom" as implying the Christian last judgment'.[13] There are, however, critics of such an interpretation who argue that the poem cannot be understood as being so evidently Christian in meaning, but must be interpreted in a broader, less specific manner.[14]

In his desire to promote Christianity and learning, Alfred founded two monasteries: a house for men on his own lands at Athelney, and a nunnery at Shaftesbury. It seems that the former was intended to follow the example of such Carolingian houses as Coebie or Fulda: to be Benedictine, dedicated to the recitation of the opus dei and to study, as Wearmouth and St Augustine's at Canterbury had once been. Asser asserts that this was partly in order to revive a monastic tradition 'which had been totally lacking in that entire race'.[15] But Alfred's monastic programme was not ambitious. He only founded these two religious houses; he did not demand precise observance of the Benedictine Rule; he was content that secular clergy should be admitted to Athelney; and he subsidized the older unreformed communities both in Wessex and Mercia. In adopting such a policy he was being realistic. The task of restoring the monastic ideal was well nigh hopeless in the late ninth century. This is well demonstrated by the fact that Alfred could not find one Englishman to fill the abbacy of Athelney and had to recruit someone from the continent.

The miserable failure of this attempt by Alfred to revive monasticism may have been in large part because of the current circumstances and the prevailing conditions in England in the previous decades. After all the rejuvenation of monasteries might have appeared to many contemporaries to have taken little account of the most pressing problems confronting the church, and to have had little claim to receive urgent attention in view of other more obvious issues demanding prompt remedial action. As we have noted, there had been a massive and serious dislocation of the church as an institution, and a series of traumatic experiences for local Christian communities and individual believers as a result of the Danish raids, wars and settlement. With buildings destroyed, ecclesiastical and pastoral breakdown on a large scale, territorial endowments fallen into secular hands, and believers in a state of shock, the recovery of monasticism may have seemed to many to be irrelevant or low on the scale of priorities. Christianity had barely survived the testing times. In the Danelaw it had a precarious hold on the inhabitants, whether they were natives or Danes who may have given up their paganism, and it may not have continued had not the reconquest been followed by measures to restore the supply of trained clergy to the lands recovered. It is understandable if, in such a situation, the maintenance of a decent level of ecclesiastical order in Wessex and English Mercia, and the restoration of the church in the Danelaw, were considered more urgent needs 'than the revivification of an institution which appeared both moribund and ill-suited to the tasks in hand'.[16] The monasteries of the seventh century whose inmates were key figures in the conversion of England, were very different from their ninth-century or tenth-century counterparts, whose roles were much more rigorously defined so that they were ill-adapted to be centres for evangelistic endeavour.

Alfred's son and then his grandson who succeeded him so successfully one after the other on the throne abandoned his premature pursuit of a monastic revival; but, like their illustrious forebear, they were zealous in their care of the church. This was shown in unspectacular but highly significant ways. The history of the church in these years, during the first decades of the tenth century is once more somewhat drab, and there are no colourful personalities or dramatic events to enliven the story. But the state of the church during that period may have been portrayed as more desperate than it was, for those who recorded the impending monastic revival were monks 'whose zeal to demonstrate the greatness of their heroes led them to display the premonastic Church in its worst guise and to conceal the magnitude of the debt which the monks owed to their secular predecessors'.[17]

The concern of Alfred's successors expressed itself in grants to religious communities. Edward the Elder completed the plans of his father for the New Minster at Winchester. Athelstan enriched almost all the minsters in England with buildings, ornaments, books and land, and he also founded Milton Abbas and Muchelney. Edmund gave Glastonbury to Dunstan to restore, and King Eadred was actively engaged in constructing Etholwold's Abingdon. All of these monarchs additionally gave help to continental religious causes.

These kings and church leaders of the first half of the tenth century also engaged in the task of diocesan reconstruction and re-organization in which extra 'assistant' bishops were provided. Archbishop Plegmund consecrated bishops for Berkshire and Wiltshire, based on Ramsbury, for Somerset, with the see at Wells, and for Devonshire, with the see at Crediton. The bishopric of Selsey was re-established; and diocesan supervision in the area of the old sees of Lindsey and Leicester was initiated by the consecration of a bishop for Dorchester-on-Thames. It would have gladdened the heart of archbishop Theodore that the new dioceses were small enough to allow effective oversight and pastoral care, although their endowments proved to be inadequate. Later, in 926, Athelstan created a new bishopric at St Germans. As the Danelaw was absorbed, episcopal oversight was provided in the south by Dorchester, and further north by an extension of the authority of the Archbishop of York into the north midlands and Lindsey. The see of North Elmham was revived in 956 to help cover East Anglia. The situation of Northumbria was less satisfactory, as it was found impossible to re-establish the bishoprics of Hexham and Whithorn, and for the whole of the tenth century the impoverished archbishopric of York had only one subordinate bishopric, Chester-le-Street, which was moved to Durham in 990. The royal appointments to bishoprics were taken very seriously by each of the kings who succeeded Alfred, and they included men of distinction.

Alfred and his descendants were concerned to maintain close links not only with the continent, but with Rome and the papacy. Alfred sent alms and gifts, and received relics and favours from Rome. He was aware of the potential benefit of papal approval and support in the exercise of his authority within England. He was pious and yet worldly-wise. He also fostered relations with the Patriarch of Jerusalem, partly again for religious and partly for diplomatic reasons. His successors carried on this external policy.

In so many ways Alfred was a saviour and exemplar for his country. It has been said that in the ninth century 'Anglo-Saxon independence and English Christianity might well have collapsed together'.[18] That they did not was to a large extent due to Alfred the Great. But credit needs also to be given to those who followed him on the throne and who so magnificently reinforced what Alfred had achieved.

Monastic revival

The inclination of the pagan Vikings to embrace the Christian faith was heightened the more vibrant Christianity was seen to be, and the more it was perceived as the fountainhead of literary, aesthetic and other developments. The monastic revival of the tenth century was therefore highly significant not only as a Christian movement of renewal, but also as a means of making Christianity more attractive, and as a factor in Christianizing the whole culture and life of the country. Why there should have been a quite sudden and dramatic revitalization of monasticism in the second half of the tenth century, when but a few decades before attempts to breath new life into it had met with such a dismal lack of success, is not easy to determine, but it is certainly bound up with the efforts of three men at the time, and two, to a lesser extent, who added a sort of postscript in the eleventh century.

In the first phase the central figures were Dunstan, Oswald and Ethelwold; and in its second phase Elfric and Wulfstan. The origins, course and content of the movement can perhaps best be depicted by an examination of the contribution which each of them made to what may be regarded as one connected series of reforms, adaptations and initiatives. The first phase was concentrated on monastic reform, and the second on the extension of that reform not only within monasteries but to the secular clergy through laws, canons and homilies. The political context for reform had also changed in the meantime, from the relatively peaceful rule of Edgar to the upheaval brought about by the renewed Danish raids during the reign of King Ethelred the Unready. But if the two parts are seen as a whole, and are taken as complementary to the developments in the local church which I will review later in this chapter, then it will be apparent that this was a most important time in the evolution of the English church.

In addition, the constant and profound interlocking of 'church' and 'state' affairs, of the 'sacred' and the 'secular' at national as well as at the local level meant that the reform of the one had great impact on the other. In pre-Conquest England there was no definition of the boundary between lay and spiritual authority. 'The lay and spiritual powers were associated in every action of the Old English state and in the working of all its principal institutions. The bishop sat beside the earl in the shire court, ecclesiastical pleas were heard in the hundred court, and the spiritual element was so strong in the king's council that it is sometimes described as a synod.' Archbishop Oda of Canterbury (941–58) wrote his *Constitutions* apparently for recitation, and in them he adamantly told King Edmund to obey his bishops, and rule justly. 'The effect of this alliance is perhaps most plainly seen in the religious colour which it imparted to Old English legislation, and in particular to that of the period between the accession of Edgar and the death of Cnut.'[19] The law codes, and the preambles and content of legislation which emanated from the king's council, frequently suggest that they originated as the canons of church synods. For example, Aethelstan's first code and his *Ordinance on Charities*, both state that they were framed on the advice of Archbishop Wulfhelm of Canterbury and other bishops, and the decisions enshrined in the text known as 1 Edmund appear to have been taken purely by the ecclesiastical wing of the royal council, the *witan*. So the revival of monasticism and all the subsequent repercussions of that movement, were not matters of purely ecclesiastical concern; they had wide implications and results. Within the church itself the end result was 'the restoration of the powers of the English church, and the efflorescence of learning'.[20]

The immediate precursory event for the English monastic revival was the European-wide revivification of reformed monasticism. The essential element in this was Rule according to an Order. Although St Benedict had laid down rules for the monastic life long since, and features of that life had been exported to Britain in the seventh century, the breakthrough came with the founding of the monastery of Cluny in south-east France in 910. There the community was subject to a stringent set of rules, which included celibacy, communal living and abstention from eating meat. This institution in particular, but others also, and all that they represented, were to play a crucial part in what was about to take place in England.

The chief architect of the English reform movement was Dunstan.[21] He was born in about the year 909, the son of a Somersetshire thegn, and educated at the small clerical community of Glastonbury. He was introduced to the court of King Athelstan by his uncle, Athelm, Archbishop of Canterbury, but it seems that he aroused enmity because of his purity of life and was expelled on some pretext. He took refuge with another uncle, Elfheah, the Bishop of Winchester, and was ordained by him as priest. He subsequently took monastic vows. On Athelstan's death he returned to court, but once more became a victim of intrigue. A turning point in his life came after the new King Edmund had a near-death experience, as a result of which he resolved to re-establish Glastonbury as a regular monastery with Dunstan as its abbot.

The continental monastic reform movement, largely associated with Cluny and Fleury, had apparently not had much impact on English church life and thinking. But Archbishop Oda, Dunstan's predecessor at Canterbury, had been a monk at Fleury, and others were touched by the new inspiration from the continent. What was going on there may have influenced Dunstan in the measures he now took to reinstate the derelict buildings. He also extended the church and added a cloister; and he assembled a monastic community which was subject to the Rule of St Benedict, possibly supplemented by the *Ordo Qualiter* of the late eighth century.

The succession of Eadred to the throne resulted in the full restoration of Dunstan to royal favour. He was numbered among the king's principal counsellors, and Glastonbury was used as a repository for treasures and archives.

Dunstan attracted disciples and drew attention to the potential for monastic revival. But, in the meantime Ethelwold and Oswald were moving towards an even stricter view of the monastic ideal. After having received the monastic habit Ethelwold went abroad in order to perfect himself in learning and in the monastic discipline. Oswald, a nephew of Archbishop Oda, ruled a community at Winchester. He was sent for further training to Fleury, and others followed him there. So, both Ethelwold and Oswald received first-hand experience of reformed continental monasticism. The king gave Ethelwold the abandoned, neglected and mean buildings and small site of the former monastery at Abingdon; which he promptly transformed into the second genuinely monastic community in England. But still, by the time King Eadred died in 955 only these two monasteries had been reformed. It was not yet a movement.

Dunstan fell into disfavour with the new monarch, Eadwig, who exiled him in 956. His time at the reformed abbey of St Peter's in Ghent, although it had no immediate consequences, gave him invaluable direct experience of the continental movement.

The indispensability of royal favour and support was then fully demonstrated with the accession of Edgar as king of Mercia in 957. Dunstan was immediately recalled, and he was appointed to the see of Worcester, to which the bishopric of London was later added. In 959 Edgar assumed authority over the whole kingdom on the death of Eadwig, and he promptly promoted Dunstan to Canterbury. It was rather ironic that the main architect of reform was himself the subject of such a blatantly disgraceful show of ecclesiastical malpractice. He was not only a pluralist by holding the sees of Worcester and London, but he had been translated uncanonically to Canterbury, and intruded into a see whose occupant still lived.

Dunstan exerted his influence by the appointment of Oswald as his successor at Worcester, and the new bishop immediately started to exercise his particular and subtle powers in the move towards reformation.

His nature held neither the deep reserve of Dunstan nor the impetuous drive toward the goal so characteristic of Ethelwold. His was, rather, a spirit of warm and genial friendliness; his spontaneous greeting of welcome to his fellow-men won for him ready response from all with whom he lived and worked. His fervour for religion in its stricter ways was no less than that of Dunstan and of Ethelwold, his practice as sincere and faithful; but his mind seems to have lacked something of the austere temperament of the one, the stern quickness of the other.[22]

One of his first acts was to establish a small community of monks at

Westbury-on-Trym under the leadership of Germanus, an ex-member of Oda's community at Winchester, who had been at Fleury.

In 963 Ethelwold became Bishop of Winchester. He held the see until his death in 984, and his dedication and drive were infectious. He

> was a man full of rushing energy, impetuous, driven by a single purpose, unencumbered by scruple of policies to be weighed and balanced. To him the cause dominated all; and to this cause the individual should bow, spirit and body, for the good of the whole. Those who submitted and followed his ideal knew him as tender, considerate, ready for their aid to sacrifice both himself and all things outside himself which he could lawfully yield. He wrecked his health, not only by his rigid abstinence from food and sleep, but by his incessant work; he spent his fortune – and he was a man of much wealth – on gifts to churches, to monasteries, and to individuals.[23]

It is even said that in a time of great famine, when the funds for relief were exhausted, he ordered the silver vessels and items of fine workmanship which constituted the treasures of the church, to be broken up and melted down to provide money for the starving poor.

Thus, within a few months of Edgar's accession the three reforming monks had been appointed to three of the greatest sees in the kingdom, and the ecclesiastical situation was transformed. The new reforming brush swept dramatically into action with the expulsion in 964 of the clerks of the Old Minster at Winchester, and their replacement by monks from Abingdon.

The reform movement was beginning to gain momentum. 'From Glastonbury, Abingdon and Westbury colonies of monks were sent to restore observance of the Benedictine Rule in old foundations and to make new plantations.'[24] The catalogue of renewal which ensued is most impressive. The monasteries of Bath, Malmesbury and Westminster were reformed; several monasteries were founded in the west country; and monasticism was extended to the Danelaw by the founding of Ramsey monastery and the restoration of the fenland monasteries at Peterborough, Ely and Thorney. By the end of the century there were forty entirely new monasteries, or old houses refounded in the southern half of England, including half-a-dozen for women.

But, although the three men at the centre of the revival were united in what they regarded as the essential principles of the reform movement, the growth was to a large extent unregulated, with each house following its own customs. It was agreed by the leaders of the movement that some sort of more explicit general direction was necessary. At their request, therefore, the king summoned a council at Winchester for the purpose of co-ordinating the revival. It was attended by many bishops, abbots and abbesses, and by monks from Fleury and Ghent, and it approved a book of monastic customs, the *Regularis Concordia*, 'The Monastic Agreement of the Monks and Nuns of the English Nation', issued about 970. This set out in detail the daily and yearly liturgical routine to be followed in future by all houses of monks and nuns in England. It made very clear the intention of the English religious to align themselves with those of Fleury, Ghent and Lorraine. It also gave substance to an underlying concept of monasticism which was not an imitation of the former Celtic codes. Each monastic house was required to elect a superior, who would usually come from among its own members, with the advice and consent of the king. The daily round of prayer within the monastery was to be supplemented by periods of work, which included teaching the oblates and the illumination of books. The monastic lands were to be worked by lay tenants in order not to intrude on the cohesion of the spiritual community inside the monastery. The members of the community were under obligation to attend a daily chapter meeting, and they were to show hospitality to strangers and to the poor. In common with the provision of the Benedictine rule, communal meals were to be taken at 'noon' and 'evening' during the summer, and once a day in winter and Lent and on certain other specified days, and the consumption of meat was restricted to the sick.

There was to be a close link between the monastery and those lay people who lived in its vicinity. Lay people were expected to attend the monastic churches to receive mass on Sundays, and in fact the buildings were soon adapted to separate them from the monks. But it was not all one-way traffic. On great feasts the monks processed in the streets. By such means the effects of the monastic reform percolated into society, and were felt by the church and the people in general. This was somewhat in contrast to the situation on the continent. In England the movement was led by bishops and archbishops who were engaged in the day by day life of the whole church, and they were concerned that the changes should not be confined to monasteries.

The *Regularis Concordia* in like manner tied together English monasticism and the English monarchy. As we have seen, the church leaders depended on the sympathy and favour of the king. But it was conversely in the interest of the king to co-operate with his archbishops and bishops. By the tenth and eleventh centuries the church commanded great influence, and it could not be ignored and affronted by the monarch without possible dire consequences for him and the unity and peace of his realm.

This working together of the church and the king is seen in the policy of replacing secular clergy by monks, which the reform movement encouraged and the monarchy supported. Thus, when Bishop Aelfwine of Elmham expelled the secular clergy from St Edmund's Abbey, Suffolk, the king, Cnut, granted the abbey a new charter, and his Norman wife Emma became patroness of the monks. The twenty monks concerned came from St Benet's Holme, Norfolk, which, together with Burton-on-Trent and Coventry, was one of three new monastic foundations.

Lastly, the reform movement stimulated a remarkable flowering of literature and the illumination of manuscripts. Bishop Ethelwold was assiduous in equipping his monasteries with books, and the practice spread. At Winchester a school of illumination and book production sprang up and grew with astonishing speed. Examples of the work undertaken include a copy of the charter granted to them by King Edgar in 966, in which there was a splendid miniature depicting the king, flanked by the patrons of the Minster, offering the charter to Christ himself. Also among the surviving items is a Benedictional, a collection of pontifical blessings for each day's mass, that belonged to Ethelwold himself, which is a superb object in black, red and gold, embellished with fine full-page miniatures. Overall, the range of high quality manuscripts produced at that time is astonishing.

The monks of Winchester, Glastonbury, Ramsey and other refounded abbeys, in addition to copying liturgical manuscripts, expressed their rekindled devotion in holy week and Easter with the introduction of ceremonies and processions, and by re-editing their sacramentaries. They also produced a number of small liturgical books for use in chapel; epistle books, collectars, troopers, or song books with the sequences, grails, or graduals with the verses of the psalm to be sung before the gospel, antiphones, with the music for the divine office, calendars, martyrologies, and benedictionals, or books of blessings. There was a tendency to replace sacramentaries, general books of rites and blessings, by pontificals and missals.

In all the artistic works produced by the tenth-century monasteries, as well as in the architecture, furniture and fittings of the monasteries and churches, continental influences are clear, and especially the tastes of

France and Italy. The crucifix over the high altar of Bury St Edmunds was modelled on the Holy Face of Lucca; and, more significantly because of its prominence in national life, the rebuilding of Westminster Abbey as the royal church of Edward the Confessor's kingdom was undertaken in the Norman-Romanesque style.

The tenth-century reform therefore had many and diverse reverberations, and it was long-lasting in what it achieved. It had its own distinctive principles which were appropriated by the church and by society at large.

> The monastic life to the English reformers as to their foreign counterparts was not primarily a state in which the individual with a 'special vocation' might devote himself wholly to God and receive guidance from a master of the spiritual life. It was rather a perfection of the clerical life and a discipline for the many, by which individuals might find salvation and the Church as a whole receive strength, dignity and order.[25]

The reform movement, although of immense importance and with wide and long-term consequences, was confined largely to the southern half of England. By 1017 it had not penetrated further north than Burton in Staffordshire and Crowland in south Lincolnshire. Restricted it may have been geographically, but the ripples went out into areas beyond the epicentre, as well as into the succeeding centuries. It 'set in being a life that was destined to endure till the Dissolution of the monasteries six hundred years later'; an 'unbroken series of generations lived the regular life and formed a sequence of tradition which, while accepting elements from without, remained in its essentials one and the same'.[26] The focus of historians has tended to be either on the monasticism of the age of Aidan, Wilfrid, Aldhelm, Bede and Boniface, or on the Norman period of Lanfranc and Anselm. But the reforms I have just reviewed played a crucial part in the evolution not only of monasticism, but of the church in England as a whole.

This was exhibited in a most public manner with the consecration of King Edgar in 973. The ceremony succinctly portrayed the way in which the relationship between ruler and people, and the nature of Anglo-Saxon kingship, had undergone a transformation under the influence of the Christian faith, invigorated by the revival. The unction received by the prince made him a Christian king, and in the service the notion of the church and people as one is made explicit. 'The duty of the king is now to "nourish, teach, defend and instruct" the Church understood as the Christian people committed by divinity to his charge.'[27]

Christianity in England owes more than is often conceded to the tenth-century monastic reform movement. It had incalculable short, medium and long-term consequences. And what was accomplished was due almost entirely to Dunstan, Ethelwold and Oswald.

> When the strong new life of monastic England in the reigns of Edgar and Ethelred is seen in a true light, the achievement of the three, and especially of Ethelwold and Dunstan, can be more justly assessed . . . they left no new impress on the form of monastic life; they changed nothing, nor did they enrich the blood of the religious world by their writings or spiritual doctrine. But in another respect they did everything: they called the dead to life; they created a great and flourishing system upon vacant soil; and to Dunstan especially, as to Augustine of Canterbury before him, are due in a very real sense the titles of patron and father of medieval England.[28]

Nonetheless, the frequent eulogies and the general, almost uncritical, praises heaped upon the three reformers have not gone unchallenged. Some are of the opinion that much was achieved, but it was from a low base as a starting point, and was therefore not as great as is often depicted. The standards of the reform and of the reformers, it is claimed by such detractors, were not particularly high in the first place, and this meant that there was not very much for the eleventh century to live up to. The result was that the impetus of the revival fell away after the death of the three prime movers.[29] But even those who raise such queries acknowledge some solid achievements. Thus, D. H. Farmer, while he reacts against the general unqualified acclaim which the movement often receives, acknowledges that it led to the foundation of many of England's principal monasteries; resulted in the peculiarly English institution of monastic cathedrals; provided most of the English bishops from the reign of Edgar until that of Cnut; initiated an evangelistic mission to Scandinavia; and generated an impressive output of high quality manuscripts which were illuminated, or enlivened with line-drawings, and gave a boost to the creation of high quality sculptures in metal and ivory, to the composition of polyphonic music and to the resuscitation of ecclesiastical architecture.[30] I have some sympathy with this perspective and interpretation of events, but in view of the somewhat depressed state of Christianity prior to the reform movement, surely even such results are impressive. And if to them is added the

ripples which went far further into the future, then justice demands that
the movement should be accorded a prominent place in any historical
narrative and analysis.

As for how long the revival lasted, and when it lost its dynamism, this
is difficult to gauge. Although the monastic reform survived a political
reaction in Mercia after the death of King Edgar in 975, the impression
is sometimes given that the movement was past its high point by then,
and that a decline had set in. Certainly it is frequently reckoned to have
been a spent force by the early decades of the eleventh century. But no
true judgment can be made on its termination, or even on the years in
which it ceased to be a major force within the church and in society
generally. It may even have continued to exercise influence until the time
of the Norman Conquest; although by then the number of monks in the
monasteries was small by later standards, and there were such irregu-
larities as the possession of property by individual monks in defiance of
one of the principal tenets of the reform. The monks also appear to have
been shallow and unimpressive intellectually, with few of the standard
patristic works in their libraries, and an evident unfamiliarity with
Latin. The contemporary biographies of Christian leaders are rather
pathetic and inadequate. The two on Dunstan are poor efforts unworthy of one of the great men of the age; and the turgid rhetoric
adopted by the biographer of Oswald tends to obscure rather than cast
light on its subject. The lives of Ethelwold are perhaps the best, but
they may well be considered inferior to the best biographies of Bede's
generation. All these shortcomings point to a church which lacked
vibrancy and spiritual depth, and was in need of further reform.

Yet those who wish to champion the persistent good effects of the
reform movement up to the time of the Norman Conquest can point to
the flowering of vernacular literature and art; the outstanding characters and achievements of the statesmanlike Archbishop Wulfstan and
the saintly Bishop Wulfstan of Worcester; and the invigorating example
of the monasteries of the Seven valley in sending helpers to the north,
soon after the Conquest, who revived Northumbrian monasticism and
eventually refounded Durham, with immense and beneficial consequences for the future.

The church in England on the eve of the Norman Conquest

It was fortunate for the church that Cnut, the longest reigning king of
England in the eleventh century before the Norman Conquest, was a

baptized Christian who demonstrated his religious sincerity by his benefactions to religious houses and his manifest concern for the welfare of the church. He was anxious to maintain political, social and religious continuity and stability, to build on the foundation which the church reform movement of the previous century and the work of local priests and lay people had established, and to co-operate with the church in all his policies. He did not want to depart from the fundamentals of what King Edgar had tried to achieve, and showed this most impressively in the code of law which he issued between 1020 and 1023, which fulfilled explicitly and in detail his former undertaking to maintain Edgar's law. He helped to ensure continuity by retaining the same bishops and senior churchmen he inherited, in contrast to the radical changes in the lay aristocracy which he introduced at that time, and in still greater contrast to the wholesale changes in ecclesiastical personnel which occurred fifty years later under William the Conqueror. He introduced legislation to assist the church in its work. He was careful in choosing those who should be elevated to the episcopate, mostly favouring monks, although the appointments in his later years were more questionable.

The archbishops and bishops gladly gave Cnut unstinted support. Thus Lyfing of Canterbury early in the reign embarked on an important mission to Rome on behalf of the king; and Wulfstan of York who had drafted law codes for King Ethelred, undertook the same task for the new king. But this harmonious and productive co-operation and consequent retention of the work of the church on a fairly even keel, if not with any spectacular results to compare with the reform movement of a few decades before, seems to have deteriorated into a period of mediocrity soon after Cnut's death in 1035; and the decline may have begun before that.

Edward the Confessor (king from 1043 to 1066) was canonized, but his reign 'seems of curiously little importance in the history of the Anglo-Saxon Church'.[31] He showed some originality by inaugurating the practice of promoting secular rather than monastic clergy to the episcopate; which is somewhat paradoxical as he is remembered as a lover of monks and their ways. But, despite his reputation, there was a general decline in the influence of monasteries during his reign. In the years preceding the Conquest there seems to have been some falling away from the previous strict Benedictine standards; and houses like Winchester and Canterbury were not what they had recently been. Evesham, under its abbot Ethelwig, and Worcester, under Wulfstan, were dedicated and productive monasteries; but apart from them and these two men the monastic life was at a rather low ebb, and there were no outstanding figures among the monks. Monastic scholarship had lost its former fervour and keenness under men like Elfric, and whilst it was not in the doldrums it was not to be compared with that of contemporary France. 'In 1066, though the English monasteries were assuredly not decadent in the commonly accepted meaning of that word, it could scarcely be said of them that this was their finest hour.'[32]

Of considerable symbolic significance was Edward's most cherished project during his declining years: the splendid new abbey designed and planned to be geographically and religiously central to the life of London. It was constructed as a glorious memento of his piety and concern to promote the good of the church. It was dedicated on Holy Innocents day, 28 December 1065, too late for the king to be present, as he was on his death-bed, but just in time to provide the setting for the consecration of William I as the victorious new king after his defeat of Harold. Structural work on the great abbey church was continued by the Normans. The building remained largely intact for centuries to come: the sanctuary and the transepts stood for two hundred and fifty years, and the nave survived for about a century longer. It was to be the spot on which all subsequent English sovereigns were to receive their hallowing.

Edward's cherished abbey was also indicative of his affinity with, and respect for, the Normans; for it was modelled on Jumièges Abbey. Emma, the Confessor's mother, was a Norman, and the king had spent the first twenty-five years of his life as an exile in Normandy. It was in the course of his lifetime that the Normans became dominant in Europe, largely through their crusades and their conquests of Sicily and most of southern Italy. Edward's Norman associations were, of course, of considerable significance in view of the rapid turn of events in the months following his death.

Westminster Abbey did not feature in the diocesan structure, which by then was well-established and reasonably stable. There were seventeen dioceses: Canterbury, York, Cornwall, Devonshire, Dorchester, Durham, East Anglia, Hereford, Lichfield, London, Ramsbury, Rochester, Selsey, Sherborne, Wells, Winchester and Worcester.[33] By 1066 the church was one of the foremost landowners in England. The archbishop of Canterbury and his monks formed an enormous lordship of some eighty-nine manors. These were scattered over eight counties ranging from as far west as Newington in Oxfordshire to as far east as

Monk's Eleigh in Suffolk. Canterbury was in fact the richest English episcopal see. It had an annual revenue of £1,750 according to Domesday Book; the second, Winchester, had over £1,000. All the other bishoprics, although well funded, were surpassed by the greater monasteries – Glastonbury, Ely, Bury St Edmund's and St Augustine's, Canterbury. In total, monasteries and nunneries accounted for between a sixth and a seventh of all the Domesday landed wealth. The accumulated wealth, land and property of the church by the time of the Norman Conquest is a measure of the extent to which it was integrated into society and secure both institutionally and as an accepted part of national life locally, regionally and centrally.

And, of course, the bishops were at the heart of the ecclesiastical system. By the eleventh century, in addition to their purely evangelistic and pastoral roles, they were also key figures in royal government as well as in the general administration of secular affairs in their own areas and nationally. 'The bishops were great men, active in society, natural advisers to the king in the witan. They were also for the most part wealthy men, responsible for the administration of extensive estates that belonged to the see or technically to the saint to whom their cathedral church was dedicated.'[34] The responsibilities resulting from the fulfilment of lordship obligations were onerous. These included the military aspects of large estates: to ensure that proper steps were taken to protect their property from outside barbarians or from cattle raiders and other disturbers of the peace. The duties increasingly encompassed such civic functions as the running of hundred courts, and engagement in other judicial and administrative business of the community. Of course there was plenty of scope for individual choice, and the expression of personal interests or predilections. Not all bishops were as warlike as Leofgar of Hereford who was killed on an expedition against the Welsh in 1056, and who played an active part in the actual fighting.

All the bishops were involved in ecclesiastical courts, and in such matters as the trial and, if found guilty, the punishment, of criminous priests. In such matters, and especially in the case of very serious crimes, there was an interaction between ecclesiastical and civil authorities. By the time of the Norman Conquest the ecclesiastical courts were well developed and defined in their functions and roles. 'Side by side therefore with the public courts and apparatus of justice with which they themselves were intimately bound, there also existed a powerful age-old tradition of episcopal jurisdiction that was indeed intensified in the course of the tenth century as knowledge of Carolingian-Frankish modifications of canon law became better known.'[35] There was in practice room for doubt and hesitation in situations where there was an overlap between the shire court, at which the bishop could preside, and the bishop's court. Both types of court were recognized as legitimate parts of the overall legal system. It was one more example of the close working together at all levels of the bishop and those who represented the crown. It placed a responsibility on the church, and on the bishops in particular, to make sure that the church continued to have its own sound and effective means of ecclesiastical jurisdiction; and the eleventh century saw some advance in this field. Archbishop Wulfstan was especially active in making known the procedure relating to public penance, and in regularizing and bringing up to date a full penitential system based on Frankish precedents.

Wulfstan was in fact one of the most important church leaders of the early eleventh century, and the most renowned intellectual figure of the late Saxon church; and he deserves special mention among the bishops of the generation after the main period of monastic reform. As Archbishop of York from 1002 to 1023 he combined the conscientious performance of his episcopal duties with prolific writing. He was active in restoring monastic life; vigilant in his care for the wellbeing of the churches for which he was responsible; and concerned to be an effective pastor and church leader. But it was in his writings that he was most distinguished. He and his friend Elfric were the most commanding figures of the intellectual revival that can be reckoned as having grown out of the movement of ecclesiastical reform initiated by Dunstan, Ethelwold and Oswald. He was not an original thinker, but he clarified and made explicit much of the teaching of the church on the proper ordering of Christian society as a whole. He concentrated especially on the place of the church in secular affairs, and more particularly on the conduct and obligations of bishops and kings. Repeatedly in homilies he reverted to the Christian duty to render obedience to lords, and above all to the king. Society was divided into those who pray, those who fight, and those who labour. The royal duty was to hold the balance between these groups, and to dispense good justice to men. He embodied this teaching in his most ambitious work, the *Institutes of Polity, Civil and Ecclesiastical*. It accorded well with the writings of the Carolingian period, and it had analogies with the works of continental contemporaries, more especially the teaching of bishops in Germany and northern France.

In their governance of dioceses, and especially in the larger ones such as Dorchester, the bishops needed much assistance. Coadjutor bishops were occasionally to be found; and at Canterbury as early as the ninth century there seems to have been a chief deacon who was singled out from among the cathedral clergy to be the principal active servant in the episcopal household. There appears to have been no attempt to lighten the burden of the diocesan bishop by territorial subdivisions of dioceses. The nearest approach to tackling the problem was perhaps the occasional use of the office of archdeacon.

Archdeacons were next after bishops in the ecclesiastical hierarchy of the secular clergy. But the use of them was rather neglected in England, possibly because of the tenth-century reform emphasis on the bishops themselves ministering to their flocks. There is no reference to archdeacons in the royal laws, but the development of the office may have come after Cnut promulgated his codes. It may have existed in London, Wells, Hereford and Exeter, but there is no good evidence of that, or indeed of any archdeacons in many other dioceses, even if they were only the bishop's personal assistants.

In the vast diocese of York the pressing need for such posts, with men who could serve in the bishop's name, may have resulted in some pre-Conquest clarification of the archdeacon's position. In a complex but interesting document known as the 'Law of the Northumbrian Priests', dating from the first quarter of the eleventh century, the archdeacon appears as a man with considerable disciplinary and legal authority over the lesser clergy. This official promulgation stipulated that if a priest neglected the bishop's summons he was to be fined twenty *oras*, normally equivalent to sixteen pence an *ora*, and he was to pay twelve *oras* if he neglected the archdeacon's summons. A fine of twenty *oras* was imposed upon a priest if he committed an offence and celebrated mass in spite of the bishop's prohibition, and he was also required to make amends for the offence he had previously committed. For a similar offence involving an archdeacon the penalty was twelve *oras*.

As with so many things to do with the church, the groundwork had been laid for a system which only flourished in the Norman period. It was after 1066 that archdeacons came into their own as the right-hand men of bishops in all dioceses.

It was to some extent the same with the post of dean. In the pre-Conquest era men holding the title *decanus* (dean) were prominent among those who gave great assistance in the administration of the complex ecclesiastical institutions, regular and secular. The tenth-century monastic reformation increased the popularity of the term 'dean', mainly to describe the chief monk after the abbot in a monastic community. Then, as the monastic reforms spread into the secular ecclesiastical sphere with the introduction of monastic chapters at some of the great cathedrals, and notably Winchester and Worcester, the title became even more common.

In reviewing this hierarchy of secular clergy, we should not lose sight of the monasteries, which continued to be a vital part of the total work and witness of the church in the land. At the time of the Norman Conquest there were thirty-five of them for monks and nine for nuns. A few of these were large institutions, but most were small. It is doubtful if more than six of them had in excess of forty inmates. Evesham, which became renowned because of Aethelwig, had only twelve monks in 1058, the same number as at Worcester when Wulfstan became prior. Even in 1100 Abingdon numbered only twenty-eight, while there were but twenty monks in the eleventh-century foundation of Bury St Edmunds in 1020, and twenty-five in another new foundation, Coventry, in 1043. Westminster, which was greatly enlarged by the Confessor, had only twelve monks when it was founded in 958. And such notable houses as Muchelney, Abbotsbury, Pershore and Gloucester were even smaller. Outstanding among all of them was Winchester. It did not have the antiquity and fine library enjoyed by Glastonbury, but it did have a magnificent church, impressive achievements in the production of illuminated works and music, the great advantage of proximity to the royal palace, an honourable connection with the most energetic and resolute reformers, and a great influence in nurturing the principal vernacular writer, Elfric.

Although the monasteries did not have the high profile of the previous generation, their persistent importance after the tenth century ended is highlighted by the lives and work of Elfric and Byrhtferth. In 987 Elfric took charge of teaching at the newly-founded monastery of Cerne, now Cerne Abbas, in Dorset. When Eynsham monastery was established in 1005 he was made its first abbot. He was one of the foremost and most gifted writers of Old English prose in the late Anglo-Saxon period. Like Wulfstan, he was profoundly concerned about wide issues of church, state and society. He provided a classic statement and exposition of the pre-Hildebrandine notion of kingship in which the monarch has a god-given right to rule once he has been chosen as king, and consecrated. He produced an important tract on chronology, *De temporibus anni*, two text books of Latin instruction, the *Grammar* and the *Colloquy*, and an impressive volume of homilies covering a wide range of mostly conventional topics.

Byrhtferth was a monk of Ramsey monastery and an important contributor to the intellectual life of late Anglo-Saxon England. Although his interests ranged over history, logic, mathematics and astronomy, he was more of a scientist than a pastoral theologian or homilist, and this distinguished him from Wulfstan and Elfric. His *Enchiridion* or *Manual* was a conspectus of scientific thought. In its depth of insight it was no advance on Bede, but it clearly set out and presented a summary of continental sources since the writings of Bede, and Byrhtferth attempted an abstract mathematical analysis. His works showed how greatly English scientific scholarship had advanced during the preceding centuries.

Of course most of the worshippers in the kingdom had little to do with any such ecclesiastical dignitaries and men of learning, or the important matters which occupied them; and they gathered in churches which, by comparison with Westminster Abbey or cathedrals, were unsubstantial and insignificant. But these local places of worship and centres of communal Christian life, and the mostly small fellowships of Christians which regularly gathered in them, were perhaps the most magnificent bequest of the church in England in 1066 to future generations.

Fortunately, there has been some excellent scholarly work on the transition of the local church in the period from the tenth to the thirteenth centuries, against the background of earlier developments. Documentary, topographical, archaeological, historical and architectural approaches have been adopted; but there is a core consensus among scholars on how the parish church evolved. There is a sequence of development which is widely accepted in its main lines, and which is most usefully summarised by John Blair:

> (i) a system, general in Anglo-Saxon England, of large parishes served by teams of priests operating from important central churches (the 'old minsters'); (ii) the rapid proliferation, between the 10th and 12th centuries, of 'local' or 'private' churches with resident priests; (iii) a major campaign, during the 11th and 12th centuries, of stone church-building at a local level; and (iv) the eclipse of the minsters, the division of their parishes between local churches and the crystallization of the modern parochial system, a process which was under way in the 11th century and complete by the 13th.[36]

It is quite possible that by as early as the first decades of the eighth century the private estate church had not only come into existence, but was fairly common. 'But there is little as yet, in churches such as these, to do more than hint at the much later emergence of the village church and parish as these would come to be understood in the tenth century.'[37] The minsters were well established and far from being replaced. There was a shortage of priests which impeded any proliferation of small, more localized churches. Also, the development of the manorial system, and the growth of thegnly authority, which were crucial in the form-ation of the local church, had not yet taken place. But change was imminent, and the weakening of the existing institutions of the church brought about by the Viking invasions may have been a contributory cause of the changes in pastoral provision, and the remarkable growth of local churches.

The replacement of the old system by the new was a protracted process, and it was not totally accomplished even by the eleventh century. Some of the oldest and most deep-rooted minsters continued their role. Some local minsters were still familiar and respected, and they enjoyed regular bequests from those of thegnly rank. During the late tenth century and up to the late eleventh century some minsters were re-founded or endowed by great magnates, notably Leifric Godiva at Leominster, Wenlock, Stow and Chester. Indeed, a distinctive feature of the reign of Edward the Confessor was the annexation of royal minsters as endowments for household chaplains. Many ex-minsters retained large parishes and abnormally large clerical staffs, as was the case with the 'archpriest' and his two colleagues who served three parochial altars in St Martin's, Dover, until 1536. But the general trend was in the direction of smaller pastoral units, and a less centralized system of pastoral care.

Exact figures on the growth in numbers of churches are not possible; neither have scholars been able to identify unambiguously what were the reasons for the sudden surge in the provision of local churches. The pattern of urban and rural settlement was undergoing fundamental change from the ninth century onwards, and many new churches are likely to have been a by product of such changes. These were years of critical re-organization of rural life. Large and complex royal, aristo-cratic or ecclesiastical estates and territories fragmented into self-contained local manors, and this was the land-base for a broader thegn class. Local communities were becoming more internally-focussed and coherent. There may well have been a 'transfer of an individual's primary allegiance from kin-group to community'.[38]

This process of economic, social and ecclesiastical change was accomplished in stages. 'Just as many large manors created in the 10th century were subdivided into smaller ones before Domesday Book, so churches of more than ordinary local status may sometimes have been founded to serve them, with parishes which fragmented in their turn.'[39]

In the fifty years after about 975 new churches emerged which operated on a scaled-down version of the old system. They can be defined as 'sub-minsters' or 'superior' estate churches. One-priest churches, which were rare before the tenth century, started to become the norm. Most of the local churches appear to have originated as lay or ecclesiastical seigneurial foundations, through devolution from minsters, or through corporate initiative; and these were not mutually exclusive categories. The drift towards local churches was mainly a matter of thegnly initiative linked to a basic shift of perception in society at large. Rather than having a devotional centre, the minster, to which all parishioners looked, there was now a concern to have a more continuous and personal pastoral provision vested in someone who was known and accepted by the community in a more personal and intimate way than in former times. In this we see the origins of the 'village priest', who seems to have emerged from about the early eleventh century.

The new local churches also had considerable financial benefits which helped to promote their multiplication and to ensure their stability. Foremost was the matter of tithes and other revenues. Tithe payments had existed well before the tenth century; but they were recommended and not compulsory, and the old minsters could not rely on that source of support. They became compulsory as a result of the enactments of Edmund (939–46) and Edgar (959–75), the former imposing ecclesiastical penalties on tithe-evaders, the latter writing payment into the law of the land. This was accompanied in many cases by an agreement about parish boundaries. Before the end of the tenth century, 'every man in England, for purposes of geld and tithing (taxation and policing), belonged to a vill; he was a member of a parish with a tithe liability; he had identifiable duties and rights'.[40]

The majority of the churches constructed before about 950 were fabricated from wood; with cathedrals and important monasteries only being built of stone. As late as 1020, when Cnut ordered a church to be built for the souls of men who had been slain in battle at Ashingdon in 1016, a chronicler thought it worthwhile to record that the church was built 'of stone and mortar'.[41] In the century after about 1050 there was a great rebuilding, when almost all the churches were reconstructed in stone. It was a remarkable and, in one sense, unique phenomenon: 'there was only one period during which the construction of such buildings in stone was practised as a general, national activity'.[42] Not only was there an expansion of the number and an improvement in the structural quality of churches, but there was a considerable amount of church enlargement. 'No longer ephemeral or informal, the local church was now a fixed point in the landscape, maintained from permanent endowments and the focus of a nascent parish community.'[43] Again, it was among ordinary people in local situations that in an unsung and unostentatious way church life was perpetuated and consolidated. But countless lords and thegns played their indispensable part.

It was the bones of a system which was to last. Of the 9000 or so parishes in England in 1700 the vast majority existed before 1150, and a very high proportion of those before 1066. And the early, pre-Norman, origin of parish churches was accompanied by an equally significant pre-Norman origin of parish priests as a distinctive group of clergy: the very backbone of the evolving parish system. 'If Normans often took the better livings, most ordinary parish priests remained English. In the Church as in the state, continuity depended above all on the status and functions of many thousands of Englishmen.'[44]

Grand gestures from kings, the establishment of bishoprics and monasteries, and policies for diocesan-wide or national church recovery had their crucial part to play in the survival of the church, but they were not the only means of forwarding the Christian cause, and of establishing the church throughout the land. The day by day task of evangelism and pastoral work, and of maintaining the faith, the fellowship and the liturgical life of the church fell on the local church. What of the faith of these ordinary local folk?

Here we touch on one of the themes I am trying to pursue throughout this work: what in modern jargon is referred to as 'popular religion'. 'Seen in the broader context of cultural conflict and accommodation, the period of reconquest and consolidation in the tenth and eleventh centuries becomes a dynamic phase for popular religion as an acculturating process.' In the local situation the form this took must have been repeated innumerable times with variations according to distinctive circumstances and personalities, but with a fundamental similarity. In those two centuries there was a growth of local churches, particularly in the Danelaw, but in other areas as well. 'Typically, a lone priest served in these new, lay-founded churches, usually a man of relatively low origin who had a rudimentary education, was isolated from the church hierarchy and the large collegiate minsters, and was called upon to meet the daily, practical needs of an agricultural population. In this environment, and through this kind of clerical agency interacting with local folk culture and domestic life, popular religion formed.'[45]

Priests, hired by lay proprietors, served their congregations on manors and in vills by combining their limited education and spiritual expertise with their knowledge of local practice. They were often born locally and spent all their lives in the same place. Their almost sole focus was on the local community. This resulted in a close interaction between the individual priest and his congregation distinctly different from the collegiate environment of the older, more remote large minster churches, centrally staffed by a group of clergy. The priest was intimately engaged in the local scene, albeit with some measure of social ambiguity as he was both a tenant of the manorial proprietor and a spiritual elder. Nevertheless, his economic status as a villein allowed him to empathize with a large proportion of his congregation. The Domesday Book frequently lumped the priest with the villeins and indicated that the priest had a share in the ploughteams.

Through his, albeit tenuous, relationships with the ecclesiastical authorities, with the aristocracy and with the peasantry the local priest played a pivotal role in the development of popular Christianity. The local church was the centre of the manorial community. It linked spiritual, social and political interests. The building with its priest became the vital locus of communal activity. Once the private chapels of lords were attached to their halls; but by the tenth century they had largely moved out and were separate buildings. These may well have been situated in the centre of the vill; and they were commonly used for a wide variety of functions other than liturgical. They were often two-celled or linear in plan, rather than just a single space, which in the earlier churches served as both nave and chancel.

In an age of widespread illiteracy, there was a great use of pictorial representation. The walls were frequently plastered and decorated with paintings which depicted biblical stories. These small local churches were typically dedicated to a saint, but they did not have relics. The saint provided an example to be followed and perhaps a conscious or unconscious replacement for the former animistic worship at springs, wells, groves and trees. The priestly duties embraced teaching, the celebration of mass, hearing confession, the administration of penance, ensuring that the Sabbath was observed, conducting the liturgy, the administration of the rites of passage, anointing the sick, and acting as pastor to local individuals; and they were supplemented by other community-based functions. The relationship of the priest to the people meant that he acquired such secular roles as law-enforcement, arbitration in disputes, distribution of alms and caring for the sick. Although there is evidence of greedy and corrupt priests, it appears that most of them conscientiously performed their varied and very extensive and demanding duties without any, or with very little, payment.

The large number of local churches which came into use in the tenth and eleventh centuries, and the development of a local ministry with wide-ranging responsibilities which brought the local priests into intimate contact with the population within small and closely-knit communities, together provided a powerful meeting between the everyday domestic and agricultural concerns of the rural people, Germanic folk customs, and the Christian faith however rudimentarily represented. Here was the dynamic, the continuity of Christian witness and the growth of the Christian faith which lay behind such public acts as Edgar's impressive coronation. Here was the key to the Christianization of late Saxon and Viking England.

By quite early in the tenth century the presence of a priest in every village community was assumed by legislators, especially in Wessex but also in most of the remaining parts of the country. Likewise, even before the reign of Athelstan (925–40), the manorial church, which is sometimes called an 'inferior' church or a church 'of the second foundation', had become a widely-recognized mark of thegnly rank. Athelstan insisted that a person who was to be considered for elevation from a ceorl to a thegn should have acquired an estate of four hides and a church. An eleventh-century text, *Of People's Ranks and Law*, stipulated that the ownership of the manorial church was among the conditions for promotion. The manorial entries in the Domesday Book show that many of these local churches had been constructed by a lord to serve the spiritual needs of those working on his estate. The church buildings were assuming a dual role. They were highly visible tokens of spiritual concern, and at the same time they were extremely public symbols of social standing. 'In 11th century England the possession of a church was looked upon as one of the attributes of thegnly rank, along with a cookhouse, a fortified gatehouse, and five hides of land.'[46] And the advantages of owning a church went far beyond the prospects of higher social status. The builder of a church and his heirs held the right to appoint the priest who would serve it, the advowson; and they enjoyed an interest in the tithes and offerings, the oblations. 'In effect, the village church was both essential to the status of the Late Saxon thegn and a part of his capital worth. Like his estate, his hall, and his weapons of war, it was a necessary element in his equipment.[47]

By the time of the Domesday Book it appears that a large number of vills had churches of their own. But the record is patchy. In Suffolk and Huntingdonshire over fifty per cent of the vills named had a church, but the national figures, although inaccurate, indicate that this may have been a better provision than in the country as a whole. It is clear that there remained over-large villages, some of which were the traditional territories of minsters, which had still to be divided, and there were new towns which needed a church. A skeleton had been provided, but it was the Normans who put so much of the flesh on the bones as there was a surge of church-building in the post-Conquest era. Estate village churches often became parish churches between the tenth and twelfth centuries. The growth of estate-sized parishes, served by a single priest, and linked with the development of manorial organization based on nucleated villages and open fields, was a process which escalated under the Normans.

The church by 1066 was integrated as never before into the very fabric of society at all levels. Its institutional centrality was evident to all, and could not be gainsaid. It was solidly and undeniably part of the daily life of peasant, thegn, lord and king. It was visible wherever any-one went in the form of churches large and small, and mostly small. For the mass of the population the church as a building was becoming an accepted part of the landscape. It represented the religious aspect of life, even if there was a great amount of surviving superstition and folk religion. For many it was the place where their baptism had taken place, and where their children had also been baptized. The last visit of the bishop would have been remembered, when he came for confirmation; and it would have been recalled how he and his chaplain sat talking to the priest while someone ran round the village to collect the children. The church was a familiar, respected and loved place of worship for many of the villagers, as they went to mass regularly on Sundays; and even when there was hay to get in they attended the service first. As they stood in the church looking towards the altar through the narrow chancel arch, they would glance around at the pictures of biblical scenes painted on the walls, but would pay particular attention as the priest blessed the housel, which was the very Paschal lamb and Christ himself, as they had been told by the priest.

If you had asked the villager what it meant to him, the church and the litanies and the mass and all that went with them, he would have found it difficult to understand your question. God made the world and there were churches for his service everywhere; the king himself had built many of them. The laws enjoined the service of God. Mercy and pity and the service of God went together, and keeping one's oath and being trustworthy.[48]

There is evidence that this pervasiveness of Christianity was typical of towns as well, but perhaps to a lesser extent. Many had more than one church, and some places like Thetford, York, Lincoln, Norwich and, of course, London had several. It may well be true with reference to large towns of pre-Conquest origin, as well as for rural communities, that 'at least three-quarters of parish churches were in position before the end of the eleventh century'.[49] Archaeology shows that small churches in Cambridge, Lincoln, Norwich and York even possessed burial grounds from the moment of their establishment.

The Christian orientation of most of the population infused and informed all their activities. Christianity impregnated every sphere of their lives. Surviving rules of lay gilds suggest that most of these associations had a spiritual aspect. In tenth-century Exeter guildsmen assembled 'for the love of God and for our souls' need, having regard both to the prosperity of our life and also to the days thereafter which we wish to be allotted to us at God's judgment', and they gave any member going on pilgrimage overseas five pence from each of his colleagues.[50] For society as a whole, and for individuals at all levels in the community, there was a substratum of Christian presuppositions. The clergy could generally rely on a concern among their flock for matters of Christian belief and conduct.

And in their teaching and preaching, these local priests in villages or towns could benefit from a substantial amount of vernacular prose in the mid-eleventh century, largely in the form of homilies written by monks. These were especially important in an age when so many of the secular priests were ill-educated. In the homilies we catch a glimpse of the teaching which was being set before the people, and which was moulding their religious outlook. Taken as a whole, the theology was sober, and the issues which commanded most attention were to do with morality and Christian conduct. The miraculous did not feature as prominently as in earlier mediaeval times. Death and judgment were frequent themes. The Trinity was expounded carefully. Baptism was held in high esteem, but confirmation hardly mentioned. Fasting and abstinence from carnal relations during Lent were emphasized; but the fast most pleasing to God was the avoidance of sin. The homilies were replete with scriptural quotations, on which there were comments with a great use of the allegorical method.

There is little if any reference to pilgrimages in the literature of the time, but they formed part of the Christian life, especially for some of the more privileged members of society. Of particular influence in encouraging this practice was King Cnut's pilgrimage to Rome in 1027. His jarl Harold followed his example in 1042. About 1056 Earl Harold made the journey, and this was followed by his younger brothers, Tostig and Gyrth, in 1061. The example of the earls was a spur to thegns and a number of people of lower social status, as we have seen with the guildsmen of Exeter. After the Norman Conquest pilgrimages were to become even more common.[51]

A pilgrim, whether bound for a distant goal overseas, such as Rome or Jerusalem, or simply heading for one of the many shrines in England, was expected to see the relics of the saints. It was widely believed that by their holy lives, often attested by miracles, and in some cases by their martyrdom, these favoured and precious servants of God were especially effective, not only as examples to imitate, but as intercessors for the living. In exceptional circumstances they might even appear to pilgrims and might still perform miracles.

So, the Normans inherited a country in which the Christian faith touched the lives of all types and conditions of people in a very profound way. Of course there was much folklore, superstition, hypocrisy and downright cynicism or disbelief, as well as lingering paganism. Mingled with genuine and deep-rooted faith there was a residue of Celtic, Roman, Romano-British, Anglo-Saxon and Viking beliefs and practices which could not be fully cast off, and which remained as a kind of subterranean remnant of past and powerful influences in the lives of an ethnically and culturally mixed population. But the Christian faith had emerged supreme; and it had become so embedded consciously and sub-consciously, corporately and in the lives of individuals, that it was in effect the authoritative, largely unchallenged determinant of religious beliefs and moral standards.

It also is clear 'that permanent government was predominantly the creation of the kings and of the Church'.[52] The making of England was not an inevitable process, and yet there is a sense in which the welding together of peoples of different ethnic origins but with the same economic background, social structure and language appears as a natural consequence of settlement and more particularly of conversion.

In the gradual but increasing awareness of common interests, and even of a feeling of common destiny, the force of a shared continental homeland was strong. It is to an extent true that 'the Anglo-Saxons could conceive of themselves as a common people because of the ancestral migration. Despite frequent political rivalries, religious disputes, and some degree of dialect variation, they could gather a sense of unity from their continental origins as they were memorialized in the central works of the culture'.[53]

But, powerful as this consciousness of a distant past was, it cannot be reckoned as the most potent factor in that emerging realization of national identity which the Anglo-Saxon period so manifestly exemplified. After all, the continental experience was ever receding into the past and becoming a dim memory even in the collective consciousness. What was more relevant was the present, continuing and ever growing and deepening experience of a people who were learning to sink differences as previous allegiances were exchanged for new loyalties. And in this transformation cerebral and emotional transmutations in the lives of countless individuals were as important as political and economic measures. There was a battle for the minds of innumerable individuals as the force of national consciousness struggled against strong local and parochial identities.

And this is where Christianity was so important. It helped not only to give a common religious commitment, but a broader sense of a unifying culture. 'Christianity was a literate civilized religion drawing sustenance from its deep roots in the experience of the Near East and Mediterranean world. As a literate religion it was also an educative force in the full Roman tradition. Men were made aware of their group unity in the religious and linguistic fields long before the political.'[54]

So, with the passage of many centuries, and after countless occasions of conflict and antagonism, there was a drawing together of the ecclesiastical and the political interests and objectives. There was not total concord, but there was an acknowledgment by all concerned that there were common purposes and common needs which were greater and more extensive than those matters over which there was actual or potential discord and conflict.

This complementary process, the *imitatio regnii/imperii* and the *imitatio sacerdotti*, was inspired up to the eleventh century less by hostile rivalry than by the natural interplay of influences between the two most active political forces in Christendom. The interpenetration was the result of a basic harmony and a common agreement on ideals. There was no real rivalry between the secular and ecclesiastical organizations. The renunciation of the monks put them apart and led them to passive acceptance of sinful government. Their hope was for pious rulers who would establish the peace in which their quiet lives could be lived. The secular church, although through its governmental claims more liable to come into conflict with the *regnum*, was not yet aggressive in temper. Each was engaged in a battle against the same or similar enemies, and each needed the help of the other.[55]

The Normans had a firm foundation on which to build both a political and a spiritual house and to implant a coherent ethical system. The years covered by this book had seen much Christian failure and inadequacy in the face of the daunting tasks of evangelizing the country, establishing a system of pastoral care for all the people, and ensuring that the church was the standard bearer for the ethical and moral values which governed individual and corporate life. So often the spirit had been willing and the flesh weak; and not infrequently even the spirit seems to have been unwilling. But there had been countless victories. Great things had been accomplished.

Three Christian achievements stand out among many which became part of the Norman inheritance. First was a most impressive form of territorial church government, with England mapped out into territorial divisions, and this formed the basis of a fully fledged parochial system. Secondly there was the freshness and vigour which the converted Anglo-Saxons infused into English Christianity. Thirdly was the remarkable contribution to learning and letters made by the church, both in Latin and in the vernacular. Christianity in England had grown to a measure of maturity over about nine hundred years of torments, tribulations and triumphs, as well as falterings and failures. It was about to face new and demanding times in the much-changed circumstances of the coming centuries, when what had been achieved in Roman, sub-Roman and Anglo-Saxon times would be tested and tried to the full.

Appendix 1

The Military, Political, Demographic, Economic and Social History of Roman Britain

Julius Caesar invaded Britain in 55 BC. He made little permanent impression on the Britons, and he returned precipitately with a number of face-saving hostages, and with the promise that he would return the following year. In 54 BC the second expedition was on a much larger scale. The disciplined Roman force encountered vigorous and determined opposition led by the able and charismatic Cassivellaunus, who was probably king of the Catuvellauni. By an adroit deployment of javelin-armed charioteers, and a skilled use of guerrilla tactics the Celtic leader and his fanatical followers were able to blunt the onslaught of the hardened and well-trained Romans. After a campaign which entailed mixed fortunes for both contending parties, terms were agreed for the termination of hostilities. Hostages were given, an annual tribute was fixed, and arrangements were made for the security of the Trinovantes from aggression.

The next invasion of Britain by Claudius in AD 43 resulted in conquest. After initial opposition the advance from the south was facilitated by the political alignments already existing in Britain as a result of previous Roman policy. The southern dynasty had a long tradition of friendship with Rome, and soon other tribes decided to become allies of the Romans. By AD 60 the governor, Suetonius Paullinus, felt confident enough of his hold on the south to launch an attack on Anglesey. Despite fearsome resistance from hordes of black-clad Celtic women and Druids yelling out curses from heaven on the invaders, victory was soon achieved and the island garrisoned. The full conquest of Wales seemed a real possibility. But far away to the east severe trouble was rapidly brewing which almost toppled the mighty Romans.

The pride of Claudius in his new province was almost unbounded, and was reflected in the conferment upon his son of the additional name of Britannicus. It also induced him to establish an ostentatious capital at Colchester, pointedly replacing the very hub of the Catuvellaunian realm. The arrogance and tact-lessness of the move was heightened by work undertaken on the site to make it a centre for the imperial cult. The indignation of some of the Britons was intense because of what was perceived as a blatant and unnecessarily provocative expression of overlordship and, perhaps, insensitivity to local religious sentiments; and it sparked off a rebellion by the Iceni under the awesome leadership of Boudicca. For some time the Iceni and the Trinovantes in particular had suffered from the exactions of Roman money-lenders, who required capital for new towns, roads, country houses in the Roman style, education in the new civilization, and other costs involved in the expensive process of romanization, and there had been maltreatment of Iceni nobility. The revolt of AD 60 was short-lived but vicious. The rebels captured Colchester, Verulamium and London with much slaughter, torture and destruction, but were then comprehensively defeated with massive losses. The reprisals to which Paullinus gave rein were so harsh that, after an investigation instigated by the Emperor Nero, he was relieved of his British command.

By 84, and largely as a result of the distinguished military exploits of three governors, Petillius Cerialis (71–74), Julius Frontinus (74–78) and Julius Agricola (78–84), there were far-reaching advances both militarily and culturally. Roman control was established over Wales, and for a time conquest in the north embraced almost the whole island before the need to move troops to more pressing theatres of war compelled curtailment.

The period of almost uninhibited expansion of the Roman Empire terminated with the death in 117 of the Emperor Trajan. From then onwards the concern was to consolidate existing gains, to find safe boundaries, and to keep the barbarians out. Trajan's successor Hadrian undertook the construction of the wall named after him to help protect the lands to the south from the marauding and ever-present threat from the Picts. It was one of the most remarkable building feats of any of the emperors. Nevertheless, the next emperor, Antoninus Pius (138–61) introduced a change of frontier policy in Britain, and the wall was abandoned. The lowlands were reconquered, and a new barrier, built of turf, was drawn across the Scottish isthmus.

It was probably early in the third century that the administration of the island was definitely rearranged into two provinces. The south, *Britannia Superior*, was administered by a consular governor, probably from a base in London. The north, *Britannia Inferior* was under a governor of praetorian rank with its centre at York.

Up to this point Roman Britain had developed in a quite satisfactory way from the point of view of Rome. There had been an overall growth and reinforcement of its prosperity. Towns had been established and had undergone a fairly relaxed and unhurried, but still noteworthy, development. There had been an impressive provision of such key elements in the infrastructure of the province as roads, administrative and military headquarters and public buildings.

For the Roman Empire as a whole change was imminent. The third century was a time of crisis. The summary given by Peter Salway seems fair and accurate:

As one contemplates the third century, the feeling that a real change has come over the Roman world is overwhelming. In the first half of the second century the empire was still expanding, in the second, despite the pressure on the Danube which at times looked very dangerous, the empire stood triumphant and unshaken. In the third century all seems changed. Inflation, military insurrection, one murdered emperor following hard on the heels of another, open autocracy, and the simultaneous breaching of the imperial defences in both the east and west look like the beginning of the end.[1]

The trauma was not felt much in Britain. Daily life was little affected by the dramatic events of Rome and the continental Empire, or by movements of alien people in far off lands. It was not until the period 268–82 that the threat of Saxon sea-raiders first became acute. Then there appears to have been a change of mood. The sudden increase in the burial of coin-hoards in unusual numbers seems to indicate greatly increased apprehension. The construction at this time of an earth fort at Richborough, which was apparently designed to create a look-out post, reinforces this impression. But such incursions into the peace and general well-being of the province were fairly localized and infrequent, even if they did presage trouble to come.

The largely undisturbed tranquillity of life seems to have continued into the fourth century. But as the century advanced there are further signs of the attacks which were to be so harrowing in the following century. In 339 there seems to have been an assault by the Picts, perhaps with assistance from the Scots who at this time were still based in Ireland, upon the unprotected lands north of Hadrian's wall. A hurried and apparently unexpected visit by the Emperor Constans in 343 was possibly the result of some severe, but unidentified, trouble the previous year. In 360 the Scots and Picts began to lay waste the regions near the frontier. The Picts were increasingly learning the advantages of sea-borne raiding, and this enabled them to pillage southern Britain. But stability and order were maintained. By 370 the province was once more enjoying firm government, and the defences were effective. But in retrospect we can see that forty years later she ceased to be part of the Roman Empire.

The troops were repeatedly withdrawn between 383 and 407, so that the defence of the island increasingly devolved upon the local population. There was reportedly a serious Saxon raid on Britain in 408; and the legions were removed in 410.

Roman Britain – demography and politics

Once the initial, first-century, phase of military activity was over, and Britain was reasonably subdued, Rome moved rapidly to establish a loosely decentralized administration which allowed overall control by the emperor while leaving the low-level administration in the hands of the traditional aristocrats. This was necessary because the Roman élite was too small to directly control each incorporated society in a massive and rapidly expanding empire. Roman Britain alone, it has been estimated, had a population at the end of the second century of almost three million, the vast majority of whom were not part of the immigrant military and civilian Romans. This is the conclusion of Frere after a full review of the data,[2] and it is broadly confirmed by Martin Millett in a careful consideration of the situation.[3]

In Britain administrative changes in the third and fourth centuries had the effect of multiplying the layers of government structure. This was accompanied by the deliberate inaccessibility of emperors, and the greater remoteness of British governors from the fount of authority. The division into two provinces in the third century was drastically modified in the fourth century when the two became four and later five. More importantly, the division of responsibility was no longer between general administration, which included command of the army in Britain, and finance, but between military and civil. In his civil role the former *legatus Augusti* of the undivided province reappeared as the *vicarius*, to whom the governors of the increased number of provinces were responsible. Unlike the *legatus Augusti*, however, the *vicarius* did not have a direct relationship with the emperor, but was responsible to the praetorian prefect of the Gauls, in whose prefecture Britain was included.

By degrees the Romans also introduced an ever more genuine and effective system of local self-government, which had already proved successful in Gaul. It was based on *civitates peregrinae*, which were self-governing communities of non-citizens. The tangible indication of this decentralization was the possession of a forum with basilica, which housed the meetings of the council and the administration of local justice. Such fora were first constructed in Chichester, Cirencester, Exeter and Winchester in the Flavian period, and the timber forum at Silchester was built about the same time. Nowhere is a pre-Flavian forum known, so it seems that the first, or at least the main, development of local government occurred in the last decades of the first century and the early years of the second century.

The general practice of Rome was to adapt what was already in existence, and it appears that this happened in Britain, especially in the south and east, where the civitates were based on the social groupings of the late pre-Roman Iron Age. The tribal landowning élites transformed themselves into the controlling powers, as *decuriones* in the Roman terminology, in the new civitates. They were thus rewarded by retaining power, and control of their tribes and wealth, and were allowed to continue a *de facto* hereditary system. This arrangement may well have been the result of an essentially *laissez-faire* administration in relation to the native society rather than the consequence of a set of deliberate acts of policy by the Roman authorities. But, whatever the balance of Roman initiative or inertia, the result was satisfactory from the viewpoint of both the Romans and the host society. 'Those already in power could thus gain or retain more by co-operation than by opposition. Retaining control, even if in a more circumscribed form, was preferable to losing it. The secret of Rome's success was that through devolution she was able to govern with minimal coercion.'[4] This model applies mostly to the south, east and midland territories; there was a departure from it in the west and north, where there is less evidence that native civil administration took root.

Roman Britain – the economy

The economy, and indeed the whole way of life of the Celtic realms at the time of the Claudian invasion, was rural. But the advent of the Roman or romanized estate-owner changed the overall scale of agricultural output. The increase in production was achieved by the cultivation of larger areas of land, not through any significant improvement in yields. The expansion was also aided by the introduction of more and better quality implements such as ploughs, iron-shod spades, scythes and even 'mechanical' reaping machines. This was combined with increased use of spelt, a form of wheat which had been introduced in the Iron Age because it was more suitable for a damp climate, rye, oats and flax, and root crops such as turnips, carrots and parsnips which provided vegetables for human consumption as well as a supplement to rape as winter feed for stock. More careful breeding together with better supplies of winter fodder improved the strains of cows, sheep and horses. Such advances were part of a long-term trend in Britain and other parts of temperate Europe towards agricultural intensification, involving a new balance of crop species, changing methods of cultivation, and new developments in horticulture and hay production. This process was of much longer duration than the period of British Roman occupation, but Roman influence helped to ensure that the province was not left on the sidelines of such changes.[5]

The Roman villa-economy permitted the continuance of old native farms. But they became part of the new organization without necessarily being adjacent to a villa or being directly run from a villa. The non-rural population, consisting mainly of the army and the dwellers in the urban areas, although not a large proportion of the total population, created an extra demand for food which needed to be satisfied. About six hundred villas are known, and there were clearly more. They prospered for much of the Roman period. They varied greatly in size. Most of the very big ones, such as Woodchester, which were about as large as a medium-sized eighteenth-century country house, with sixty or more rooms, were built around the end of the third century. Many villas were enlarged or improved in the fourth century. It was at that time that most of the mosaic pavements characteristic of villa luxury were laid; and, as we will see, this is when mosaic chi-rho symbols are mostly to be found. It is all indicative of prosperity, and the ability to make money in a developed economy. The beginning of the end for villas as the focus for an agricultural system can probably be pinpointed to the increased barbarian incursions of the late 360s. Villas were sitting targets for wandering bands of raiders. Some survived until well into the fifth century, although they may well have contracted in size as part of a decline in the standard of living of the owners.

Nonetheless, up to the late fourth century there was widespread prosperity in the province. The abundance of coins which have been unearthed suffice to show that late Roman Britain enjoyed a well-established money economy. Economic sophistication is also demonstrated by the growth of such industries as pottery, the mining of silver, gold, lead, copper, iron and coal, forestry, the quarrying of stone, the manufacture of bronze objects, as well as a more extensive and organized system for trading. The expansion of the pottery industry was a good example of the changes effected. In the early Roman period Britain had depended heavily on imports for its pottery requirements. By the fourth century it had become self-sufficient in this produce, as in others. There were about a dozen centres for the production of pottery for ordinary use, and the items manufactured were widely used.

Economic health was also reflected in the development of towns. About a hundred walled places have been identified and, though some of these were so small that they should be regarded as villages rather than towns, some were large. London was foremost with 330 acres within its walls, which could have held 30,000 people. At an early stage it became the financial centre of the province, possibly acting in that role before the Boudiccan rebellion. Cirencester had 240 acres, *Verulamium* (St Albans) and Wroxeter 200 each; which implies that they may have had populations of over 15,000. Using the same measure, there were approximately a score of other places which could have had populations of between 2,000 and about 10,000. They, like the villas, experienced decline around and after the Roman withdrawal as part of a general economic deterioration. 'Economically the province seems to die very rapidly at the beginning of the fifth century.'[6]

Roman Britain – social life

When the Romans arrived they encountered nothing in Britain which remotely resembled their idea of what a town should be like, let alone a city.[7] This was unacceptable: for towns were focal points of Roman life and activity throughout the empire. They set about remedying what they regarded as an intolerable deficiency by the deliberate foundation of Colchester in 49 as a chartered *colonia*. A similar procedure was adopted for Lincoln and Gloucester before the end of the first century. Later a fourth well-attested *colonia*, York, appeared. Some of the towns, such as Canterbury, Rochester or Silchester, succeeded pre-Roman *oppida* on the same site; others, like Colchester, *Verulamium*, Chichester or Dorchester (Dorset), also succeeded their native predecessors, but on a nearby, freshly chosen, site. Lesser status towns were named *vicus*, or, as a community of intermediate rank between a vicus and a colonia, a *munici-pium*.

In the towns the streets were in the main laid out at right angles to one another, thus forming rectangular blocks of land, or *insulae*, between them. It was usual to have two main streets to carry the through flows of traffic, which intersected at the centre of the town; these were referred to as *cardo maximus* and *decumanus maximus*. The forum and basilica, the principal public build-ings, were normally located in one of the four insulae, as shown in a fine way by Cirencester and Silchester. Occasionally, when a town expanded, a fresh alignment was introduced for the new streets, as at Wroxeter; or some elements of an earlier, unplanned street system were preserved when a new grid was con-structed, as at Silchester and Caistor-by-Norwich. With the passage of time, subsidiary roads were often built, perhaps to allow additional access to a par-ticular building, and this effectively reduced the size of insulae, as at Leicester and Canterbury.

The larger towns were provided with amenities far superior to those of the pre-Roman oppida. In addition to well-paved, spacious streets and covered porticoes, there was running water supplied from a remarkable system of aqueducts, good sewage and surface water disposal, public lavatories and bath-houses, entertainments, including in some cases an amphitheatre with wild-beasts matched against each other as in bear-baiting and cock-fighting, amusements, including public executions, educational facilities, and a reason-able standard of comfort in private dwellings, especially for the more wealthy. And the proportion of more prosperous citizens apparently increased throughout the Roman period. In Britain, as in other parts of the Empire, most townspeople in the earlier years were probably involved in trade and lived over or in their shops. With increased wealth more luxurious separate living accommodation tended to be provided for those who prospered most. They then enjoyed such additional facilities as underfloor heating on the hypocaust principle, and their houses had masonry, masonry and cob, or half-timbered walls, instead of a wooden structure with walls made of wattle and daub which was characteristic of the unprepossessing artisan houses and workshops which gave way to the grand merchant residences. As the dwellings increased in size and elaborateness they would have included two or more wings situated around an enclosed courtyard which was frequently laid out as a garden. 'The overall effect of the reduction in the density of occupation and the increased scale of the buildings was to make many of these towns appear as garden cities.'[8]

In contrast to the high-class homes, there might have been areas within some towns occupied by small huts for the poor. These shanty towns were, however, not typical. It appears that many of the authorities may not have allowed them to develop. The very poor, other than retainers and slaves, who would be accommodated on their master's premises, would have lived in the countryside where a peasant class, whether free or bound to the land, would find some opportunity to scratch a living.

Smaller towns and settlements would not have benefitted from some of the provisions in the more important centres. Indeed, many of them were little more than military vici or local rural markets with ephemeral buildings and a not very sophisticated way of life. There was some up-grading in the third and fourth centuries, when more substantial buildings were erected, but they often remained very much humble cousins of the illustrious urban complexes just described.

There was no clear cut division between town and country. Farms and farmhouses were to be found in towns as well as the country, as at Silchester and Cirencester, and some trades such as pottery were active in both towns and the countryside. Some of the new colonies, as at Colchester, Lincoln and Gloucester, were designed to give retired veterans a stake in the land, and the inhabitants, although they lived for the most part in the town concerned, cultivated allotments in the surrounding country. For most of the countryside the agricultural exploitation was either in the form of peasant settlements or villas and their estates. The former, whether villages or single farmsteads, still broadly continued and developed the pre-Roman field system. The farmers sometimes even retained the use of pre-Roman grain-storage pits and the ancestral round huts of wood or stone in an irregular layout. The only signs of improvement were the gradual disappearance of the storage pits, and the occasional replacement of the round huts by rectangular cottages, as at Park Brow, Sussex, and Studland, Dorset.

The villas were a crucial element in a new social as well as economic system which grew out of and beside the old, and they increased in number and importance in the latter half of the Roman period in Britain. As we have already seen, they represented the advanced thinking, and the application of capital and new technologies and methods, of the men of wealth and enterprise. The owners had close political and business connections with the towns, and villas therefore tended to cluster near towns and to lie not far from roads. For instance, there were about thirty known villas of quality within a reasonable commuting distance of Bath.[9]

The villa owners were the rural élite. The structure of the villas reflected this and also the growing romanization of manners. The basic design remained the same throughout Roman times. There was a symmetrical facade with a central entrance, which in some villas was more elaborate than others when it was the exterior to a tripartite winged corridor plan with a corridor and wings at the back as well as at the front. There was usually at least one bath-suite, and the appearance of a central dining-room, larger in size than the other rooms, was a further sure sign of increasing culture and romanization, as was the presence of a courtyard either behind lengthened wings or totally enclosed. Such large establishments were served by a household of numerous domestic slaves and agricultural workers; and they were the centres of large estates. Many villas were progressively enlarged well into the fourth century, as with the town dwellings of successful merchants.[10]

But in parallel with this trend there was also a proliferation, especially during the third century, of smaller villas, including a number of cottage-type buildings such as Barton Farm. This represented a popularization of the villa idea: 'taste for rural *Romanitas* had moved down the social and economic scale so that more modest members of the community, hitherto presumably satisfied with a traditional timber dwelling, began to construct villas for themselves.'[11] It was one more evidence of a continuing process of romanization which took place through to at least the first half of the fourth century, but the villas remained a small proportion of the total number of settlements.

In the changing settlement pattern in the Roman period another feature of significance was the more widespread occurrence of small nucleated agricultural settlements. These did not have the same mediaeval tenurial implications of later villages, but they were in many respects similar to such communities. They were akin to the less-developed small Roman towns, and overlapped with them in function, although many were not located on the major roads.[12]

Some scholars think that the whole social structure established by the Romans, and typified in the villas and the towns, evaporated, especially after 410. 'In reality there was no grand apocalyptic orgy of destruction, merely a slow decline until all attempts to keep up appearances were abandoned. The way of life enjoyed by the privileged minority in towns and villas simply passed away and everyone reverted to a lifestyle that had much in common with that of their Iron Age ancestors.'[13]

What had taken place during the almost four centuries of continuous Roman presence was a process whereby two ways of life merged to form a civilization with a dual character. 'Romano-British culture arose from the impact of the civilization of Rome upon the Celtic people of Britain; the result, however, was not a replacement of cultures, but rather what can broadly be described as a synthesis.'[14]

Appendix 2

Glossary

Ambulatory A covered area for walking around the outside of a building.

Apse Semicircular or polygonal extension, usually in a church where it most frequently occurs at the east end of the building.

Barrows Prehistoric structures for communal burial, usually in the form of long or round barrows.

Benedictional In the Western church this was the liturgical book which contained the formulae of the bishop's blessings for use in the mass.

Bretwalda An Old English term which means either 'wide ruler' or 'ruler of Britain'. It is used to describe those kings who exercised overlordship over other kings and whose sway therefore extended well beyond their own kingdom.

Burh A fortified town such as those which played such an important part in the defences of King Alfred the Great.

Cella The central, principal, room of a temple, usually containing the cult statue and sacred objects.

Chancel The east end area of a church, where the altar or communion table is placed, originally shut off by a screen from the nave.

Chi-rho The Christian cross-like motif which incorporated the first two letters of the Greek word *Christos*. The sign was sometimes accompanied by the two Greek letters, the alpha and omega.

Clerestory That part of the external wall of a church above the aisle roofs which frequently contains a series of windows.

Collectars A liturgical book containing the collects.

Danegeld A tax on land which was levied at various times to buy off Danish attackers or pay the settled Danes to avoid attack.

Danelaw That region of England which was most fully settled by the Danes from the ninth century onwards. It was centred on East Anglia, the East Midlands and Yorkshire, and it developed social and legal characteristics which helped to distinguish it from the rest of England.

Demesne Land occupied freehold instead of being leased to tenants.

Double minster Monastery in which there were separate but adjacent institutions for men and women, with the two under the supervision of one person, almost invariably an abbess.

Ealdorman A nobleman who exercised authority within a shire or group of shires on behalf of the king. After the Danish conquest of Cnut the term was gradually replaced by the Anglo-Scandinavian word *earl*.

Epigraphy The science which is concerned with the study, deciphering and interpretation of inscriptions.

Extra-mural Outside the walls of any town or city.

Graduals Book of hymns and prayers.

Hagiography The writing of the lives of saints.

Henges Prehistoric stone circles and the related earthen rings.

Hide A word which originally donated the amount of land required to support a family. But probably by the early eighth century it was used as a notional unit in the assessment of land for services and taxes, and it continued to have this meaning until after the Norman Conquest.

Housel The eucharist.

Hundred A subdivision of a shire.

Iconography The study of ancient images, statues, and engravings on objects such as gems.

Intra-mural Within the walls of any town or city.

Martyrium A chapel or shrine erected in memory of a martyr.

Minster A church covering a large territory for pastoral purposes, served by a community of clergy, but not necessarily monastic.

Missals Book containing the services of the mass for a year.

Muniment Title deed or charter.

Narthex A porch or anteroom located at the west end of a church, originally provided for women or converts under instruction.

Nave The central, middle, part of a church, which extends from the chancel, or choir, to the main entrance.

Nymphaeum A shrine dedicated to nymths, which were semi-divine beings associated with water, fountains or trees.

Pallium A stole given by the pope to an archbishop in token of his archiepiscopal status, which was made of white wool and decorated with dark purple crosses.

Podium An artificial platform for a temple and its surrounds.

Pontificals In the Western church it was the book containing the prayers and ceremonies for rites used by a bishop, such as confirmation and holy orders.

Reliquary A small shrine, casket or other form of container to house a relic or relics.

Rune A letter or character of the old Teutonic and Scandinavian alphabets.

Sacramentary Book which prescribes the ritual to be followed at the celebration of the sacraments.

Sarsens Prehistoric standing stones.

Scriptorium The room which was set apart in a religious community for the writing and decoration of manuscripts.

Temenos The sacred precinct or enclosure surrounding a temple, the limits of which were usually defined by a wall or a ditch.

Thegn A close follower of a lord with special status and privileges.

Tithe A tenth part of the annual produce of land payable in later Saxon times to the church.

Wapentake The word used in the Danelaw as the equivalent to the hundred.

Witan The chief council of an Anglo-Saxon king.

Appendix 3

Some Key Dates

BC

55   Caesar's first invasion of Britain

AD

43   Roman invasion under Aulus Plautius in the reign of the Emperor Claudius

60   Rebellion of the Iceni under Boudicca

84   Agricola's victory at *Mons Graupius*

*c.*122–33   Building of Hadrianic frontier

*c.*143   Building of Antonine frontier

*c.*200   Perhaps, the arrival of the first Christians

208–11   Earliest likely date for the martyrdom of Alban, Aaron and Julius

314   British bishops at the Council of Arles

359   British bishops at the Council of Ariminum

367–70   Picts, Scots and Saxons assault Britain. Hadrianic frontier overthrown for third time; restored by Theodosius

410   The Emperor Honorius writes to the *civitates* of Britain, and tells them they must defend themselves

415?   Birth of St Patrick (died 493?)

420   Death of Pelagius (born *c.*380)

*c.*425–55   Reign of Vortigern

429   First visit of Germanus to Britain

447   Second visit of Germanus

*c.*455   Saxon rebellion against the British

*c.*460–80   Age of Ambrosius Aurelianus

*c.*490   Battle of *Mons Badonicus*

*c.*522   Birth of St Columba (Columcille)

*c.*540   Birth of Gregory the Great

*c.*577   Battle of *Dyrham* and West Saxons capture Bath, Gloucester and Cirencester

597   Arrival of St Augustine (died 613). Death of St Columba

601   Death of St David

602–3   Conference between St Augustine and representative British bishops

	and other leaders at St Augustine's Oak
616	Bishop Mellitus driven from London. King Eabald converted
617	Edwin becomes king of Northumbria (died 633)
625	Paulinus sent to Northumbria
627	Edwin of Northumbria converted
631	Bishop Felix arrives in East Anglia
634	Oswald becomes king of Northumbria. Birinus arrives in Wessex
635	Mission of Aidan to Lindisfarne
642	Oswy becomes king of Northumbria (died 670)
651	Agilbert consecrated Bishop of Dorchester
653	Peada baptized. Mission to Mid-Angles. Second mission to Essex
654	Cedd consecrated Bishop of the East Saxons
c.660	Caedmon born (died 680)
661	Colman succeeds Finan as Bishop of Lindisfarne. Wilfrid at Ripon
664	Synod of Whitby
665	Consecrations of Wilfrid and Chad. Third mission to Essex
669	Theodore of Tarsus arrives as Archbishop of Canterbury. Wilfrid consecrated Bishop of York. Chad becomes Bishop of Lichfield
671	Hadrian founds the School of Canterbury
672	Council of Hereford
673	Division of East-Anglian diocese
674	Benedict Biscop founds Wearmouth monastery
675	Aldhelm Abbot of Malmesbury. Possible date of birth of Boniface
678	Division of the diocese of York
679	Division of the Mercian diocese
680	Council of Hatfield. Wilfrid evangelizes Sussex. Monasteries of Jarrow and Gloucester founded
687	Death of Cuthbert (born c.634)
690	Death of Theodore, Archbishop of Canterbury. Willibrord goes to Frisia
699	Guthlac arrives at Crowland
c.700	Birth of Willibald (died 786)
702	Council of Easterfield
705	West Saxon diocese divided. Aldhelm Bishop of Sherborne. Council of Nidd
709	Death of Aldhelm and Wilfrid (born c.634)
735	Death of Bede (born c.671)
747	Council of Clofesho
755	Martyrdom of Boniface
757	Accession of Offa as king of Mercia (died 796)
786	Legatine councils
793	Lindisfarne attacked by Vikings
802	Restoration of the rights of Canterbury

804	Death of Alcuin
816	Council of Chelsea
849	Birth of Alfred the Great (died 899)
851	Vikings winter in Thanet and attack London and Canterbury
865	Great Danish army lands in East Anglia
866–67	Danes attack Northumbria
867–68	Danes move into Mercia
869	Martyrdom of King Edmund of East Anglia
871	Danes defeated at Ashdown. Accession of Alfred
c.872	Birth of Edward the Elder (died 924)
878	Baptism of Guthram
c.894	Birth of Athelstan (died 939)
921	Birth of Edmund, King of Wessex (died 946)
943	Edgar the Peaceable born (died 975)
960	Dunstan installed as Archbishop of Canterbury
963	Ethelwold consecrated Bishop of Winchester
c.966	Birth of Ethelred II (the Unready) (died 1016)
984	Death of Ethelwold, Bishop of Winchester
988	Death of Dunstan, Archbishop of Canterbury
992	Death of Oswald, Archbishop of York
c.1012	Death of Aelfric, Abbot of Eynsham
1014	Death of Sweyn Forkbeard
1016	Death of Edmund Ironside
1023	Death of Wulfstan, Archbishop of York
1035	Death of Cnut, or Canute (born c.996)
1042	Edward (the Confessor) becomes king
1062	Wulfstan consecrated Bishop of Worcester
1065	Dedication of Westminster Abbey. Death of Edward the Confessor
1066	Battle of Hastings; the death of King Harold II; the Norman Conquest under William 1.

Abbreviations

A	*Antiquity*
AA	*Archaeologia Aeliana*
AJ	*Antiquaries Journal*
AmJ	*Ampleforth Journal*
Arc	*Archaelogia*
ArchJ	*Archaeological Journal*
ASE	*Anglo-Saxon England*
B	*Britannia*
BAR	British Archaeological Reports
BMQ	*British Museum Quarterly*
C	*Celtica*
CA	*Current Archaeology*
CHJ	*Cambridge Historical Review*
CMCS	*Cambridge Medieval and Celtic Studies*
EHR	*English Historical Review*
F	*Folklore*
H	*History*
HT	*History Today*
JBAA	*Journal of the British Archaeological Association*
JEH	*Journal of Ecclesiastical History*
JRA	*Journal of Roman Archaeology*
JRS	*Journal of Roman Studies*
JTA	*Journal of Theoretical Archaeology*
JTS	*Journal of Theological Studies*
JWCI	*Journal of the Warberg and Courtauld Institutes*
LH	*Landscape History*
MA	*Mediaeval Archaeology*
MS	*Monastic Studies*
NH	*Northern History*
OJA	*Oxford Journal of Archaeology*
Ox	*Oxoniensia*
PBA	*Proceedings of the British Academy*
SC	*Studio Celtica*

SCH	*Studies in Church History*
TRHS	*Transactions of the Royal Historical Society*
TS	*Theological Studies*
WHR	*Welsh Historical Review*

Bibliography

Abrams, L. and Carley, J. P. (eds), *The Archaeology and History of Glastonbury*, Woodbridge 1991

Addyman, P. and Morris, R., *The Archaeological Study of Churches*, London 1976

Adomnan of Iona, *Life of St Columba*, trans R.Sharpe, Harmondsworth 1995

Alcock, J. P., 'Celtic water cults in Roman Britain', *ArchJ*, 112, 1965, pp. 1–12

Alcock, J., 'Classical Religious Beliefs and Burial Practice in Roman Britain', *ArchJ*, 137, 1980, pp. 50–85

Alcock, L., 'Roman Britons and Pagan Saxons: An Archaeological Appraisal', *WHR*, 3, 1967, pp. 229–49.

Alcock, Leslie, *Arthur's Britain. History and Archaeology AD 367–634*, Harmondsworth 1971

Alexander, J. J. G., *Insular Manuscripts, 6th to the 9th Centuries*, London 1978

Alexander, M. (ed), *The Earliest English Poems*, Harmondsworth 1966

Alexander, M. (trans), *Beowulf. A Verse Translation*, Harmondsworth 1973

ApSimon, A. M., 'The Roman temple at Brean Down, Somerset', Proceedings of the University of Bristol Spelaeological Society, 10, 1965, pp. 195–258

Arnold, C. J., *Roman Britain to Saxon England*, London 1984

Ashe, Geoffrey, *King Arthur's Avalon. The Story of Glastonbury*, London 1957

Backhouse, Janet, *The Lindisfarne Gospels*, Oxford 1981

Bailey, R. N. and O'Sullivan, D., 'Excavations over St Wilfrid's Crypt at Hexham; 1978', AA, 5th series 7, 1979, pp. 145–78

Banton, N., 'Monastic reform and the unification of tenth-century England', *SCH*, 18, 1982, pp. 71–85 .

Barley, M. W. and Hanson, R. P. C. (eds), *Christianity in Roman Britain 300–700*, Leicester 1968

Barlow, Frank, *The English Church 1000–1066*, 2nd edn London 1979

Barnard, S., 'The matres of Roman Britain', *Arch.J*, 142, 1985, pp. 237–45

Bassett, S., 'Churches in Worcester before and after the conversion of the Anglo-Saxons', *AJ*, 69, 1989, pp. 225–56

Bassett, Steven (ed), *The Origins of Anglo-Saxon Kingdoms*, Leicester 1989

Bately, J. M., *The Anglo-Saxon Chronicle: texts and textual relationships*, Reading Medieval Studies, Reading 1991

Bateson, M., 'The Origin and Early Histories of Double Monasteries', *TRHS*, New Series, 13, 1899, pp. 137–98.

Battiscombe, G. (ed), *The Relics of St Cuthbert*, Oxford 1986

Beard, M. and Reynolds, J. (eds), *Image and Mystery in the Roman World*, Gloucester 1988

Bede, *Historiam Ecclesiasticam (HE) see* Colgrave and Mynore (eds), *Bede's Ecclesiastical History*

Berg, K., 'The Gosforth Cross', *JWCI*, 21, 1958, pp. 27–43

Bieler, L., *The Life and Legend of St Patrick*, Dublin 1948

Bieler, L., 'The "Creeds" of St Victorinus and St Patrick', *TS*, ix, 1949, pp. 121–24

Bieler, L., *The Works of St Patrick*, London 1953

Birley, A. R., *The People of Roman Britain*, London 1979

Blagg, T., 'Roman religious sites in the British landscape', *LH*, 8, 1986, pp. 16–24

Blair, Peter Hunter, *An Introduction to Anglo-Saxon England*, Cambridge 1956

Blair, Peter Hunter, *The World of Bede*, Cambridge 1970

Blair, P. Hunter, *Roman Britain and Early England 55 BC-AD 871*, London 1975

Blair, P. Hunter, *Northumbria in the Days of Bede*, London 1976

Blair, W. J. (ed), *Ministers and Parish Churches: the Local Church in Transition 950–1200*, Oxford 1988

Blair, W. J., *Saint Frideswide: Patron of Oxford*, Oxford 1989

Blair, W. J. and Sharpe, R. (eds), *Pastoral Care before the Parish*, Leicester 1992

Bonner, G., 'Bede and Medieval Civilization', *ASE* 2, 1973, pp. 71–90

Bonner, G. (ed), *Famulus Christi: Essays in Commemoration of the Thirteenth Century of the Birth of the Venerable Bede*, London 1976

Bonner, G., Rollason, David and Stancliffe, Clare (eds), *St Cuthbert, his Cult and his Community to AD 1200*, Woodbridge, Suffolk, 1989

Bonser, W., 'Survivals of Paganism in Anglo-Saxon England', The Birmingham Archaeological Society, LVI, 1932, pp. 37–76

Bonser, W., 'The Magic of Saint Oswald', *A*, IX, 1935, pp. 418–23

Boon, G. C., 'A temple of Mithras at Caernarvon-*Segontium*, *Archaeol Cambrensis*, 109, 1960, pp.136–72

Boon, G. C., 'A Roman sculpture rehabilitated: the Pagan's Hill dog', *B*, 20, 1989, pp. 201–17

Born, H., 'The pagan revival in the west at the end of the fourth century' in Momigliano (ed), *The Conflict between Christianity and Paganism in the Fourth Century*, pp. 193–218

Bradley, Ian, *The Celtic Way*, London 1993

Bradley, Ian, *Columba. Pilgrim and Penitent*, Glasgow 1996

Bradley, S. A. J. (ed and trans), *Anglo-Saxon Poetry*, London 1982

Branigan, Keith, *Roman Britain. Life in an Imperial Province*, London 1980

Branigan, K. and Fowler, P. J. (eds), *The Roman West Country*, Newton Abbot 1976

Branston, Brian, *The Lost Gods of England*, 2nd edn London 1974

Brendan, Lehane, *Early Celtic Christianity*, London 1968

Bright, William, *Chapters of Early English Church History*, Oxford 1888

Brooks, D. A., 'Gildas's *De Excidio*, its revolutionary meaning and purpose', *SC*, 18/19, 1983/4, pp. 1–10

Brooks, N. P., 'England in the ninth century: the crucible of defeat', *TRHS*, 5th series, 29, 1979, pp. 1–20

Brooks, N. P., *Early History of the Church of Canterbury*, Leicester 1984

Brooks, N. P. and Cupitt, C. (eds), *St Oswald of Worcester: Life and Influence*, Leicester 1996

Brown, D., *Anglo-Saxon England*, London 1978

Brown, George Hardin, *Bede the Venerable*, Boston, Mass. 1987

Brown, P. D. C., 'The Church at Richborough', *B*, 2, 1971, pp. 225–31

Brown, P. R. L., 'Pelagius and his supporters: Aims and Environment', *JTS*, XIX, 1968, pp. 93–114

Brown, P. R. L., *Relics and Social Status in the Age of Gregory of Tours*, Reading 1977

Brown, Peter [R. L.], *Augustine of Hippo. A Biography*, London 1967

Brown, Peter [R. L.], *The Cult of the Saints: Its Rise and Function in Latin Christianity*, Chicago and London 1981

Brown, T. J., 'Northumbria and the Book of Kells', *ASE*, I, 1972, pp. 281–46

Bruce-Mitford, R. L. S., 'The art of the Codex Amiatinus', *JBAA*, 32, 1969, pp. 1–25

Bruce-Mitford, R. L. S., *Aspects of Anglo-Saxon Archaeology*, London 1974

Bruce-Mitford, R. L. S., *The Sutton Hoo Ship Burial*, 3rd edn London 1979

Bruhl, C. R., 'Problems of continuity of Roman *civitates* as illustrated by the interpretation of cathedral and *palatium*' in Hodges and Hobley (eds), *The Rebirth of Towns in the West*, pp. 43–46

Brundage, J. A., *Law, Sex and Christian Society in Medieval Europe (500–1500)*, Chicago 1987

Bulloch, J., *The Life of the Celtic Church*, Edinburgh 1963

Bullough, D. A. and Wormald, C. P. (eds), *Ideal and Reality in Early Medieval Europe: studies presented to J.M. Wallace-Hadrill*, Oxford 1983

Burl, Aubrey, *Prehistoric Avebury*, London 1979

Burl, Aubrey, *Rites of the Gods*, London 1981

Burl, Aubrey, *The Stonehenge People: Life and Death at the World's Greatest Stone Circle*, London 1987

Burnham, B. C. and Davies, J. L. (eds), *Conquest, Co-existence, and Change*, Cambridge 1990

Bury, J. B., 'The Origin of Pelagius', *Hermathena*, xiii, 1905, pp. 26–35

Butler, L. A. S. and Morris, R. K. (eds), *The Anglo-Saxon Church: Papers on history, architecture, and archeaology in honour of Dr H.M.Taylor*, London 1986

Campbell, J., 'The First Century of English Christianity', *AmJ*, 76, 1971, pp. 12–29

Campbell, J., 'Observations on the conversion of England', *AmJ*, 78, 1973, pp. 12–26

Campbell, James, *Essays in Anglo-Saxon History*, London 1986

Campbell, James (ed), *The Anglo-Saxons*, new edn London 1991

Carmichael, Alexander (collector), *Carmina Gadelica. Hymns and Incantations*, Edinburgh 1992

Carver, M. (ed), *The Age of Sutton Hoo*, Woodbridge 1992

Casey, P. J. (ed), *The End of Roman Britain*, BAR 71, Oxford 1979

Casey, P. J., 'Excavations at Lydney Park, Gloucester', University of Durham and University of Newcastle-on-Tyne Archaeological Reports for 1980, 1981, pp. 30–32

Cassidy, B. (ed), *The Ruthwell Cross*, Princeton 1992

Chadwick, Henry, *The Early Christian Church*, Harmondsworth 1967

Chadwick, N. K. (ed), *Studies in Early British History*, Cambridge 1954

Chadwick, N. K. (ed), *Studies in Early British History*, Cambridge 1958

Chadwick, N. K., *The Age of the Saints in the Early Celtic Church*, Oxford 1961

Chadwick, N. K., *The Druids*, Cardiff 1966

Chadwick, Nora, *The Celts*, Harmondsworth 1970

Christiansen, E., 'Canute and his World', *HT*, 36, November 1986, pp. 34–39

Clancy, Thomas Owen and Markus, Gilbert, *Iona. The Earliest Poetry of a Celtic Monastery*, Edinburgh 1995

Clayton, M., *The Cult of the Virgin Mary in Anglo-Saxon England*, Cambridge 1990

Cleary, Esmonde, *The Ending of Roman Britain*, London 1989

Colgrave, B. (ed and trans), *Eddius Stephanus, Life of St Wilfred*, Cambridge 1927

Colgrave, B. (ed and trans), *Anon. Life of Pope Gregory*, Lawrence, USA 1968

Colgrave, B. (ed and trans), *Felix's Life of Guthlac*, Cambridge 1956

Colgrave, B., 'Earliest Saints' Lives Written in England', *PBA*, 44, 1958, pp. 35–60

Colgrave, B. (ed and trans), *Two Lives of Cuthbert*, Cambridge 1940

Colgrave, Bertram, and Mynors, R.A.B. (eds), *Bede's Ecclesiastical History of the English People*, Oxford 1969

Collingwood, R.G. and Richmond, I.A., *The Archaeology of Roman Britian*, London 1969

Collins, Roger, *Early Medieval Europe 300–1000*, London 1991

Cooper, Janet M., *The Last Four Anglo-Saxon Archbishops of York*, York 1970

Corrain, D. O., Breatnach, L and McKone, K. (eds), *Sagas, Saints and Story-tellers*, Maynooth 1989

Cotterell, Leonard, *Seeing Roman Britain*, new edn London 1956

Cramp, Rosemary J., 'Beowulf and Archaeology', *MA*, 1, 1957, pp. 57–77

Cramp, R., 'A Reconsideration of the Monastic Site at Whitby' in Higgit, John, and Spearman, R. Michael (eds), *The Age of Migrating Ideas*, Edinburgh 1993, pp. 64–73

Crummy, P., 'A Roman church in Colchester', *CA*, 120, 1990, pp. 406–8

Cubitt, C. R., *Anglo-Saxon Church Councils c. 650 -c. 850*, Leicester 1995

Cunliffe, Barry, and Davenport, Peter, *The Temple of Sulis Minerva at Bath*, Oxford University Committee for Archaeology Monographs, 7, Oxford 1985

Cunliffe, Barry, *Wessex to AD 1000*, London 1993

Cunliffe, Barry, *Roman Bath*, London 1995

Cutts, Edward, *Augustine of Canterbury*, London 1895

Daniels, R., 'Hartlepool', *CA*, 104, April 1987, pp. 273–77

Daniels, R., 'The Anglo-Saxon Monastery at Church Close, Hartlepool, Cleveland', *AJ*, 145, 1988, pp. 158–210

Dark, K. R., 'Celtic Monastic Archaeology: Fifth to Eighth Centuries', *MS*, 14, 1983, pp. 17–29

Dark, K. R., *Civitas to Kingdom. British Political Continuity 300–800*, Leicester 1994

Darlington, R. R., 'Ecclesiastical Reform in the late Old English period', *EHR*, LI, 1936, pp. 385-428 .

Davies, J. G., *The Origin and Development of Early Christian Church Architecture*, London 1952

Davies, W., 'The Myth of the Celtic Church' in Edwards and Lane (eds), *The Early Church*, pp. 12–21

Davis, R. H. C., *A History of Medieval Europe from Constantine to Saint Louis*, London and New York 1970

Davis, R. H. C., 'Alfred the Great: Propaganda and Truth', *H*, 56, 1971, pp. 169–82

Davis, R. H. C., *From Alfred the Great to Stephen*, London 1991

Deanesely, Margaret, 'Early English and Gallic Minsters', *TRHS*, 4th series, 23, 1941, pp. 25–69

Deanesley, Margaret, *The Pre-Conquest Church in England*, London 1961

Deanesley, Margaret, *Sidelights on the Anglo-Catholic Church*, London 1962

Dickinson, T., Rahtz, P. and Watts, L. (eds), *Anglo-Saxon Cemeteries*, Oxford 1980

Dodwell, C. R., *Anglo-Saxon Art: a New Perspective*, Manchester 1982

Donaldson, Christopher, *Martin of Tours*, Norwich 1980

Douglas, D. C. (ed), *English Historical Documents: II (1042–1189)*, 2nd edn London 1980

Downey, R., Soffe, G. and King, A., 'The Hayling Island Temple and Religious Connections across the Channel' in Rodwell (ed), *Temples, Churches and Religion in Roman Britain*, pp. 289–304

Drewett, P., *The South East to AD 1000*, London 1988

Drury, P. J., 'Neo-classical Religious Buildings in Iron Age and Roman Britain: A Review' in Rodwell (ed), *Temples, Churches and Religion in Roman Britain*, pp. 45–78

Duckett, Eleanor Shipley, *Anglo-Saxon Saints and Scholars*, New York 1947

Duckett, Eleanor Shipley, *St Dunstan of Canterbury. A study of Monastic Reform in the Tenth Century*, London 1953

Duckett, Eleanor Shipley, *Alcuin, Friend of Charlemagne*, London 1955

Dumville, D. N., 'Sub-Roman Britain – History and Legend', *H*, 62, 1977, pp. 173–92

Dumville, D. N., 'Late seventh-or eighth-century evidence for the British transmission of Pelagius', *CMCS*, 10, Winter 1985, pp. 39–52

Dumville, D. N., *Liturgy and the ecclesiastical history of late Anglo-Saxon England*, Woodbridge 1992

Dumville, D. M., *Wessex and England from Alfred to Edgar: Six Essays on Political, Cultural and Ecclesiastical Revival*, Woodbridge 1992

Dumville, D. N. with Abrams, L. et al., *Saint Patrick, AD 493–1993*, Woodbridge 1993

Duncan, A. A. M., *Scotland: The Making of the Kingdom*, revd edn Edinburgh 1978

Dunnett, R., 'The Excavations of the Roman Theatre at Gosbecks', *B*, 2, 1971, pp. 27–47

Edwards, N. and Lane, A. (eds), *The Early Church in Wales and the West*, Oxford 1992

Ellis, Peter Berresford, *The Druids*, London 1994

Ellis-Davidson, H. R., *Gods and Myths of Northern Europe*, London 1964

Ellison, A., *Excavations at West Hill, Uley: 1977. The Romano-British Temple*, Bristol 1978

Ellison, A., 'Natives, Romans and Christians on West Hill, Uley: an Interim Report on the excavation of a Ritual Complex of the First Millennium AD' in Rodwell (ed), *Temples, Churches and Religion in Roman Britain*, pp. 305–28

Ellison, A. and Henig, M., 'Head of Mercury from Uley, Gloucestershire', *A*, LV, 1981, pp. 43, 44.

Ericksen, R. T., 'Syncretistic Symbolism and the Christian Roman mosaic at Hinton St Mary: A Closer Reading', Proceedings of the Dorset Natural History and Archaeological Society, CII, 1980, pp. 434–38

Evans, A. C., *The Sutton Hoo Ship Burial*, London 1986

Evans, J., 'Settlement and society in northwest England in the fourth century' in Wilson, P. R., Jones, R. F. J. and Evans, D. M. (eds), *Settlement and Society in the Roman North*, Bradford 1984, pp. 43–48

Evison, V. I., *Dover: Buckland Anglo-Saxon Cemetery*, London 1987

Falkus, M., and Gillingham, J. (eds), *Historical Atlas of Britain*, revd edn London 1987

Farrell, R. T. (ed), *Bede and Anglo-Saxon England*, BAR 48, Oxford 1978

Ferguson, J., *The Religions of the Roman Empire*, London 1970

Fernie, E., *The Architecture of the Anglo-Saxons*, London 1983

Filmer-Sankey, W., Hawkes, S. Chadwick, Campbell, J., and Brown, D. (eds), *Anglo-Saxon Studies in Archaeology and History*, 5, Oxford 1992

Finberg, H. P. R. 'Continuity or Cataclysm' in Finberg, H. P. R., *Lucerna*, Leicester 1964, pp. 1–20.

Finlay, Ian, *Columba*, London 1979

Finucane, R. C., *Miracles and Pilgrims. Popular Beliefs in Medieval England*, London 1977

Fisher, D. J. V., 'The Anti-monastic Reaction in the Reign of King Edward the Martyr', *CHJ*, x, 3, 1952, pp. 254–70

Fisher, D. J. V., 'The Church in England between the death of Bede and the Danish Invasions', *TRHS*, 5th series, 2, 1952, pp. 1–19

Fisher, D. J. V., *The Anglo-Saxon Age c.400–1042*, London 1973

Fisher, E. A., *An Introduction to Anglo-Saxon Architecture*, London 1959

Fisher, E. A., *The Greater Anglo-Saxon Churches*, London 1962

Fleming, R., 'Monastic Lands and England's Defence in the Viking Age', *EHR*, 100, 1985, pp. 247-65 .

Fletcher, Eric, 'Early Kentish Churches', *MA*, 19, 1965, pp. 16–31

Fletcher, E. and Meates, G. W., 'The Ruined Church of Stone-by-Faversham', *AJ*, 49, 1969, pp. 273–94

Fletcher, E. and Meates, G. W., 'The Ruined Church of Stone-by-Faversham: Second Report', *AJ*, 57, 1977, pp. 67–72

Fletcher, Richard, *Who's Who in Roman Britain and Anglo-Saxon England*, London 1989

Flint, V. I. J., *The Rise of Magic in Early Medieval Europe*, Oxford 1991

Foakes-Jackson, F. J., *A History of the Christian Church from the Earliest Times to the Death of St Leo the Great, AD 461*, London 1905

Foley, W. T., *Images of Sanctity in Eddius Stephanus' Life of Bishop Wilfrid. An Early English Saint's Life*, Lampeter 1992

Ford, Boris (ed), *Cambridge Cultural History of Britain: Vol 1 Early Britain*, Cambridge 1992

Fox, Robin Lane, *Pagans and Christians in the Mediterranean world from the second century AD to the conversion of Constantine*, London 1986

France, N. E. and Gobel, B. M., *The Romano-British Temple at Harlow*, Gloucester 1985

Frantzen, A. J., *The Literature of Penance in Anglo-Saxon England*, New Brunswick, New Jersey 1986

Frend, W. H. C., 'Religion in Roman Britain in the Fourth Century', *JBAA*, 3rd series, 18, 1955, pp. 1–18

Frend, W. H. C., 'Ecclesia Britannica: Prelude or Dead End?', *JEH*, 30, 1979, pp. 129–44

Frend, W. H. C., *The Rise of Christianity*, London 1984

Frend, W. H. C., 'Pagans, Christians, and the "barbarian conspiracy" of AD 367 in Roman Britain', *B*, 23, 1992, pp. 121–31

Frere, Sheppard, *Britannia. A History of Roman Britain*, 3rd edn London 1987

Frere, S. S., 'The Silchester Church: The Excavation by Sir Ian Richmond in 1961', *Arc*, 105, 1975, pp. 277–302

Frere, S. S., *Verulamium Excavations*, 2 vols, London 1972, 1983

Gallyon, Margaret, *The Early Church in Eastern England*, Lavenham 1973

Gallyon, Margaret, *The Early Church in Wessex and Mercia*, Lavenham 1980

Gameson, R., *The Role of Art in the Later Anglo-Saxon Church*, Oxford 1995

Gascoign, C. J. B., *Alcuin: his life and work*, London 1904

Gatch, Milton McC., *Preaching and Theology in Anglo-Saxon England: Aelfric and Wulfstan*, Toronto 1977

Gelling, M., 'Place-names and Anglo-Saxon paganism', *University of Birmingham Historical Journal*, 8, 1961–62, pp. 7–25

Gelling, M., *Signposts to the Past-Place Names and the History of England*, London 1978

Gelling, M., *The West Midlands in the Early Middle Ages*, Leicester 1992

Gilchrist, R., *Gender and Material Culture: the archaeology of religious women*, London 1994

Gildas, *The Ruin of Britain see* Winterbottom (ed and trans)

Gilmour, B., 'The Anglo-Saxon church at St Paul-in-the-Bail, Lincoln', *MA*, 23, 1979, pp. 214–18

Godfrey, John, *The Church in Anglo-Saxon England*, Cambridge 1962

Godfrey, J, *The English Parish: 600–1300*, London 1969

Goodburn, R., *The Roman Villa, Chedworth*, London 1972

Goodchild, R. and Kirk, J. R., 'The Romano-Celtic Temple at Woodeaton', *Ox*, 19, 1954, pp. 15-37

Gordon, Richard, 'Who worshipped Mithras ?', *JRA*, 7, 1994, pp. 459–74

Gougaud, Louis, *Christianity in Celtic Lands. A History of the Churches of the Celts, their origin, their development, influence and mutual relations*, Dublin 1992

Graham-Campbell, J., *The Viking World*, New Haven, New York 1980

Green C. J. S., 'The Cemetery of a Romano-British Christian Community at

306 Christianity in England from Roman Times to the Reformation

Poundbury, Dorchester, Dorset' in Pearce (ed), *The Early Church in Western Britain and Ireland*, pp. 61–76

Green, Miranda, *The Gods of Roman Britain*, Princes Risborough 1983

Green, Miranda, *The Gods of the Celts*, Gloucester 1986

Green, M. J., *The Religions of Civilian Roman Britain*, BAR 24, Oxford 1976

Green, M. (ed), *The Celtic World*, London 1995

Greenaway, George William, *Saint Boniface. Three Biographical Studies for the Twelfth Century Festival*, London 1955

Greene, K., 'A Christian Monogram from Richborough, Kent', *B*, 5, 1974, pp. 393–95

Greenfield, E. and Taylor, M.V., 'The Romano-British Shrines at Brigstock, Northants', *AJ*, 43, 1963, pp. 228–63

Grimes, W. F., *The Excavation of Roman and Medieval London*, London 1968

Haddan, A. W. and Stubbs, W., *Councils and Ecclesiastical Documents relating to Great Britain and Ireland*, 3 vols, Oxford 1859–71

Hamer, R. (ed and trans), *A Choice of Anglo-Saxon Verse*, London 1970

Hamerow, H. F., 'Settlement Mobility and the "Middle Saxon Shift": Rural Settlements and Settlement Patterns in Anglo-Saxon England', *ASE*, 20, 1991, pp. 1–17

Hanson, R. P. C., *St Patrick, a British Missionary Bishop*, Nottingham 1965

Hanson, R. P. C., *Saint Patrick. His Origins and Career*, Oxford 1968

Harries, J., 'The rise of Christianity' in Wacher (ed), *The Roman World*, pp. 796–811

Haverfield, F., *The Romanization of Roman Britain*, 2nd edn Oxford 1912

Hawkes, S. C. and Dunning, G. C., 'Soldiers and Settlers in Roman Britain', *MA*, 5, 1961, pp. 1–70

Hawkes, S. C., 'A late Roman buckle from *Tripontium*', Transactions of the Birmingham and Warwickshire Archaeological Society, 85, 1973, pp. 145–59

Hayes, A., *Archaeology of the British Isles*, London 1993

Heighway, C. M., *Anglo-Saxon Gloucestershire*, Gloucester 1987

Henderson, George, *From Durrow to Kells: the Insular Gospel-books*, London 1987

Henig, M., 'Seasonal Feasts in Roman Britain', *OJA*, 50, 1982, pp. 213–23

Henig, Martin, *Religion in Roman Britain*, London 1984

Henig, Martin, and King, Anthony (eds), *Pagan Gods and Shrines of the Roman Empire*, Oxford University Committee for Archaeology Monographs, 8, Oxford 1986

Herbert, M., *Iona, Kells and Derry: the History and Hagiography of the Monastic Familia of Columba*, Oxford 1988

Herren, M. W., 'Gildas and Early British Monasticism' in Bammesberger, A. and Wollmann, A. (eds), *Britain 400–600: Language and History*, Heildelberg 1990, pp. 65–78

Higham, N. J., *The Northern Counties to AD 1000*, London 1986

Higham, N. J., *Rome, Britain and the Anglo-Saxons*, London 1992

Higham, N. J., *The Kingdom of Northumbria AD 350–1100*, Stroud 1993

Higham, N. J., *The English Conquest. Gildas and Britain in the fifth century*, Manchester 1994

Higham, N. J., *An English Empire. Bede and the early Anglo-Saxon kings*, Manchester and New York 1995

Hill, D., *An Atlas of Anglo-Saxon England*, Oxford 1981

Hills, C., 'The Archaeology of Anglo-Saxon England in the Pagan Period: a Review', *ASE*, 8, 1979, pp. 297–330

Hinton, D. A., 'Sutton Hoo Reviewed', *AJ*, 150, 1993, pp. 508–13

Hoare, F. R., *The Western Fathers. Being the lives of Saints Martin of Tours, Ambrose, Augustine of Hippo, Honoratus of Arles and Germanus of Auxerre*, London and New York 1954

Hodges, R., *The Anglo-Saxon Achievement*, London 1989

Hodges, R. and Hobley, B. (eds), *The Rebirth of Towns in the West, AD 700–1050*, London 1988

Hodgkin, R. H., *A History of the Anglo-Saxons*, 2 vols, Oxford 1939

Hollis, S., *Anglo-Saxon Women and the Church*, Woodbridge 1992

Hood, A. B. E. (ed and trans), Patrick, *Confessio, Epistola, Dicta*, London and Chichester 1978

Hooke, D. (ed), *Anglo-Saxon Settlements*, Oxford 1988

Hooper, N., 'Edgar the Aetheling: Anglo-Saxon Prince, Rebel and Crusader', *ASE*, 14, 1985, pp. 197–214

Horne, P., 'Romano-Celtic temples in the third century' in King, A. and Henig, M. (eds), *The Roman West in the Third Century*, Oxford 1981, pp. 21–26

Howe, Nicholas, *Migration and Mythmaking in Anglo-Saxon England*, New Haven and London, 1989

Howorth, H. H., *St Augustine of Canterbury*, London 1913

Hughes, K., *The Church in Early Irish Society*, London 1966

Hughes, K., 'The Celtic Church: is this a valid concept?', *CMCS*, 50, 1981, pp. 1–20

Hunt, William, *The English Church from its Foundation to the Norman Conquest (597–1066)*, London 1901

Huskinson, J., 'Some Pagan Mythological Figures and their Significance in Early Christian Art', Papers of the British School in Rome, 42, 1974, pp. 68–97

Hutchinson, V. J., *Bacchus in Roman Britain: the Evidence for his Cult*, 2 vols, Oxford 1986

Hutton, Ronald, *The Pagan Religions of the Ancient British Isles. Their Nature and Legacy*, Oxford 1991

Hyslop, M., 'The Two Cemeteries at Chamberlain's Barn, Leighton Buzzard, Bedfordshire', *AJ*, 120, 1963, pp. 161–200

Jenkins, F., 'St Martin's Church at Canterbury; a survey of the earliest structural features', *MA*, 9, 1965, pp. 11–15

Jenkins, F., 'Preliminary Report on the Excavations at the Church of St Pancras at Canterbury', *Canterbury Archaeology*, 1976, pp. 4–5

John, E., 'The King and the Monks in the Tenth-Century Reformation' in John, E. (ed), *Orbis Britanniae and Other Studies*, Leicester 1966, pp. 154–80

Johns, Catherine, and Potter, Timothy, *The Thetford Treasure: Roman Jewellery and Silver*, London 1983

Johnson, S., *Later Roman Britain*, London 1980

Jolly, Karen Louise, *Popular Religion in Late Saxon England. Elf Charms in Context*, North Carolina 1996

Jones, A., 'The Significance of the Regal Consecration of Edgar in 973', *JEH*, 33, 3, July 1982, pp. 375–90 .

Jones, B. and Mattingly D., *An Atlas of Roman Britain*, London 1990

Jones, Gwyn, *A History of the Vikings*, 2nd edn London 1985

Keynes, S., 'A Tale of Two Kings: Alfred the Great and Aethelred the Unready', *TRHS*, 5th series, 36, 1986, pp. 195–217

Keynes, S. and Lapidge, M. (trans), *Alfred the Great. Asser's Life of King Alfred and other contemporary sources*, Harmondsworth 1983

King, A., 'The Roman Church at Silchester Reconsidered', *OJA*, II, 1983, pp. 225–37

Kirby, D. P., 'Bede and the Pictish Church', *Innes Review*, 24, 1973, pp. 6–25

Kirby, D. P. (ed), *Saint Wilfrid at Hexham*, Newcastle upon Tyne 1974

Knowles, D., *The Monastic Order in England. A History of its development from the times of St Dunstan to the Fourth Lateran Council 943–1216*, Cambridge 1940

Krautheimer, R., *Three Christian Capitals: topography and politics*, Berkeley 1983

Laing, L., *The Archaeology of Late Celtic Britain and Ireland c.400–1200 AD*, London 1975

Laing, Lloyd and Laing, Jennifer, *Anglo-Saxon England*, London 1979

Lapidge, M., and Herren, M., *Aldhelm: the Prose Works*, London 1979

Lapidge, M., and Dumville, D. N. (eds), *Gildas: New Approaches*, Woodbridge 1984

Lapidge, M. and Gneuss, H. (eds), *Learning and Literature in Anglo-Saxon England*, Cambridge 1985

Lawson, M.K., *Cnut. The Danes in England in the Early Eleventh Century*, London and New York 1993

Leech, R. H., 'The excavation of a Romano-British farmstead and cemetery on Bradley Hill, Somerton, Somerset', *B*, 12, 1981, pp. 177–270

Leech, R. H., 'The excavation of a Romano-Celtic temple and later cemetery on Lamgatt Beacon, Somerset', *B*, 17, 1986, pp. 259–328

Lehane, Brendan, *Early Celtic Christianity*, new edn London 1994

Levison, W., 'St Alban and St Albans', *A*, 15, 1941, pp. 337–59

Levison, Wilhelm, *England and the Continent in the Eighth Century*, Oxford 1946

Lewis, M. J. T., *Temples in Roman Britain*, Cambridge 1966

Linsell, Tony, *Anglo-Saxon Runes*, Pinner 1992

Liversidge, Joan, *Britain in the Roman Empire*, London 1973

Loyn, H. R., *Anglo-Saxon England and the Norman Conquest*, 2nd edn London 1968

Loyn, H. R., *The Governance of Anglo-Saxon England 500–1087*, London 1984

Loyn, H. R., *The Making of the English Nation*, London 1991

Loyn, Henry, *The Vikings in Britain*, Oxford 1994

Mackie, E. W., *Science and Society in Prehistoric Britain*, London 1977

McWhirr, A. (ed), *Archaeology and History of Cirencester*, Oxford 1976

McWhirr, Alan, *Roman Gloucestershire*, Gloucester 1981

McWhirr, A., Viner, L. and Wells, C., *Cirencester Excavations II: Romano-British Cemeteries at Cirencester*, Cirencester 1982

Magnusson, M. and Palsson, H. (trans), *Orkneyinga Saga*, Harmondsworth 1981

Malory, Sir Thomas, *Le Morte D'Arthur*, 2 vols, London 1906

Markus, R. A., *From Augustine to Gregory the Great*, London 1983

Mason, Emma, *St Wulfstan of Worcester, c.1008–1095*, Oxford 1990

Mawer, C. F., *Evidence for Christianity in Roman Britain. The Small Finds*, Oxford 1995

Mayr-Harting, Henry, *The Coming of Christianity to Anglo-Saxon England*, London 1972

Meaney, A. L., 'Women, Witchcraft, and Magic' in Scragg, D. G.(ed), *Superstition and Popular Medicine in Anglo-Saxon England*, Manchester 1989, pp. 9–40

Meaney, A. and Hawkes, S. C., *Two Anglo-Saxon Cemeteries at Winnall, Winchester, Hampshire*, London 1970

Meates, G. W., *The Roman Villa at Lullingstone, Kent, Vol 1*, Kent Archaeological Society, Chichester 1979

Meates, G. W., *The Roman Villa at Lullingstone, Kent, Vol II*, Kent Archaeological Society, Maidstone 1988

Menzies, Lucy, *St Columba of Iona*, Glasgow 1949

Merrifield, R., 'Art and religion in Roman London – an inquest on the sculptures of Londinium' in Munby, J. and Henig, M. (eds), *Roman Life and Art in Britain*, 2 vols, Oxford 1977, Vol II, pp. 375–406

Merrifield, R., *The Archaeology of Ritual and Magic*, London 1987

Mews, S. (ed), *Religion and National Identity*, Oxford 1982

Meyvaert, P., 'Bede and the Church Paintings at Wearmouth/Jarrow', *ASE*, 8, 1979, pp. 63–78

Miket, R. and Burgess, C. (eds), *Between and Beyond the Walls*, Edinburgh 1984

Miller, M., 'Starting to Write History: Gildas, Bede and Nennius', *WHR*, 8, 1977, pp. 456–65

Millett, Martin, *The Romanization of Britain. An Essay in Archeological Interpretation*, Cambridge 1990

Momigliano, A. (ed), *The Conflict between Paganism and Christianity in the Fourth Century*, Oxford 1963

Morris, John R., 'Pelagian Literature', *JTS*, 16, April 1965, pp. 26–60

Morris, John R., 'The Dates of the Celtic Saints', *JTS*, 17, 1966, pp. 342–91

Morris, John R., 'The Date of St Alban', *Herefordshire Archaeology*, 1, 1968, pp.1–8

Morris, John R., *The Age of Arthur. A History of the British Isles from 350 to 650*, London 1973

Morris, J. (ed and trans), *Nennius, British History and The Welsh Annals*, London and Chichester 1980

Morris, R., *The Church in British Archaeology*, Council for British Archaeology 47, London 1983

Morris, R., *Churches in the Landscape*, London 1989

Morris R., 'Baptismal places: 600–800' in Wood, I. and Lund, N. (eds), *Peoples and Places in Northern Europe 500–1600. Essays in Honour of Peter Hayes Sawyer*, Woodbridge 1991, pp. 15–24

Murray, Sister C., *Rebirth and Afterlife. A study of the transmutation of some pagan imagery in early Christian funerary art*, Oxford 1981

Myres, J. N. L., 'Pelagius and the End of Roman Rule in Britain', *J RS*, 50, 1960, pp. 21–36

Myres, J. N. L., *Anglo-Saxon Pottery and the Settlement of England*, Oxford 1969

Myres, J. N. L., *The English Settlements*, Oxford 1986

Nash-Williams, V. E., *The Early Christian Monuments of Wales*, Cardiff 1950

Nordenfalk, C., *Celtic and Anglo-Saxon Painting*, New York 1977

O'Croinin, D., *Early Medieval Ireland, 400–1200*, London 1995

Okasha, E., *Corpus of Early Christian Inscribed Stones of South-West Britain 500–1100*, London 1993

Olson, B. L., *Early Monasteries in Cornwall*, Woodbridge 1989

Ortenberg, V., *The English Church and the Continent in the Tenth and Eleventh Centuries: Cultural, Spiritual and Artistic Exchanges*, Oxford 1992

O'Sullivan, T. D., *The De Excidio of Gildas. Its Authenticity and Date*, Leiden 1978

Owen, Gale R., *Rites and Religions of the Anglo-Saxons*, Newton Abbott and London 1981

Painter, K. S., 'Villa and Christianity in Roman Britain', *BMQ*, 35, 1971, pp. 157–75

Painter, K. S., *The Water Newton Early Christian Silver*, London 1977

Parsons, David (ed), *Tenth-Century Studies. Essays in Commemoration of the Millenium of the Council of Winchester and Regularis Concordia*, London and Chichester 1975

Pearce, S. M. (ed), *The Early Church in Western Britain and Ireland*, Oxford 1982

Pearce, S. M., 'Estates and Church Sites in Dorset and Gloucestershire: The Emergence of a Christian Society' in Pearce (ed), *The Early Church in Western Britain and Ireland*, pp. 117–35

Pearce, S. M., 'The Early Church in the Landscape: the Evidence from North Devon', *ArchJ*, 142, 1985, pp. 255–75

Philpott, R., *Burial Practices in Roman Britain*, Oxford 1991

Piggot, S., *The Druids*, London 1968

Platt, Colin, *The Parish Churches of Medieval England*, London 1981

Porter, H. M., *The Celtic Church in Somerset. With a Chapter on North Devon*, Bath 1971

Plummer, C. (ed), *Baedae Historia Ecclesiastica gentis Anglorum: Venerabilis Baedae Opera Historica*, 2 vols, Oxford 1896

Plummer, C., *Life and Times of Alfred the Great*, 1902

Potter, T. W. and Johns, C., *Roman Britain*, London 1992

Powell, T. G. E., *The Celts*, 2nd edn London 1980

Radford, C. A. R., 'The Early Church in Strathclyde and Galloway', *MA*, 11, 1967, pp. 105–26

Radford, C. A. R., 'The Archaeological Background on the Continent' in Barley and Hanson (eds), *Christianity in Roman Britain 300–700*, pp. 19–36

Radford, C. A. R., 'Christian Origins in Britain', *MA*, 15, 1971, pp. 1–12

Rahtz, P. A., 'The Roman Temple at Pagans Hill, Chew Stoke, N.Somerset', *Procedings of the Somerset Archaeological and Natural History Society*, 96, 1951, pp. 112–42

Rahtz, P. and Watts, L., 'The end of Roman temples in the west of Britain' in Casey (ed), *The End of Roman Britain*, pp. 183–210

Rahtz, P., Dickinson, T. and Watts, L. (eds), *Anglo-Saxon Cemeteries*, Oxford 1980

Ramsay, N., Sparks, M., and Tatton-Brown, T. (eds), *St Dunstan. His Life, Times and Cult*, Woodbridge 1992

Raw, B. C., *Anglo-Saxon Crucifixion Iconography and the Art of the Monastic Revival*, Cambridge 1990

Redknap, M., *The Christian Celts*, Cardiff 1991

Reece, R. (ed), *Burial in the Roman World*, Council of British Archaeology Research Report 22, London 1977

Rees, B. R., *Pelagius: A Reluctant Heretic*, Woodbridge 1988

Reuter, T. (ed), *The Greatest Englishman*, Exeter 1980

Reynolds, P. L., *Marriage in the Western Church: The Christianization of Marriage during the Patristic and Early Medieval Periods*, Leiden 1994

Richards, J., *Consul of God*, London 1981

Richmond, I., *Archaeology and the Afterlife in Pagan and Christian Imagery*, Oxford 1950

Richmond, I. and Gillam, J. P., 'The Temple of Mithras at Carrawburgh', *AA*, 4, 29, 1951, pp. 1–92

Richmond, I. A., *Roman Britain*, Harmondsworth 1955

Ridyard, S. J., *The Royal Saints of Anglo-Saxon England: A Study of West Saxon and East Anglian Cults*, Cambridge 1988

Rivet, A. L. F., *Town and Country in Roman Britain*, London 1958

Rivet, A. L. F. (ed), *The Roman Villa in Britain*, London 1969

Rivet, A. L. and Smith, C., *The Placenames of Roman Britain*, London 1979

Roberts, A. (trans), *Works of Sulpitius Severus*, London 1894

Robinson, G. W. (trans), *The Life of St Boniface by Willibald*, Cambridge, Mass. 1916

Robinson, J. Armitage, *The Times of St Dunstan*, Oxford 1969

Rodwell, Warwick (ed), *Temples, Churches and Religion in Roman Britain*, BAR, 77, Oxford 1980

Rodwell, Warwick, 'Temple archaeology: problems of the present and portents for the future' in Rodwell (ed), *Temples, Churches and Religion in Roman Britain*, pp. 211–41

Rodwell, W., 'The Origins of Wells Cathedral', *A*, 56, 1982, pp. 215–18

Rodwell, W., *Wells Cathedral: Excavations and Discoveries*, 3rd edn Wells 1987

Rodwell, W. and Bentley, J., *Our Christian Heritage*, London 1984

Rodwell, W. J. and Rodwell, K. A., *Rivenhall: investigations of a villa, church and village 1950-1977*, London 1985

Rodwell, W. and Rowley, T. (eds), *Small Towns of Roman Britian*, BAR, 15, Oxford 1975

Rollason, David W. (ed), *Cuthbert: Saint and Patron*, Durham 1987

Rollason, David W., *Saints and Relics in Anglo-Saxon England*, Oxford 1990

Rollason, David W., *The Mildrith Legend: A Study in Early Medieval Hagiography*, Leicester 1982

Rose, H. J., *Ancient Roman Religion*, London 1948

Ross, Anne, *Pagan Celtic Britain: Studies in Inconography and Tradition*, London 1967

Ross, Anne, *The Pagan Celts*, London 1986

Rumble, A. (ed), *The Reign of Canute*, Leicester 1994

Ryan, John, *Irish Monasticism. Origins and Early Development*, London 1992

Salman, W. A., *Churches and Royal Patronage. A History of The Royal Patronage in the Churches of England and Wales*, Cowbridge and Bridgend 1983

Salway, P., *Roman Britain*, Oxford 1981

Salway, P. and Blair, J., *The Oxford History of Britain: Vol. 1 Roman and Anglo-Saxon Britain*, Oxford 1992

Sawyer, P. H., *From Roman Britain to Norman England*, London 1978

Sawyer, P. H., *The Age of the Vikings*, 2nd edn London 1971

Sawyer, P. H., *Kings and Vikings*, London 1982

Scott, E., *Theoretical Roman Archaeology*, Aldershot, Avebury 1993

Scott, S., 'An outline of a new approach for the interpretation of Romano-British mosaics, and some comments on the possible significance of the Orpheus mosaics of fourth-century Roman Britain', *JTA*, 2, 1992, pp. 29–35

Scott, S., 'A theoretical framework for the study of Romano-British villa mosaics' in Scott (ed), *Theoretical Roman Archaeology*, pp. 103–14

Scragg, D. G., *Superstition and Popular Medicine in Anglo-Saxon England*, Manchester 1989

Selkirk, A., 'St Paul in the Bail', *CA*, 129, 1992, pp. 376–79

Sharpe, R., 'Gildas as a Father of the Church' in Lapidge and Dumville (eds), *Gildas: New Approaches*, pp. 193–205

Sharpe, R. (trans), Adomnan of Iona, *Life of St Columba*, Harmondsworth 1995

Sims-Williams, P., 'Gildas and the Anglo-Saxons', *CMCS*, 6, 1983, pp. 1–30

Sims-Williams, P., 'The Settlement of England in Bede and the Chronicle', *ASE*, 12, 1983, pp. 1–41

Sims-Williams, P., *Religion and Literature in Western England, 600–800*, Cambridge 1990

Sladden, John C., *Boniface of Devon: Apostle of Germany*, Exeter 1980

Small, A., Thomas, C. and Wilson, D., *St Ninian's Isle and its Treasure*, London 1973

Smith, A., 'St Augustine of Canterbury in History and Tradition', *F*, 89, 1978, pp. 23–38

Smith, L. M. (ed), *The Making of Britain: The Dark Ages*, Basingstoke 1984

Smyth, A. P., *Warlords and Holy Men: Scotland AD 80–1000*, Edinburgh 1989

Smyth, A. P., *King Alfred the Great*, Oxford 1995

Speake, G., *Posses Hlaewe: a Saxon Bed Burial on Swallowcliffe Down*, London 1989

Stafford, P., *The East Midlands in the Early Middle Ages*, Leicester 1985

Stancliffe, Clare and Cambridge, Eric (eds), *Oswald. Northumberland King to European Saint*, Stamford 1995

Stanley, E. G., 'The Quest for Anglo-Saxon Paganism', *Notes and Queries*, 11,

1964, pp. 204–9, 242–50, 282–87, 324–331, 455–463, and 12, 1965, pp. 9–17, 203–7, 285–93, 322–27

Stenton, F. M., *Anglo-Saxon England*, 3rd edn Oxford 1971

Stevens, C. E., 'The British Sections of the "Notitia Dignitatum"', *AJ*, 97, 1940, pp. 125–54

Stevenson, J., *Creeds, Councils and Controversies – Documents illustrative of the history of the Church AD 337–461*, London 1966

Storms, G., *Anglo-Saxon Magic*, The Hague 1948

Swanton, M., *Anglo-Saxon Prose*, London 1975

Swanton, Michael (ed and trans), *The Anglo-Saxon Chronicle*, London 1996

Symons, T. (ed and trans), *Regularis Concordia*, London 1953

Talbot, C. H. (trans), *The Anglo-Saxon Missionaries in Germany*, London 1954

Taylor, H. M.and Taylor, J., *Anglo-Saxon Architecture*, 2 vols, Cambridge 1965

Taylor, H. M., *Anglo-Saxon Architecture*, Vol 3, Cambridge 1978

Taylor, H. M., 'The position of the altar in early Anglo-Saxon churches', *AJ*, 53, 1973, pp. 52–58

Taylor, H. M. and Younge, D. D., 'The Ruined Church of Stone-By-Faversham: A Re-Assessment', *AJ*, 138, 1981, pp.118–45

Taylor, Thomas, *The Celtic Christianity of Cornwall*, Felinfach 1995

Thirsk, J. (ed), *Land, Church and People: Essays presented to H.P.R. Finberg*, Reading 1970

Thomas, C., *The Early Christian Archaeology of North Britain*, Oxford 1971

Thomas, C., *Britain and Ireland in Early Christian Times AD 400–800*, London 1971

Thomas, C., *Bede, Archaeology and the Cult of Relics*, Jarrow 1973

Thomas, Charles, *Christianity in Roman Britain to AD 500*, London 1981

Thomas, Charles, 'East and West: Tintagel, Mediterranean Imports and the Early Insular Church' in Pearce (ed), *The Early Church in Western Britain and Ireland*, pp. 17–34

Thomas, Charles, 'Recognising Christian origins: an archaeological and historical dilemma' in Butler and Morris (eds), *The Anglo-Saxon Church*, pp. 121–25

Thomas, Charles, *Tintagel: Arthur and Archaeology*, London 1993

Thomas, Charles, *And Shall These Mute Stones Speak?: post-Roman inscriptions in Western Britain*, Cardiff 1994

Thompson, A. H. (ed), *Bede. His Life, Times and Writing*, Oxford 1935

Thompson, E. A., 'Britain AD 406–410', *B*, 8, 1977, pp. 303–18

Thompson, E. A., 'Gildas and the History of Britain', *B*, 10, 1979, pp. 203–26

Thompson, E. A., *Saint Germanus of Auxerre and the End of Roman Britain*, Woodbridge 1984

Thorpe, Benjamin (ed and trans), Aelfric, Abbot of Eynsham, *The Homilies of the Anglo-Saxon Church*, London 1844

Todd, Malcolm, *Roman Britain*, London 1981

Todd, Malcolm, *The South West to AD 1000*, London 1987

Todd, Malcolm (ed), *Research on Roman Britain 1960–89*, Britannia Monograph Series, London 1989

Tolkien, J. R. R. and others, *Angles and Britons*, Cardiff 1963

Toynbee, J. M. C., 'Christianity in Roman Britain', *JBAA*, 3rd series, 16, 1953, pp. 1–24

Toynbee, J. M. C., 'The Christian Roman Mosaic, Hinton St Mary, Dorset', Procedings of the Dorset Natural History and Archaeological Society, 85, 1964, pp. 116–21

Toynbee, J. M. C., *Death and Burial in the Roman World*, London 1971

Toynbee, J. M. C., *The Roman Art Treasures from the Temple of* Mithras, London and Middlesex Archeological Society Special Paper, 7, London 1986

Turville-Petre, R. O. G., *Myth and Religion of the North*, London 1964

Vermascren, M. J., *Cybele and Atys. The Myth and the Cult*, London 1977

Victory, S., *The Celtic Church in Wales*, London 1977

Wacher, John, *The Towns of Roman Britain*, London 1974

Wacher, John, *Roman Britain*, London 1978

Wacher, J. (ed), *The Roman World*, 2 vols, London 1987

Wait, G. A., *Ritual and Religion in Iron Age Britain*, BAR, 149, Oxford 1985

Wall, J., 'Christian Evidences in the Roman Period: The Northern Counties, Parts I and II', *AA*, 4th series, 43, 1965, pp. 201–25; 4th series, 44, 1966, pp. 147–64

Wallace-Hadrill, J. M., *Early Medieval History*, Oxford 1975

Wallace-Hadrill, J. M., *The Frankish Church*, Oxford 1983

Wallace-Hadrill, J. M., *Bede's Ecclesiastical History of the English People: A Historical Commentary*, Oxford 1988

Walsh, M., *Roots of Christianity*, London 1986

Ward, Benedicta, *The Venerable Bede*, London 1990

Warin, A., *Wilfrid: AD 634 to 709*, York 1992

Watts, D., *Christians and Pagans in Roman Britain*, London 1991

Watts, D., *Religion in Late Roman Britain*, London and New York 1998

Webb, J. F. and Farmer, D. H. (eds and trans), *The Age of Bede*, Harmondsworth 1983

Webster, Graham, *The British Celts and their Gods under Rome*, London 1986

Webster, L. and Backhouse, J., *The Making of England: Anglo-Saxon Art and Culture AD 600-900*, London 1991

Wedlake, W. J., *The Excavation of the Shrine of Apollo, Nettleton, Wiltshire 1956–71*, London 1982

Welch, M., *Discovering Anglo-Saxon England*, Pennsylvania 1992

West, Stanley and Plouvicz, Judith, 'The Romano-British site at Icklingham', East Anglian Archaeology, 3, 1976, pp. 63–126

Wheeler, R. E. M., *Maiden Castle, Dorset*, London 1943

Wheeler, R. E. M. and Wheeler, T. V., *Report on the excavation of the prehistoric, Roman and post-Roman site in Lydney Park, Gloucestershire*, London 1932

White, R. B., 'Excavations at Arfryn, Bodedern, long-cist cemeteries and the origins of Christianity in Britain', Anglesey Antiquarian Society and Field Club Transactions, 1971–72, pp. 19–51

Whitelock, D., *The Beginnings of English Society*, London 1952

Whitelock, D. (ed), *English Historical Documents:Vol I, c.550–1042*, 2nd edn London 1979

Whitelock, D., Brett, M. and Brooks, C. N. L. (eds), *Councils and Synods with other documents relating to the English Church. Part I 871–1066*, Oxford 1981

William of Malmesbury, *The Kings Before the Norman Conquest*, Llanerch 1989

Williams, A., Smyth, A. P. and Kirby, D. P., *A Biographical Dictionary of Dark Age Britain: England, Scotland and Wales c.500–c.1050*, London 1991

Williams, Hugh, *Christianity in Early Britain*, Oxford 1912

Wilson, D. M., 'The Vikings' Relationship with Christianity in Northern England', *JBAA*, 3rd series, 30, 1967, pp. 37–46

Wilson, David M., *The Anglo-Saxons*, Harmondsworth 1971

Wilson, D. M (ed), *The Archaeology of Anglo-Saxon England*, London 1976

Wilson, D. M., *Anglo-Saxon Art from the Seventh Century to the Norman Conquest*, London 1984

Wilson, D., *Anglo-Saxon Paganism*, London and New York 1992

Wilson, P. A., 'Romano-British and Welsh Christianity: Continuity or Discontinuity?', *WHR*, 3, 1966, pp. 5–21, 103–20

Winterbottom, M., *Three Lives of English Saints*, London 1972

Winterbottom, M. (ed and trans), *Gildas, The Ruin of Britain and other works*, London and Chichester 1978

Wood, I. N., 'The fall of the western empire and the end of Roman Britain', *B*, 18, 1987, pp. 251-62

Wood, Ian, 'Northumbria and its Churches', *NH*, 27, 1991, pp. 273–75

Wood, M., *In Search of the Dark Ages*, revd edn London 1991

Woodward, Ann, *Shrines and Sacrifice*, London 1992

Woodward, Ann, and Leach, Peter, *The Uley Shrines: Excavation of a Ritual Complex on West Hill, Uley, Gloucestershire 1977–9*, London 1993

Wormald, C. P., *Ideal and Reality in Frankish and Anglo-Saxon Society*, Oxford 1983

Wright, N., 'Did Gildas read Orosius?', *CMCS*, 9, 1985, pp. 31–42

Wright, R. P., 'A Revised Restoration of the Inscription on the Mosaic Pavement found in the Temple at Lydney Park, Gloucestershire', *B*, 16, 1985, pp. 248–49

Yorke, B. (ed), *Bishop Aethelwold: Studies in his Career and Influence*, Woodbridge 1988
Yorke, B., *Kings and Kingdoms in Early Anglo-Saxon England*, London 1990
Yorke, B., *Wessex in the Early Middle Ages*, Leicester 1995
Youngs, S. (ed), *The Work of Angels*, London 1989

Notes

In general, works will be referred to only by author's surname and shortened title. Publication details will be found in the Bibliography.

Preface

1. Kenneth Hylson-Smith, *The Churches in England from Elizabeth I to Elizabeth II*, Vol I: *1558–1688*, Vol 2: *1689–1833*, Vol 3: *1833 –1998*, London 1996, 1997, 1998.
2. The only comprehensive work covering the history of the English church for the whole period from Roman times to 1066 is Deanesly, *The Pre-Conquest Church in England*. Those which cover particular parts of this period include Bright, *Chapters of Early English Church History*, Godfrey, *The Church in Anglo-Saxon England*, Mayr-Harting, *The Coming of Christianity to Anglo-Saxon England*, Thomas, *Christianity in Roman Britain*, Watts, *Christians and Pagans in Roman Britain*, and Williams, *Christianity in Early Britain*.

Introduction

1. Hayes, *Archaeology of the British Isles*, p. 11.
2. Bassett (ed), *The Origins of Anglo-Saxon Kingdoms*, p. 3.
3. R. P. C. Hanson, 'Summary and Prospects' in Barley and Hanson (eds), *Christianity in Roman Britain*, p. 211.
4. Martin Henig, 'Religion in Roman Britain' in Todd (ed) *Research on Roman Britain*, p. 232.
5. Hutton, *The Pagan Religions*, pp. 340, 341.
6. Woodward, *Shrines and Sacrifice*, p. 10.
7. Green, *The Gods of the Celts*, p. 7.
8. Ross, *Pagan Celtic Britian*, p. 28.
9. Bernard Colgrave, 'Historical Introduction' in Colgrave and Mynors (eds), *Bede's Ecclesiastical History*, p. xviii.
10. For an explanation of this see P. Hunter Blair, *Bede's Ecclesiastical History of the English Nation and its Importance Today*, Jarrow Lecture 1959, and

also Campbell, *Essays in Anglo-Saxon History*, pp. 1–48.

11. Wallace-Hadrill, *Bede's Ecclesiastical History*, p. 5.
12. Bernard Colgrave, 'Historical Introduction' in Colgrave and Mynors (eds), *Bede's Ecclesiastical History*, pp. xxxiv, xxxv.
13. Benedicta Ward, 'Miracles and History', in Bonner (ed), *Famulus Christi*, p. 70.
14. See Simms-Williams, 'Gildas and the Anglo-Saxons'.
15. Miller, 'Starting to Write History'.
16. See Lapidge and Dumville (eds), *Gildas: New Approaches*.
17. Myres, *The English Settlements*, p. 13.
18. Higham, *An English Empire*, p. 74.
19. Malcolm Todd, 'Preface' in Todd (ed), *Research on Roman Britain*, p. xi.
20. Charles Thomas, 'Churches in Late Roman Britain' in Rodwell (ed), *Temples, Churches and Religion*, p. 129.
21. See Morris, *The Church in British Archaeology*.
22. Wilson, *Anglo-Saxon Paganism*, p. 2.
23. Mawer, *Evidence for Christianity in Roman Britain*, p. 142.
24. Barlow, *The English Church*, pp. 23, 24.
25. Plummer, *Baedae Opera Historica*, Vol II, p. 28.
26. I Corinthians 13, 12.

1. Non-Christian Religion in Pre-Roman and Roman Britain

1. The following historiographical comment owes much to Burl, *Prehistoric Avebury*.
2. Ibid., p. 8.
3. MacKie, *Science and Society in Prehistoric Britain*, p. 151.
4. See Hutton, *The Pagan Religions*, p. 97.
5. Burl, *Prehistoric Avebury*, p. 200.
6. For the use of the term 'Celt' see Millett, *The Romanization of Britain*, p. 10.
7. Green, *The Gods of the Celts*, p. 1. For the Celts in general see Chadwick, *The Celts* and Powell, *The Celts*.
8. Rivet, *Town and Country*, p. 33.
9. Hayes, *Archaeology of the British Isles*, p. 93.
10. See Colin Haselgrove, 'The Later Iron Age in Southern Britain and Beyond' in Todd (ed), *Research on Roman Britain*, pp. 1–18.
11. For these examples I am indebted to Green, *The Gods of the Celts*, pp. 17–19.
12. See A. Ellison, 'Natives, Romans and Christians on West Hill, Uley: an Interim Report on the excavation of a Ritual Complex of the First Millenium AD' in Rodwell (ed), *Temples, Churches and Religion*, pp. 305–28.

13. For good accounts and comments on temples in the Roman period see Rodwell (ed),*Temples, Churches and Religion* and Woodward, *Shrines and Sacrifice.*

14. But see I. C. G. Burrow, 'Roman material from hillforts' in Casey (ed), *The End of Roman Britain*, pp. 212–29.

15. The nearest approach to such a study is Woodward, *Shrines and Sacrifice.*

16. Gougaud, *Christianity in Celtic Lands*, p. 5.

17. Ross, *Pagan Celtic Britain*, and *The Pagan Celts.*

18. Webster, *The British Celts and their Gods.*

19. See Henig, *Religion in Roman Britain.*

20. Chadwick, *The Celts*, p. 154.

21. Ross, *Pagan Celtic Britain*, p. 27.

22. For the examples in this paragraph see Green, *The Gods of the Celts*, pp. 148, 149, 156, 157.

23. For the study of the Lydney shrine see Wheeler and Wheeler, *Report on the . . . site in Lydney Park.*

24. J. P. Alcock, Celtic water cults in Roman Britain'.

25. Ross, *Pagan Celtic Britain*, p. 365.

26. S. Barnard, 'The matres of Roman Britain'.

27. Ross, *Pagan Celtic Britain*, p. 265.

28. For a further elaboration on the gods and goddesses mentioned in this present section, see Webster, *The British Celts and their Gods*, ch 3.

29. Woodward, *Shrines and Sacrifice*, p. 79. This is a book to which the present section on Roman views of Druidism is greatly indebted.

30. See, for example, H. J. M. Green, 'Religious Cults in Roman Godmanchester' in Henig and King (eds), *Pagan Gods*, pp. 29–55.

31. Graham Webster, 'What the Britons required from the gods as seen through the pairing of Roman and Celtic deities and the character of votive offerings' in Henig and King, *Pagan God,* p. 61.

32. See Henig, *Religion in Roman Britain*, p. 84.

33. See Green, *The Gods of Roman Britain*, pp. 31–33.

34. Ellison and Henig, 'Head of Mercury from Uley, Gloucestershire'.

35. Henig, *Religion in Roman Britain*, p. 27.

36. Wacher, *Roman Britain*, p. 226.

37. See Lewis, *Temples in Roman Britain*, pp. 57–72 and Millett, *The Romanization of Britain*, p. 105.

38. See for example, Frere, 'The Silchester Church'.

39. S. S. Frere, *Verulamium Excavations*, Vol II, pp. 73–74.

40. Dunnett, 'The Excavations of the Roman Theatre at Gosbecks'.

41. Bennet, 'The Topography of Roman Canterbury'.

42. For a summary of such edifices see Woodward, *Shrines and Sacrifice* and Wacher, *Roman Britain*, pp. 229–32, but also see Leech, 'The excavation of a Romano-Celtic temple'.

43. Henig, *Religion in Roman Britain*, p. 98. This is a book to which the present account of Mithraism, and the section in general, owes much.
44. Vermascren, *Cybele and Atys*, pp. 138–39.
45. See ibid., pp. 101–7, 131–37.
46. See Henig, *Religion in Roman Britain*, pp. 113–16. This present section also owes much to Green, *The Gods of Roman Britain*.
47. The following account of the association of Sulis and Minerva at Bath is based on Cunliffe, *Roman Bath*.
48. Barry Cunliffe, 'The Sanctuary of Sulis Minerva at Bath: a brief review' in Henig and King (eds), *Pagan Gods*, p. 2.
49. Ibid., p. 12.
50. I am indebted for these examples to P. Hunter Blair, *Roman Britain*, p. 151 and to Wacher, *Roman Britain*, p. 224.
51. For these last two examples I am indebted to Henig, *Religion in Roman Britain*, pp. 61, 62.
52. Catherine Johns, 'Faunus at Thetford: an early Latin deity in Late Roman Britain' in Henig and King (eds), *Pagan Gods*, p. 102.
53. Miranda Green 'Jupiter, Taranis and the Solar Wheel' in Henig and King (eds), *Pagan Gods*, p. 65.
54. Ibid., p. 65.
55. Ellison, *Excavations at West Hill, Uley: 1977* and 'Natives, Romans and Christians on West Hill, Uley', Ellison and Henig, 'Head of Mercury from Uley, Gloucestershire' and Woodward and Leach, *The Uley Shrines*.
56. Wedlake, *The Excavation of the Shrine of Apollo*.
57. R. H. Leech, 'The excavation of a Romano-Celtic temple'.
58. Henig, *Religion in Roman Britain*, p. 22.
59. Peter D. Horne, 'Roman or Celtic Temples? A case study' in Henig and King (eds), *Pagan Gods*, p. 23.
60. Watts, *Religion in Late Roman Britain*, p. 115.
61. Isabelle Fauduet, 'Cult and Ritual Practices at Argentomagus, Indre, France' in Henig and King (eds), *Pagan Gods*, p. 25.
62. Watts, *Religion in Late Roman Britain*, p. 131.
63. J. Alcock, 'Classical Religious Beliefs and Burial Practice in Roman Britain'.
64. Watts, *Religion in Late Roman Britain*, p. 9. But see also Watts, *Christians and Pagans*, pp. 209–14.
65. Miranda Green, 'Jupiter, Taranis and the Solar Wheel' in Henig and King (eds), *Pagan Gods*, p.65.
66. Wacher, *Roman Britain*, p. 223.

2. *Christianity in Roman Britain to c. 410: Its History*

1. For a summary of the military, political, demographic, economic and social history of Roman Britain, see Appendix 1.
2. William Blake, 'Jerusalem'.
3. See Bright, *Chapters of Early English Church History*, pp. 1,2.
4. Thomas, *Christianity in Roman Britain*, p. 18.
5. Toynbee, 'Christianity in Roman Britain', p. 2.
6. Deanesly, *The Pre-Conquest Church*, p. 5.
7. Bede, *HE*, i.4, p. 24.
8. Wallace-Hadrill, *Bede's Ecclesiastical History*, p. 11.
9. Dark, *Civitas to Kingdom*, p. 36.
10. Wedlake, *The Excavation of the Shrine of Apollo*.
11. Watts, *Christians and Pagans*, p. 142.
12. Radford, 'Christian Origins in Britain', p. 1.
13. The site was re-excavated by Sir Ian Richmond in 1961, and reported in Frere, 'The Silchester Church'.
14. Ibid.
15. King, 'The Roman Church at Silchester reconsidered', pp. 235, 236.
16. See P. D. C. Brown, 'The Church at Richborough'.
17. This description is based on the report by Crummy, 'A Roman church in Colchester'.
18. See ApSimon, 'The Roman temple at Brean Down, Somerset' and Leech, 'The excavation of a Romano-Celtic temple '.
19. Wedlake, *The Excavation of the Shrine of Apollo*.
20. Watts, *Christians and Pagans*, p. 88.
21. Ibid., pp. 88, 89.
22. P. Rahtz in Reece (ed), *Burial in the Roman World*, p. 54.
23. See Salway, *Roman Britain*, pp. 731, 732.
24. Thomas, *Christianity in Roman Britain*, p. 181. See also Meates, *The Roman Villa at Lullingstone, Kent, Vol II*.
25. See Toynbee, 'The Christian Roman Mosaic, Hinton St Mary, Dorset'.
26. Ericksen, 'Syncrotistic Symbolism and the Christian Roman mosaic at Hinton St Mary'.
27. E. W. Black, 'Christian and Pagan hopes of salvation in Romano-British mosaics' in Henig and King (eds), *Pagan Gods*, p. 147.
28. Radford, 'Christian Origins in Britain'.
29. Rodwell and Bentley, *Our Christian Heritage*, p. 9.
30. For the examples just cited I am indebted to the summary in Green, *The Gods of Roman Britain*, pp. 68–71.
31. See Thomas, *Christianity in Roman Britain*, pp. 101–103.
32. West and Plouvicz, 'The Romano-British site at Icklingham'.
33. Toynbee, 'Christianity in Roman Britain'.

34. Painter, 'Villa and Christianity in Roman Britain'.
35. Toynbee, 'Christianity in Roman Britain'.
36. Frend, 'Religion in Roman Britain in the Fourth Century'.
37. See Williams, *Christianity in Early Britain*, ch 4, Morris, 'The date of St Alban', Thomas, *Christianity in Roman Britain*, p. 48 and James Campbell, 'The End of Roman Britain' in Campbell (ed), *The Anglo-Saxons*, p.11.
38. See Levison, 'St Alban and St Albans'.
39. James Campbell, 'The First Christian Kings' in Campbell (ed), *The Anglo-Saxons*, p. 51.
40. Bede, *HE*, 1.7, p. 26.
41. Ibid., p. 30.
42. Ibid., p. 32.
43. Ibid., p. 32.
44. Ibid., p. 32.
45. Ibid., p. 34.
46. Ibid., p. 34.
47. Winterbottom (ed), *Gildas, The Ruin of Britain*, 12, p. 51.
48. Deanesly, *The Pre-Conquest Church in England*, p. 7.
49. For the life, work and influence of Martin of Tours see Roberts (trans), *Works of Sulpitius Severus*, Vol 11, ch 2, and Donaldson, *Martin of Tours*. See also Hoare, *The Western Fathers*.
50. W. H. C. Frend, 'The Christianization of Roman Britain' in Barley and Hanson (eds), *Christianity in Britain*, p. 43.
51. Donaldson, *Martin of Tours*, p. 9.
52. W. H. C. Frend, 'The Christianization of Roman Britain' in Barley and Hanson (eds), *Christianity in Britain*, p. 44.
53. Winterbottom (ed), *Gildas, The Ruin of Britain*, 12, p. 20.
54. Bede, *HE*, 1.7, p. 34.
55. St Hilary of Poitiers, *De synodis*, Prol and ch 11 in Haddan and Stubbs (eds), *Councils and Ecclesiastical Documents*, Vol 1, p. 9.
56. Athanasius, *Ad Iovinianum imp.*, p. 2 in Haddan and Stubbs (eds), *Councils and Ecclesiastical Documents*, Vol 1, pp. 7,8.
57. Plummer, *Baedae Opera Historica*, Vol 11, p. 20.
58. Wallace-Hadrill, *Bede's Ecclesiastical History*, p. 13.
59. Green, *The Gods of Roman Britain*, p. 71.
60. See H. Boon, 'The pagan revival in the west at the end of the fourth century' in Momigliano (ed), *The Conflict between Paganism and Christianity*, pp. 193–218 and Watts, *Christians and Pagans*.
61. See Toynbee, 'Christianity in Roman Britain', p. 3.
62. See Frend, *The Rise of Christianity*, pp. 608–9.
63. Henig, *Religion in Roman Britain*, pp. 13, 14.
64. See Watts, *Christians and Pagans* and *Religion in Late Roman Britain*.

65. Watts, *Religion in Late Roman Britain*, p. 23.
66. Dark, *Civitas to Kingdom*, p. 34.
67. Millett, *The Romanization of Britain*, pp. 195, 196.
68. Henig, *Religion in Roman Britain*, p. 214.
69. E. W. Black, 'Christian and Pagan hopes of salvation in Romano-British mosaics' in Henig and King (eds), *Pagan Gods*, p. 157.
70. Chadwick, *The Celts*, p. 192.
71. See Boon, 'A temple of Mithras at Caernarvon-*Segontium*'.
72. See Grimes, *The Excavation of Roman and Medieval London*.
73. See Richmond and Gillam, 'The Temple of Mithras at Carrawburgh'.
74. See Johns and Potter, *The Thetford Treasure*.
75. Dark, *Civitas to Kingdom*, p. 32.
76. Ibid., p. 32.
77. Watts, *Christians and Pagans*, p. 214.
78. Toynbee, 'Christianity in Roman Britain'.
79. Frend, 'Religion in Roman Britain in the Fourth Century'.
80. Henig, *Religion in Roman Britain*, pp. 12, 13.
81. Thomas, *Christianity in Roman Britain*, pp. 13, 14.
82. Watts, *Christians and Pagans*, p. xi.
83. Ibid., p. 221.
84. Martin Henig, 'Religion in Roman Britain' in Todd (ed), *Research on Roman Britain*, p. 230.
85. See Thomas, *Tintagel*.

3. *Christianity in Roman Britain to c.410: Its Main Features*

1. Rodwell and Bentley, *Our Christian Heritage*, p.9.
2. Thomas, *Christianity in Roman Britain*, p. 137.
3. W. H. C. Frend, 'The Christianization of Roman Britain' in Barley and Hanson (eds), *Christianity in Britain*, p. 40.
4. R. C. P. Hanson, 'Summary and Prospects' in Barley and Hanson (eds), *Christianity in Britian*, p. 208.
5. Watts, *Christians and Pagans*.
6. Dark, *Civitas to Kingdom*, p. 36. This is a book to which the present section is greatly indebted.
7. Branigan, *Roman Britain*, pp. 272, 273.
8. See Thomas, *Christianity in Roman Britain*, Watts, *Christians and Pagans* and C. Thomas, 'Recognising Christian origins: an archaeological and historical dilemma' in Butler and Morris (eds), *The Anglo-Saxon Church*, pp. 121–5.
9. Leech, 'The excavation of a Romano-British farmstead and cemetery.'
10. West and Plouvicz, 'The Romano-British site at Icklingham'.
11. Dark, *Civitas to Kingdom*, p. 58.

12. Ibid., p. 196.
13. Hayes, *Archaeology of the British Isles*, p. 108.
14. Watts, *Christians and Pagans*, p. 227.
15. Merrifield, *The Archaeology of Ritual and Magic*, p. 83.
16. Ross, *Pagan Celtic Britain*, pp. 28, 29.
17. Merrifield, *The Archaeology of Ritual and Magic*, p. 83.
18. Watts, *Christians and Pagans*, pp. 221, 223.
19. Ibid., p. 224.
20. This section owes much to Thomas, *Christianity in Roman Britain*.
21. This was the view favoured by Salway; see *Roman Britain*, p. 273.
22. Thomas, *Christianity in Roman Britain*, pp. 198, 200.
23. This whole description is based on the summary by Wedlake, *The Excavation of the Shrine of Apollo*, pp. ixx, xx.
24. Ibid., p. ixx.
25. Ibid.
26. The following account of Christian worship and liturgy is indebted to Chadwick, *The Early Christian Church*, ch 18.
27. Philpott, *Burial Practices in Roman Britain*, p. 240.
28. Thomas, *Christianity in Roman Britain*, p. 230. I am once more indebted to Thomas in this section on Christian burial and cemeteries.
29. See Collingwood and Richmond, *The Archaeology of Roman Britain*.
30. See Reece (ed), *Burial in the Roman World*.
31. See Radford, 'Christian Origins in Britain'.
32. See Reece (ed), *Burial in the Roman World*.
33. See Wacher, *The Towns of Roman Britain*, and Rodwell and Rowley (eds), *Small Towns of Roman Britain*.
34. See P. A. Rahtz, 'Pagan and Christian by the Severn Sea' in Abrams and Carley (eds), *The Archaeology and History of Glastonbury*, pp. 3–37.
35. See Philpott, *Burial Practices in Roman Britain*.
36. See C. A. R. Radford, 'The Early Church in Strathclyde and Galloway', 'The Archaeological Background on the Continent' and 'Christian Origins in Britain'.
37. Thomas, *Christianity in Roman Britain*, p. 231.
38. Woodward, *Shrines and Sacrifice*, p. 96.
39. The description of the Poundbury cemetery is indebted to Woodward, *Shrines and Sacrifice*.
40. Thomas, *Christianity in Roman Britain*, pp. 238, 239.
41. Woodward, *Shrines and Sacrifice*, p. 97.
42. M. Todd, 'Margidunum and Ancaster' in Rodwell and Rowley (eds), *Small Towns of Roman Britain*, pp. 211–23.
43. P. A. Rahtz, 'Late Roman cemeteries and beyond' in Reece (ed), *Burial in the Roman World*, pp. 53–64.
44. Thomas, *Christianity in Roman Britain*, p. 237.

45. Foakes-Jackson, *A History of the Christian Church*, p. 238.
46. Rollason, *Saints and Relics*, p. 12.
47. Ibid., p. 14.
48. Winterbottom (ed), *Gildas, The Ruin of Britain*, 4.4, p. 17.
49. Ibid., 10.2, p. 19.
50. Brooks, *The Early History*, p. 20.
51. For the excavations at Stone-by-Faversham, see Fletcher and Meates, 'The Ruined Church of Stone-by-Faversham' and 'The Ruined Church of Stone-by-Faversham: Second Report'. For subsequent interpretation see Taylor andYounge, 'The Ruined Church of Stone-by-Faversham: A Re-Assessment'.
52. Rollason, *Saints and Relics*, p. 15. For the work on Wells, see Rodwell, 'The Origins of Wells Cathedral', 'From Mausoleum to Minster: The Early Development of Wells Cathedral' in Pearce (ed), *The Early Church*, pp. 49–59, and *Wells Cathedral: Excavations and Discoveries*.
53. Bede, *HE*, v.22, 554.
54. This whole section owes much to Rollason, *Saints and Relics*.
55. Gougaug, *Christianity in Celtic Lands*, p. 20.
56. Ibid., p. 27.

4. Sub-Roman Britain

1. Stenton, *Anglo-Saxon England*, p. 1.
2. Myres, *The English Settlements*, p. 1.
3. James Campbell, 'The End of Roman Britain' in Campbell (ed), *The Anglo-Saxons*, p. 20.
4. Morris, *The Age of Arthur*, pp. xiii, xiv.
5. John Morris, 'Historical Introduction' in Winterbottom (ed), *Gildas, The Ruin of Britain*, p. 1.
6. James Campbell, 'The Lost Centuries' in Campbell (ed), *The Anglo-Saxons*, p. 29.
7. Dark, *Civitas to Kingdom*.
8. Ibid., p. xiii.
9. Myres, *The English Settlements*, p. 2.
10. See, for instance, Bassett (ed), *The Origins of Anglo-Saxon Kingdoms*.
11. See especially Dark, *Civitas to Kingdom* and Millett, *The Romanization of Britain*.
12. Hayes, *Archaeology of the British Isles*, p. 114.
13. Dark, *Civitas to Kingdom*, pp. xii, xiii. But see the whole of this important book for an exposition of this and other related themes.
14. See Thompson, *Saint Germanus*, and the comment by Millett, *The Romanization of Britain*, p. 227.
15. Winterbottom (ed), *Gildas, The Ruin of Britain*, 23, p. 26.

16. Ibid., 25, pp. 27, 28.
17. Morris (ed), *Nennius, British History*, 48, p. 33.
18. Winterbottom (ed), *Gildas, The Ruin of Britain*, 20.1, pp. 23, 24.
19. The site seems to have been in the west, as the Welsh Annals record a second battle in 665. On linguistic grounds Morris makes a strong case for Bath (see his note in Winterbottom [ed], *Gildas, The Ruin of Britain*, note 26.1, p. 151).
20. For these comments I am indebted to Higham, *The English Conquest*, pp. 50, 51.
21. 'Introductory list of dates' in Morris (ed), *Nennius, The Welsh Annals*, p. 45.
22. Morris (ed), *Nennius, British History*, 56, p. 35.
23. 'Introductory list of dates' in Nennius, *The Welsh Annals*, p. 45.
24. Stenton, *Anglo-Saxon England*, pp. 3,4.
25. James Campbell, 'The Lost Centuries' in Campbell (ed), *Anglo-Saxon England*, p. 27.
26. Morris, *The Age of Arthur*, p. xiii.
27. See, for instance, H. F. Hamerow, 'Settlement Mobility and the "Middle Saxon Shift"'.
28. Hayes, *Archaeology of the British Isles*, p. 115.
29. Millett, *The Romanization of Britain*, p. 230.
30. For these comments, and this conclusion, see James Campbell, 'The Lost Centuries' in Campbell (ed), *The Anglo-Saxons*, pp. 23, 24.
31. A most useful study of the origins of Anglo-Saxon dynasties is Bassett (ed), *The Origins of Anglo-Saxon Kingdoms*.
32. See Dark, *Civitas to Kingdom*, p. 95.
33. Cleary, *The Ending of Roman Britain*, p. 144.
34. Edward James, 'The origins of barbarian kingdoms: the continental evidence' in Bassett (ed), *The Origins of Anglo-Saxon Kingdoms*, p. 52.

5. Christianity in Sub-Roman Britain

1. The following account of Anglo-Saxon gods is largely based on Hodgkin, *A History of the Anglo-Saxons*, Vol 1, pp. 19f. and Hutton, *The Pagan Religions*, pp. 265–80.
2. Hodgkin, *A History of the Anglo-Saxons*, Vol 1, pp. 72, 73.
3. Hutton, *The Pagan Religions*, p. 279.
4. Ibid., p. 262.
5. Thompson, *St Germanus*, p. 16.
6. Mayr-Harting, *The Coming of Christianity*, pp. 29, 30.
7. Hanson, *Saint Patrick* (1968), pp. 34, 35.
8. This passage is based on Dark, *Civitas to Kingdom*, p. 55.
9. See Donaldson, *Martin of Tours*, pp. 136–40.

10. Bede, *HE*, iii.4, p. 222.
11. Hanson, *St Patrick*, p. 199.
12. See L. Bieler, 'St Patrick and the British Church' in Barley and Hanson (eds), *Christianity in Roman Britain* , p. 128.
13. Dark, *Civitas to Kingdom*, pp. 62, 63.
14. Bede, *HE*, i.14, p. 48.
15. Ibid., p. 48.
16. Rodwell and Bentley, *Our Christian Heritage*, p. 37.
17. Brown, *Augustine of Hippo*, p. 341.
18. Chadwick, *The Early Christian Church*, p. 228.
19. Thompson, *St Germanus*, p. 22.
20. Ibid., p. 17.
21. Constantius, *The Life of St Germanus*, ch. XIV in Hoare, *The Western Fathers*, p. 297.
22. Alcock, *Arthur's Britain*, p. 133.
23. Bede, *HE*, i.20, pp. 62, 64.
24. This whole section is indebted to Hughes, *The Church in Early Irish Society* and 'The Celtic Church', Ryan, *Irish Monasticism* and Youngs (ed), *The Work of Angels*.
25. Hughes, 'The Celtic Church', p. 15.
26. Ryan, *Irish Monasticism*, p. 110.
27. Williams, *Christianity in Early Britain*, pp. 393, 394.
28. Fisher, *The Anglo-Saxon Age*, p. 60.
29. Higham, *The English Conquest*, pp. 159, 160.

6. Christianity in England from the Late Sixth Century to 664

1. Hodgkin, *A History of the Anglo-Saxons*, Vol 1, pp. 245, 246.
2. For the life and works of Pope Gregory I, see Richards, *Consul of God*.
3. Fletcher, *Who's Who*, p. 29.
4. Colgrave (ed and trans), *Anon, Life of Pope Gregory*, p. 91.
5. Gregory may have chosen Augustine because he was a monk, the prior of Gregory's own monastery, bound to Gregory by the vow of obedience. His companions were likewise monks with the same obedience owed to the pope, and, especially after Augustine was appointed abbott, they were committed in obedience to their leader.
6. These quotations are from Bede, *HE*, i.23, p. 68.
7. For comments on these letters see Deanesly, *The Pre-Conquest Church*, pp. 46–48.
8. Bede, *HE*, i.25, p. 72.
9. P. Ewald and L. M. Hartmann (eds), *Gregorii I papae registrum epistolarum*, Berlin 1887–90, Vol 8, p. 29.
10. For the origins of Kent and its early history see Nicholas Brooks, 'The

creation and early structure of the kingdom of Kent' in Bassett (ed), *The Origins of Anglo-Saxon Kingdoms*, pp. 55–74.

11. Brooks, *The Early History*, p. 7. This is a book to which this whole present section is indebted.
12. For comments on St Martin's church, and generally on the early years of the Christian mission in Kent, see Brooks, *The Early History*.
13. Bede, *HE*, i.25, p. 74.
14. Ibid., p. 76.
15. Ibid., i.26, pp. 76, 78.
16. See the comments of Brooks in *The Early History*, p. 11.
17. This letter from Gregory to Mellitus is quoted by Bede, *HE*, i.30, pp. 106, 108.
18. Ibid., ii.2, pp. 134, 136.
19. Deanesly, *The Pre-Conquest Church*, pp. 58, 59.
20. Steven Bassett, 'Church and diocese in the West Midlands: the transition from British to Anglo-Saxon control' in Blair and Sharpe (eds), *Pastoral Care before the Parish*, p. 39.
21. Godfrey, *The Church in Anglo-Saxon England*, p. 90.
22. Ibid., p. 91.
23. Bede, *HE*, ii.4, p. 144.
24. Brooks, *The Early History*, p. 64.
25. See Evans, *The Sutton Hoo Ship Burial*, to which these present comments are indebted, and especially pp. 61, 63, 107, 108.
26. Bede, *HE*, ii.6, p. 154.
27. Blair, *The World of Bede*, p. 88.
28. Mayr-Harting, *The Coming of Christianity*, pp. 67, 68.
29. Bede, *HE*, ii.13, p. 182.
30. Ibid., pp. 182, 184.
31. Ibid., p. 184.
32. Rosemary Cramp, 'The Making of Oswald's Northumbria' in Stancliffe and Cambridge (eds), *Oswald*, p. 20.
33. See Welch, *Discovering Anglo-Saxon England*, p. 121.
34. See Wallace-Hadrill, *Bede's Ecclesiastical History*, p. 95.
35. Morris, *Churches in the Landscape*, p. 131.
36. Bede, *HE*, ii.16, p. 192.
37. Selkirk, 'St Paul in the Bail'. This is an article to which the present comments are greatly indebted.
38. See B. Gilmour, 'The Anglo-Saxon church at St Paul-in-the-Bail, Lincoln'.
39. This section is indebted to Gallyon, *The Early Church in Eastern England*.
40. Gallyon, *The Early Church in Wessex and Mercia*, p. vii.
41. Bede, *HE*, ii.20, p. 206.
42. Mayr-Harting, *The Coming of Christianity*, p. 69.

43. Gougaug, *Christianity in Celtic Lands*, p. 129.
44. For the life and work of St Columba see especially *Vita Columbae* (*Life of St Columba*), the classic life written by Adomnan, the eighth abbot of Iona, between 688 and 692, Bede's *EH,* Bradley, *Columba,* Finlay, *Columba,* Menzies, *St Columba,* Clancy and Markus, *Iona,* and Herbert, *Iona, Kells and Derry.*
45. Adomnan, *Life of St Columba,* III.3, p. 207.
46. Thomas Charles-Edwards, 'The social background to Irish *peregrinatio*', *C,* 11, 1976, p. 56.
47. 'The second preface', in Adomnan, *Life of St Columba,* p. 105.
48. In crossing from Ulster to the west coast of Scotland Columba was following in the path of countless intrepid forebears, known by their Roman name of *Scoti,* who had come particularly from the *tuath* or kingdom of Dal Riata in Antrim. By the time of Columba's birth the numbers who had made the perilous journey and settled were sufficient to form a second Dal Riata whose boundaries corresponded with the modern region of Argyll.
49. Bradley, *Columba,* pp. 16, 17.
50. Ibid., p. 65.
51. Clancy and Markus, *Iona,* pp. 8, 9.
52. Iona was the main channel by which the Christian faith and the Irish-Latin culture reached Northumbria in the seventh century. Nevertheless, it is clear from Bede's writings that the direct link between England and Ireland was significant.
53. Stancliffe and Cambridge (eds), *Oswald,* p. 1.
54. Bede, *HE,* iii.3, p. 218.
55. Ibid., p. 220.
56. Clare Stancliffe, 'Oswald, Most Holy and Most Victorious King of the Northumbrians' in Stancliffe and Cambridge (eds), *Oswald,* p. 66.
57. See Mayr-Harting, *The Coming of Christianity,* pp. 94, 95.
58. See W. Bonser, 'The Magic of St Oswald'.
59. For this incident see Bede, *HE,* iii.14, p. 258.
60. Apparently Bede distinguished between the Middle Angles and the Mercians, although it is clear that by this time they were within the dominion of the Mercians. It is not certain where they resided, but it would have been in an area which included Leicestershire and Northamptonshire.
61. Deanesly, *The Pre-Conquest Church,* p. 83.
62. For this suggestion, and comments on it, see Mayr-Harting, *The Coming of Christianity,* pp. 107, 108.
63. Bede, *HE,* ii.2, p. 138.
64. Bright, *Chapters of Early English Church History,* p. 79.
65. See chapters 7 and 9 for an explanation and discussion of minsters and double minsters.

66. Some, such as Stenton (*Anglo-Saxon England*, p. 129), are of the opinion that it was 663, but there are good grounds for preferring 664.
67. Bede, *HE*, iii.25, p. 300.
68. Morris, *The Age of Arthur*, p. 310.
69. Loyn, *Anglo-Saxon England*, p. 5.
70. Fisher, *The Anglo-Saxon Age*, pp. 66, 67. This is a book to which the comments in this and the following paragraph are indebted.
71. Stenton, *Anglo-Saxon England*, p. 125.

7. *Christianity in England from 664 to the Late Eighth Century*

1. Stenton, *Anglo-Saxon England*, p. 130.
2. For the life, works and teaching of Theodore, see Mayr-Harting, *The Coming of Christianity*.
3. Deanesly, *The Pre-Conquest Church*, p. 104.
4. Bede, *HE*, iv.2, p. 332.
5. Mayr-Harting, *The Coming of Christianity*, p. 131. This is a book to which the whole of this present section is greatly indebted.
6. See S. Bassett, 'Churches in Worcester'.
7. Deanesly, *The Pre-Conquest Church*, p. 109.
8. Ibid., p. 126.
9. Bede, *HE*, iv.2, p. 334.
10. Claim made by Brooks, *The Early History*, p. 72 and endorsed by Wallace-Hadrill, *Bede's Ecclesiastical History*, p. 137.
11. See Wallace-Hadrill, *Bede's Ecclesiastical History*, p. 137.
12. Mayr-Harting, *The Coming of Christianity*, p. 129.
13. Eddius Stephanus, *Life of Wilfrid* in Webb and Farmer (eds), *The Age of Bede*, p. 118.
14. Ibid., p. 122.
15. Ibid., p, 123.
16. Ibid., p. 128.
17. In addition to Eddius, this short account of the life of Wilfrid owes much to Fletcher, *Who's Who*, pp. 50–57.
18. Stenton, *Anglo-Saxon England*, p. 145.
19. D. P. Kirby, 'Northumbria in the time of Wilfrid' in Kirby (ed), *Saint Wilfrid*, p. 23.
20. D. H. Farmer, 'Saint Wilfrid' in Kirby (ed), *Saint Wildred*, p. 35.
21. Bede, *Life of Cuthbert* in Webb and Farmer (eds), *The Age of Bede*, pp. 55, 56.
22. Ibid., p. 65.
23. See ibid., p. 55.
24. See especially Battiscombe (ed), *The Relics of St Cuthbert* and Bonner, Rollason and Stancliffe (eds), *St Cuthbert*.

25. For the life and works of Aldhelm see especially Lapidge and Herren (eds), *Aldhelm*.
26. Stenton, *Anglo-Saxon England*, p. 177.
27. Hodgkin, *A History of the Anglo-Saxons*, Vol 2, p. 416.
28. Fisher, 'The Church in England', p. 19.
29. Plummer, *Baedae Opera Historica*, Vol 1, pp. 405–23.
30. Brooks, *The Early History*, p. 111.
31. Ibid., p. 111.
32. Ibid., p. 111.
33. C. P. Wormald, 'Bede, the Bretwaldas and the origins of the *Gens Anglorum*' in Bullough and Wormald (eds), *Ideal and Reality in Early Medieval Europe*, p. 128.
34. Brooks, *The Early History*, p. 315.
35. Swanton (ed), *The Anglo-Saxon Chronicle*, pp. 56, 67.
36. Cubitt, Anglo-Saxon Church Councils, p. 11.
37. Hodgkin, *A History of the Anglo-Saxons*, Vol 2, p. 424.
38. For these and other poems and poetry of the era and in the Anglo-Saxon period in general, see Bradley (trans and ed), *Anglo-Saxon Poetry*.
39. For these comments see Fisher, *The Anglo-Saxon Age*, pp. 160, 161.
40. Peter Wormald, 'The Age of Bede and Aethelbald' in Campbell (ed), *The Anglo-Saxons*, p. 72.
41. Hamerow, 'Settlement Mobility and the "Middle Saxon Shift"', pp. 7, 8.
42. Bassett (ed), *The Origins of Anglo-Saxon Kingdoms*, p. 20.
43. See especially, Blair (ed), *Ministers and Parish Churches* and Blair and Sharpe (eds), *Pastoral Care before the Parish*.
44. John Blair and Richard Sharpe, 'Introduction' in Blair and Sharpe (eds), *Pastoral Care Before the Parish*, pp. 2, 3.
45. John Blair, 'Minster Churches in the Landscape' in Hooke (ed), *Anglo-Saxon Settlements*, pp. 35, 36.
46. John Godfrey, 'The Place of the Double Monastery in the Anglo-Saxon Minster System' in Bonner (ed), *Famulus Christi*, p. 344.
47. See ibid.
48. The following comments are based on Cubitt, *Anglo-Saxon Church Councils*, pp. 116–18.
49. Ibid., p. 118.
50. The following section is greatly indebted to Rodwell and Bentley, *Our Christian Heritage*, especially ch 2.
51. Stenton, *Anglo-Saxon England*, p. 157.
52. See Theodore's *Penitential* in Haddon and Stubbs (eds), *Councils and Ecclesiastical Documents*, p. 190.
53. See ibid., pp. 12, 183–85, 192.
54. See ibid., p. 177.
55. See ibid., pp. 184–5.

56. Bede, *HE*, iv.27, p. 432.
57. Sims-Williams, *Religion and Literature*, p. 119.
58. For the excavation of Hartlepool, see Daniels, 'Hartlepool' and 'The Anglo-Saxon Monastery at Church Close, Hartlepool'.
59. For the older view that the concept of double monasteries came from the Irish church, see Bateson, 'The Origin and Early Histories of Double Monasteries'.
60. Stenton, *Anglo-Saxon England*, p. 162.
61. John Godfrey, 'The Place of the Double Monastery in the Anglo-Saxon Minster System' in Bonnor, *Famulus Christi*, p. 347.
62. See Fisher, 'The Church in England', p. 18.
63. Gallyon, *The Early Church in Wessex and Mercia*, p. 21.
64. Blair, *Northumbria in the Days of Bede*, p. 63.
65. Ibid., pp. 142, 143.
66. Jolly, *Popular Religion*, p. 27.
67. For a life of Guthlac, see Colgrave (trans), *Felix's Life of St Guthlac*.
68. Ridyard, *The Royal Saints*, p. 250.
69. Flint, *The Rise of Magic*, p. 407.
70. Ibid., p. 407.
71. Ibid., p. 33.
72. Mayr-Harting, *The Coming of Christianity*, p. 220.
73. Two good translations are Alexander (trans), *Beowulf* and Bradley (trans and ed), *Anglo-Saxon Poetry*, pp. 411–94.
74. Michael Alexander, 'Introduction' to Alexander (trans), *Beowulf*, p. 29.
75. For the eighth-century continental missionary work see especially Greenaway, *Saint Boniface*, Levison, *England and the Continent*, and Talbot, *The Anglo-Saxon Missionaries*. For the main primary sources, see Levison, p. 2.
76. See Levison, *England and the Continent*, pp. 26f.
77. Ibid., p. 48.
78. Talbot, *The Anglo-Saxon Missionaries*, p. viii.
79. Mayr-Harting, *The Coming of Christianity*, p. 146.
80. Eddius, *Life of Wilfrid* in Webb and Farmer (eds), *The Age of Bede*, p. 132.
81. Levison, *England and the Continent*, p. 51.
82. For the life and works of Willibrord see expecially Levison, *England and the Continent* and Alcuin, *The Life of St Willibrord* in Talbot, *The Anglo-Saxon Missionaries*.
83. For the life and works of St Boniface see especially Willibald, *The Life of St Boniface* and 'The Correspondence of St Boniface' in Talbot, *The Anglo-Saxon Missionaries*, pp. 65–149, Greenaway, *Saint Boniface*, and Levison, *England and the Continent*.
84. Willibald, *The Life of St Boniface* in Talbot, *The Anglo-Saxon Missionaries*, p. 47.

85. Talbot, *The Anglo-Saxon Misionaries*, p. xiv.
86. Ibid., p. xv.
87. Simeon of Durham (attrib), quoted in Whitelock (ed), *English Historical Documents*, p. 247.

8. *The Vikings in England to 1066*

1. Loyn, *The Vikings in Britain*, p. 1.
2. Hayes, *Archaeology of the British Isles*, p. 127.
3. Ibid., p. 125.
4. Ibid., p. 129.
5. Loyn, *The Vikings in Britain*, p. 4. This is a book to which the present section owes much.
6. Wallace-Hadrill, *Early Medieval History*, p. 98.
7. These comments are based on Hutton, *The Pagan Religions*, p. 283. This is a book to which this whole present section is greatly indebted.
8. Sawyer, *Kings and Vikings*, p. 133.
9. Patrick Wormald, 'The Ninth Century' in Campbell (ed), *The Anglo-Saxons*, p. 148.
10. For this comment see ibid., pp. 148, 149.
11. H. Petrie and T. Sharpe (eds), *Monumenta Historica Britannica*, London 1848, p. 509. See the entry under the year 789 in Swanton (ed and trans), *The Anglo-Saxon Chronicle*, pp. 54, 55.
12. Whitelock (ed), *English Historical Documents*, no. 193.
13. Sawyer, *The Age of the Vikings*, pp. 202–3.
14. D. M. Metcalf, 'Anglo-Saxon Coins 2: Alfred to Edgar' in Campbell (ed), *The Anglo-Saxons*, p. 130.
15. Patrick Wormald, 'The Ninth Century' in Campbell (ed), *The Anglo-Saxons*, p. 142.
16. Ibid., p. 145.
17. Hodgkin, *A History of the Anglo-Saxons*, Vol II, p, 517.
18. Simon Keynes and Michael Lapidge, 'Introduction' in Keynes and Lapidge (trans), *Alfred the Great*, p. 10.
19. Hodgkin, *A History of the Anglo-Saxons*, Vol II, p. 609.
20. See ibid., ch 17.
21. Keynes and Lapidge (trans), *Alfred the Great*, p. 110.
22. Stenton, *Anglo-Saxon England*, p. 357.
23. Fisher, *The Anglo-Saxon Age*, p. 272.
24. For the life of Cnut, see Lawson, *Cnut*.
25. Ibid., pp. 173–74.
26. Loyn, *The Vikings in Britain*, p. 66.
27. Lawson, *Cnut*, p. 214.
28. Stenton, *Anglo-Saxon England*, p. 470.

29. Ibid., p. 488.
30. Eric John, 'The Age of Edgar' in Campbell (ed), *The Anglo-Saxons*, p. 172. This is an article to which the present section is greatly indebted.
31. Ibid., p. 181.
32. Sawyer, *Kings and Vikings*, p. 105.

9. *Christianity in the Age of the Vikings*

1. For the Council of Chelsea see Cubitt, *Anglo-Saxon Church Councils*, ch 7, pp. 191–203.
2. Stenton, *Anglo-Saxon England*, p. 433. This is a book to which the present section owes much.
3. See Deanesly, *The Pre-Conquest Church*, p. 244.
4. Swanton (ed and trans), *The Anglo-Saxon Chronicle*, pp. 54, 56.
5. Ibid., pp. 55, 57.
6. Deanesly, *The Pre-Conquest Church*, p. 245.
7. Swanton (ed and trans), *The Anglo-Saxon Chronicle*, p. 71.
8. Wilson, 'The Vikings' Relationship with Christianity in Northern England', p. 37.
9. See Berg, 'The Gosforth Cross'.
10. Stenton, *Anglo-Saxon England*, p. 434.
11. Ibid., p. 434.
12. King Alfred's 'Preface' to his translation of Pope Gregory's *Pastoral Care* in Keynes and Lapidge (trans), *Alfred the Great*, pp. 124, 125.
13. Deanesly, *The Pre-Conquest Church*, p. 264.
14. See, for example, Michael Alexander, 'Introduction' in Alexander (trans), *Beowulf*, p. 39.
15. Keynes and Lapidge (trans), *Alfred the Great*, p. 103.
16. Fisher, *The Anglo-Saxon Age*, p. 281.
17. Ibid., p. 282.
18. Deanesly, *The Pre-Conquest Church*, p. 230.
19. Stenton, *Anglo-Saxon England*, p. 546.
20. Deanesly, *The Pre-Conquest Church*, p. 276.
21. For the life and works of Dunstan see especially Duckett, *St Dunstan*.
22. Ibid., pp. 138, 139.
23. Ibid., p. 111.
24. Fisher, *The Anglo-Saxon Age*, p. 288.
25. Knowles, *The Monastic Order*, p. 44.
26. Ibid., p. 31.
27. Jones, 'The Significance of the Regal Consecration of Edgar in 973', p. 389.
28. Knowles, *The Monastic Order*, p. 56.
29. For a discussion of this see David Parsons, 'Introduction' in Parsons (ed), *Tenth-Century Studies*, pp. 1–3, and D.H. Farmer, 'The Progress of the

Monastic Revival' in Parsons (ed), *Tenth-Century Studies*, ch 2, pp. 10–19.

30. See ibid., pp. 10, 11.

31. Godfrey, *The Church in Anglo-Saxon England*, p. 407.

32. Ibid., p. 407.

33. For this list and the comments below see Barlow, *The English Church*, pp. 208f.

34. Loyn, *The Governance of Anglo-Saxon England*, pp. 154, 155. This is a book to which the present section is greatly indebted.

35. Ibid., p. 157.

36. W. J. Blair, 'Introduction: from Minster to Parish Church' in Blair (ed), *Minsters and Parish Churches*, p. 1. This is an excellent volume on the subject it covers, and because of the light it throws on the English church in the period reviewed. The present work is greatly indebted to it.

37. Platt, *The Parish Churches of Medieval England*, p. 1.

38. Morris, *Churches in the Landscape*, p. 167. For issues raised in the present section relating to the churches in the tenth and eleventh centuries see ibid., ch 4, and W.J. Blair, 'Introduction' in Blair (ed), *Minsters and Parish Churches*, pp. 1–19.

39. W. J. Blair, 'Introduction' in Blair (ed), *Ministers and Parish Churches*, p. 7.

40. Platt, *The Parish Churches of Medieval England*, p. 4.

41. Swanton (ed), *The Anglo-Saxon Chronicle (F)*, sub anno 1017, p. 155, n.9.

42. Richard K. Morris, 'Churches in York and its Hinterland: Building Patterns and Stone Sources in the 11th and 12th Centuries' in Blair (ed), *Minsters and Parish Churches*, p. 191.

43. W. J. Blair, 'Introduction' in Blair (ed), *Minsters and Parish Churches*, p. 10.

44. James Campbell, 'Epilogue' in Campbell (ed), *The Anglo-Saxons*, p. 245.

45. Jolly, *Popular Religion*, p. 39. The whole of the present section owes much to this most stimulating book.

46. Morris, *The Church in British Archaeology*, p. 71.

47. Platt, *The Parish Churches of Medieval England*, p. 3. This is a book to which the present section is greatly indebted.

48. Deanesly, *The Pre-Conquest Church*, p. 351. The previous paragraph is also base on Deanesly, p. 351.

49. Morris, *Churches in the Landscape*, p. 169.

50. Whitelock (ed), *English Historical Documents*, p. 605.

51. See Barlow, *The English Church*, p. 291.

52. Loyn, *The Governance of Anglo-Saxon England*, p. xiv. This is a book to which the present section is greatly indebted.

53. Howe, *Migration and Mythmaking*, p. 6.

54. Loyn, *The Governance of Anglo-Saxon England*, p. xiv.

55. Ibid., p. 3.

Appendix 1. The Military, Political, Demographic, Economic and Social History of Roman Britain

1. Salway, *Roman Britain*, p. 239.
2. See Frere, *Britannia*, pp. 301, 302.
3. Millett, *The Romanization of Britain*, pp. 181–85.
4. Ibid., p. 99. This is a most valuable work on the subject it explores with such creative thoroughness.
5. See Martin Jones, 'Agriculture in Roman Britain: the dynamics of change' in Todd (ed), *Research on Roman Britain*, pp. 127–34.
6. Michael Fulford, 'The Economy of Roman Britain' in Todd (ed), *Research in Roman Britain*, p. 198; but see the whole of this article.
7. The following account of Roman towns owes much to Wacher, *Roman Britain*, ch 3.
8. Millett, *The Romanization of Britain*, p. 134.
9. See Cunliffe, *Roman Bath*, p. 109.
10. Of particular value as descriptions and appraisals of villas are Frere, *Britannia*, ch 12, and Salway, *Roman Britain*, ch 19.
11. Millett, *The Romanization of Britain*, p. 186, and fig. 77, p. 188.
12. Ibid., pp. 205f, on which these comments are based.
13. Hayes, *Archaeology of the British Isles*, p. 113.
14. Frere, *Britannia*, p. 295.

Index